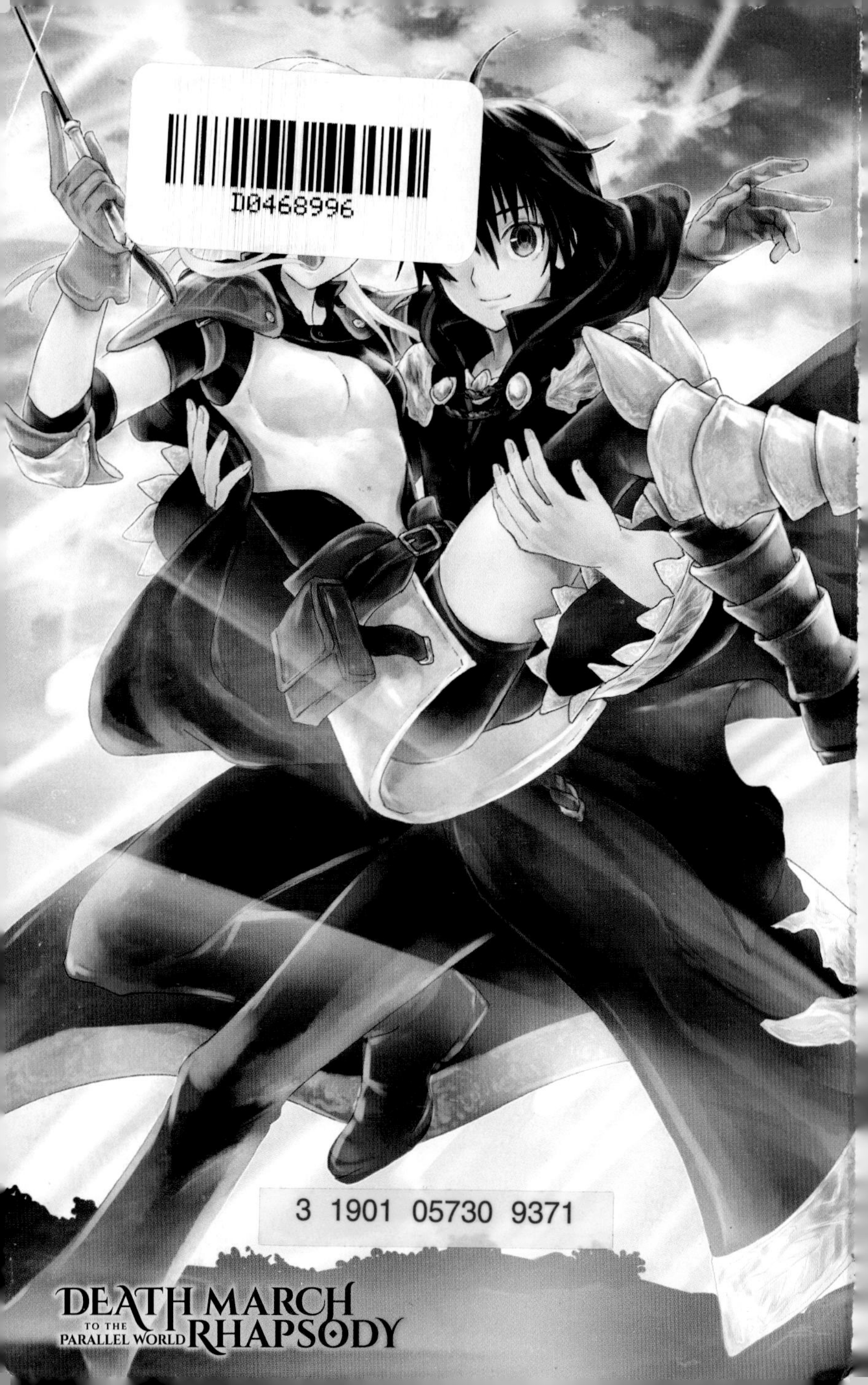
DEATH MARCH
TO THE PARALLEL WORLD RHAPSODY

CONTENTS

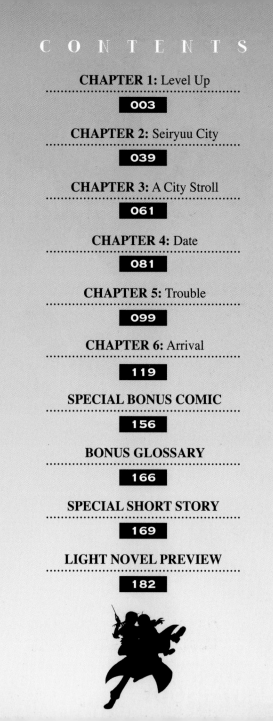

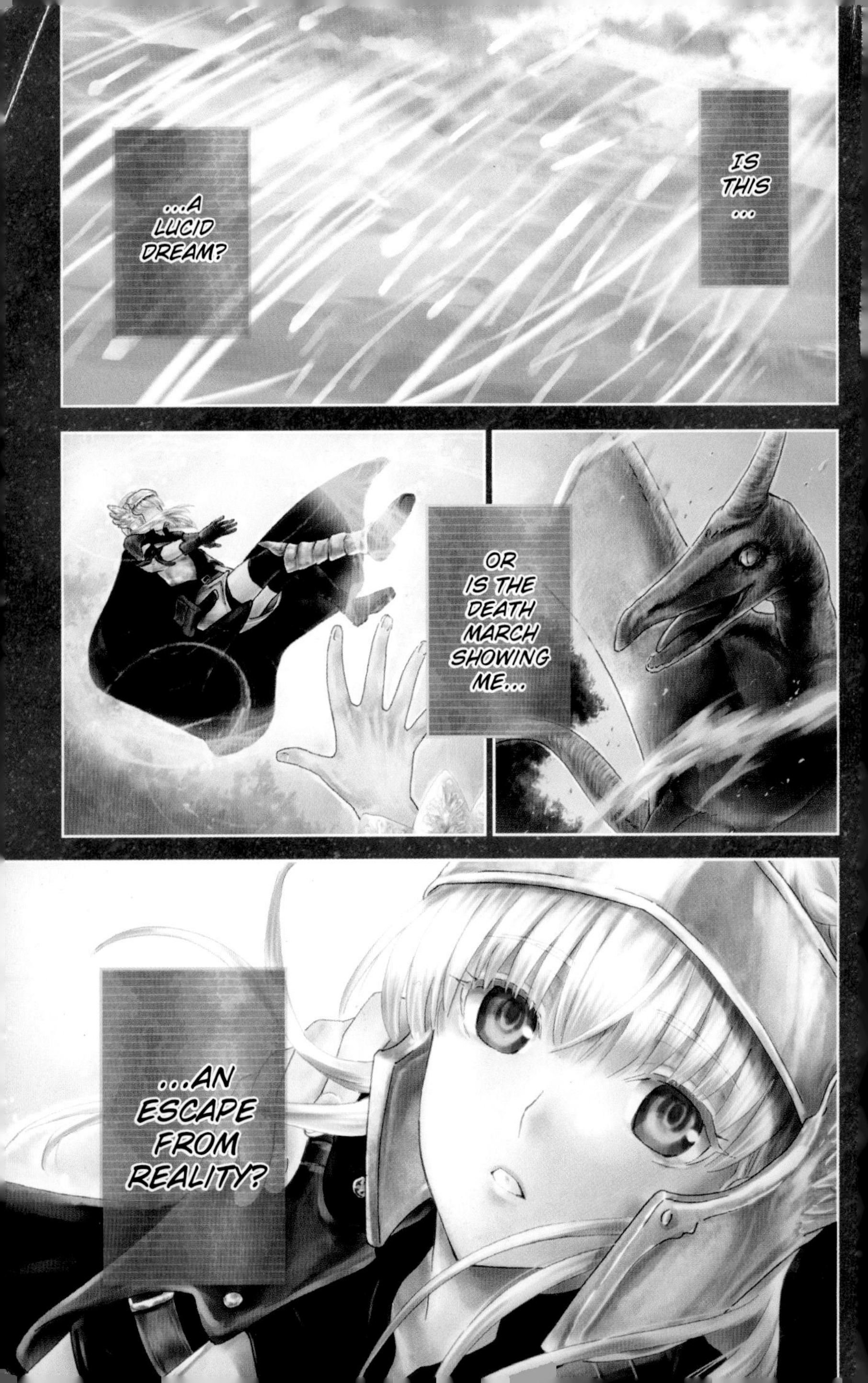
IS THIS...
...A LUCID DREAM?
OR IS THE DEATH MARCH SHOWING ME...
...AN ESCAPE FROM REALITY?

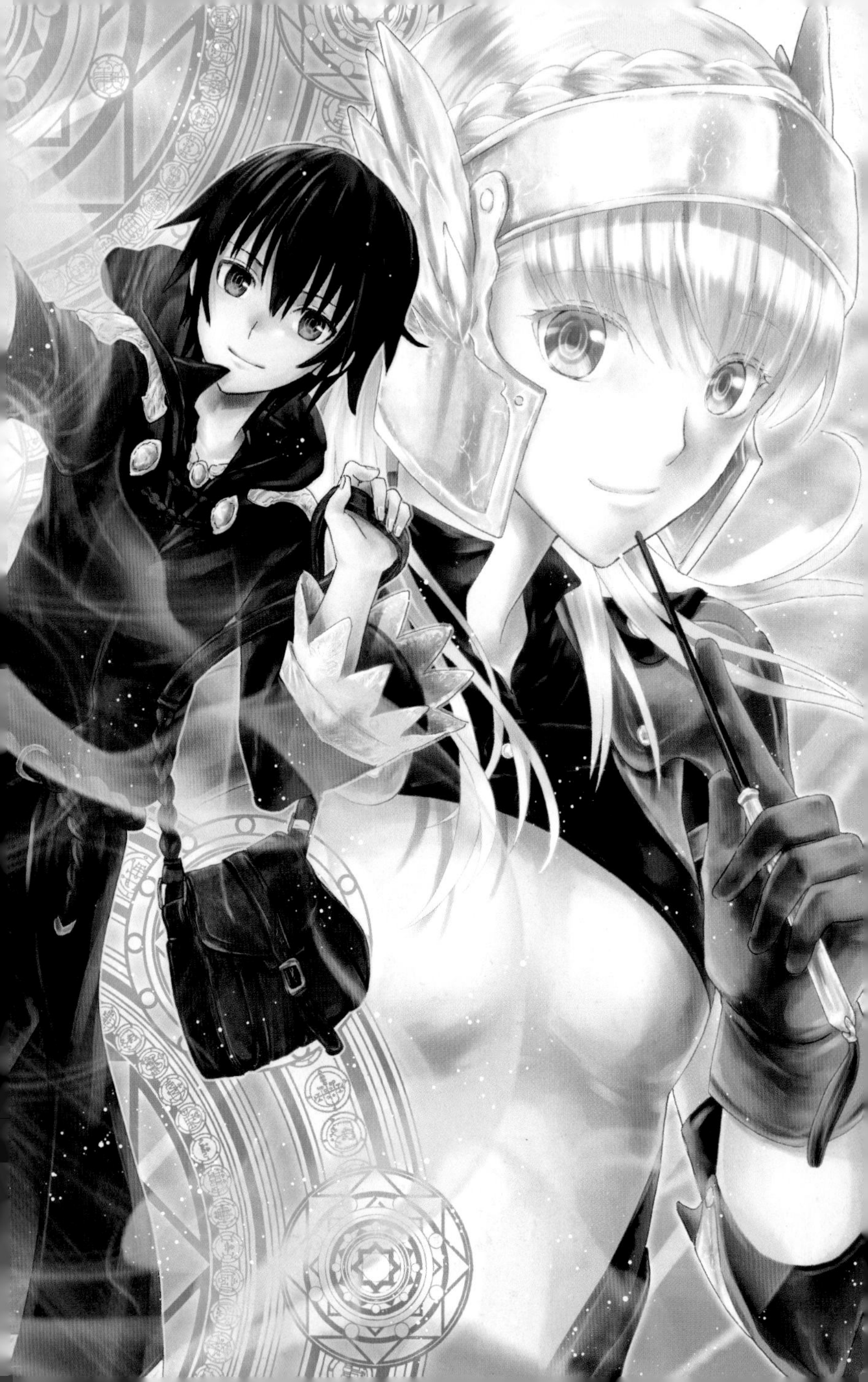

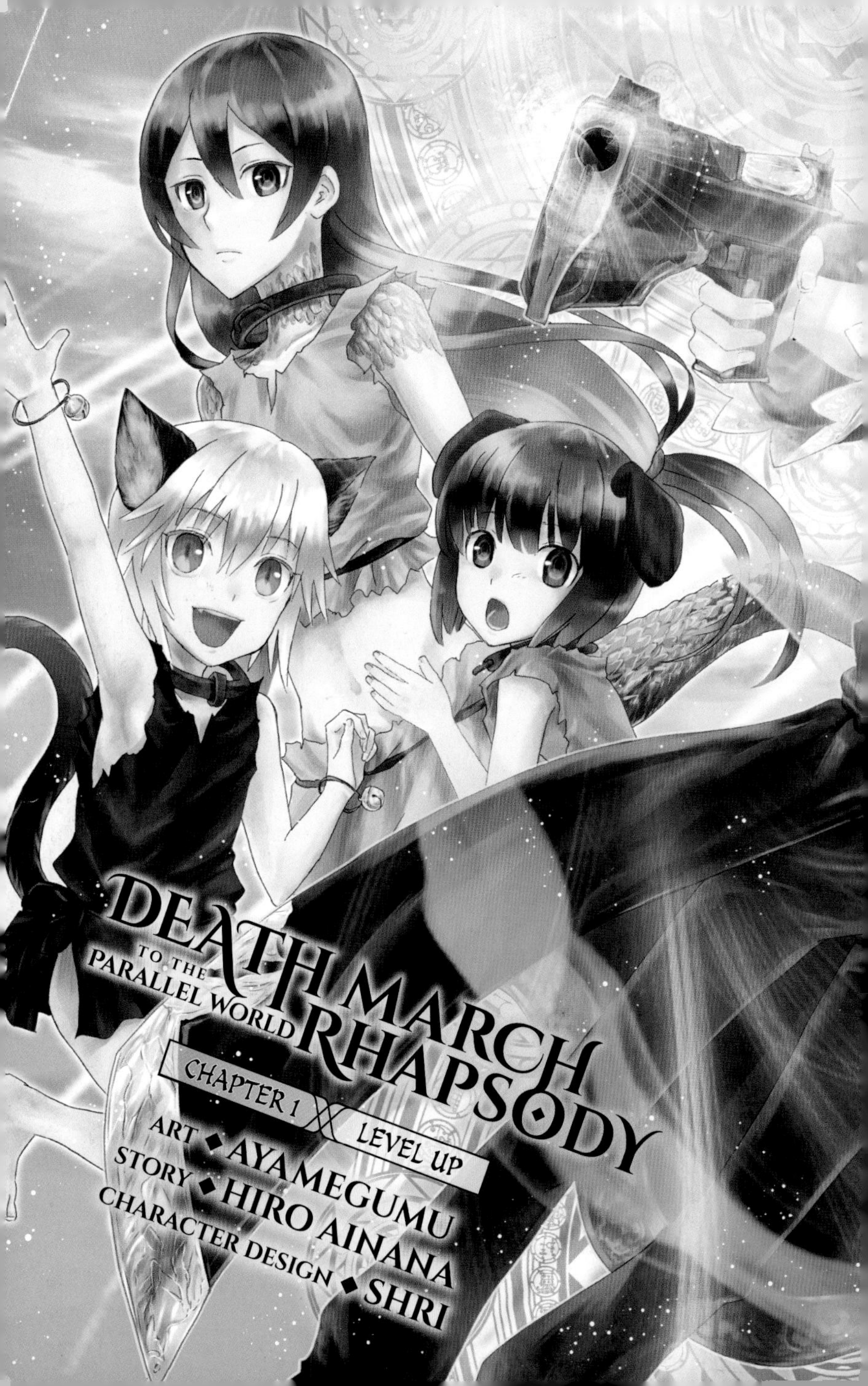
DEATH MARCH TO THE PARALLEL WORLD RHAPSODY
CHAPTER 1 LEVEL UP
ART ◆ AYAMEGUMU
STORY ◆ HIRO AINANA
CHARACTER DESIGN ◆ SHRI

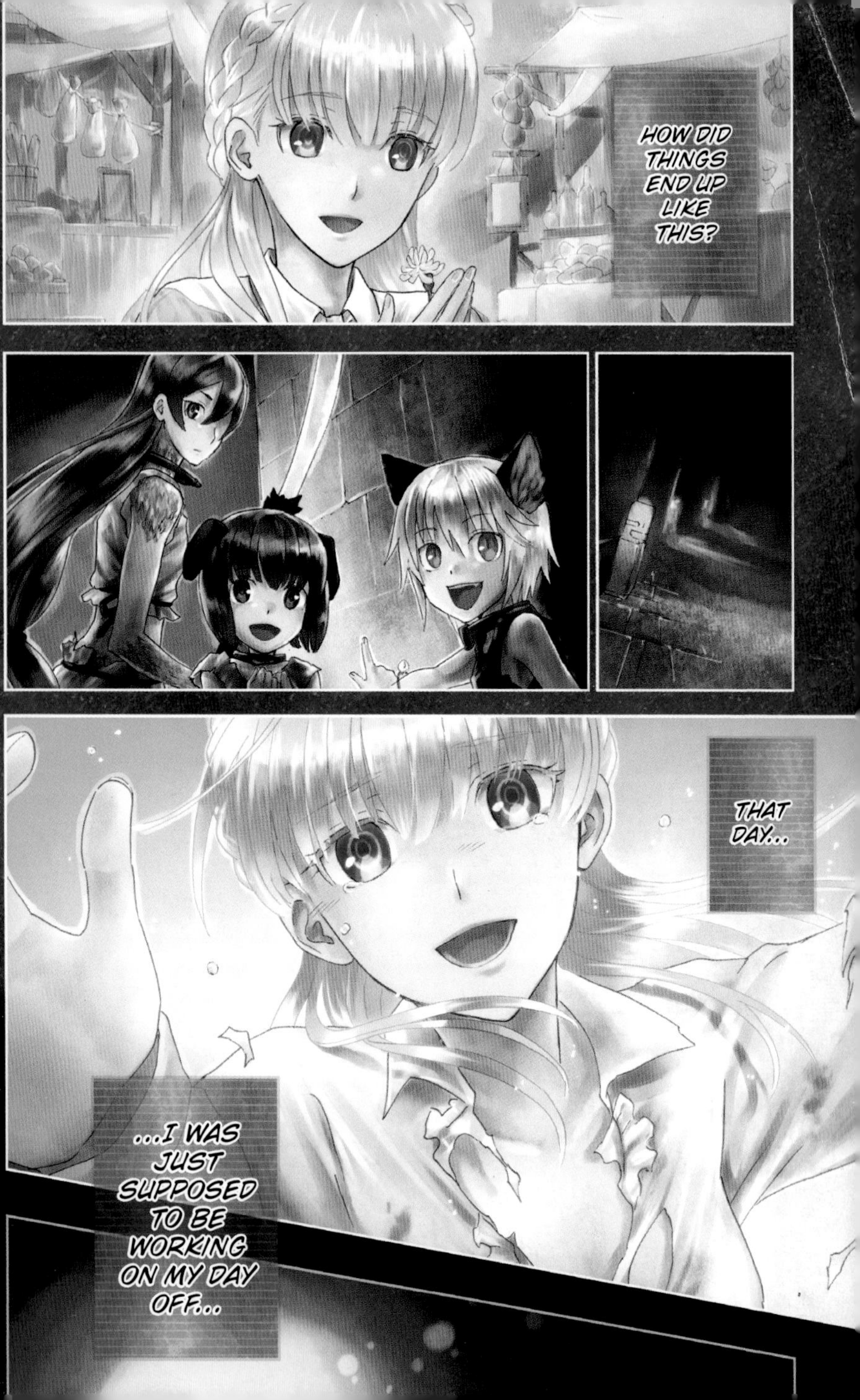
HOW DID THINGS END UP LIKE THIS?
THAT DAY...
...I WAS JUST SUPPOSED TO BE WORKING ON MY DAY OFF...

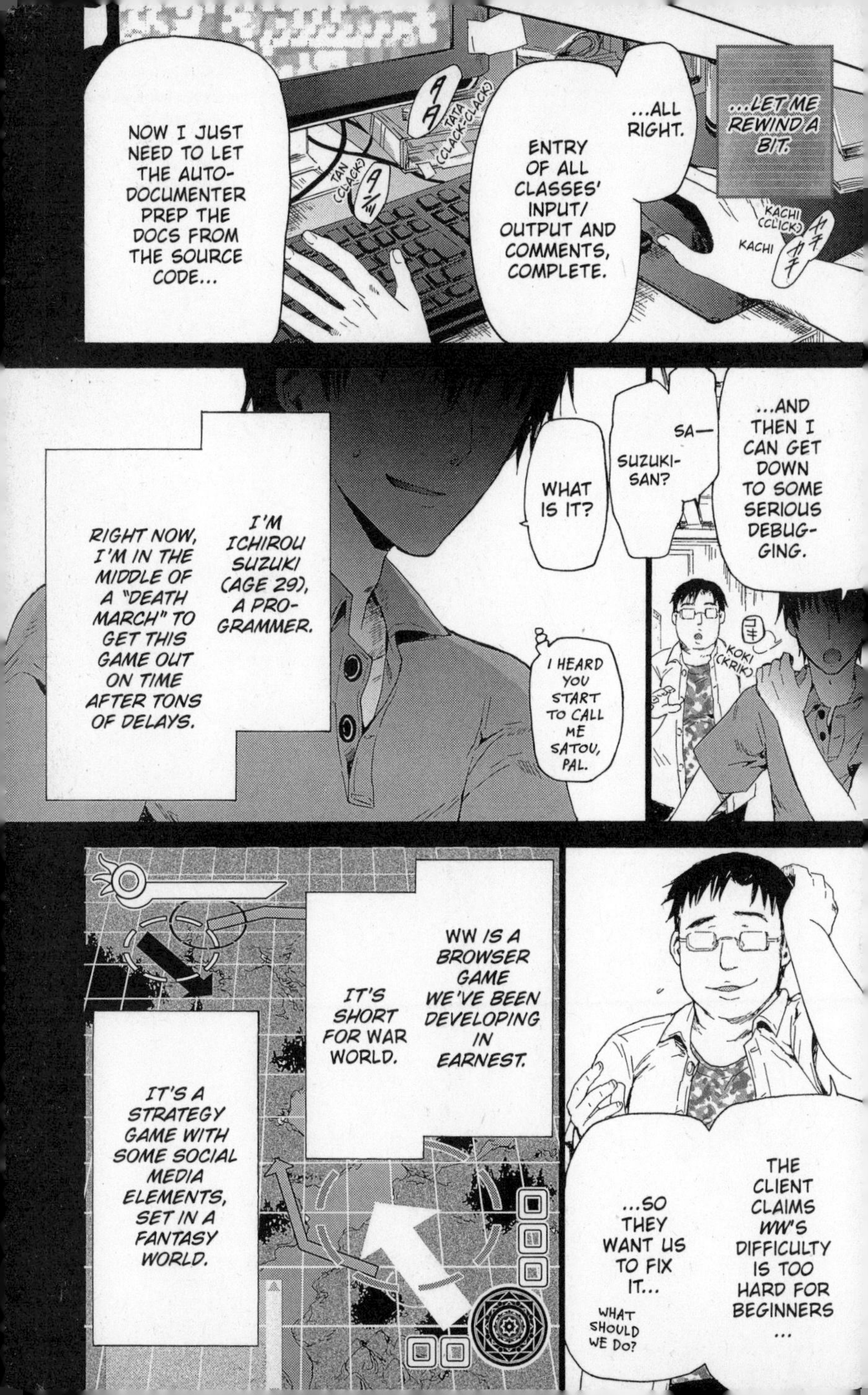
...LET ME REWIND A BIT.
KACHI (CLICK)
KACHI
...ALL RIGHT.
ENTRY OF ALL CLASSES' INPUT/OUTPUT AND COMMENTS, COMPLETE.
TATA (CLACK-CLACK)
TAN (CLACK)
NOW I JUST NEED TO LET THE AUTO-DOCUMENTER PREP THE DOCS FROM THE SOURCE CODE...
...AND THEN I CAN GET DOWN TO SOME SERIOUS DEBUGGING.
SA—
SUZUKI-SAN?
WHAT IS IT?
KOKI (KRIK)
I HEARD YOU START TO CALL ME SATOU, PAL.
I'M ICHIROU SUZUKI (AGE 29), A PROGRAMMER.
RIGHT NOW, I'M IN THE MIDDLE OF A "DEATH MARCH" TO GET THIS GAME OUT ON TIME AFTER TONS OF DELAYS.
THE CLIENT CLAIMS WW'S DIFFICULTY IS TOO HARD FOR BEGINNERS...
...SO THEY WANT US TO FIX IT...
WHAT SHOULD WE DO?
WW IS A BROWSER GAME WE'VE BEEN DEVELOPING IN EARNEST.
IT'S SHORT FOR WAR WORLD.
IT'S A STRATEGY GAME WITH SOME SOCIAL MEDIA ELEMENTS, SET IN A FANTASY WORLD.

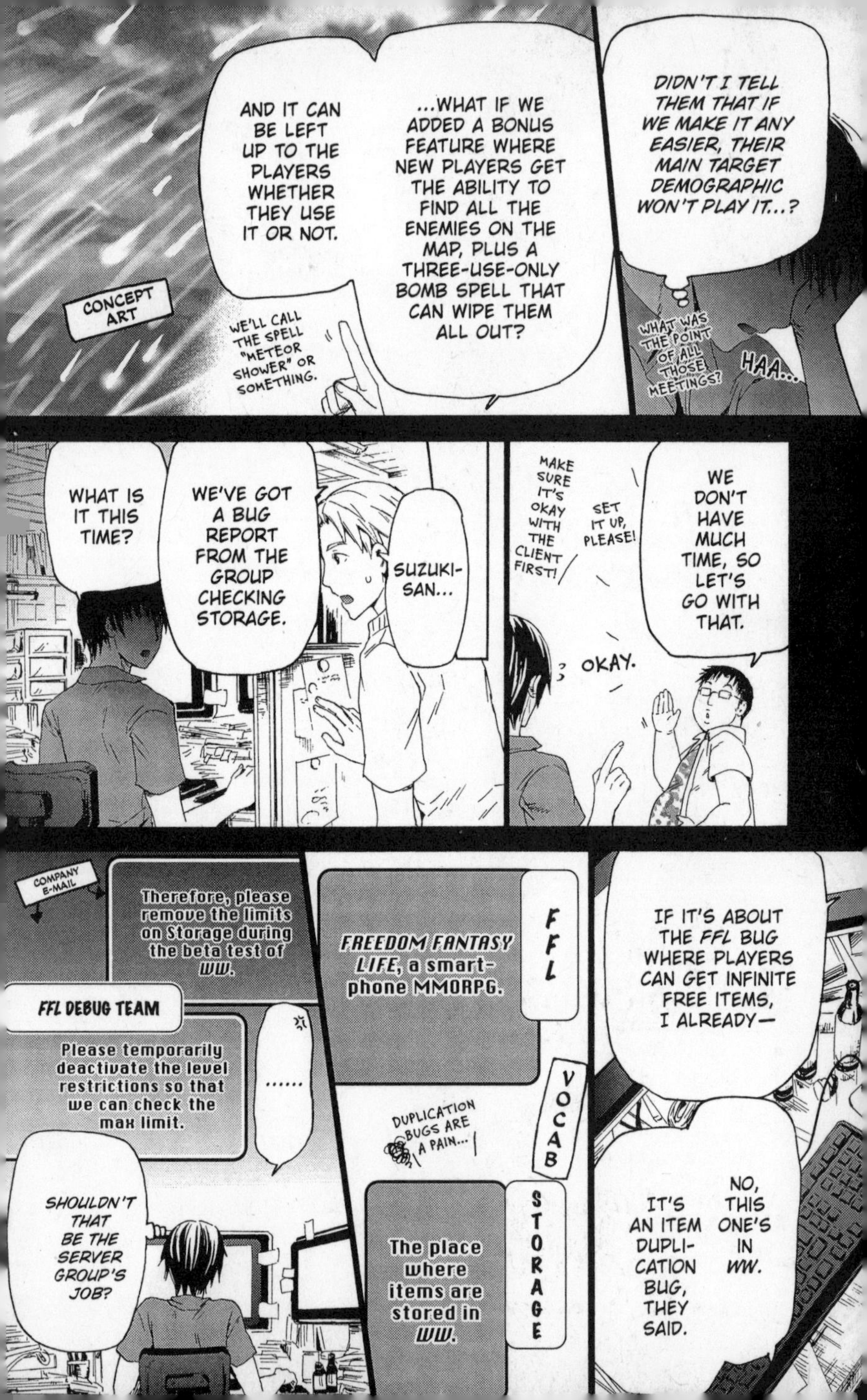

DIDN'T I TELL THEM THAT IF WE MAKE IT ANY EASIER, THEIR MAIN TARGET DEMOGRAPHIC WON'T PLAY IT...?
WHAT WAS THE POINT OF ALL THOSE MEETINGS?
HAA...
...WHAT IF WE ADDED A BONUS FEATURE WHERE NEW PLAYERS GET THE ABILITY TO FIND ALL THE ENEMIES ON THE MAP, PLUS A THREE-USE-ONLY BOMB SPELL THAT CAN WIPE THEM ALL OUT?
AND IT CAN BE LEFT UP TO THE PLAYERS WHETHER THEY USE IT OR NOT.
WE'LL CALL THE SPELL "METEOR SHOWER" OR SOMETHING.
CONCEPT ART
WE DON'T HAVE MUCH TIME, SO LET'S GO WITH THAT.
SET IT UP, PLEASE!
MAKE SURE IT'S OKAY WITH THE CLIENT FIRST!
OKAY.
SUZUKI-SAN...
WE'VE GOT A BUG REPORT FROM THE GROUP CHECKING STORAGE.
WHAT IS IT THIS TIME?
IF IT'S ABOUT THE FFL BUG WHERE PLAYERS CAN GET INFINITE FREE ITEMS, I ALREADY—
NO, THIS ONE'S IN WW.
IT'S AN ITEM DUPLICATION BUG, THEY SAID.
FFL
FREEDOM FANTASY LIFE, a smartphone MMORPG.
VOCAB
STORAGE
The place where items are stored in WW.
DUPLICATION BUGS ARE A PAIN...
COMPANY E-MAIL
Therefore, please remove the limits on Storage during the beta test of WW.
FFL DEBUG TEAM
Please temporarily deactivate the level restrictions so that we can check the max limit.
......
SHOULDN'T THAT BE THE SERVER GROUP'S JOB?

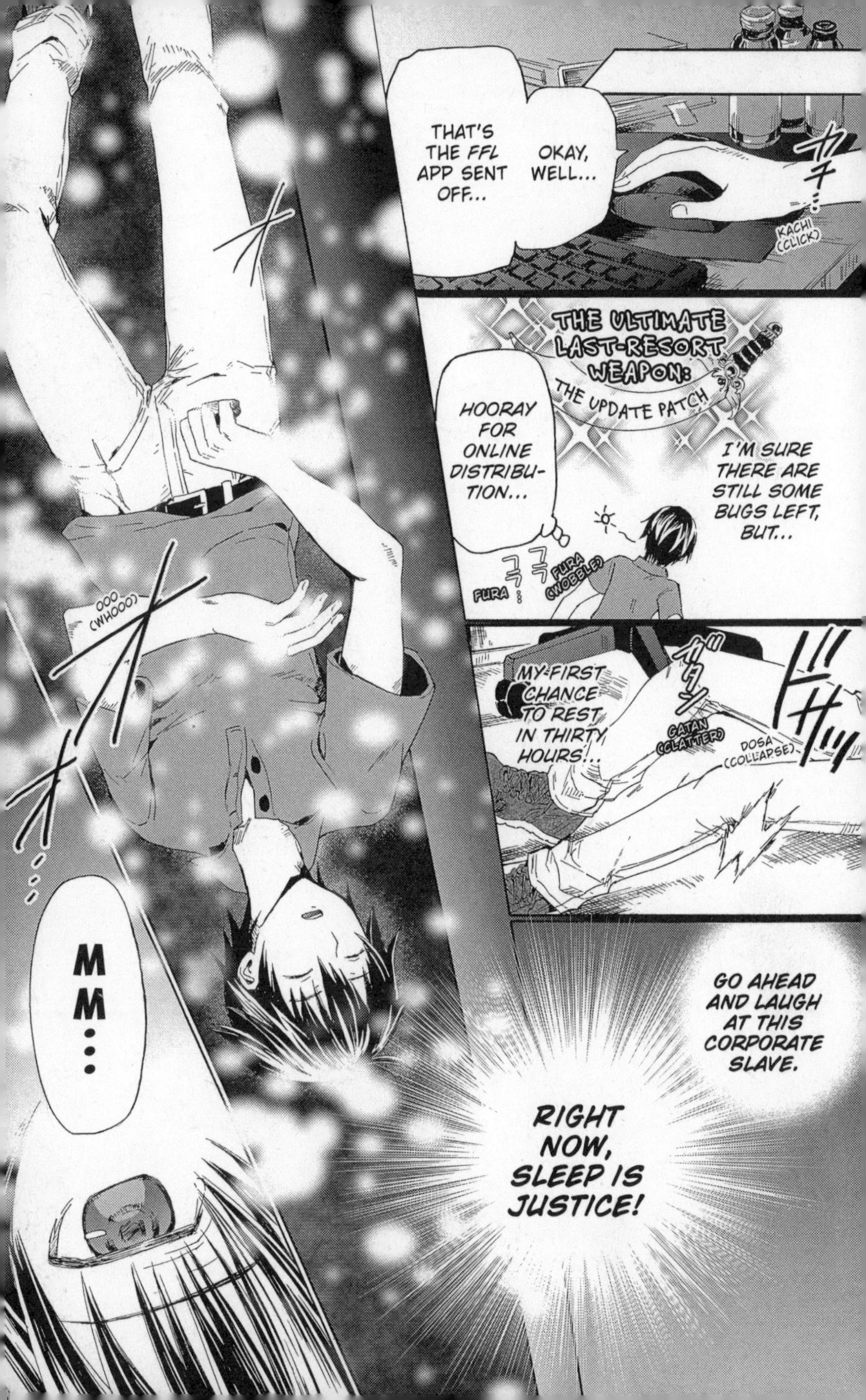
OKAY, WELL...
THAT'S THE FFL APP SENT OFF...
KACHI (CLICK)
THE ULTIMATE LAST-RESORT WEAPON: THE UPDATE PATCH
I'M SURE THERE ARE STILL SOME BUGS LEFT, BUT...
HOORAY FOR ONLINE DISTRIBUTION...
FURA (WOBBLE)
FURA
DOSA (COLLAPSE)
GATAN (CLATTER)
MY FIRST CHANCE TO REST IN THIRTY HOURS...
GO AHEAD AND LAUGH AT THIS CORPORATE SLAVE.
RIGHT NOW, SLEEP IS JUSTICE!
OOO (WHOOO)
MM...

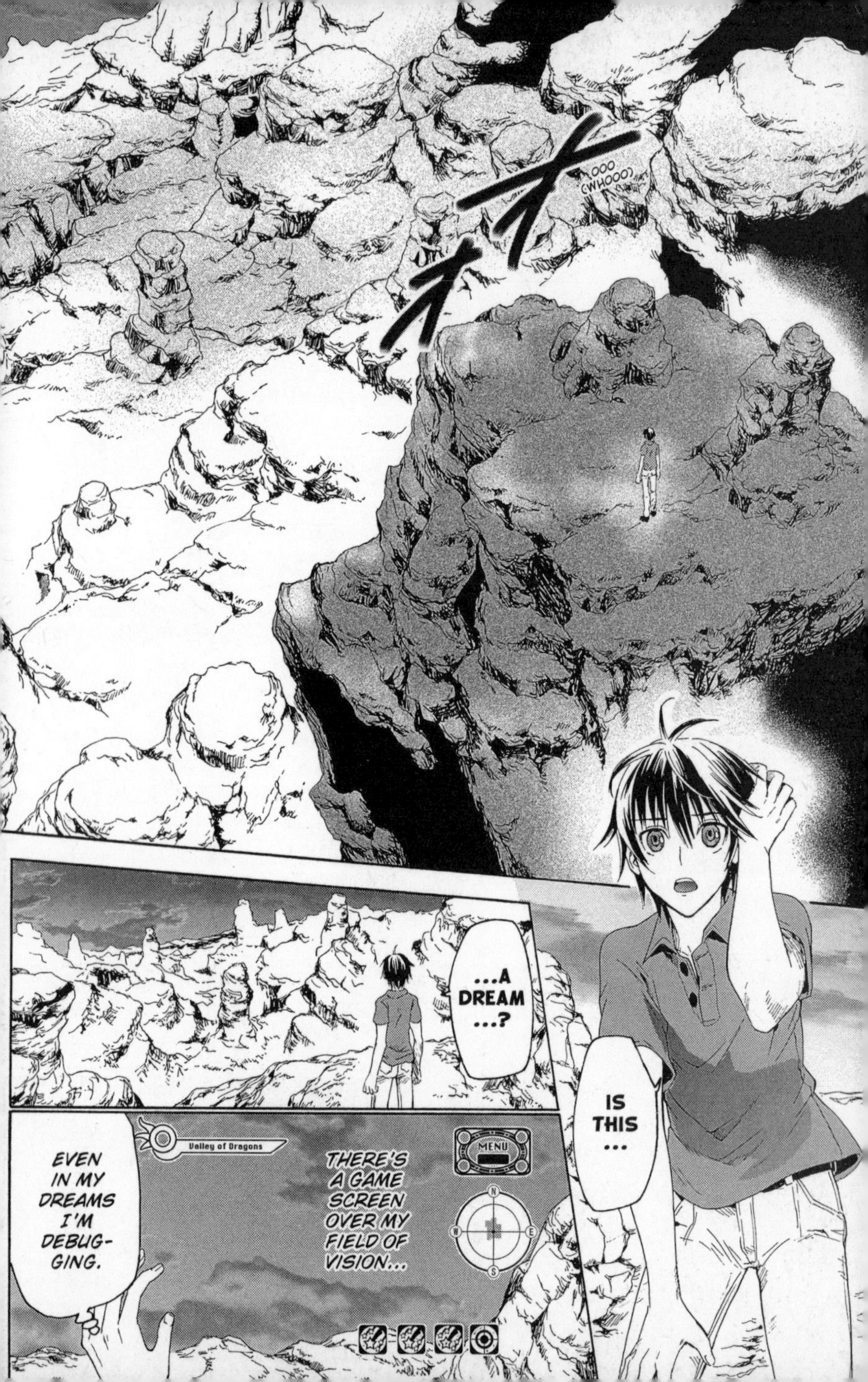
OOO
(WHOOO)
IS THIS...
...A DREAM...?
Valley of Dragons
MENU
N
E
S
W
THERE'S A GAME SCREEN OVER MY FIELD OF VISION...
EVEN IN MY DREAMS I'M DEBUG-GING.

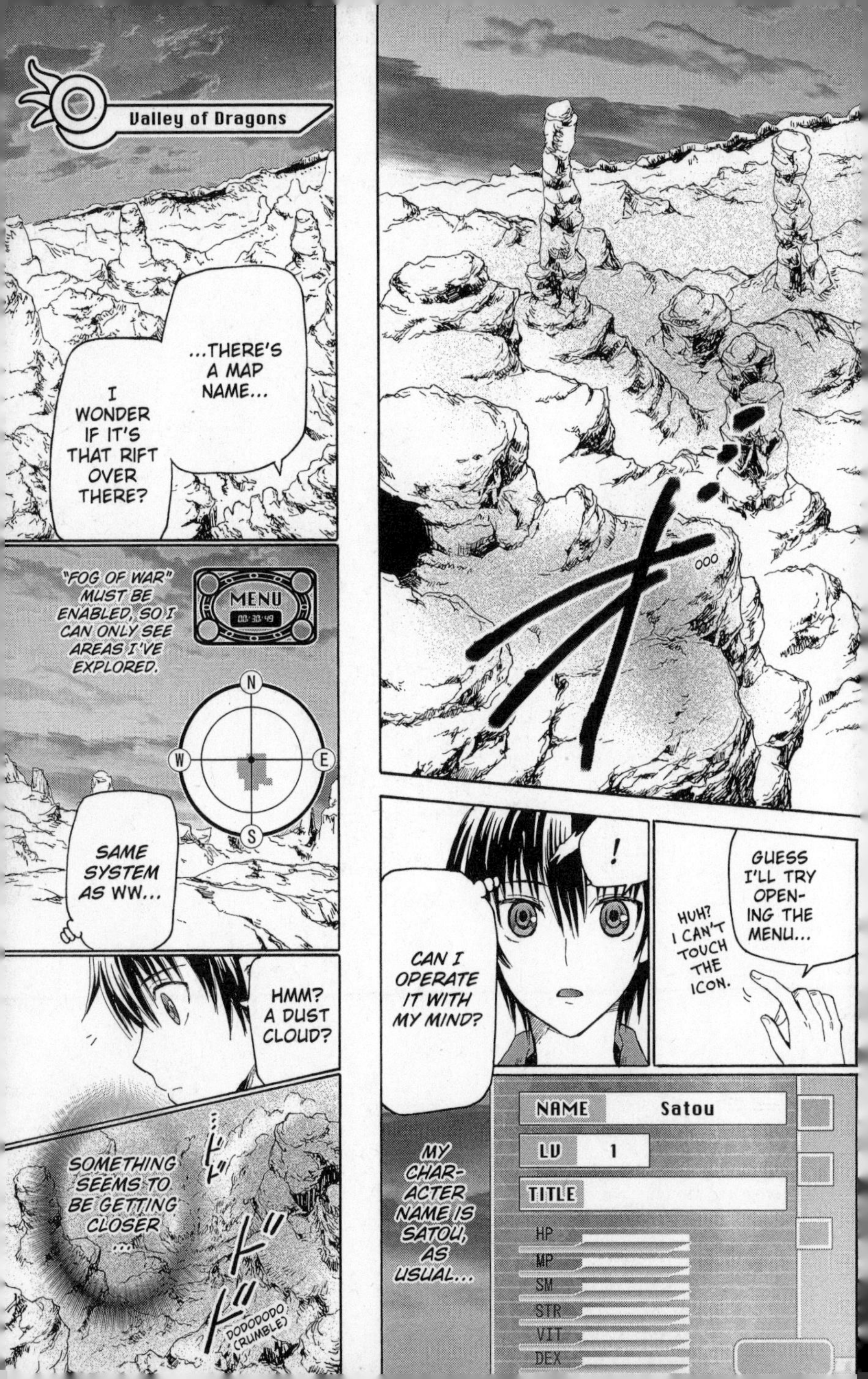
ooo
GUESS I'LL TRY OPENING THE MENU...
HUH? I CAN'T TOUCH THE ICON.
!
CAN I OPERATE IT WITH MY MIND?
NAME
Satou
LV
1
TITLE
HP
MP
SM
STR
VIT
DEX
MY CHARACTER NAME IS SATOU, AS USUAL...
Valley of Dragons
...THERE'S A MAP NAME...
I WONDER IF IT'S THAT RIFT OVER THERE?
MENU
00:30:49
"FOG OF WAR" MUST BE ENABLED, SO I CAN ONLY SEE AREAS I'VE EXPLORED.
N
W
E
S
SAME SYSTEM AS WW...
HMM? A DUST CLOUD?
SOMETHING SEEMS TO BE GETTING CLOSER...
DODODODO (RUMBLE)

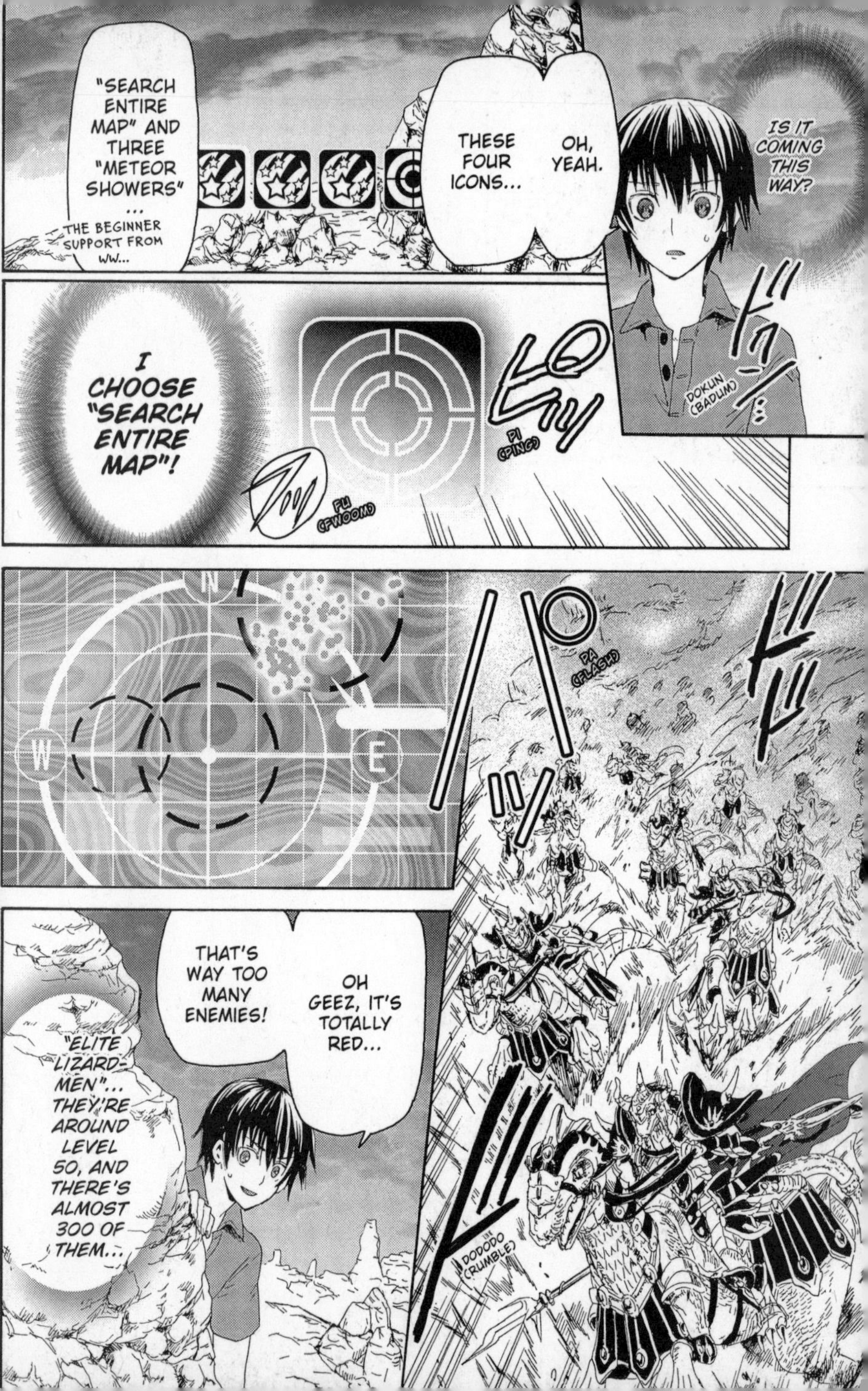
IS IT COMING THIS WAY?
OH, YEAH.
THESE FOUR ICONS...
"SEARCH ENTIRE MAP" AND THREE "METEOR SHOWERS" ... THE BEGINNER SUPPORT FROM WW...
DOKUN (BADUM)
PI (PING)
I CHOOSE "SEARCH ENTIRE MAP"!
FU (FWOOM)
PA (FLASH)
N
W
E
OH GEEZ, IT'S TOTALLY RED...
THAT'S WAY TOO MANY ENEMIES!
"ELITE LIZARD-MEN"... THEY'RE AROUND LEVEL 50, AND THERE'S ALMOST 300 OF THEM...
DODODO (RUMBLE)

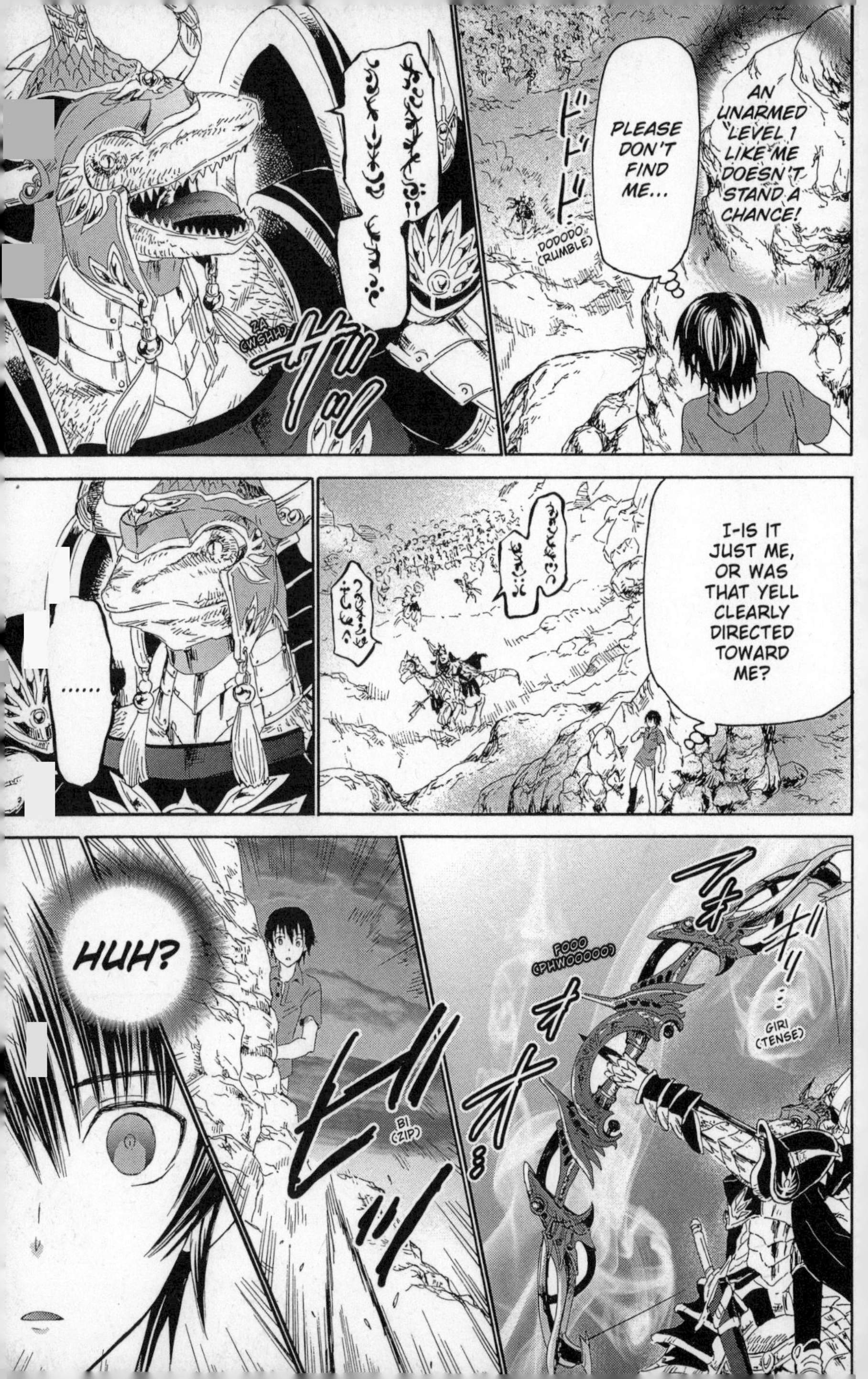
AN UNARMED LEVEL 1 LIKE ME DOESN'T STAND A CHANCE!
PLEASE DON'T FIND ME...
DODODO (RUMBLE)
ZA (WSHHH)
I-IS IT JUST ME, OR WAS THAT YELL CLEARLY DIRECTED TOWARD ME?
......
GIRI (TENSE)
FOOO (PHWOOOOO)
BI (ZIP)
HUH?

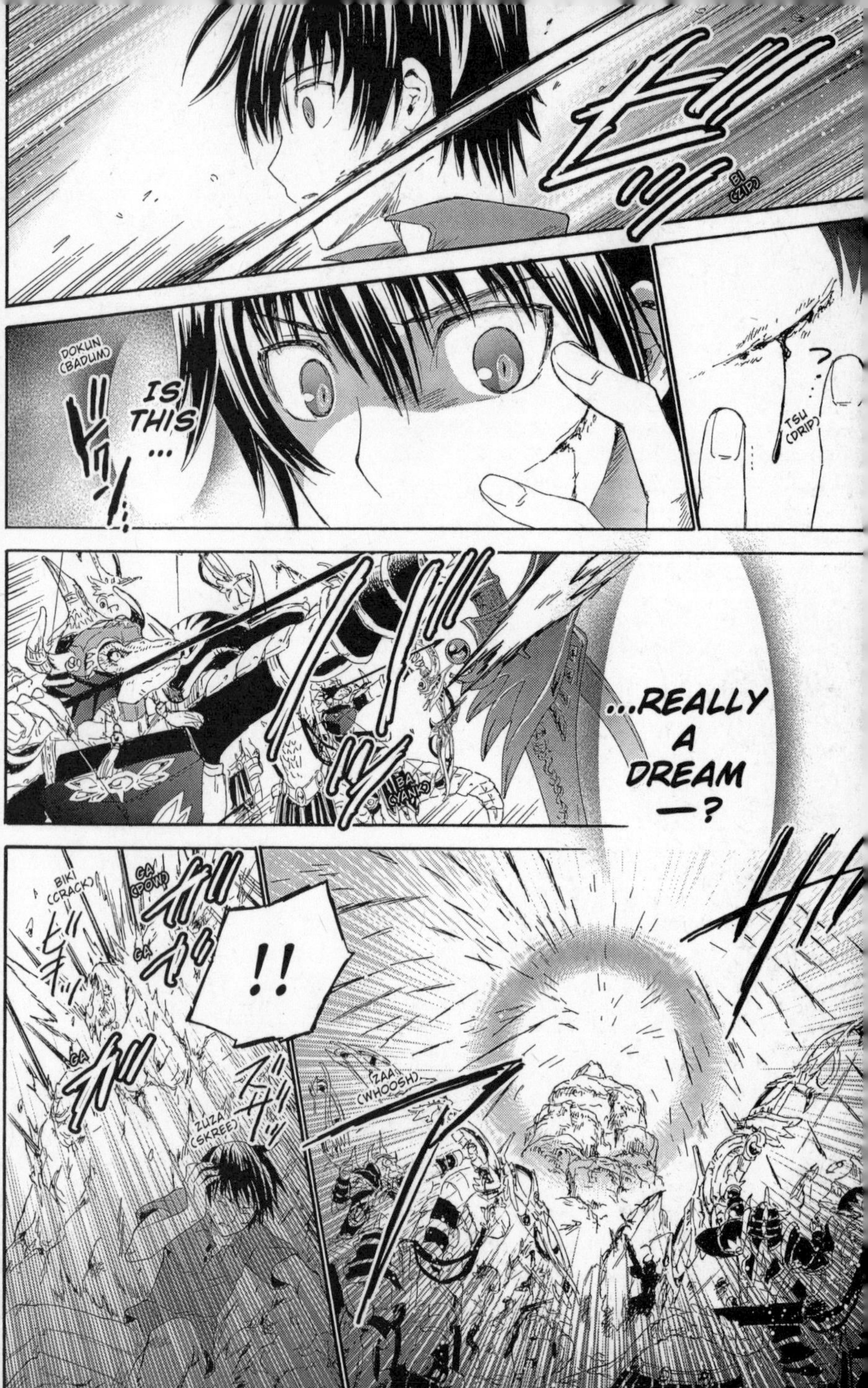
BI (ZIP)
TSU (DRIP)
DOKUN (BADUM)
IS THIS ...
...REALLY A DREAM —?
BA (YANK)
ZAA (WHOOSH)
!!
ZUZA (SKREE)
GA (POW)
BIKI (CRACK)
GA
GA

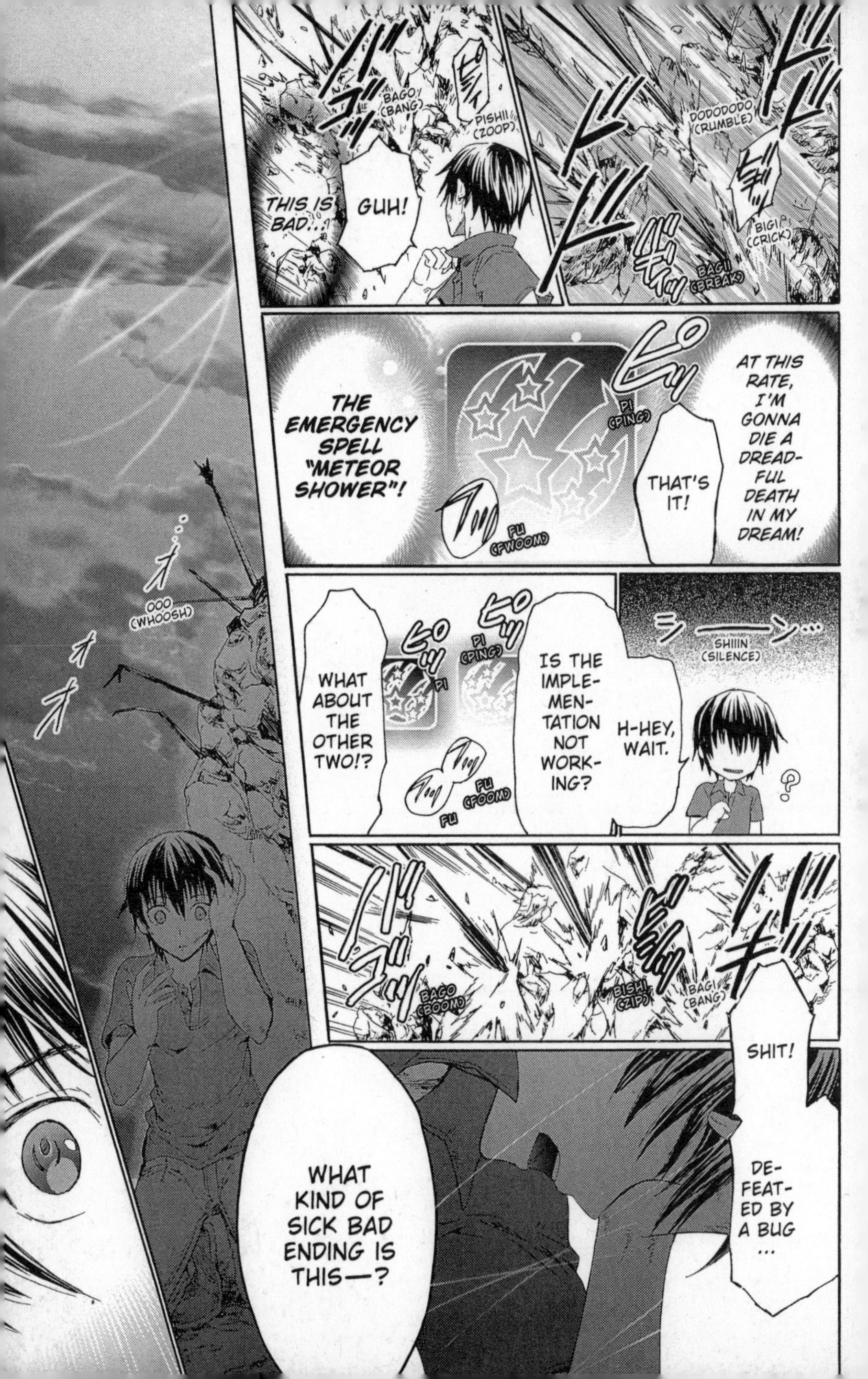
DODODODO (RUMBLE)
BIGI (CRICK)
BAGI (BREAK)
PISHII (ZOOP)
GUH!
BAGO (BANG)
THIS IS BAD...
AT THIS RATE, I'M GONNA DIE A DREADFUL DEATH IN MY DREAM!
THAT'S IT!
PI (PING)
THE EMERGENCY SPELL "METEOR SHOWER"!
FU (FWOOM)
SHIIIN (SILENCE)
H-HEY, WAIT.
IS THE IMPLEMENTATION NOT WORKING?
PI (PING)
PI
WHAT ABOUT THE OTHER TWO!?
FU (FOOM)
FU
BAGI (BANG)
BISHI (ZIP)
BAGO (BOOM)
SHIT!
DEFEATED BY A BUG...
WHAT KIND OF SICK BAD ENDING IS THIS—?
OOO (WHOOSH)

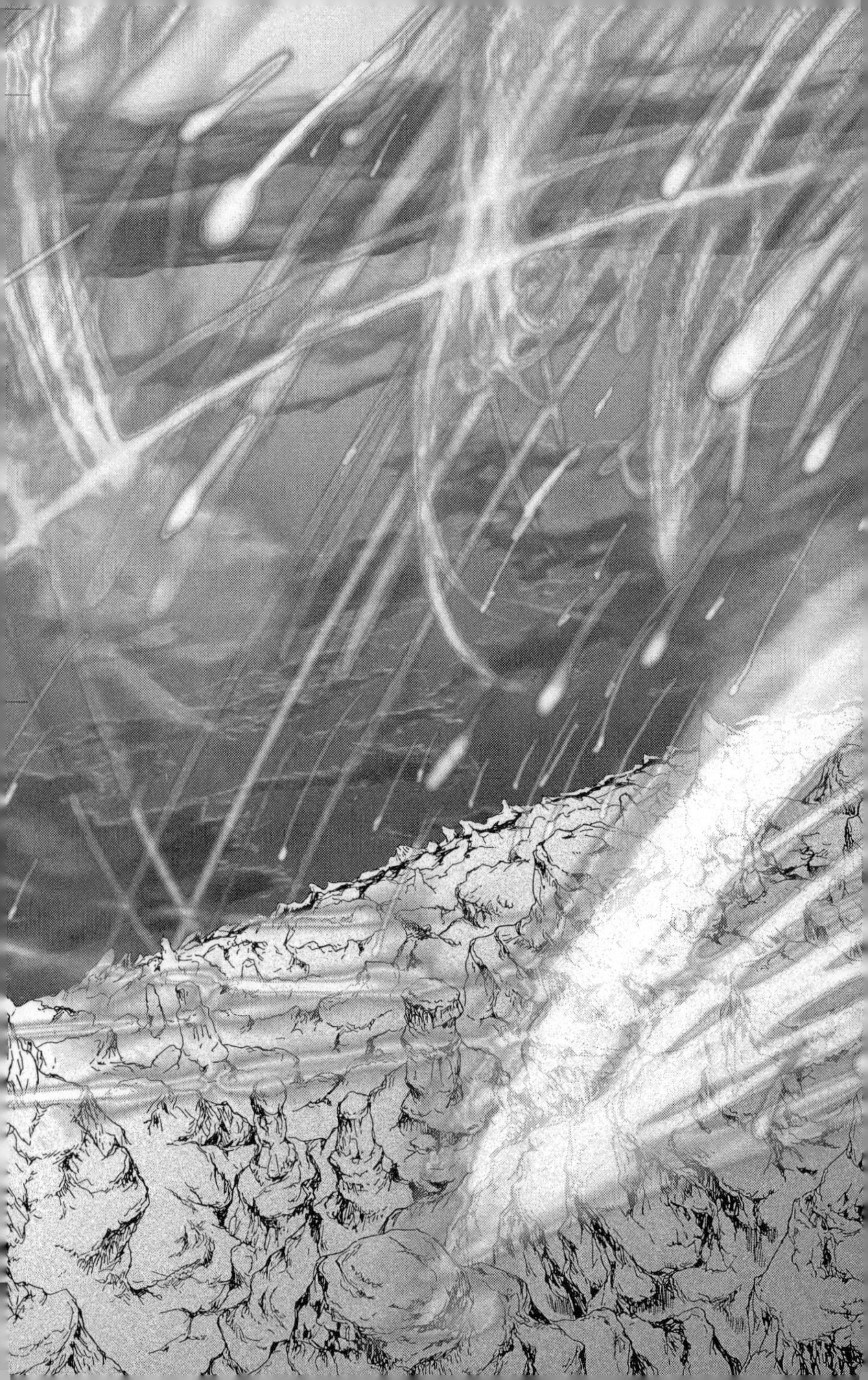

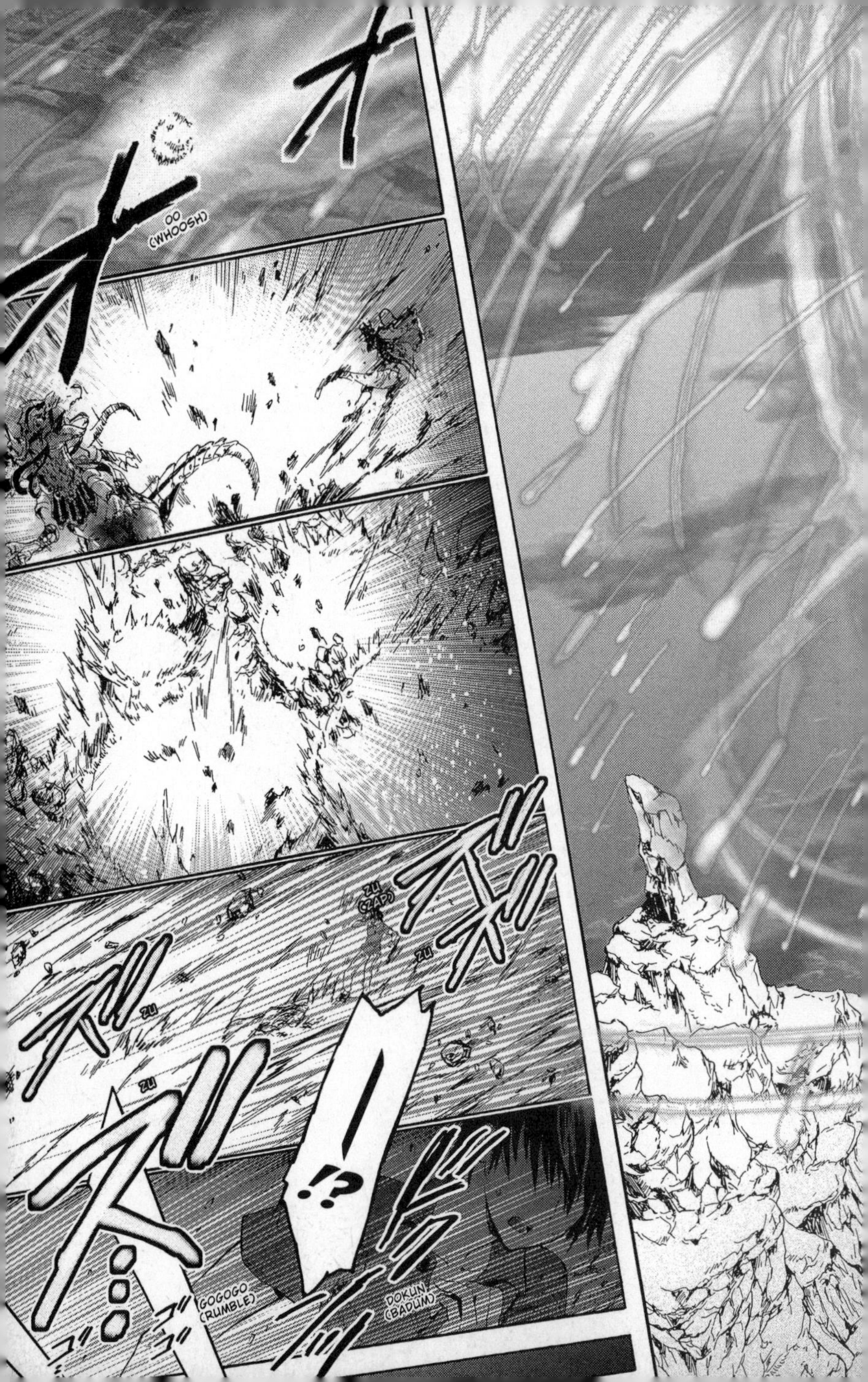
OO
(WHOOSH)
ZU
(ZAP)
ZU
ZU
ZU
!?
DOKUN
(BADUM)
GOGOGO
(RUMBLE)

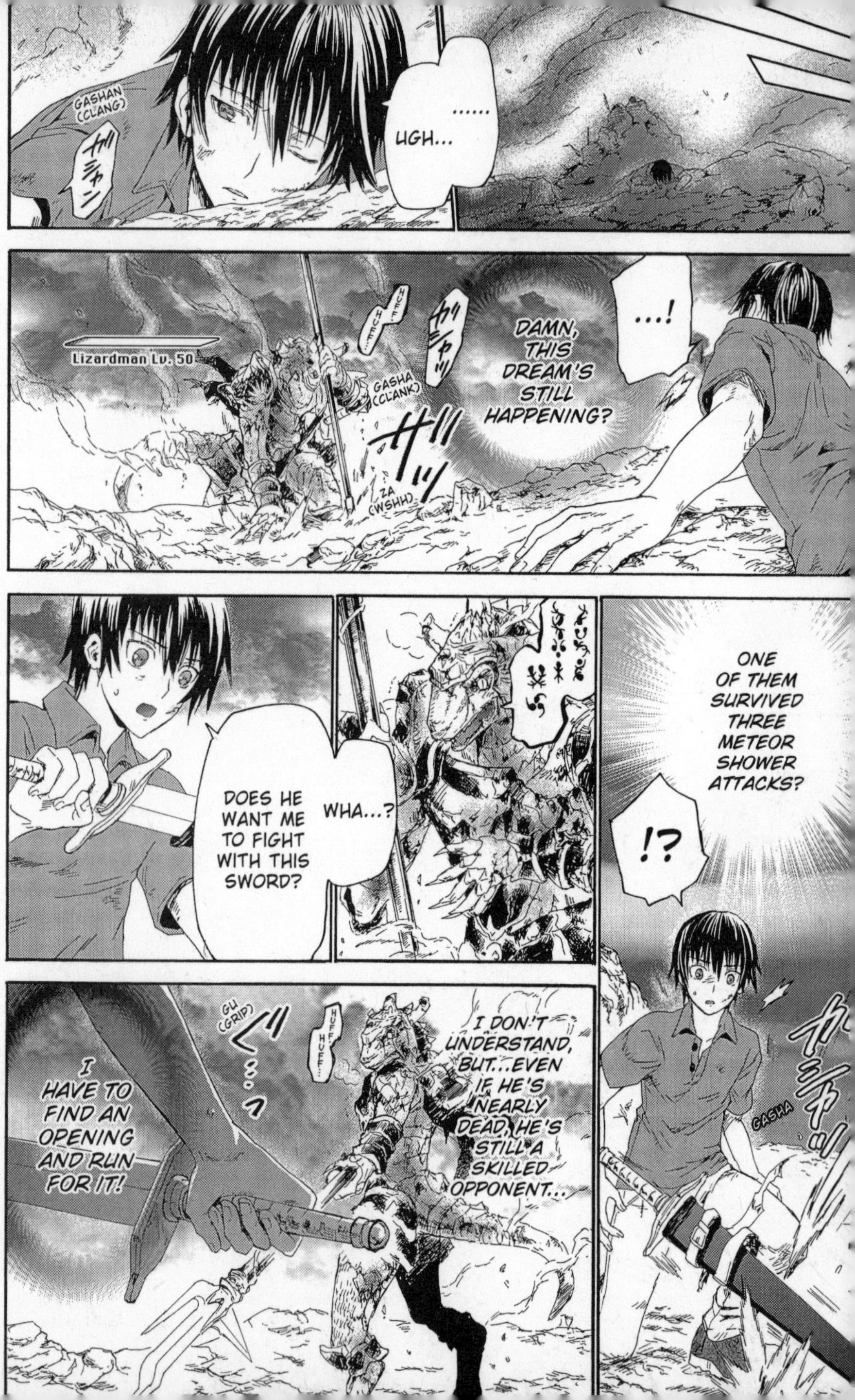
......
UGH...
GASHAN (CLANG)
...!
DAMN, THIS DREAM'S STILL HAPPENING?
HUFF... HUFF...
GASHA (CLANK)
ZA (WSHH)
Lizardman Lv. 50
ONE OF THEM SURVIVED THREE METEOR SHOWER ATTACKS?
!?
WHA...?
DOES HE WANT ME TO FIGHT WITH THIS SWORD?
GASHA
I DON'T UNDERSTAND, BUT...EVEN IF HE'S NEARLY DEAD, HE'S STILL A SKILLED OPPONENT...
HUFF... HUFF...
GU (GRIP)
I HAVE TO FIND AN OPENING AND RUN FOR IT!

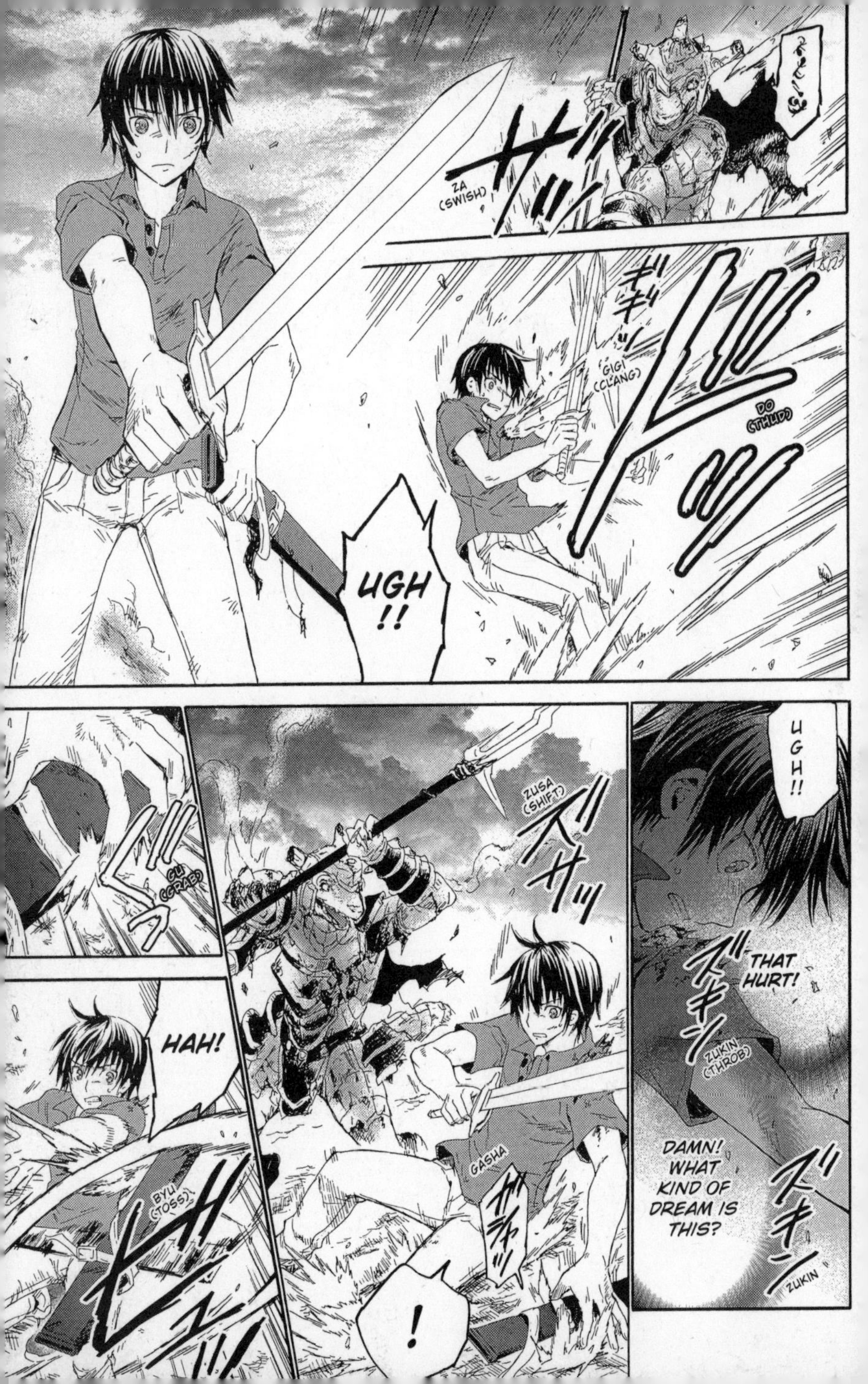
ZA (SWISH)
GIGI (CLANG)
DO (THUD)
UGH !!
UGH!!
THAT HURT!
ZUKIN (THROB)
DAMN! WHAT KIND OF DREAM IS THIS?
ZUKIN
ZUSA (SHIFT)
GASHA
!
GU (GRAB)
HAH!
BYU (TOSS)

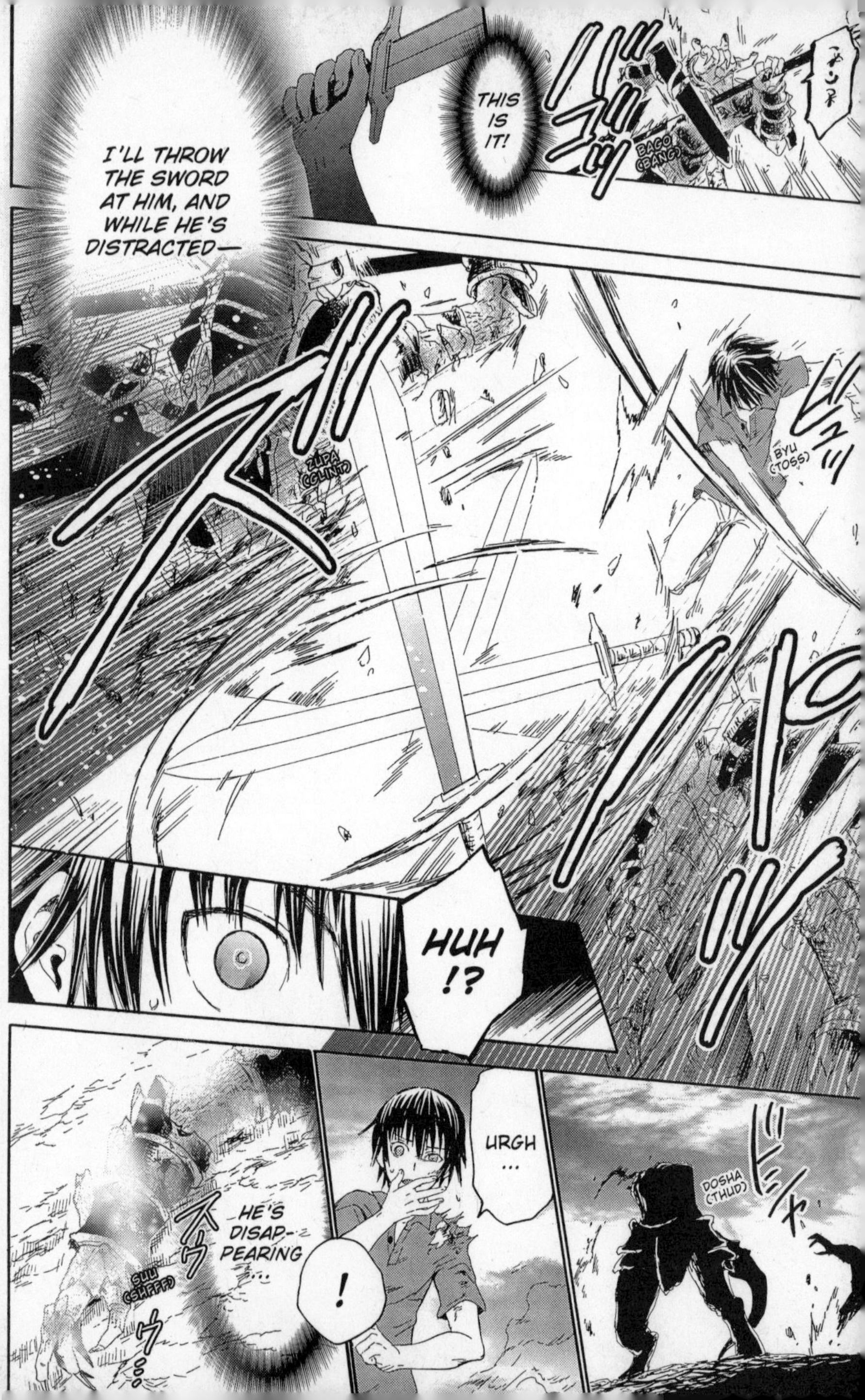
BAGO (BANG)
THIS IS IT!
I'LL THROW THE SWORD AT HIM, AND WHILE HE'S DISTRACTED—
BYU (TOSS)
ZUPA (GLINT)
HUH!?
DOSHA (THUD)
URGH...
!
HE'S DISAPPEARING...
SUU (SHFFF)

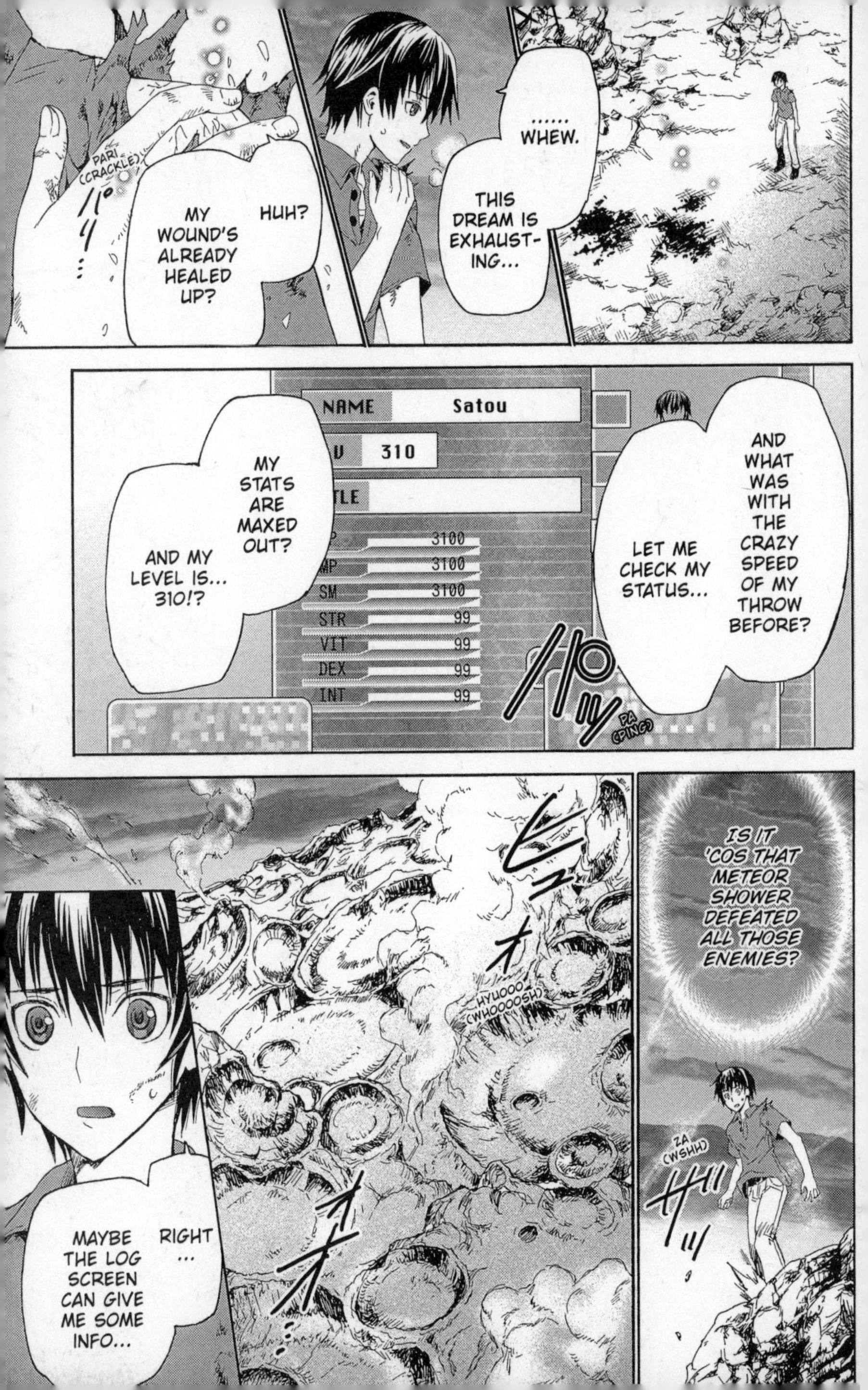......
WHEW.
THIS DREAM IS EXHAUSTING...
HUH?
MY WOUND'S ALREADY HEALED UP?
PARI (CRACKLE)
AND WHAT WAS WITH THE CRAZY SPEED OF MY THROW BEFORE?
LET ME CHECK MY STATUS...
PA (PING)
NAME Satou
V 310
TLE
P 3100
MP 3100
SM 3100
STR 99
VIT 99
DEX 99
INT 99
MY STATS ARE MAXED OUT?
AND MY LEVEL IS... 310!?
IS IT 'COS THAT METEOR SHOWER DEFEATED ALL THOSE ENEMIES?
ZA (WSHH)
HYUOOO (WHOOOOSH)
RIGHT...
MAYBE THE LOG SCREEN CAN GIVE ME SOME INFO...

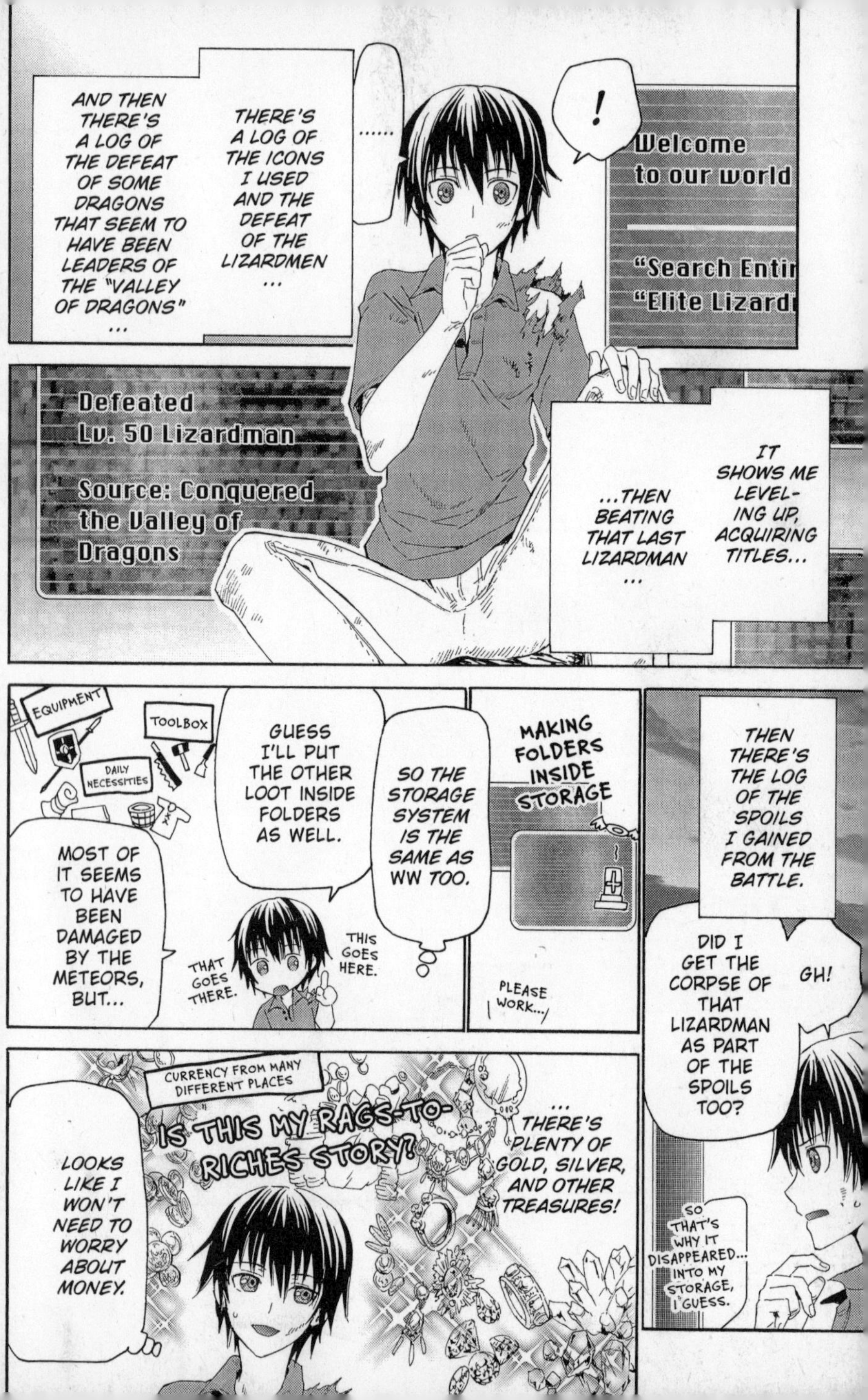
!
Welcome to our world
"Search Entir
"Elite Lizard
......
THERE'S A LOG OF THE ICONS I USED AND THE DEFEAT OF THE LIZARDMEN ...
AND THEN THERE'S A LOG OF THE DEFEAT OF SOME DRAGONS THAT SEEM TO HAVE BEEN LEADERS OF THE "VALLEY OF DRAGONS" ...
IT SHOWS ME LEVELING UP, ACQUIRING TITLES...
...THEN BEATING THAT LAST LIZARDMAN ...
Defeated Lv. 50 Lizardman
Source: Conquered the Valley of Dragons
THEN THERE'S THE LOG OF THE SPOILS I GAINED FROM THE BATTLE.
GH!
DID I GET THE CORPSE OF THAT LIZARDMAN AS PART OF THE SPOILS TOO?
SO THAT'S WHY IT DISAPPEARED... INTO MY STORAGE, I GUESS.
MAKING FOLDERS INSIDE STORAGE
PLEASE WORK...
SO THE STORAGE SYSTEM IS THE SAME AS WW TOO.
GUESS I'LL PUT THE OTHER LOOT INSIDE FOLDERS AS WELL.
THIS GOES HERE.
THAT GOES THERE.
EQUIPMENT
TOOLBOX
DAILY NECESSITIES
MOST OF IT SEEMS TO HAVE BEEN DAMAGED BY THE METEORS, BUT...
... THERE'S PLENTY OF GOLD, SILVER, AND OTHER TREASURES!
CURRENCY FROM MANY DIFFERENT PLACES
IS THIS MY RAGS-TO-RICHES STORY!?
LOOKS LIKE I WON'T NEED TO WORRY ABOUT MONEY.

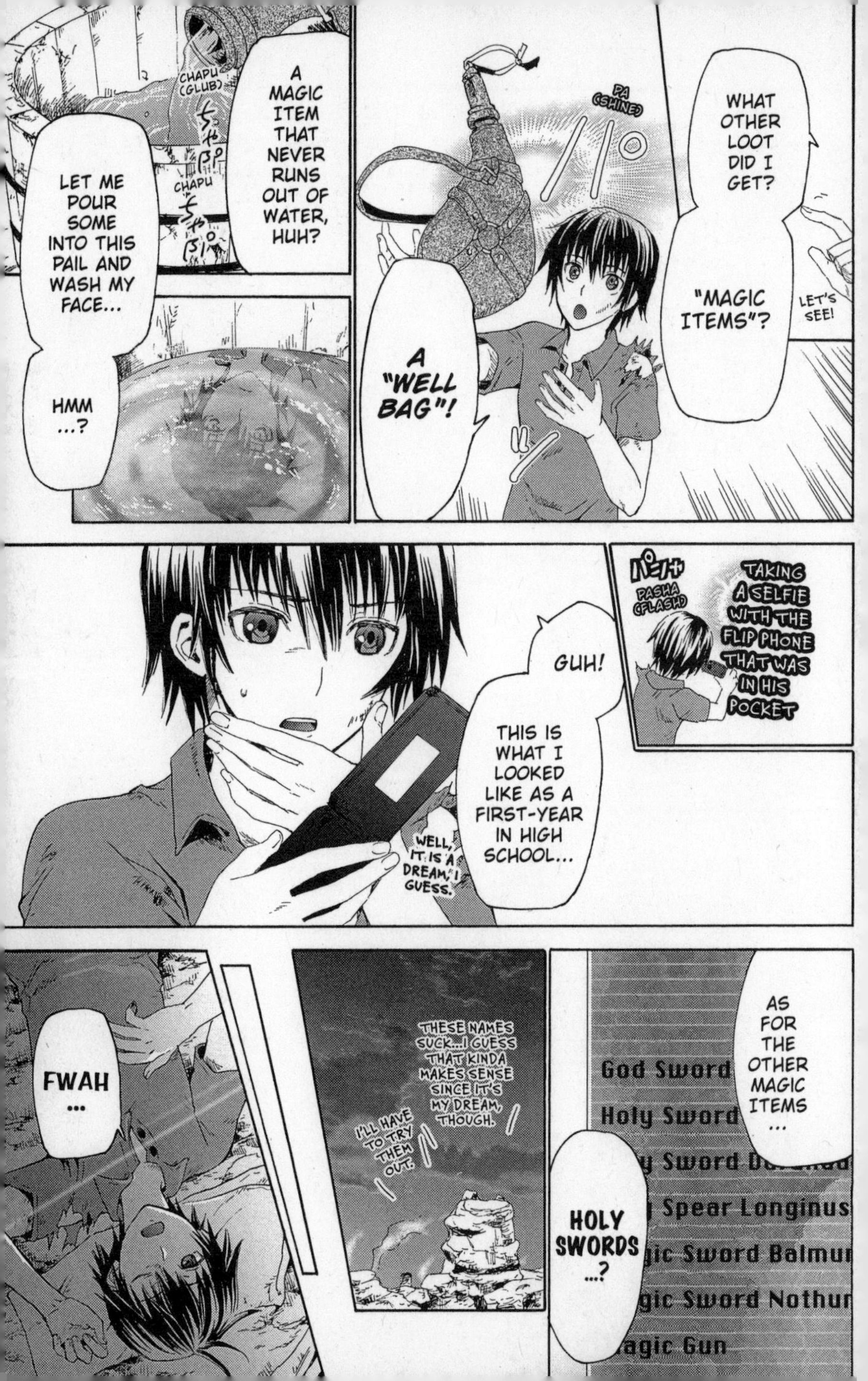
WHAT OTHER LOOT DID I GET?
LET'S SEE!
"MAGIC ITEMS"?
PA (SHINE)
A "WELL BAG"!
A MAGIC ITEM THAT NEVER RUNS OUT OF WATER, HUH?
CHAPU (GLUB)
CHAPU
LET ME POUR SOME INTO THIS PAIL AND WASH MY FACE...
HMM ...?
パシャ
PASHA (FLASH)
TAKING A SELFIE WITH THE FLIP PHONE THAT WAS IN HIS POCKET
GUH!
THIS IS WHAT I LOOKED LIKE AS A FIRST-YEAR IN HIGH SCHOOL...
WELL, IT IS A DREAM, I GUESS.
AS FOR THE OTHER MAGIC ITEMS ...
God Sword
Holy Sword
Spear Longinus
HOLY SWORDS ...?
THESE NAMES SUCK...I GUESS THAT KINDA MAKES SENSE SINCE IT'S MY DREAM, THOUGH.
I'LL HAVE TO TRY THEM OUT.
FWAH ...

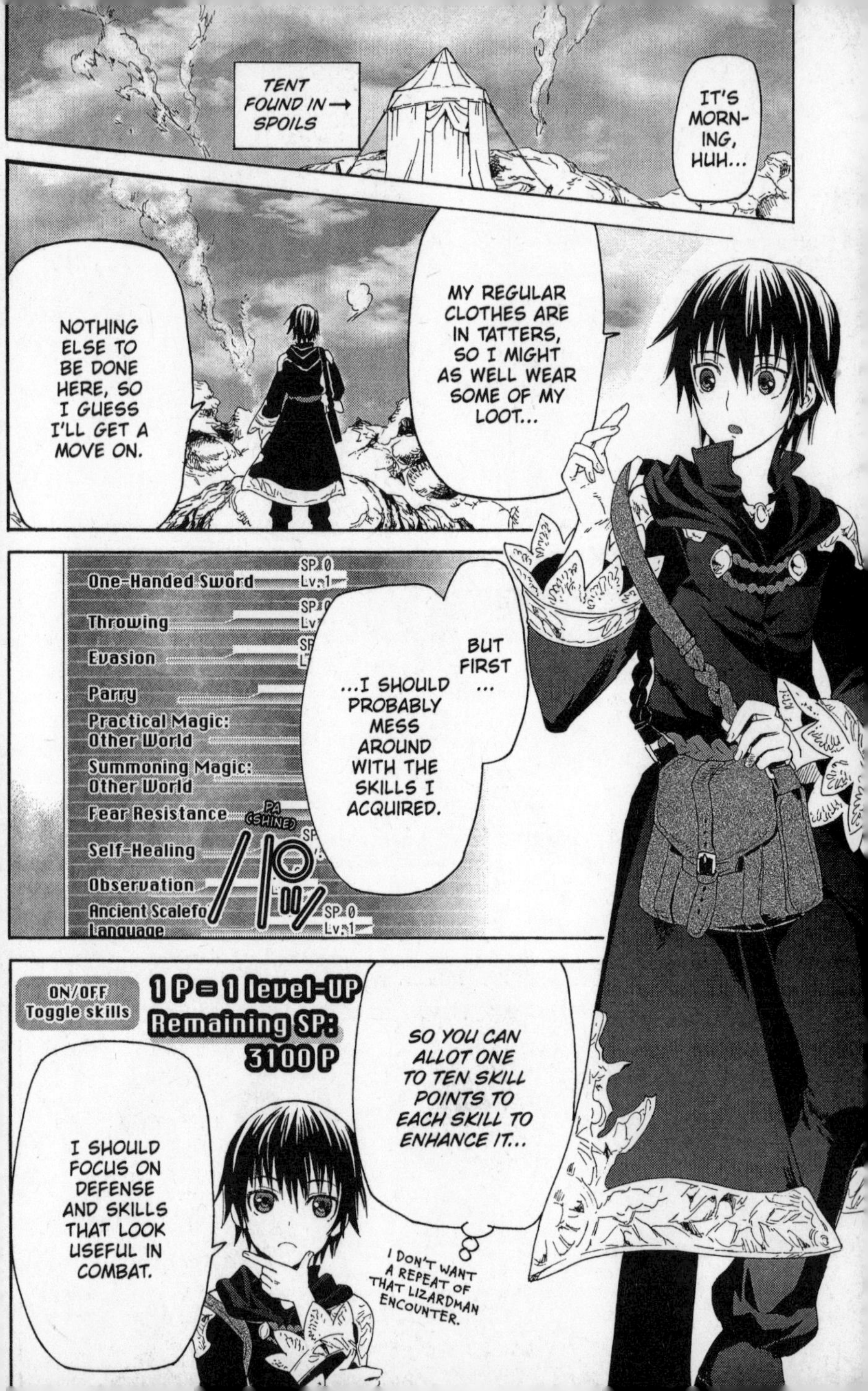
IT'S MORNING, HUH...
TENT FOUND IN SPOILS →
MY REGULAR CLOTHES ARE IN TATTERS, SO I MIGHT AS WELL WEAR SOME OF MY LOOT...
BUT FIRST...
...I SHOULD PROBABLY MESS AROUND WITH THE SKILLS I ACQUIRED.
NOTHING ELSE TO BE DONE HERE, SO I GUESS I'LL GET A MOVE ON.
One-Handed Sword SP 0 Lv. 1
Throwing
Evasion
Parry
Practical Magic: Other World
Summoning Magic: Other World
Fear Resistance
Self-Healing
Observation
Ancient Scalefo Language SP 0 Lv. 1
PA (SHINE)
SO YOU CAN ALLOT ONE TO TEN SKILL POINTS TO EACH SKILL TO ENHANCE IT...
ON/OFF Toggle skills
1 P = 1 level-UP
Remaining SP: 3100 P
I SHOULD FOCUS ON DEFENSE AND SKILLS THAT LOOK USEFUL IN COMBAT.
I DON'T WANT A REPEAT OF THAT LIZARDMAN ENCOUNTER.

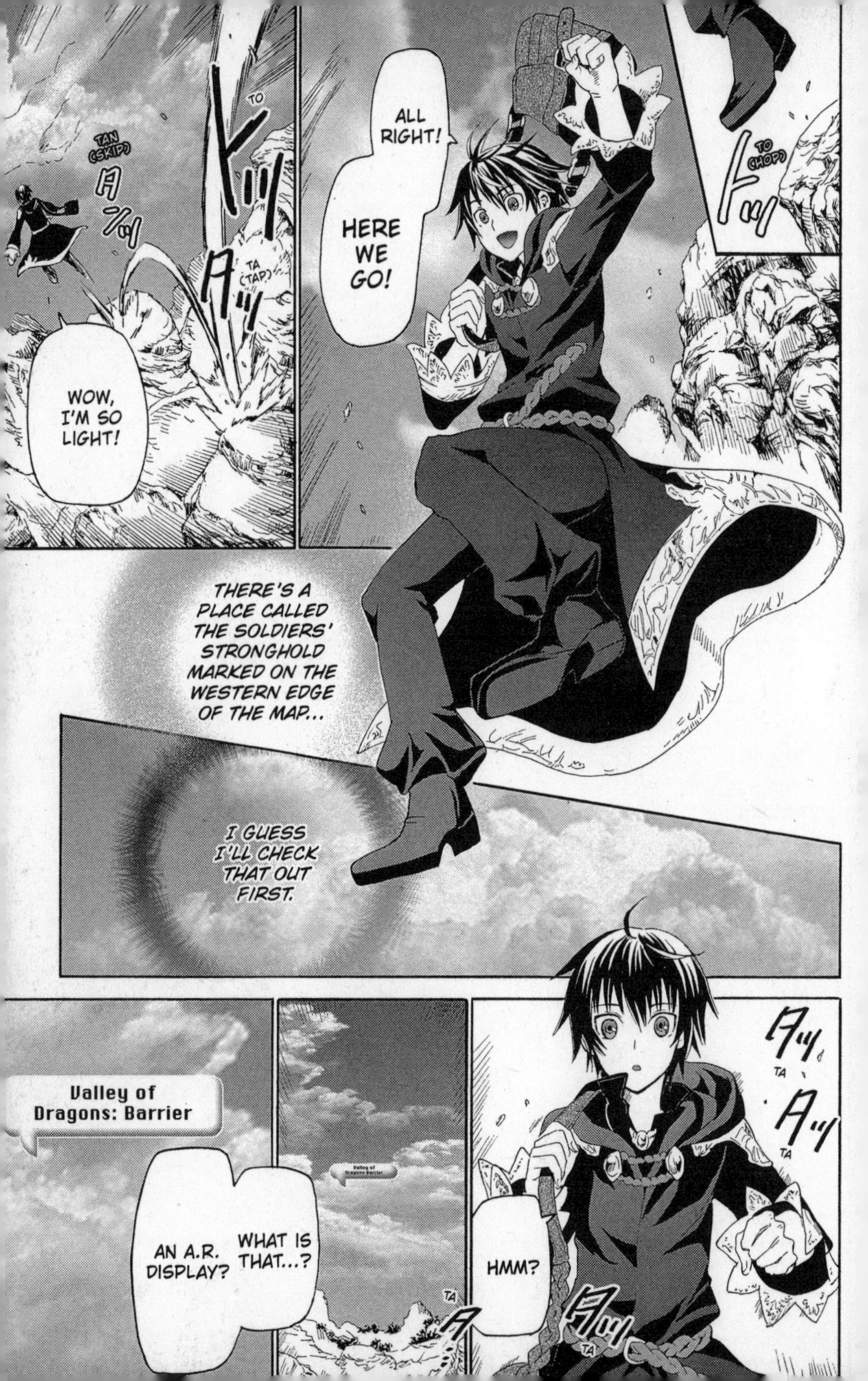
TO (CHOP)
ALL RIGHT!
HERE WE GO!
TO
TAN (SKIP)
TA (TAP)
WOW, I'M SO LIGHT!
THERE'S A PLACE CALLED THE SOLDIERS' STRONGHOLD MARKED ON THE WESTERN EDGE OF THE MAP...
I GUESS I'LL CHECK THAT OUT FIRST.
TA
TA
HMM?
TA
Valley of Dragons Barrier
TA
Valley of Dragons: Barrier
WHAT IS THAT...?
AN A.R. DISPLAY?

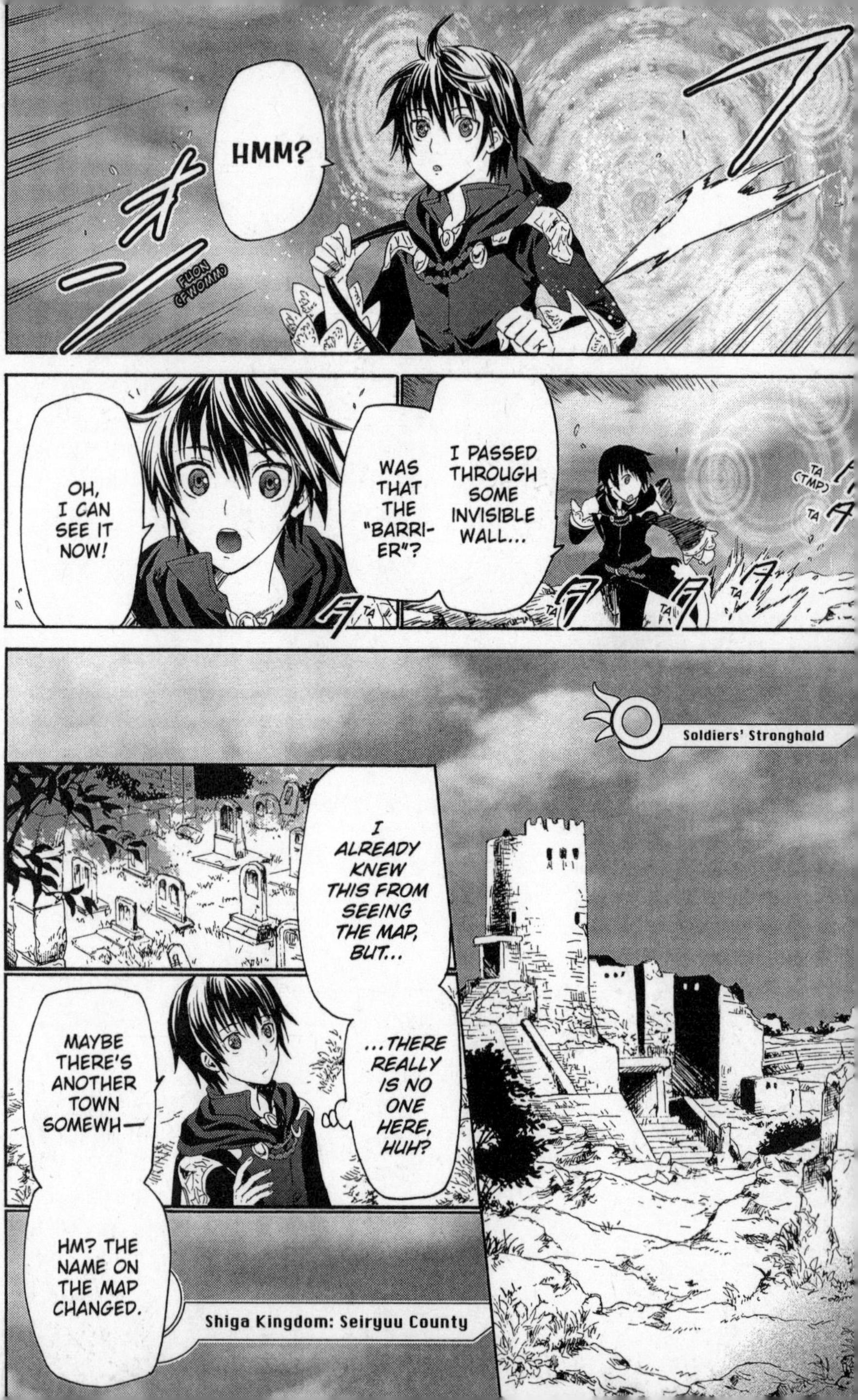
HMM?
FUON (FWOMM)
TA (TMP) TA
TA TA TA
I PASSED THROUGH SOME INVISIBLE WALL...
WAS THAT THE "BARRIER"?
TA
OH, I CAN SEE IT NOW!
Soldiers' Stronghold
I ALREADY KNEW THIS FROM SEEING THE MAP, BUT...
...THERE REALLY IS NO ONE HERE, HUH?
MAYBE THERE'S ANOTHER TOWN SOMEWH—
HM? THE NAME ON THE MAP CHANGED.
Shiga Kingdom: Seiryuu County

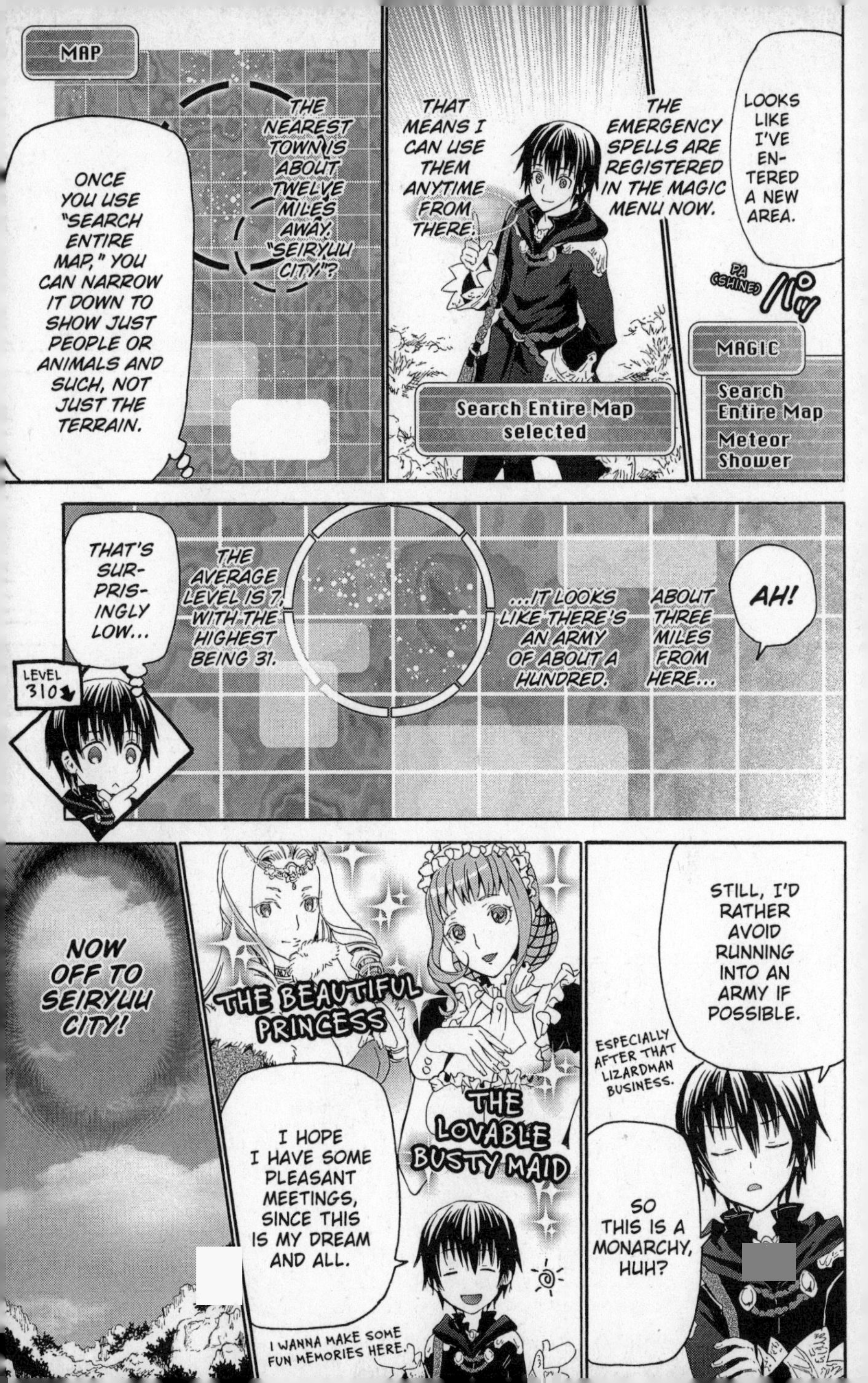
LOOKS LIKE I'VE EN-TERED A NEW AREA.
PA (SHINE) パッ
MAGIC
Search Entire Map
Meteor Shower
THE EMERGENCY SPELLS ARE REGISTERED IN THE MAGIC MENU NOW.
THAT MEANS I CAN USE THEM ANYTIME FROM THERE.
Search Entire Map selected
MAP
THE NEAREST TOWN IS ABOUT TWELVE MILES AWAY. "SEIRYUU CITY"?
ONCE YOU USE "SEARCH ENTIRE MAP," YOU CAN NARROW IT DOWN TO SHOW JUST PEOPLE OR ANIMALS AND SUCH, NOT JUST THE TERRAIN.
AH!
ABOUT THREE MILES FROM HERE...
...IT LOOKS LIKE THERE'S AN ARMY OF ABOUT A HUNDRED.
THE AVERAGE LEVEL IS 7, WITH THE HIGHEST BEING 31.
THAT'S SUR-PRIS-INGLY LOW...
LEVEL 310
STILL, I'D RATHER AVOID RUNNING INTO AN ARMY IF POSSIBLE.
ESPECIALLY AFTER THAT LIZARDMAN BUSINESS.
SO THIS IS A MONARCHY, HUH?
THE BEAUTIFUL PRINCESS
THE LOVABLE BUSTY MAID
I HOPE I HAVE SOME PLEASANT MEETINGS, SINCE THIS IS MY DREAM AND ALL.
I WANNA MAKE SOME FUN MEMORIES HERE.
NOW OFF TO SEIRYUU CITY!

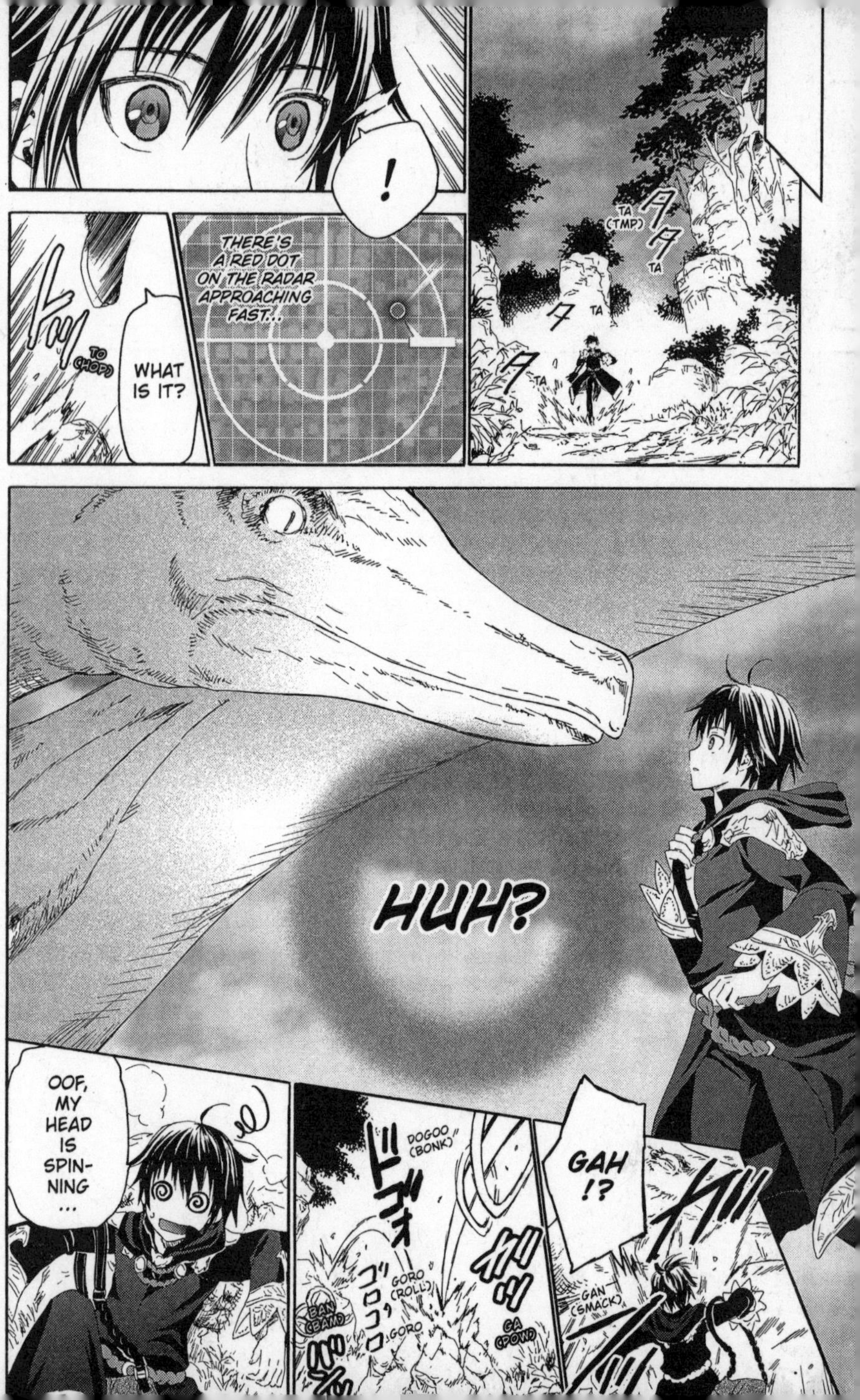
TA (TMP)
TA
TA
TA
!
THERE'S A RED DOT ON THE RADAR APPROACHING FAST...
TO (HOP)
WHAT IS IT?
HUH?
GAN (SMACK)
GAH!?
DOGOO (BONK)
GORO (ROLL)
GORO
GA (POW)
BAN (BAM)
OOF, MY HEAD IS SPINNING...

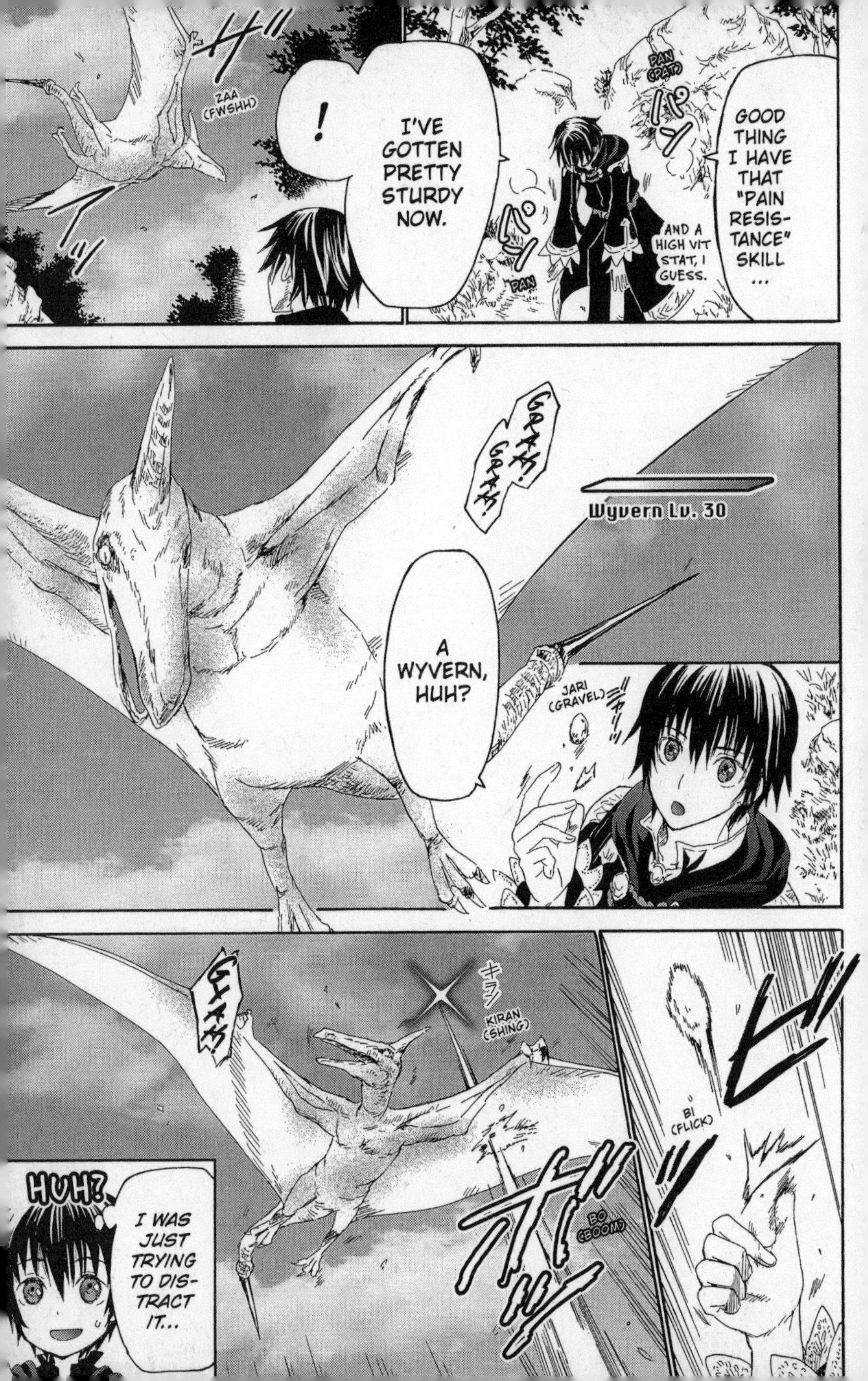
PAN (PAT)
GOOD THING I HAVE THAT "PAIN RESIS-TANCE" SKILL...
AND A HIGH VIT STAT, I GUESS.
PAN
!
I'VE GOTTEN PRETTY STURDY NOW.
ZAA (FWSHH)
GRAAA! GRAAA!
Wyvern Lv. 30
A WYVERN, HUH?
JARI (GRAVEL)
BI (FLICK)
BO (BOOM)
KIRAN (SHING)
HUH?
I WAS JUST TRYING TO DIS-TRACT IT...

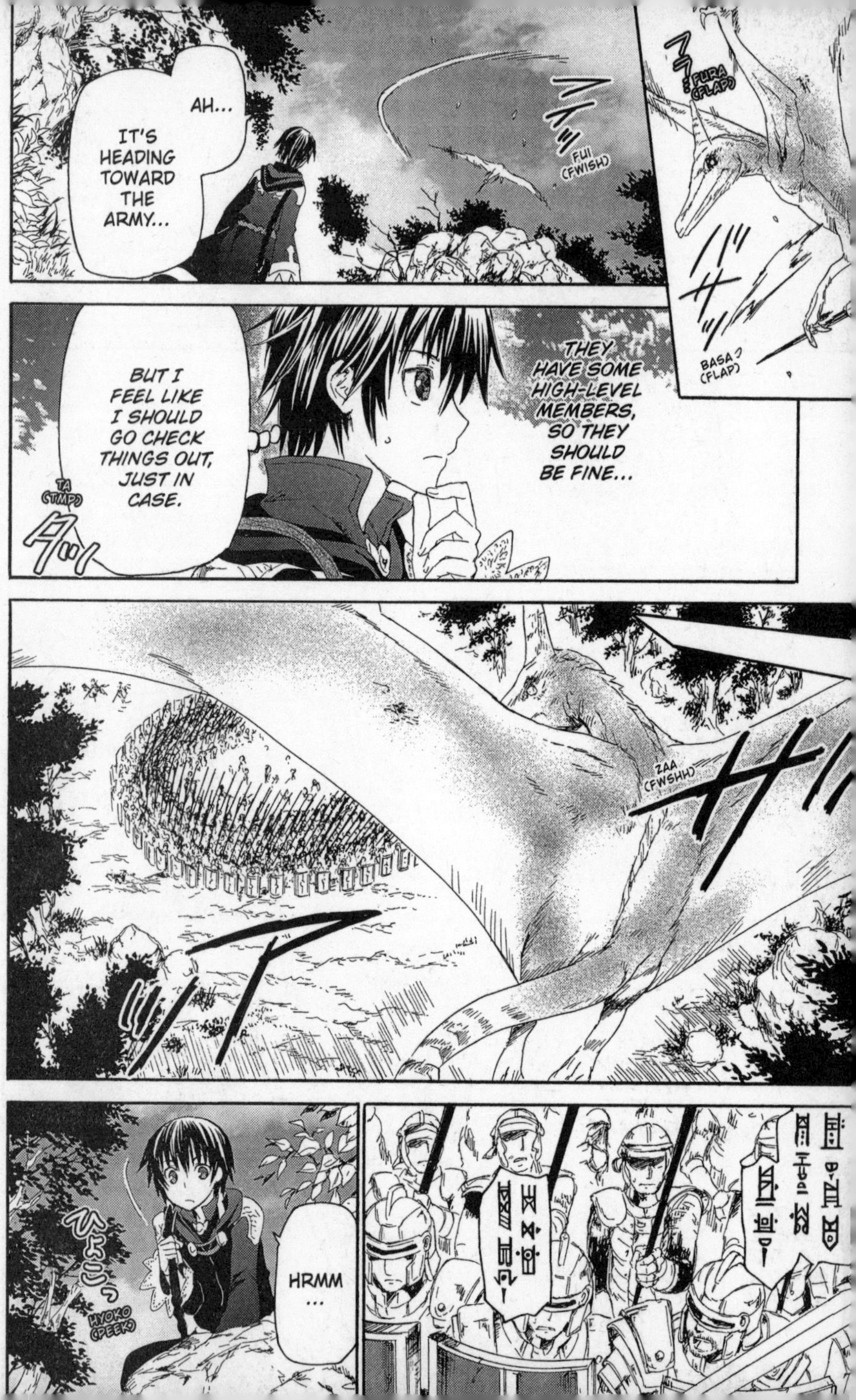
FURA (FLAP)
BASA (FLAP)
FUI (FWISH)
AH...
IT'S HEADING TOWARD THE ARMY...
THEY HAVE SOME HIGH-LEVEL MEMBERS, SO THEY SHOULD BE FINE...
BUT I FEEL LIKE I SHOULD GO CHECK THINGS OUT, JUST IN CASE.
TA (TMP)
ZAA (FWSHH)
HRMM...
HYOKO (PEEK)

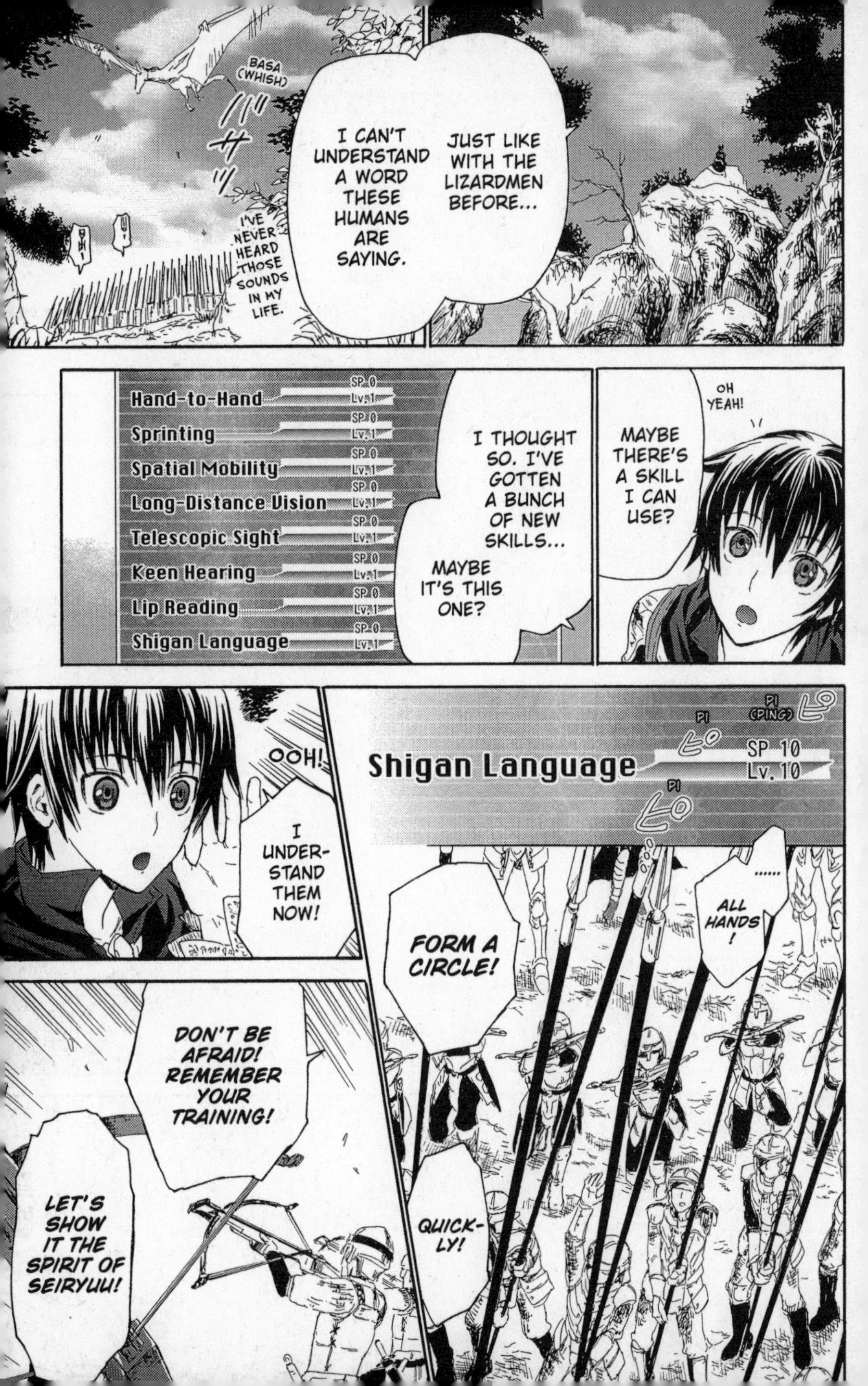
JUST LIKE WITH THE LIZARDMEN BEFORE...
I CAN'T UNDERSTAND A WORD THESE HUMANS ARE SAYING.
BASA (WHISH)
I'VE NEVER HEARD THOSE SOUNDS IN MY LIFE.
OH YEAH!
MAYBE THERE'S A SKILL I CAN USE?
I THOUGHT SO. I'VE GOTTEN A BUNCH OF NEW SKILLS...
MAYBE IT'S THIS ONE?
Hand-to-Hand SP. 0 Lv. 1
Sprinting SP. 0 Lv. 1
Spatial Mobility SP. 0 Lv. 1
Long-Distance Vision SP. 0 Lv. 1
Telescopic Sight SP. 0 Lv. 1
Keen Hearing SP. 0 Lv. 1
Lip Reading SP. 0 Lv. 1
Shigan Language SP. 0 Lv. 1
PI (PING)
PI
PI
Shigan Language SP 10 Lv. 10
OOH!
I UNDERSTAND THEM NOW!
......
ALL HANDS!
FORM A CIRCLE!
QUICKLY!
DON'T BE AFRAID! REMEMBER YOUR TRAINING!
LET'S SHOW IT THE SPIRIT OF SEIRYUU!

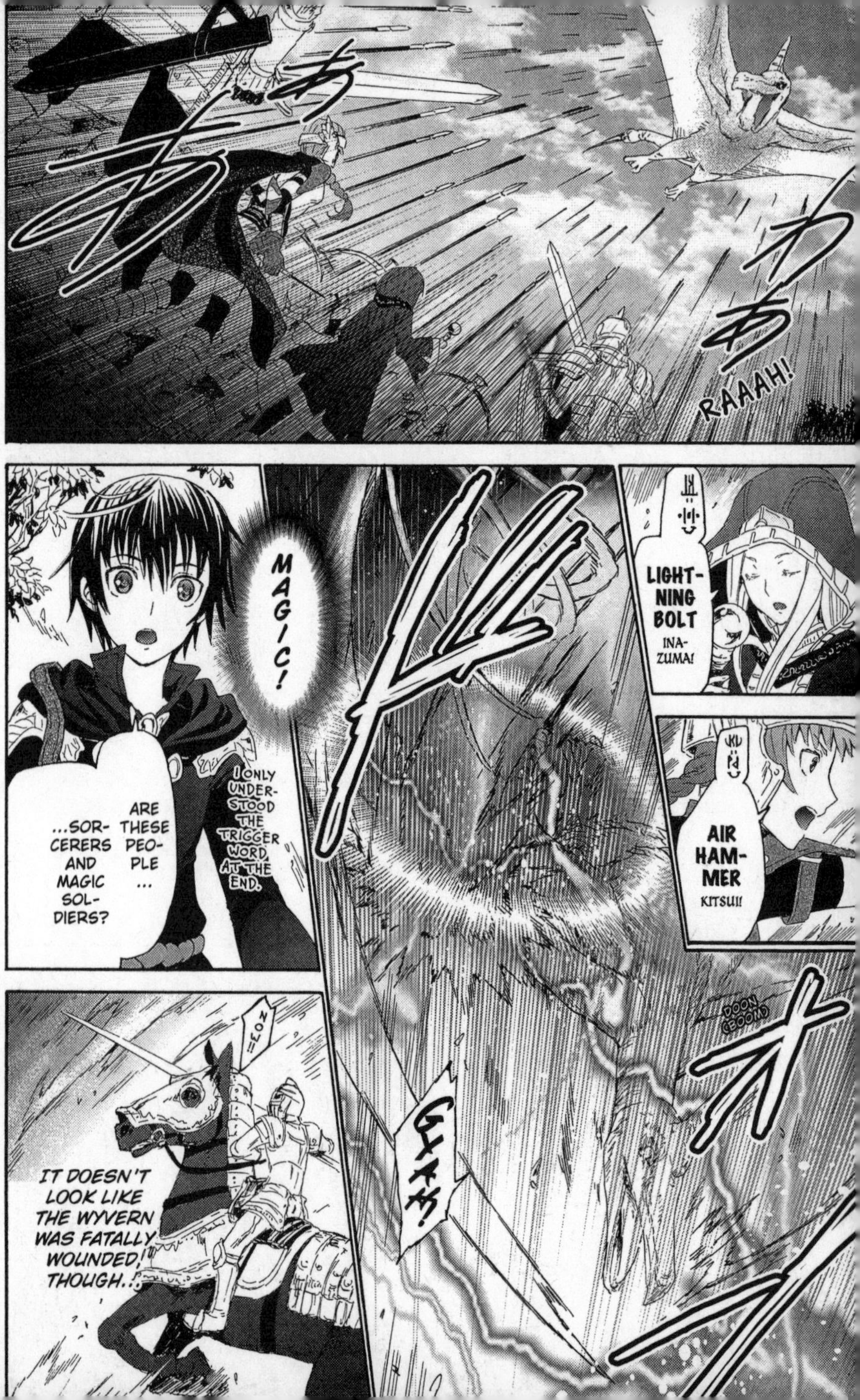

RAAAH!
LIGHTNING BOLT
INAZUMA!
AIR HAMMER
KITSUI!
DOON (BOOM)
GYAAH!
MAGIC!
I ONLY UNDERSTOOD THE TRIGGER WORD AT THE END.
ARE THESE PEOPLE...
...SORCERERS AND MAGIC SOLDIERS?
NOW!!
IT DOESN'T LOOK LIKE THE WYVERN WAS FATALLY WOUNDED, THOUGH...

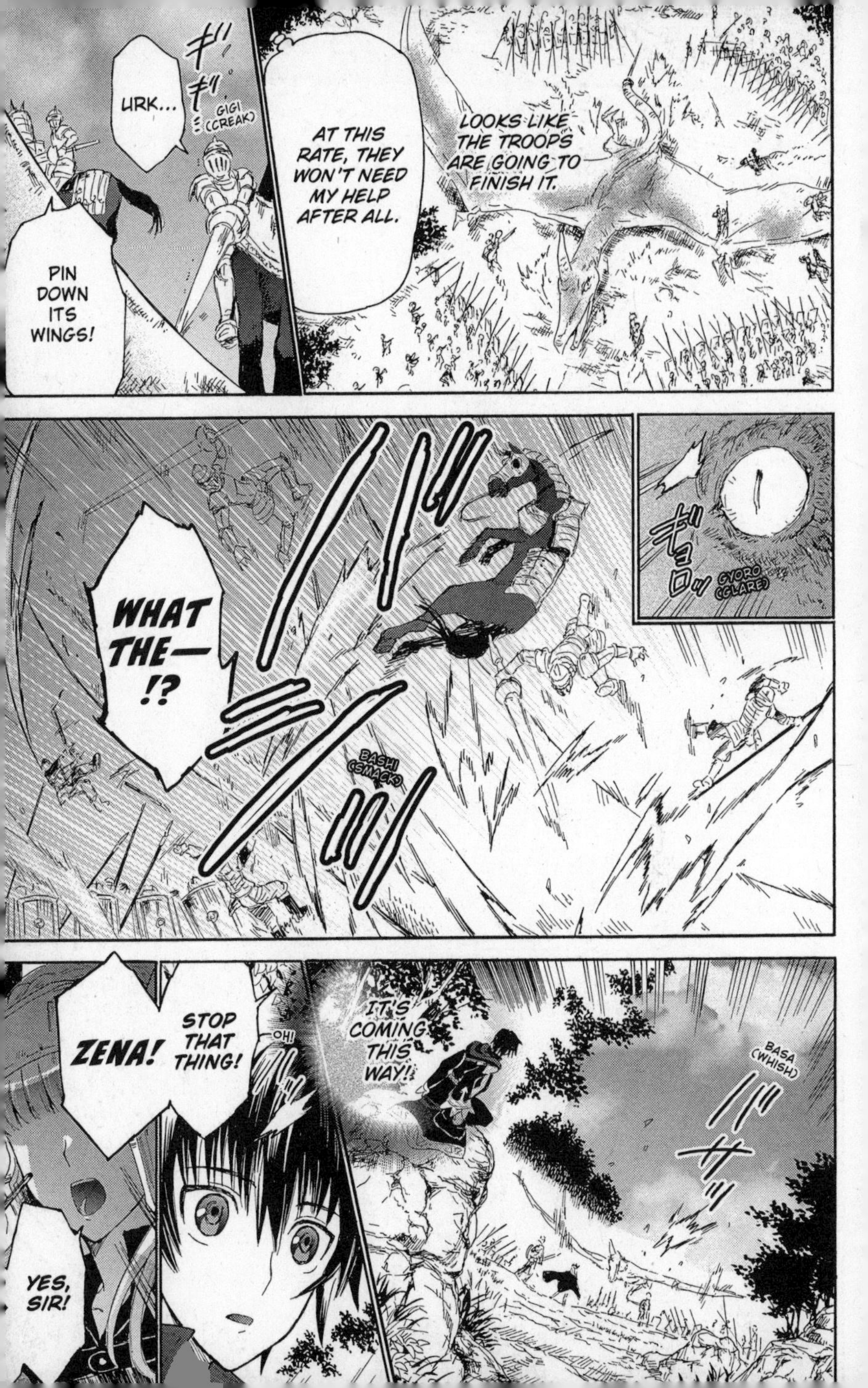
LOOKS LIKE THE TROOPS ARE GOING TO FINISH IT.
AT THIS RATE, THEY WON'T NEED MY HELP AFTER ALL.
GIGI (CREAK)
URK...
PIN DOWN ITS WINGS!
GYORO (GLARE)
BASHI (SMACK)
WHAT THE—!?
BASA (WHISH)
IT'S COMING THIS WAY!
OH!
STOP THAT THING!
ZENA!
YES, SIR!

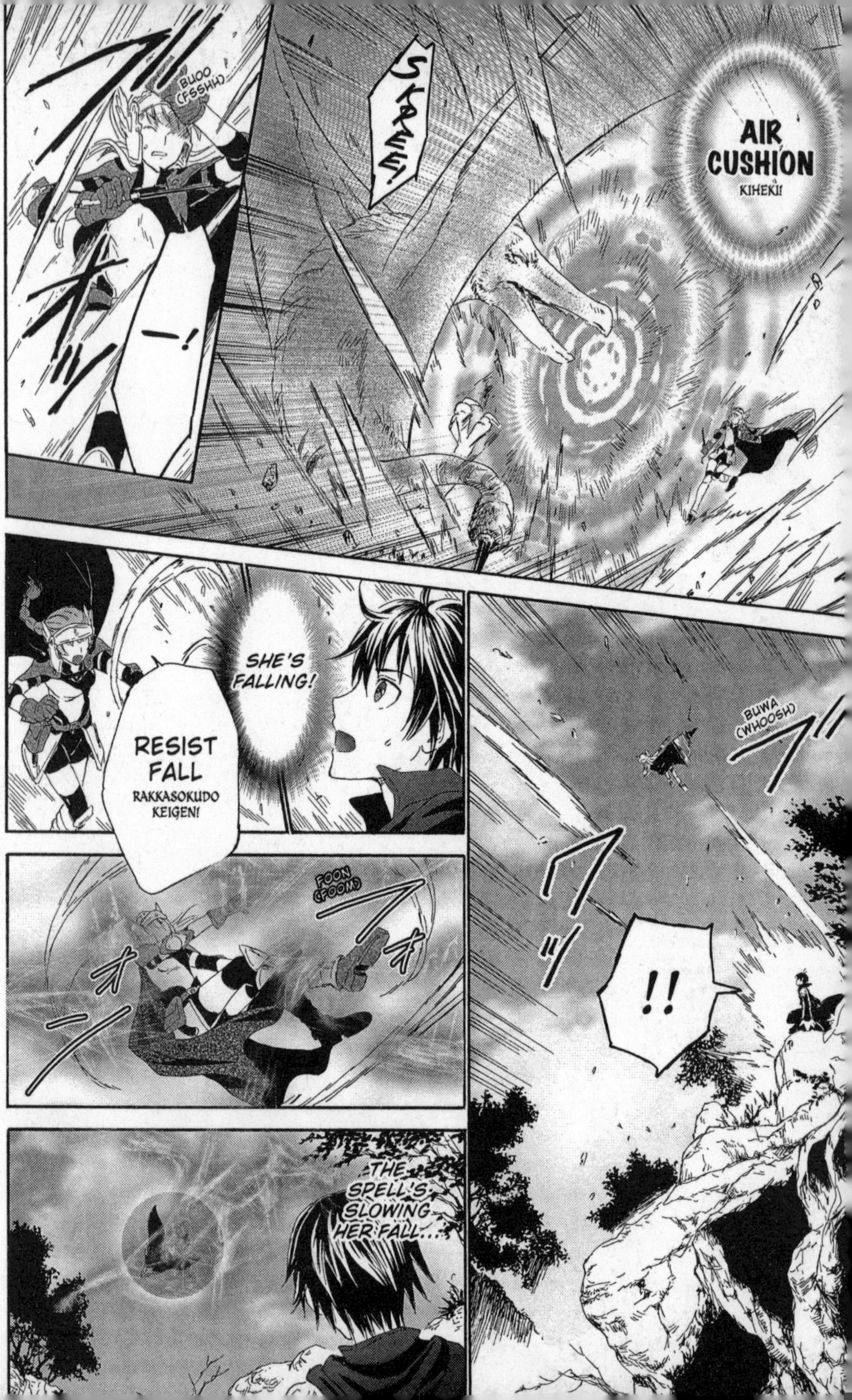
AIR CUSHION
KIHEKI!
SKREEE!
BUOO (FSSHH)
BUWA (WHOOSH)
!!
SHE'S FALLING!
RESIST FALL
RAKKASOKUDO KEIGEN!
FOON (FOOM)
THE SPELL'S SLOWING HER FALL...

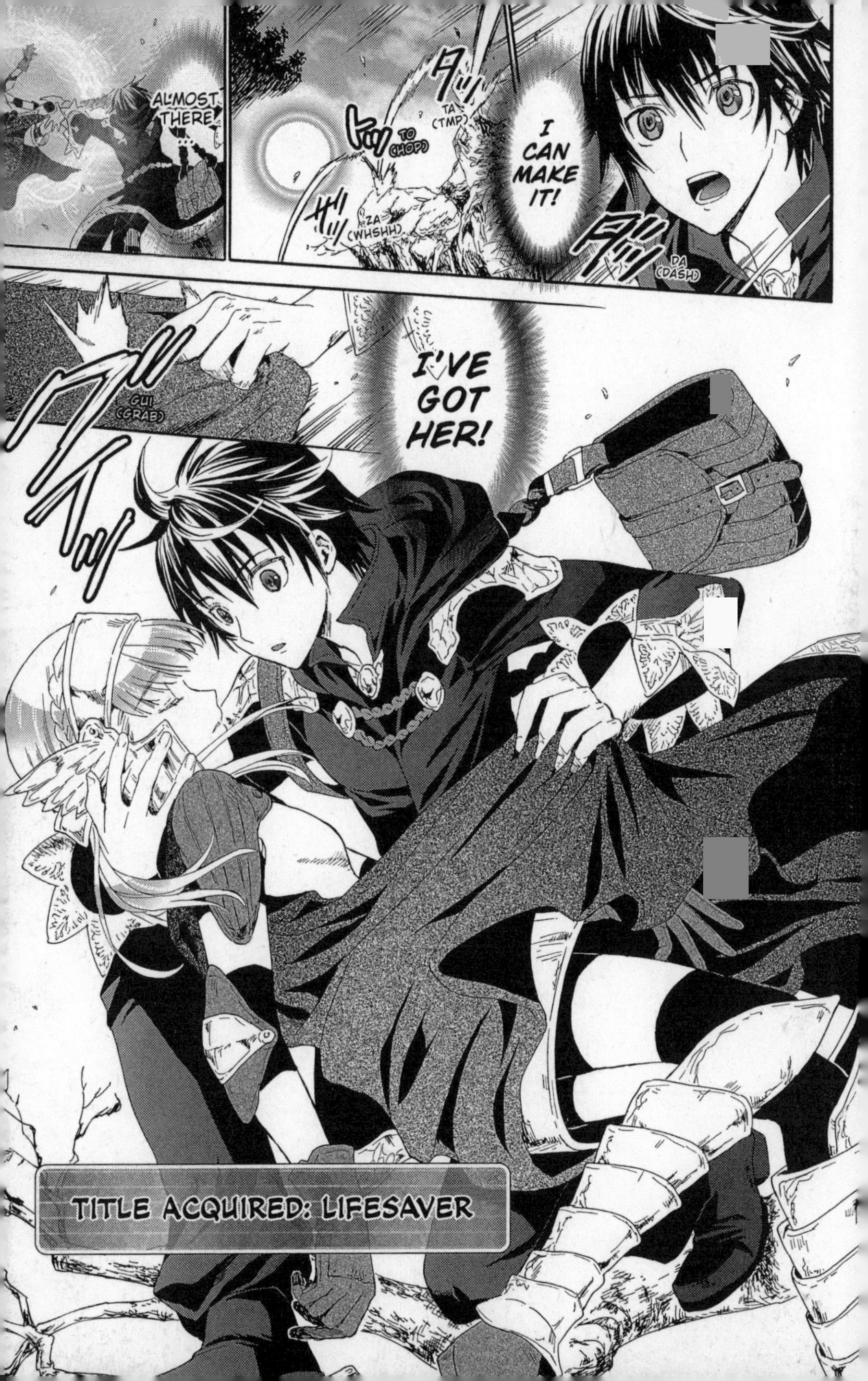
I CAN MAKE IT!
DA (DASH)
TA (TMP)
TO (HOP)
ZA (WHSHH)
ALMOST THERE...
I'VE GOT HER!
GUI (GRAB)
TITLE ACQUIRED: LIFESAVER

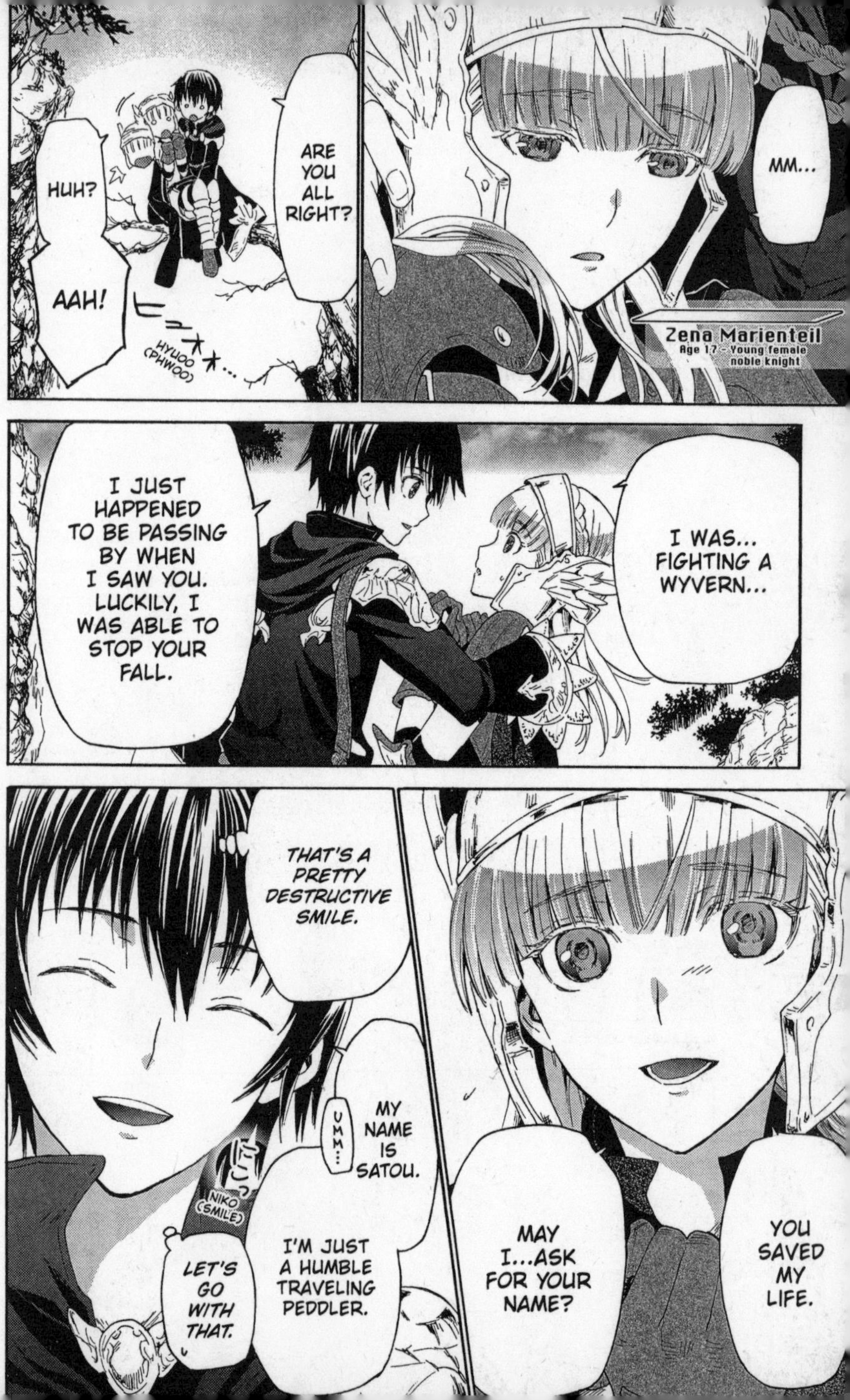
MM...
Zena Marienteil
Age 17 - Young female noble knight
ARE YOU ALL RIGHT?
HUH?
AAH!
HYUOO (PHWOO)
I WAS... FIGHTING A WYVERN...
I JUST HAPPENED TO BE PASSING BY WHEN I SAW YOU. LUCKILY, I WAS ABLE TO STOP YOUR FALL.
YOU SAVED MY LIFE.
MAY I...ASK FOR YOUR NAME?
THAT'S A PRETTY DESTRUCTIVE SMILE.
UMM...
MY NAME IS SATOU.
NIKO (SMILE)
I'M JUST A HUMBLE TRAVELING PEDDLER.
LET'S GO WITH THAT.

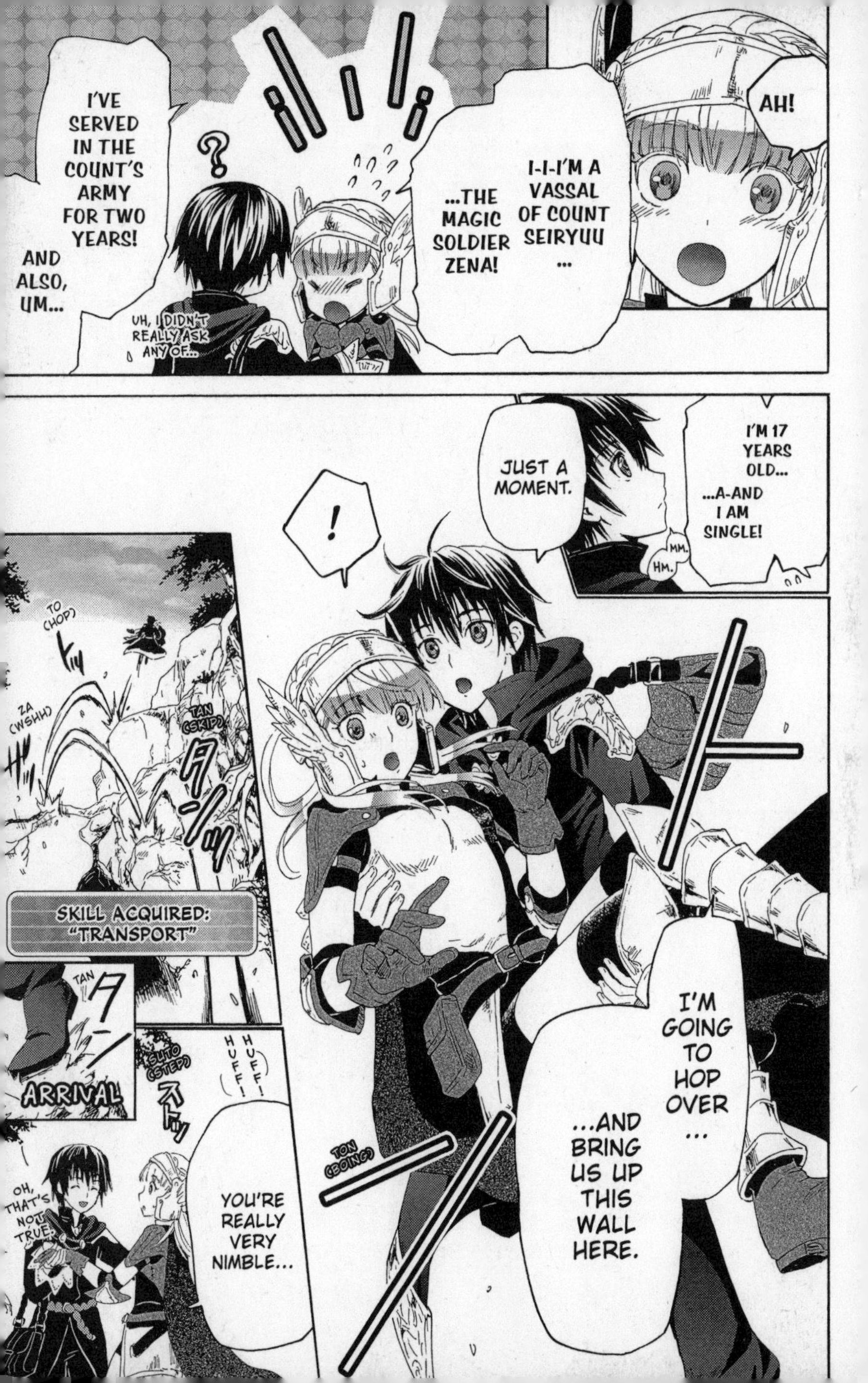
AH!
I-I-I'M A VASSAL OF COUNT SEIRYUU ...
...THE MAGIC SOLDIER ZENA!
I'VE SERVED IN THE COUNT'S ARMY FOR TWO YEARS!
AND ALSO, UM...
UH, I DIDN'T REALLY ASK ANY OF...
I'M 17 YEARS OLD...
...A-AND I AM SINGLE!
MM. HM.
JUST A MOMENT.
!
I'M GOING TO HOP OVER ...
...AND BRING US UP THIS WALL HERE.
TON (BOING)
TO (HOP)
ZA (WSHH)
TAN (SKIP)
SKILL ACQUIRED: "TRANSPORT"
TAN
ARRIVAL
SUTO (STEP)
HUFF! HUFF!
YOU'RE REALLY VERY NIMBLE...
OH, THAT'S NOT TRUE.

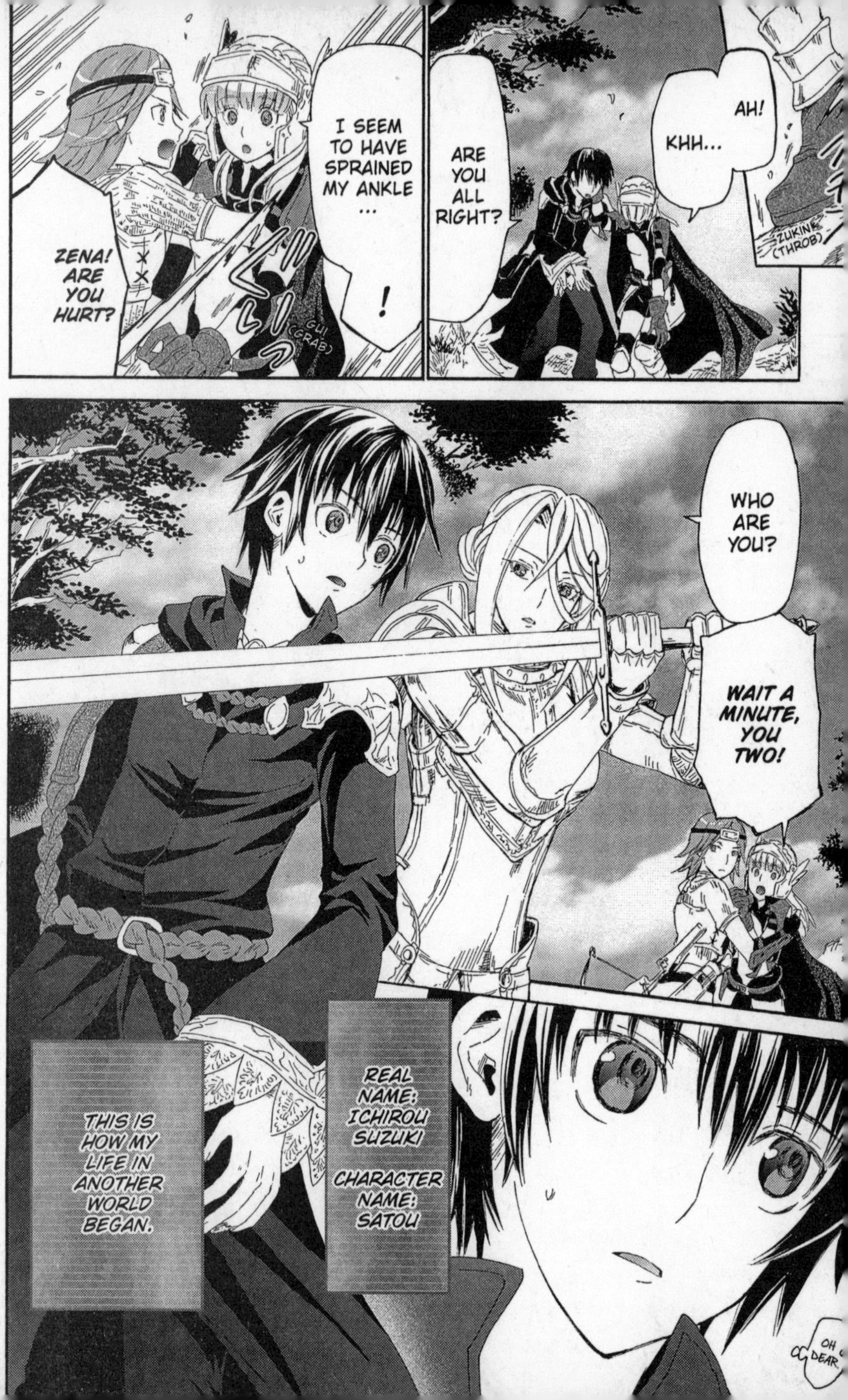
AH!
KHH...
ZUKIN (THROB)
ARE YOU ALL RIGHT?
I SEEM TO HAVE SPRAINED MY ANKLE...
!
ZENA! ARE YOU HURT?
GUI (GRAB)
WHO ARE YOU?
WAIT A MINUTE, YOU TWO!
OH DEAR.
REAL NAME: ICHIROU SUZUKI
CHARACTER NAME: SATOU
THIS IS HOW MY LIFE IN ANOTHER WORLD BEGAN.

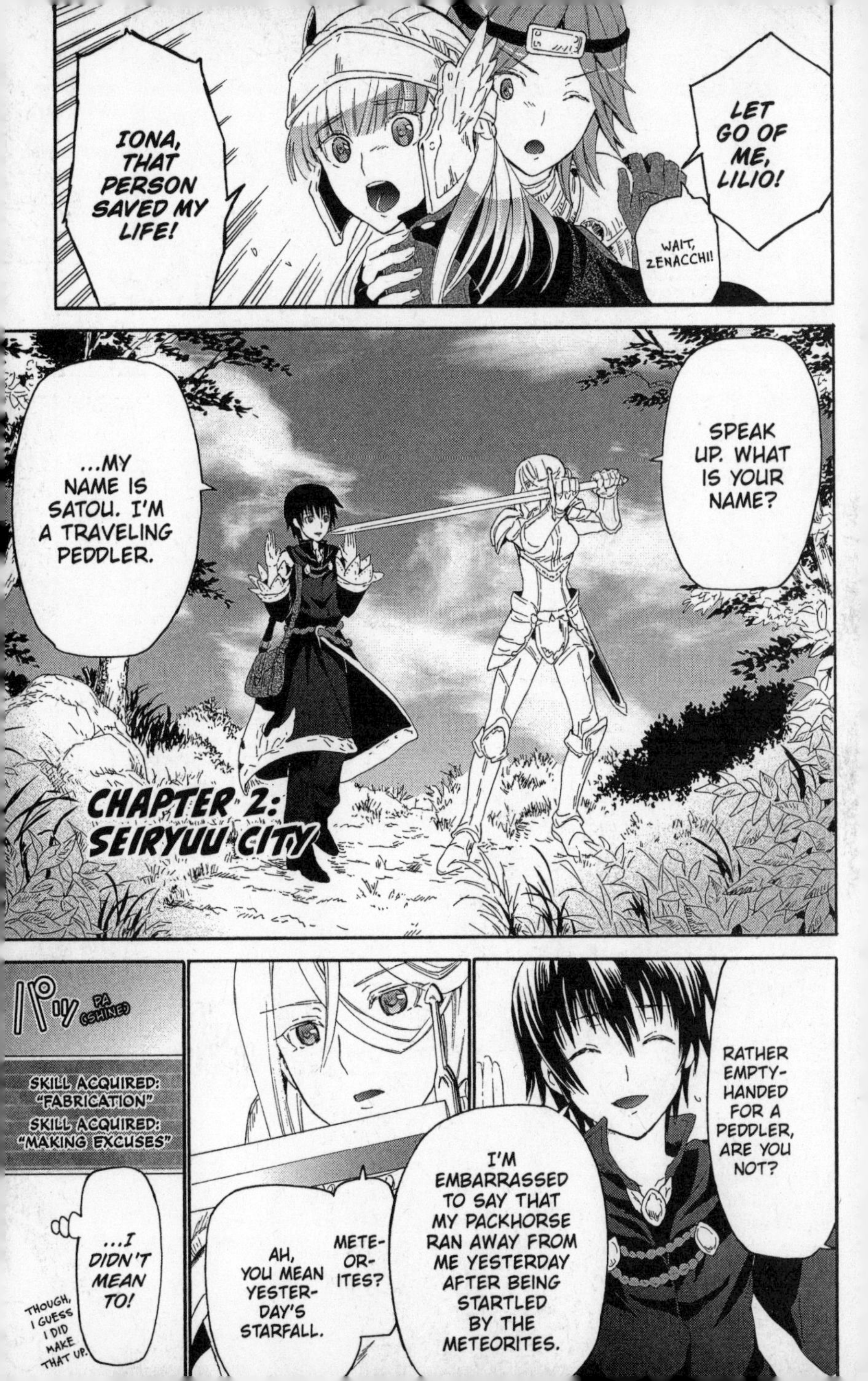
LET GO OF ME, LILIO!
WAIT, ZENACCHI!
IONA, THAT PERSON SAVED MY LIFE!
SPEAK UP. WHAT IS YOUR NAME?
...MY NAME IS SATOU. I'M A TRAVELING PEDDLER.
CHAPTER 2: SEIRYUU CITY
RATHER EMPTY-HANDED FOR A PEDDLER, ARE YOU NOT?
I'M EMBARRASSED TO SAY THAT MY PACKHORSE RAN AWAY FROM ME YESTERDAY AFTER BEING STARTLED BY THE METEORITES.
METE-OR-ITES?
AH, YOU MEAN YESTER-DAY'S STARFALL.
パッ
PA (SHINE)
SKILL ACQUIRED: "FABRICATION"
SKILL ACQUIRED: "MAKING EXCUSES"
...I DIDN'T MEAN TO!
THOUGH, I GUESS I DID MAKE THAT UP.

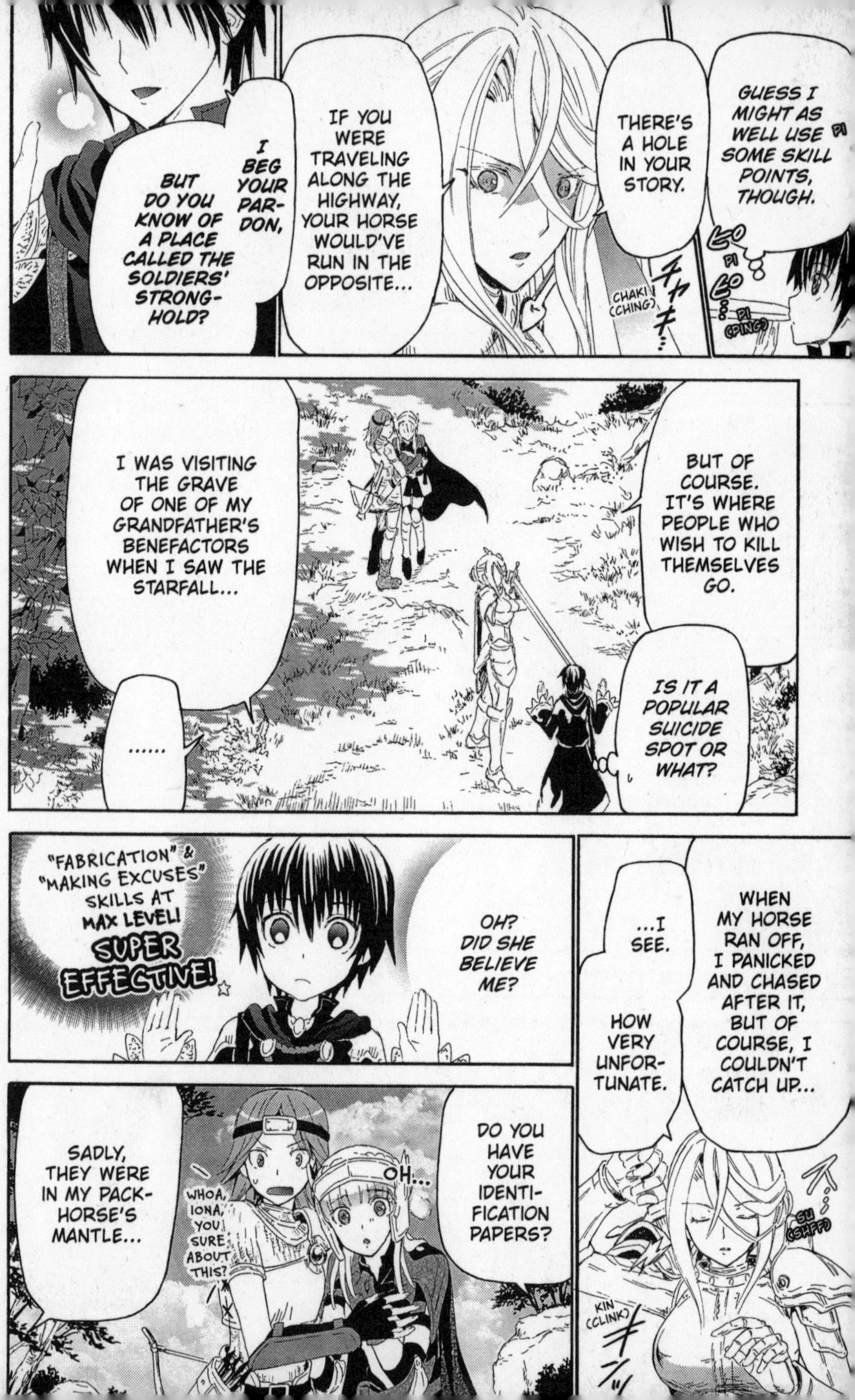
GUESS I MIGHT AS WELL USE SOME SKILL POINTS, THOUGH.
PI
PI
PI (PING)
THERE'S A HOLE IN YOUR STORY.
CHAKI (CHING)
IF YOU WERE TRAVELING ALONG THE HIGHWAY, YOUR HORSE WOULD'VE RUN IN THE OPPOSITE...
I BEG YOUR PARDON,
BUT DO YOU KNOW OF A PLACE CALLED THE SOLDIERS' STRONGHOLD?
BUT OF COURSE. IT'S WHERE PEOPLE WHO WISH TO KILL THEMSELVES GO.
IS IT A POPULAR SUICIDE SPOT OR WHAT?
I WAS VISITING THE GRAVE OF ONE OF MY GRANDFATHER'S BENEFACTORS WHEN I SAW THE STARFALL...
......
WHEN MY HORSE RAN OFF, I PANICKED AND CHASED AFTER IT, BUT OF COURSE, I COULDN'T CATCH UP...
...I SEE.
HOW VERY UNFORTUNATE.
SU (SHFF)
KIN (CLINK)
OH? DID SHE BELIEVE ME?
"FABRICATION" & "MAKING EXCUSES" SKILLS AT MAX LEVEL!
SUPER EFFECTIVE!
DO YOU HAVE YOUR IDENTIFICATION PAPERS?
OH...
WHOA, IONA, YOU SURE ABOUT THIS?
SADLY, THEY WERE IN MY PACK-HORSE'S MANTLE...

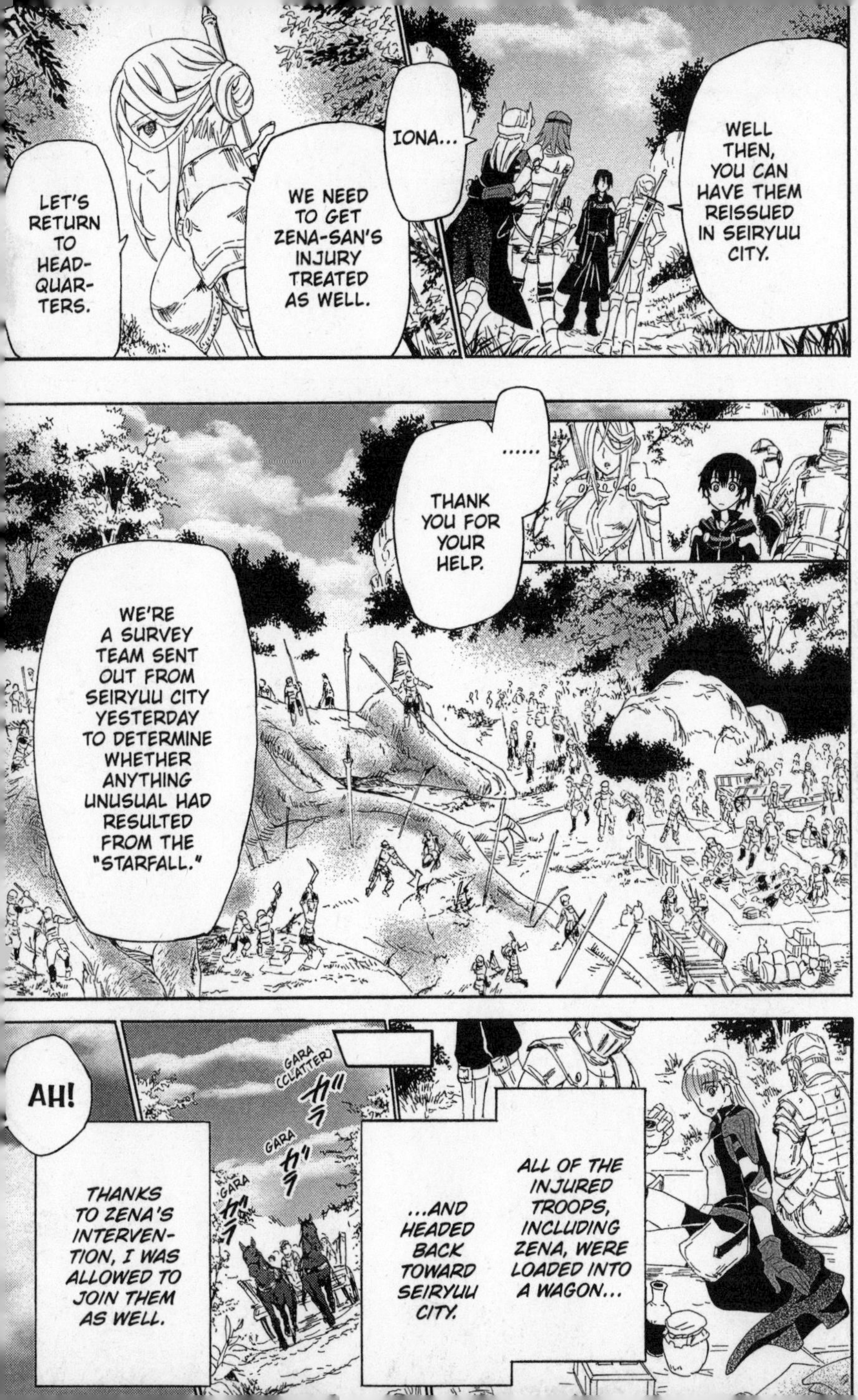
WELL THEN, YOU CAN HAVE THEM REISSUED IN SEIRYUU CITY.
IONA...
WE NEED TO GET ZENA-SAN'S INJURY TREATED AS WELL.
LET'S RETURN TO HEAD-QUARTERS.
......
THANK YOU FOR YOUR HELP.
WE'RE A SURVEY TEAM SENT OUT FROM SEIRYUU CITY YESTERDAY TO DETERMINE WHETHER ANYTHING UNUSUAL HAD RESULTED FROM THE "STARFALL."
ALL OF THE INJURED TROOPS, INCLUDING ZENA, WERE LOADED INTO A WAGON...
...AND HEADED BACK TOWARD SEIRYUU CITY.
GARA (CLATTER)
GARA
GARA
AH!
THANKS TO ZENA'S INTERVEN-TION, I WAS ALLOWED TO JOIN THEM AS WELL.

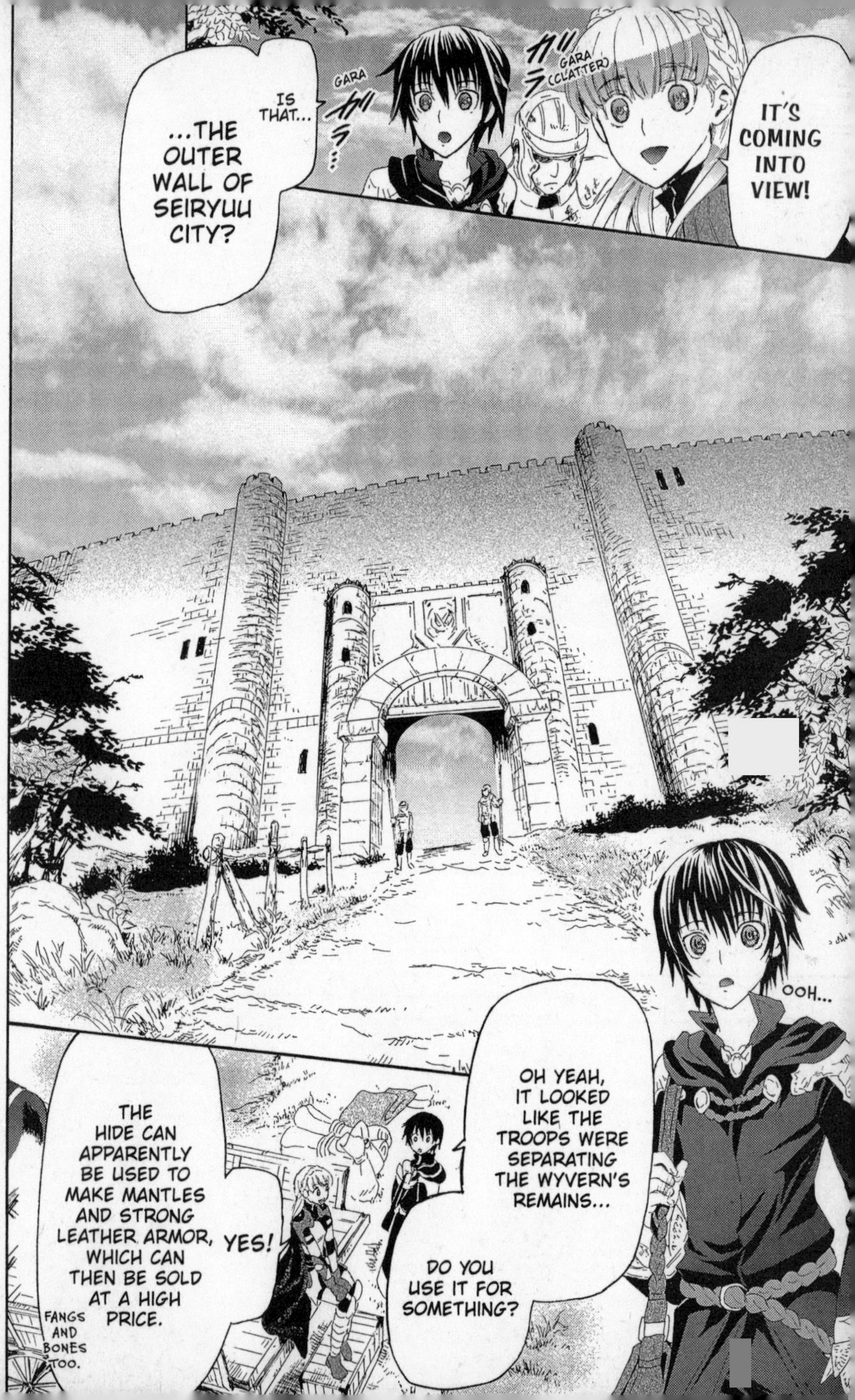
IT'S COMING INTO VIEW!
GARA (CLATTER)
GARA
IS THAT...
...THE OUTER WALL OF SEIRYUU CITY?
OOH...
OH YEAH, IT LOOKED LIKE THE TROOPS WERE SEPARATING THE WYVERN'S REMAINS...
DO YOU USE IT FOR SOMETHING?
YES!
THE HIDE CAN APPARENTLY BE USED TO MAKE MANTLES AND STRONG LEATHER ARMOR, WHICH CAN THEN BE SOLD AT A HIGH PRICE.
FANGS AND BONES TOO.

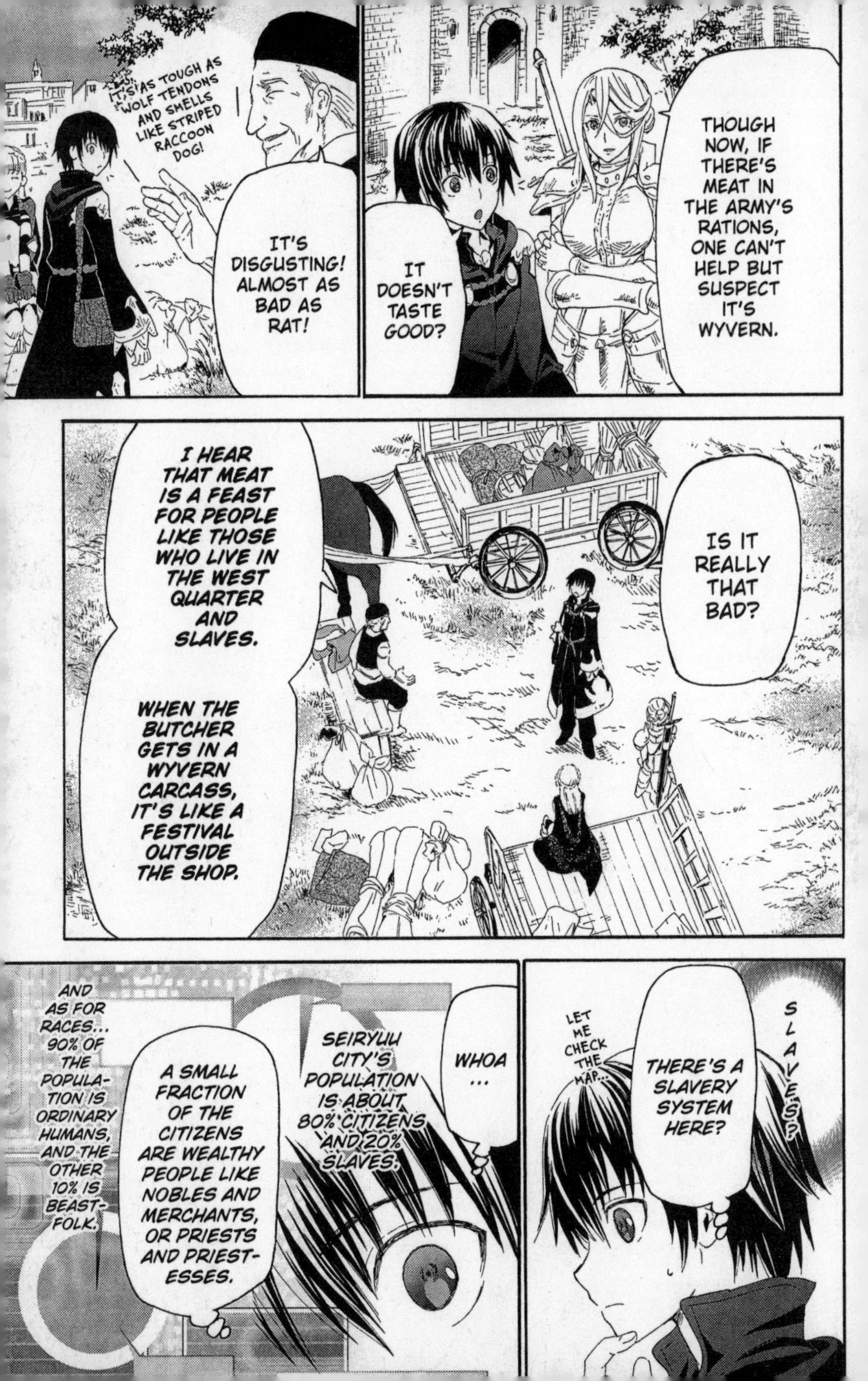
THOUGH NOW, IF THERE'S MEAT IN THE ARMY'S RATIONS, ONE CAN'T HELP BUT SUSPECT IT'S WYVERN.
IT DOESN'T TASTE GOOD?
IT'S DISGUSTING! ALMOST AS BAD AS RAT!
IT'S AS TOUGH AS WOLF TENDONS AND SMELLS LIKE STRIPED RACCOON DOG!
IS IT REALLY THAT BAD?
I HEAR THAT MEAT IS A FEAST FOR PEOPLE LIKE THOSE WHO LIVE IN THE WEST QUARTER AND SLAVES.
WHEN THE BUTCHER GETS IN A WYVERN CARCASS, IT'S LIKE A FESTIVAL OUTSIDE THE SHOP.
SLAVES?
THERE'S A SLAVERY SYSTEM HERE?
LET ME CHECK THE MAP...
WHOA...
SEIRYUU CITY'S POPULATION IS ABOUT 80% CITIZENS AND 20% SLAVES.
A SMALL FRACTION OF THE CITIZENS ARE WEALTHY PEOPLE LIKE NOBLES AND MERCHANTS, OR PRIESTS AND PRIESTESSES.
AND AS FOR RACES... 90% OF THE POPULATION IS ORDINARY HUMANS, AND THE OTHER 10% IS BEASTFOLK.

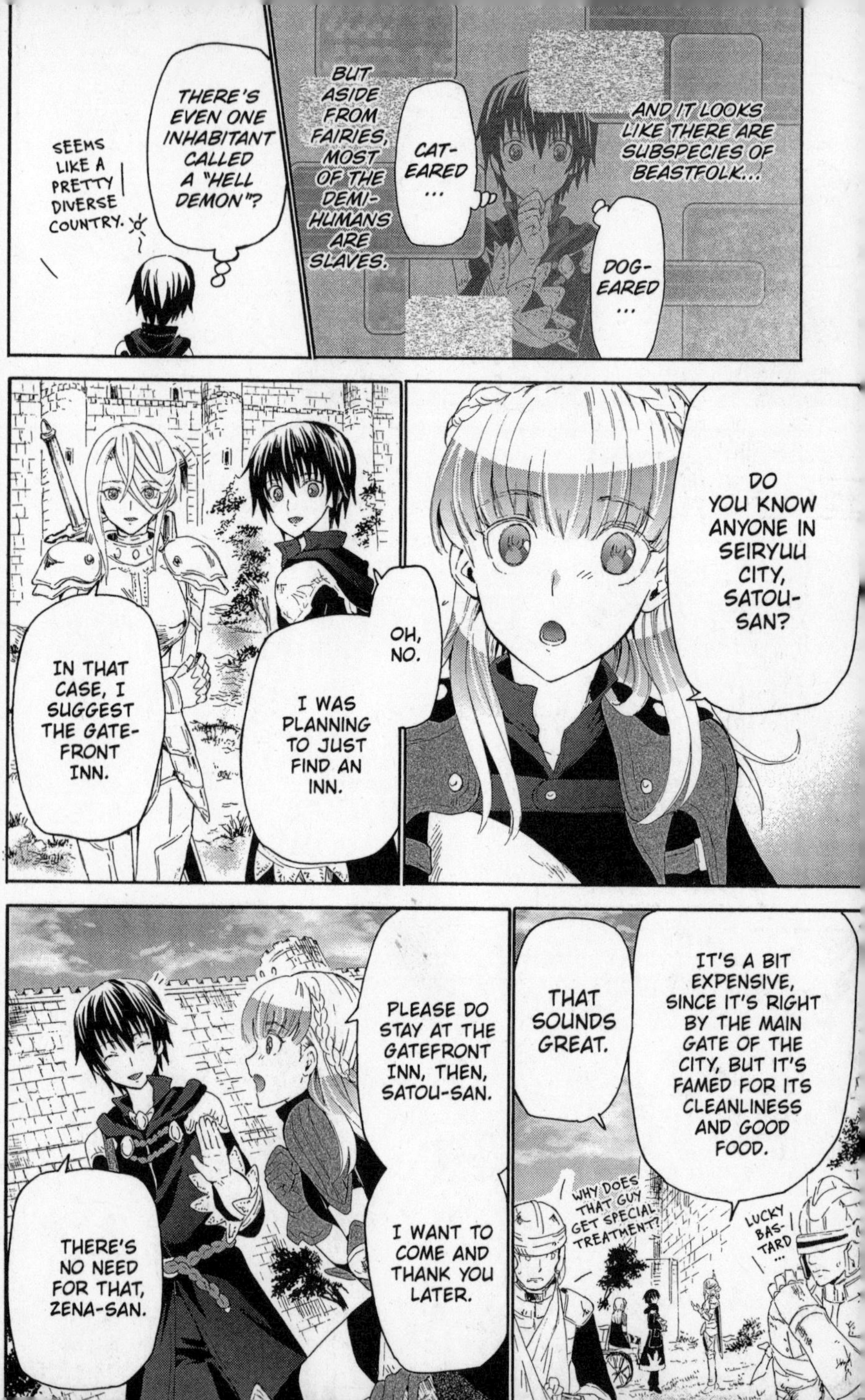
AND IT LOOKS LIKE THERE ARE SUBSPECIES OF BEASTFOLK...
DOG-EARED...
CAT-EARED...
BUT ASIDE FROM FAIRIES, MOST OF THE DEMI-HUMANS ARE SLAVES.
THERE'S EVEN ONE INHABITANT CALLED A "HELL DEMON"?
SEEMS LIKE A PRETTY DIVERSE COUNTRY.
DO YOU KNOW ANYONE IN SEIRYUU CITY, SATOU-SAN?
OH, NO.
I WAS PLANNING TO JUST FIND AN INN.
IN THAT CASE, I SUGGEST THE GATE-FRONT INN.
IT'S A BIT EXPENSIVE, SINCE IT'S RIGHT BY THE MAIN GATE OF THE CITY, BUT IT'S FAMED FOR ITS CLEANLINESS AND GOOD FOOD.
THAT SOUNDS GREAT.
LUCKY BASTARD...
WHY DOES THAT GUY GET SPECIAL TREATMENT?
PLEASE DO STAY AT THE GATEFRONT INN, THEN, SATOU-SAN.
I WANT TO COME AND THANK YOU LATER.
THERE'S NO NEED FOR THAT, ZENA-SAN.

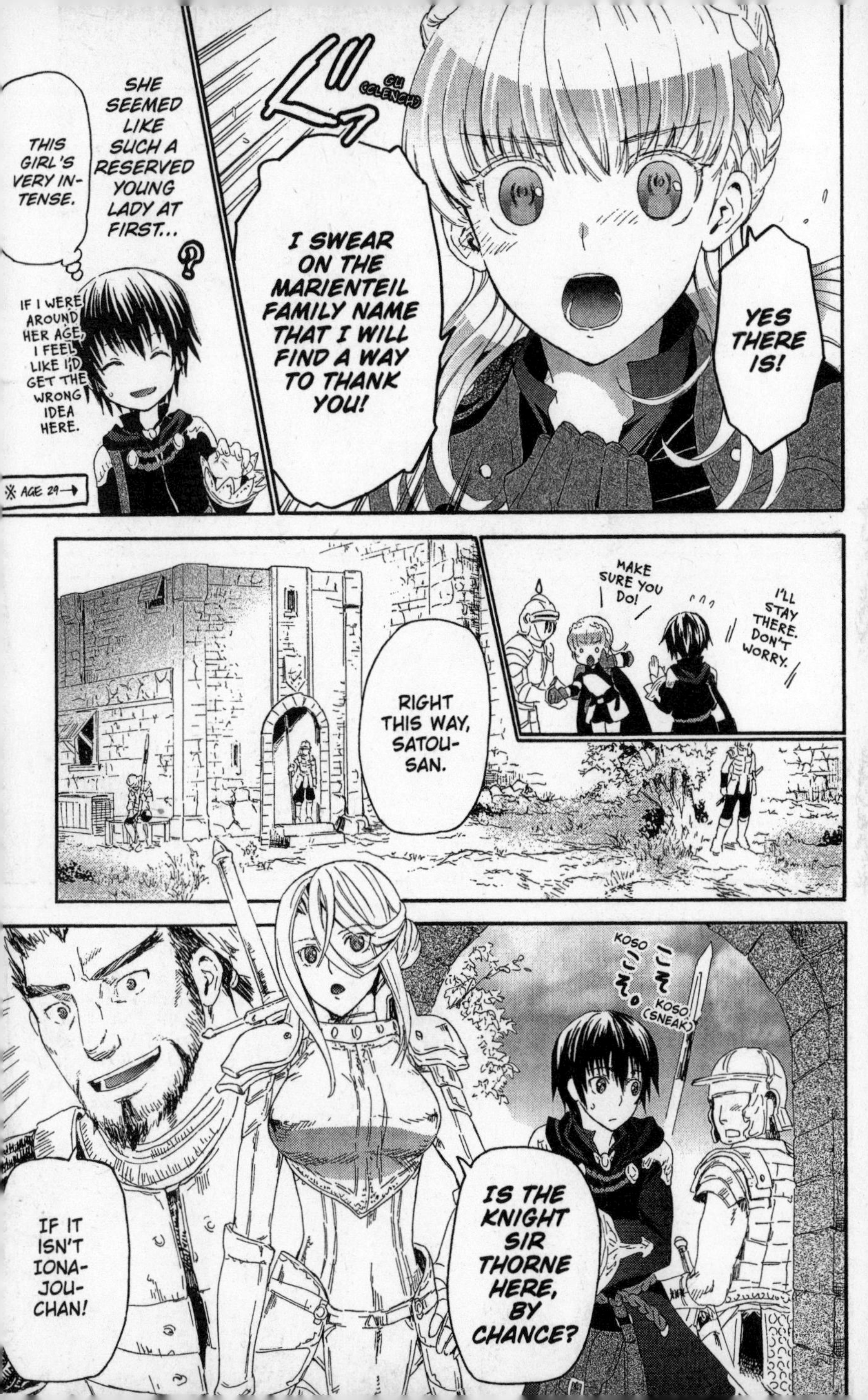
GU (CLENCH)
YES THERE IS!
I SWEAR ON THE MARIENTEIL FAMILY NAME THAT I WILL FIND A WAY TO THANK YOU!
SHE SEEMED LIKE SUCH A RESERVED YOUNG LADY AT FIRST...
THIS GIRL'S VERY IN-TENSE.
?
IF I WERE AROUND HER AGE, I FEEL LIKE I'D GET THE WRONG IDEA HERE.
※ AGE 29→
I'LL STAY THERE. DON'T WORRY.
MAKE SURE YOU DO!
RIGHT THIS WAY, SATOU-SAN.
KOSO こそ
KOSO こそ (SNEAK)
IS THE KNIGHT SIR THORNE HERE, BY CHANCE?
IF IT ISN'T IONA-JOU-CHAN!

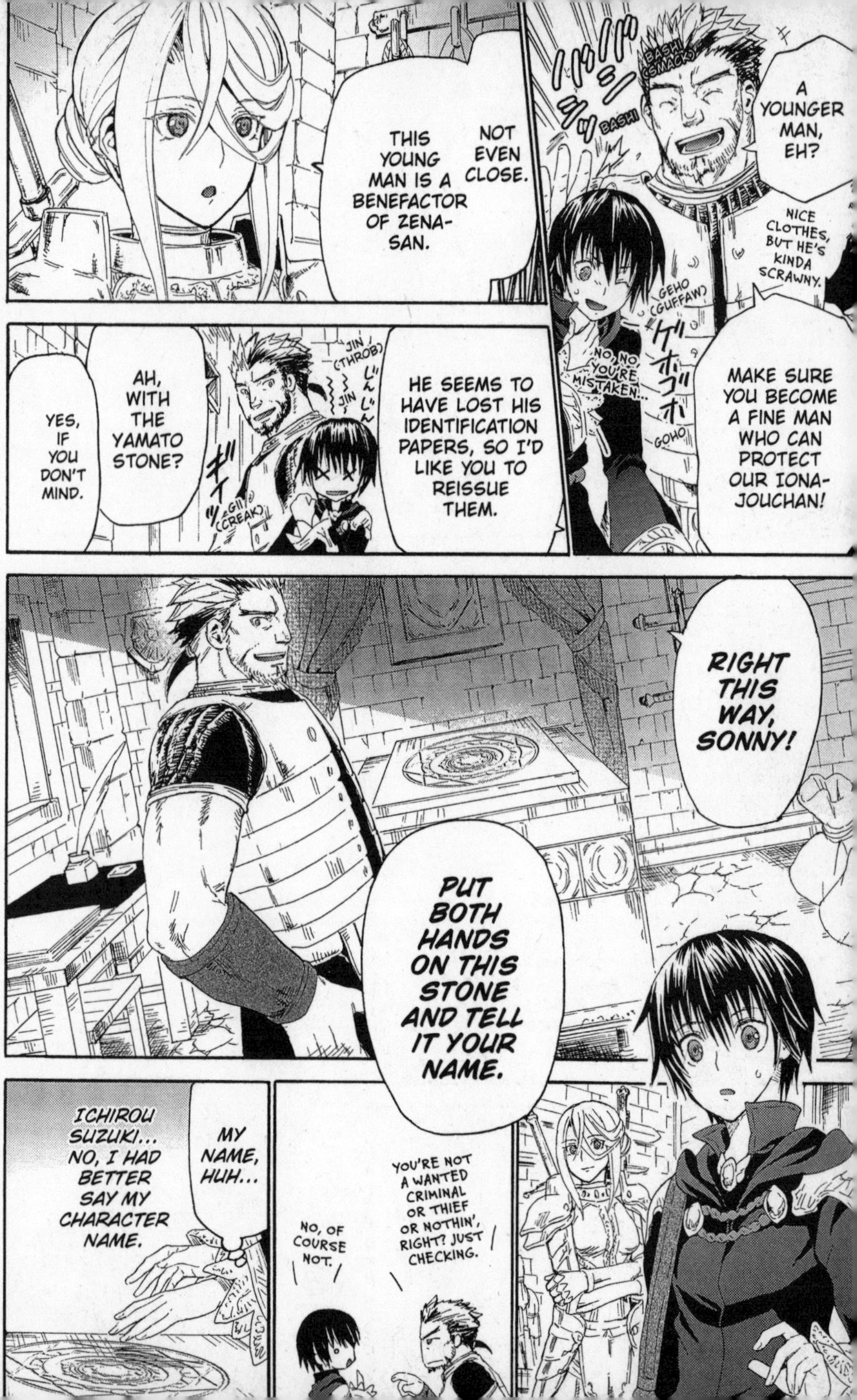
BASHI (SMACK)
BASHI
A YOUNGER MAN, EH?
NICE CLOTHES, BUT HE'S KINDA SCRAWNY.
GEHO (GUFFAW)
NO, NO, YOU'RE MISTAKEN...
GOHO
MAKE SURE YOU BECOME A FINE MAN WHO CAN PROTECT OUR IONA-JOUCHAN!
NOT EVEN CLOSE.
THIS YOUNG MAN IS A BENEFACTOR OF ZENA-SAN.
HE SEEMS TO HAVE LOST HIS IDENTIFICATION PAPERS, SO I'D LIKE YOU TO REISSUE THEM.
JIN (THROB) JIN
AH, WITH THE YAMATO STONE?
GII (CREAK)
YES, IF YOU DON'T MIND.
RIGHT THIS WAY, SONNY!
PUT BOTH HANDS ON THIS STONE AND TELL IT YOUR NAME.
YOU'RE NOT A WANTED CRIMINAL OR THIEF OR NOTHIN', RIGHT? JUST CHECKING.
NO, OF COURSE NOT.
MY NAME, HUH...
ICHIROU SUZUKI... NO, I HAD BETTER SAY MY CHARACTER NAME.

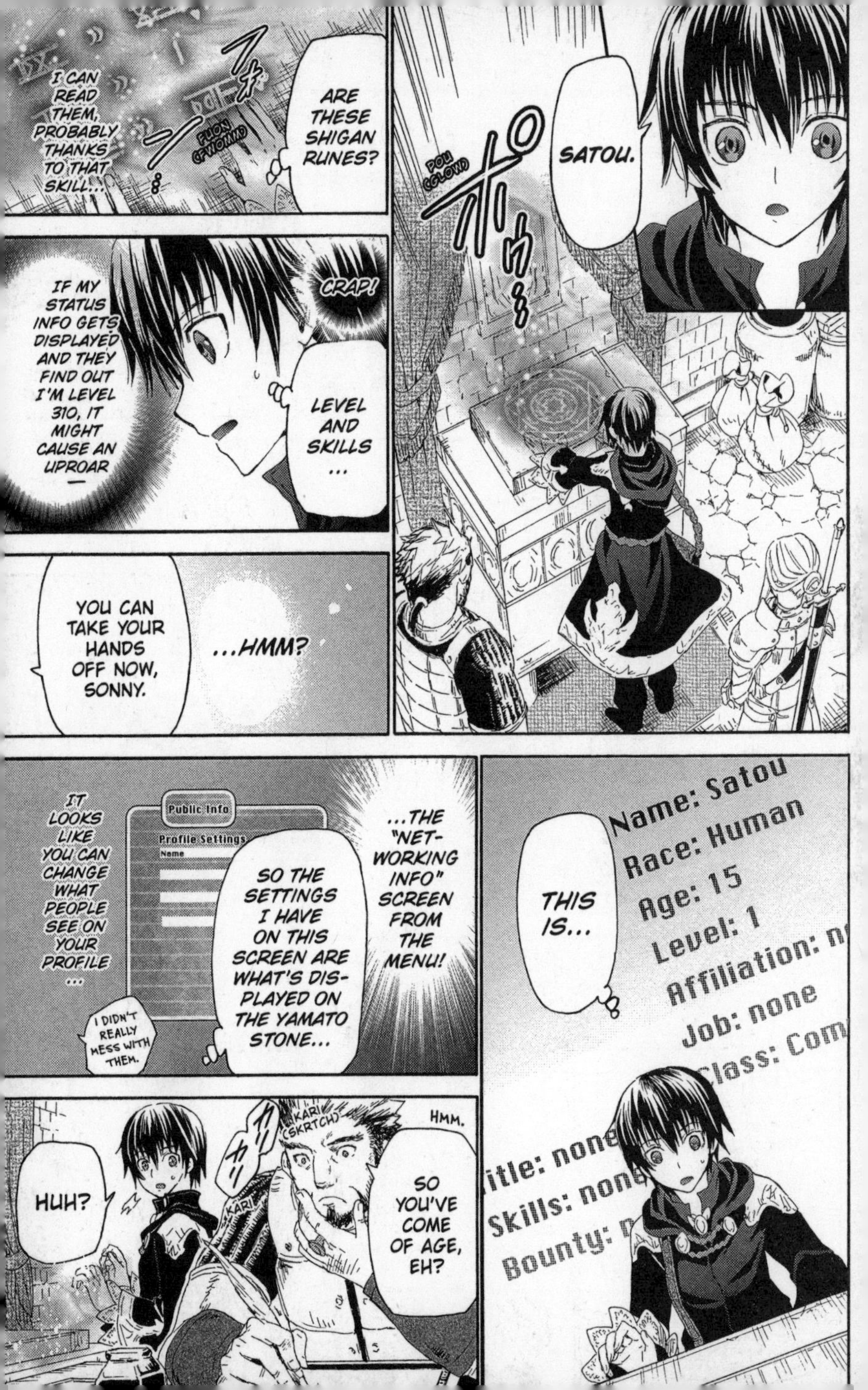
SATOU.
POU (GLOW)
ARE THESE SHIGAN RUNES?
FUON (FWOMM)
I CAN READ THEM, PROBABLY THANKS TO THAT SKILL...
CRAP!
LEVEL AND SKILLS...
IF MY STATUS INFO GETS DISPLAYED AND THEY FIND OUT I'M LEVEL 310, IT MIGHT CAUSE AN UPROAR—
...HMM?
YOU CAN TAKE YOUR HANDS OFF NOW, SONNY.
Name: Satou
Race: Human
Age: 15
Level: 1
Affiliation: n
Job: none
Class: Com
itle: none
Skills: none
Bounty: n
THIS IS...
...THE "NETWORKING INFO" SCREEN FROM THE MENU!
SO THE SETTINGS I HAVE ON THIS SCREEN ARE WHAT'S DISPLAYED ON THE YAMATO STONE...
Public Info
Profile Settings
Name
IT LOOKS LIKE YOU CAN CHANGE WHAT PEOPLE SEE ON YOUR PROFILE...
I DIDN'T REALLY MESS WITH THEM.
HMM.
KARI (SKRTCH)
KARI
SO YOU'VE COME OF AGE, EH?
HUH?

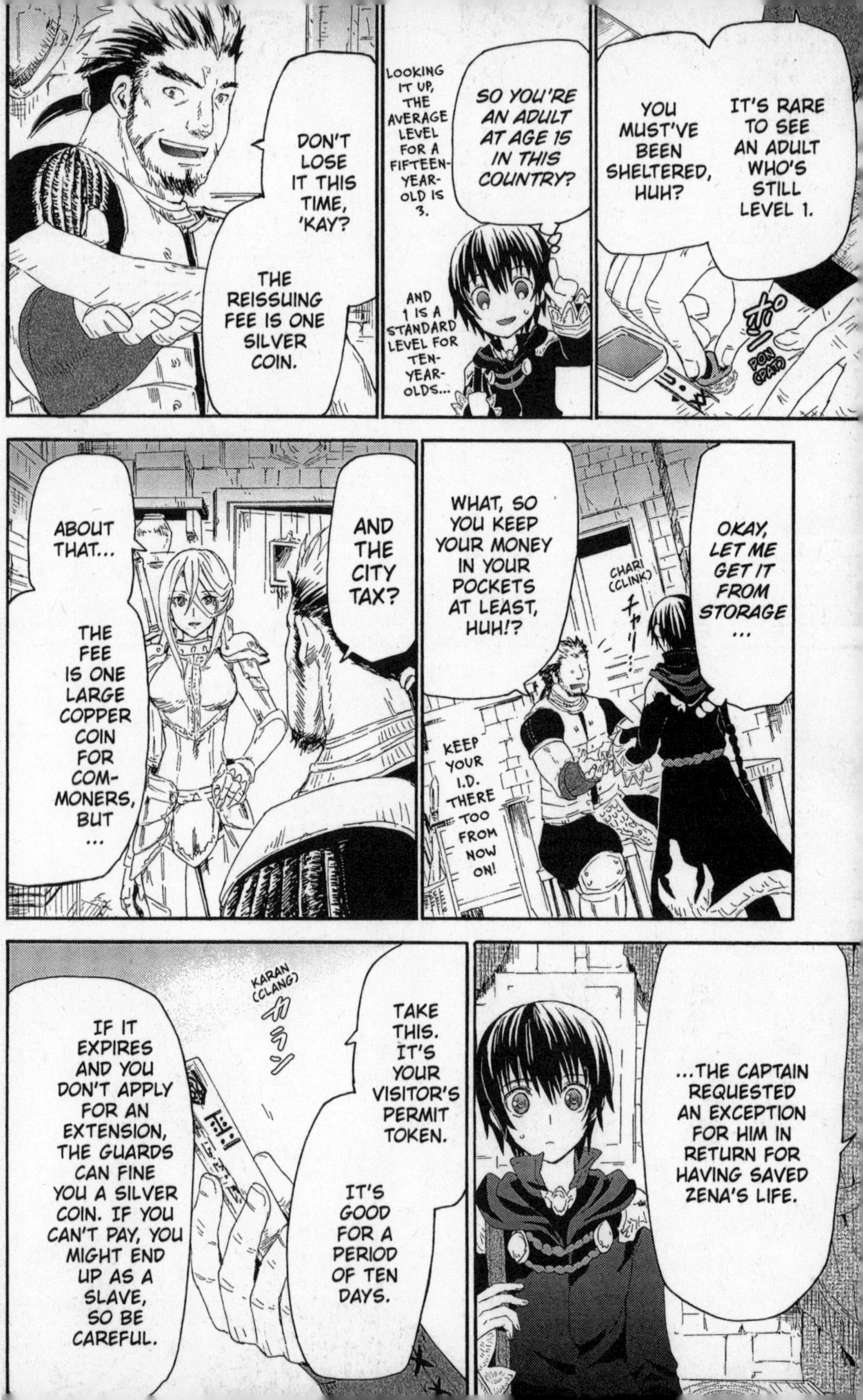
IT'S RARE TO SEE AN ADULT WHO'S STILL LEVEL 1.
YOU MUST'VE BEEN SHELTERED, HUH?
PON (PAT)
SO YOU'RE AN ADULT AT AGE 15 IN THIS COUNTRY?
LOOKING IT UP, THE AVERAGE LEVEL FOR A FIFTEEN-YEAR-OLD IS 3.
AND 1 IS A STANDARD LEVEL FOR TEN-YEAR-OLDS...
DON'T LOSE IT THIS TIME, 'KAY?
THE REISSUING FEE IS ONE SILVER COIN.
OKAY, LET ME GET IT FROM STORAGE...
CHARI (CLINK)
WHAT, SO YOU KEEP YOUR MONEY IN YOUR POCKETS AT LEAST, HUH!?
KEEP YOUR I.D. THERE TOO FROM NOW ON!
AND THE CITY TAX?
ABOUT THAT...
THE FEE IS ONE LARGE COPPER COIN FOR COMMONERS, BUT...
...THE CAPTAIN REQUESTED AN EXCEPTION FOR HIM IN RETURN FOR HAVING SAVED ZENA'S LIFE.
TAKE THIS. IT'S YOUR VISITOR'S PERMIT TOKEN.
KARAN (CLANG)
IT'S GOOD FOR A PERIOD OF TEN DAYS.
IF IT EXPIRES AND YOU DON'T APPLY FOR AN EXTENSION, THE GUARDS CAN FINE YOU A SILVER COIN. IF YOU CAN'T PAY, YOU MIGHT END UP AS A SLAVE, SO BE CAREFUL.

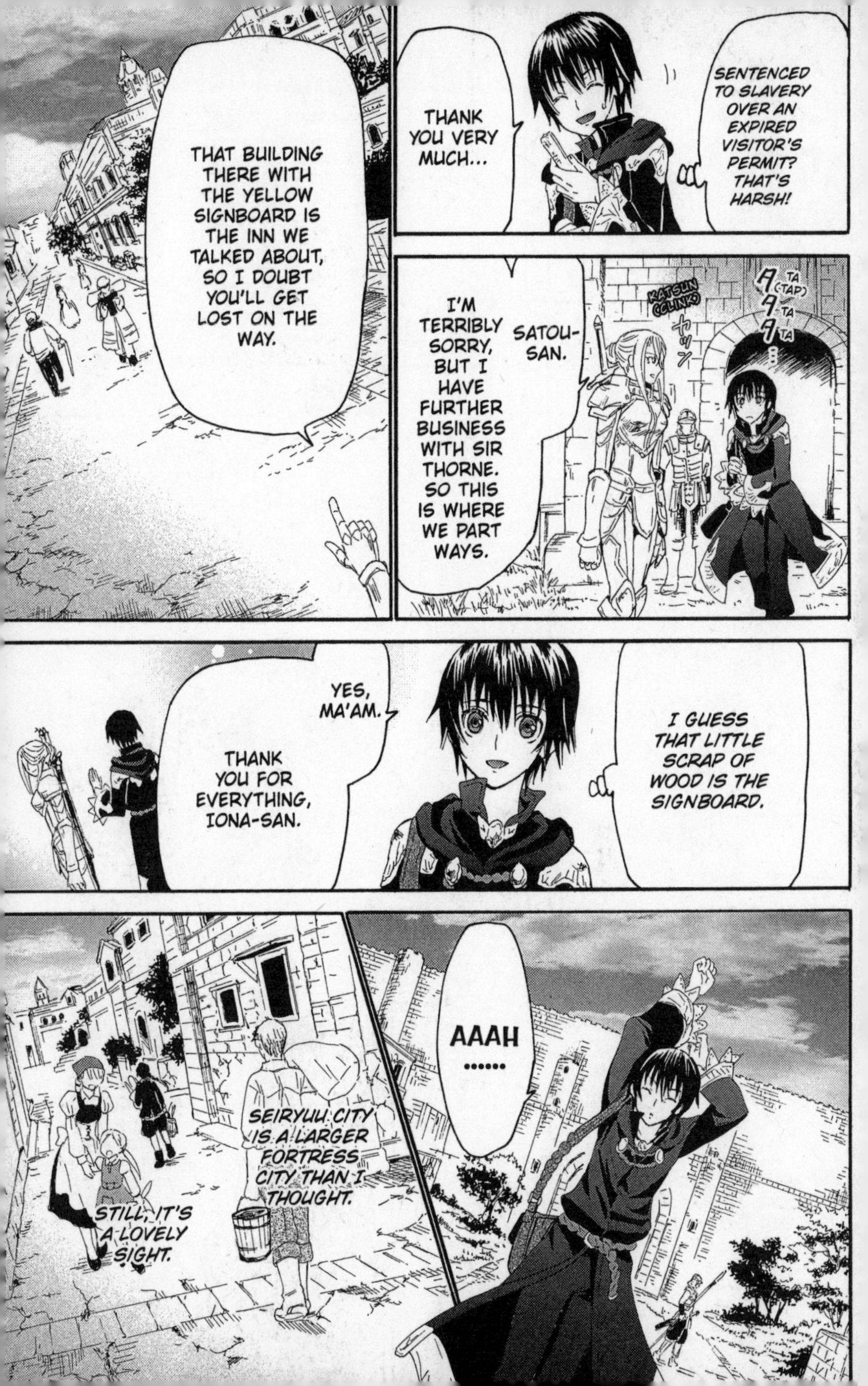
SENTENCED TO SLAVERY OVER AN EXPIRED VISITOR'S PERMIT? THAT'S HARSH!
THANK YOU VERY MUCH...
TA (TAP) TA TA
KATSUN (CLINK)
SATOU-SAN.
I'M TERRIBLY SORRY, BUT I HAVE FURTHER BUSINESS WITH SIR THORNE. SO THIS IS WHERE WE PART WAYS.
THAT BUILDING THERE WITH THE YELLOW SIGNBOARD IS THE INN WE TALKED ABOUT, SO I DOUBT YOU'LL GET LOST ON THE WAY.
I GUESS THAT LITTLE SCRAP OF WOOD IS THE SIGNBOARD.
YES, MA'AM.
THANK YOU FOR EVERYTHING, IONA-SAN.
AAAH ......
SEIRYUU CITY IS A LARGER FORTRESS CITY THAN I THOUGHT.
STILL, IT'S A LOVELY SIGHT.

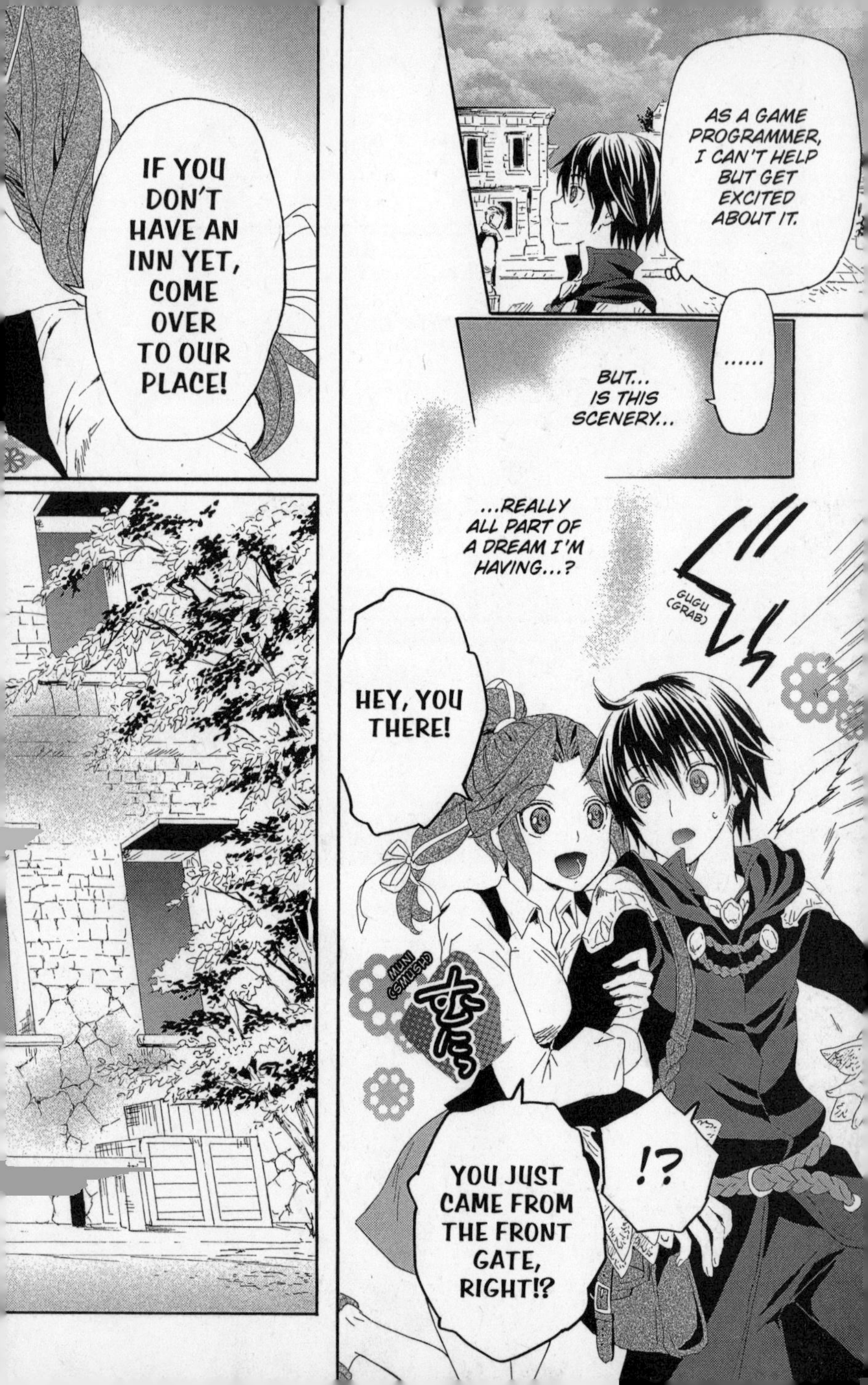
AS A GAME PROGRAMMER, I CAN'T HELP BUT GET EXCITED ABOUT IT.
......
BUT... IS THIS SCENERY...
...REALLY ALL PART OF A DREAM I'M HAVING...?
GUGU (GRAB)
HEY, YOU THERE!
!?
MUNI (SMUSH)
YOU JUST CAME FROM THE FRONT GATE, RIGHT!?
IF YOU DON'T HAVE AN INN YET, COME OVER TO OUR PLACE!

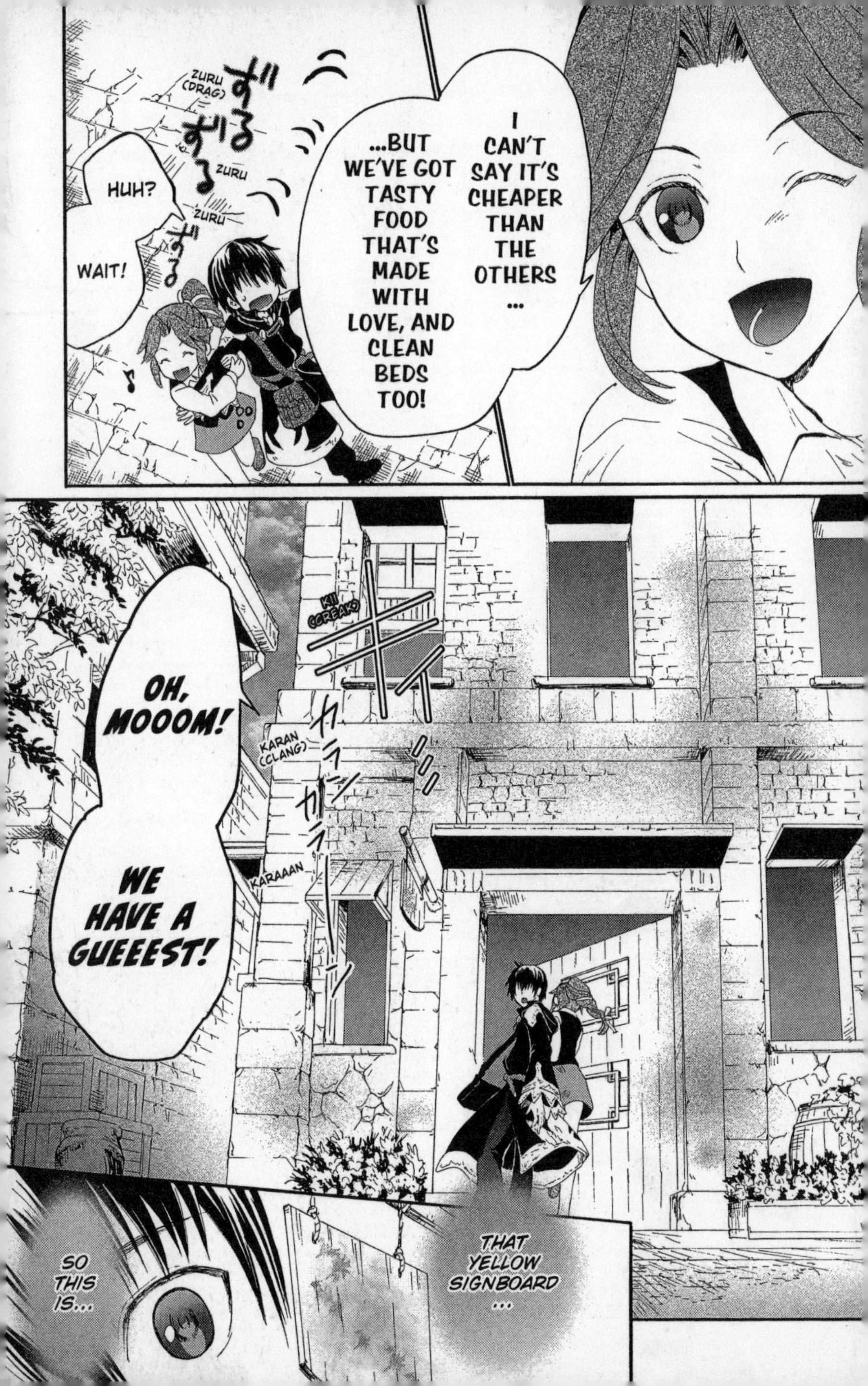
I CAN'T SAY IT'S CHEAPER THAN THE OTHERS...
...BUT WE'VE GOT TASTY FOOD THAT'S MADE WITH LOVE, AND CLEAN BEDS TOO!
ずるずる
ZURU (DRAG)
ZURU
ずる
ZURU
HUH?
WAIT!
キィ
KII (CREAK)
OH, MOOOM!
WE HAVE A GUEEEST!
カラン
KARAN (CLANG)
カラーン
KARAAAN
THAT YELLOW SIGNBOARD...
SO THIS IS...

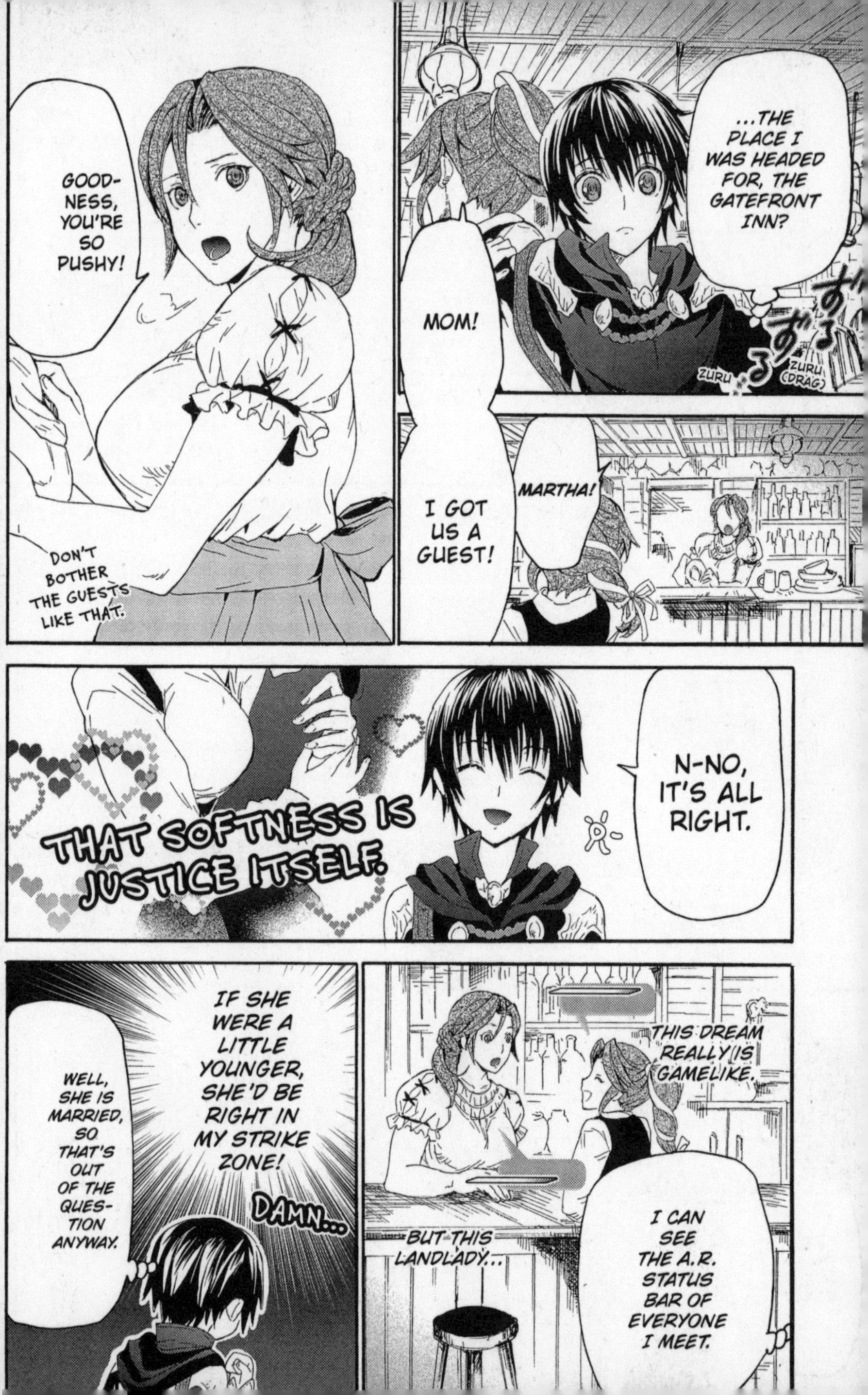
...THE PLACE I WAS HEADED FOR, THE GATEFRONT INN?
MOM!
ずるずる
ZURU ZURU (DRAG)
MARTHA!
I GOT US A GUEST!
GOODNESS, YOU'RE SO PUSHY!
DON'T BOTHER THE GUESTS LIKE THAT.
N-NO, IT'S ALL RIGHT.
THAT SOFTNESS IS JUSTICE ITSELF.
THIS DREAM REALLY IS GAMELIKE.
I CAN SEE THE A.R. STATUS BAR OF EVERYONE I MEET.
BUT THIS LANDLADY...
IF SHE WERE A LITTLE YOUNGER, SHE'D BE RIGHT IN MY STRIKE ZONE!
DAMN...
WELL, SHE IS MARRIED, SO THAT'S OUT OF THE QUESTION ANYWAY.

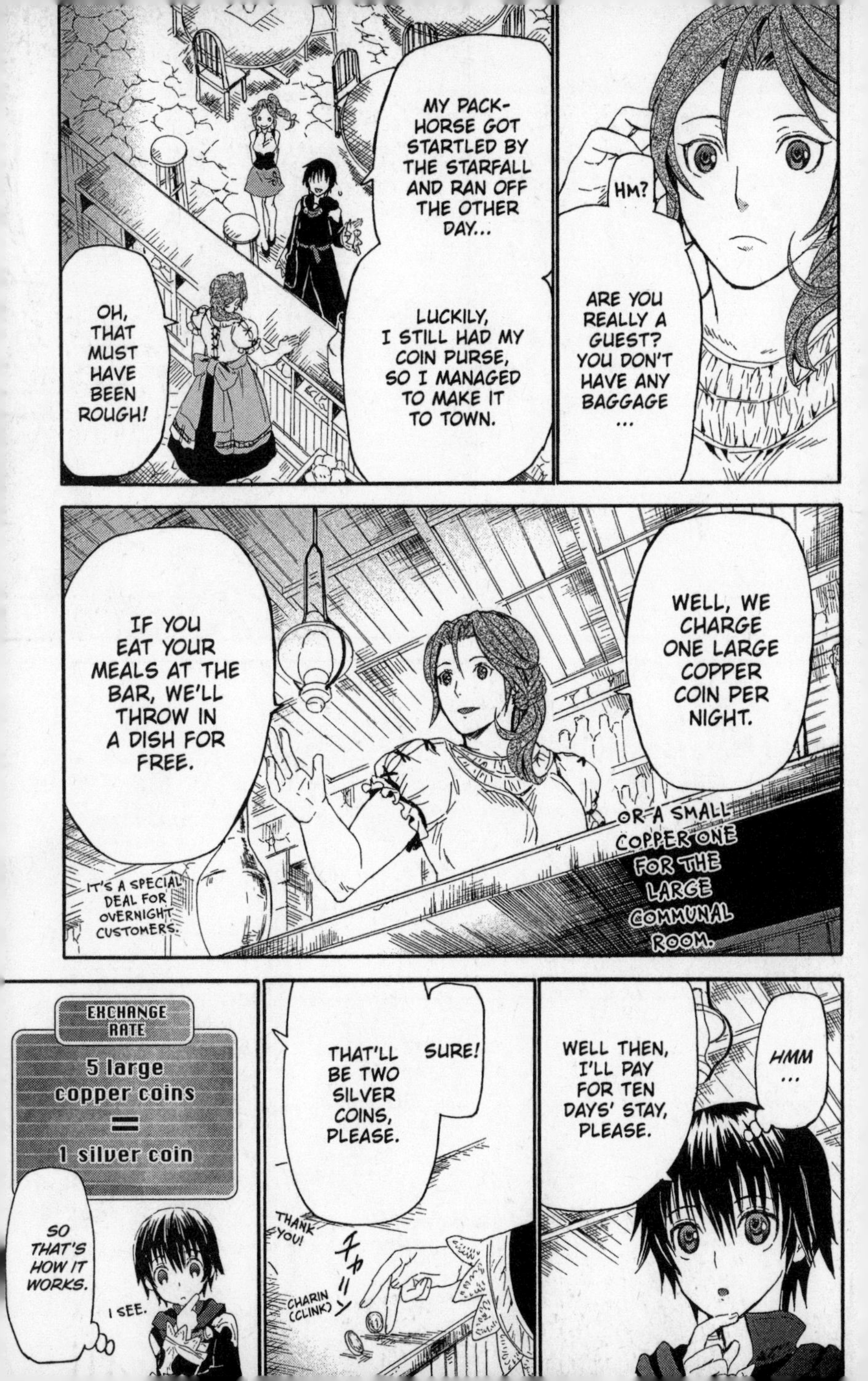
HM?
ARE YOU REALLY A GUEST? YOU DON'T HAVE ANY BAGGAGE...
MY PACK-HORSE GOT STARTLED BY THE STARFALL AND RAN OFF THE OTHER DAY...
LUCKILY, I STILL HAD MY COIN PURSE, SO I MANAGED TO MAKE IT TO TOWN.
OH, THAT MUST HAVE BEEN ROUGH!
WELL, WE CHARGE ONE LARGE COPPER COIN PER NIGHT.
OR A SMALL COPPER ONE FOR THE LARGE COMMUNAL ROOM.
IF YOU EAT YOUR MEALS AT THE BAR, WE'LL THROW IN A DISH FOR FREE.
IT'S A SPECIAL DEAL FOR OVERNIGHT CUSTOMERS.
HMM...
WELL THEN, I'LL PAY FOR TEN DAYS' STAY, PLEASE.
SURE!
THAT'LL BE TWO SILVER COINS, PLEASE.
THANK YOU!
チャリン
CHARIN (CLINK)
EXCHANGE RATE
5 large copper coins = 1 silver coin
SO THAT'S HOW IT WORKS.
I SEE.

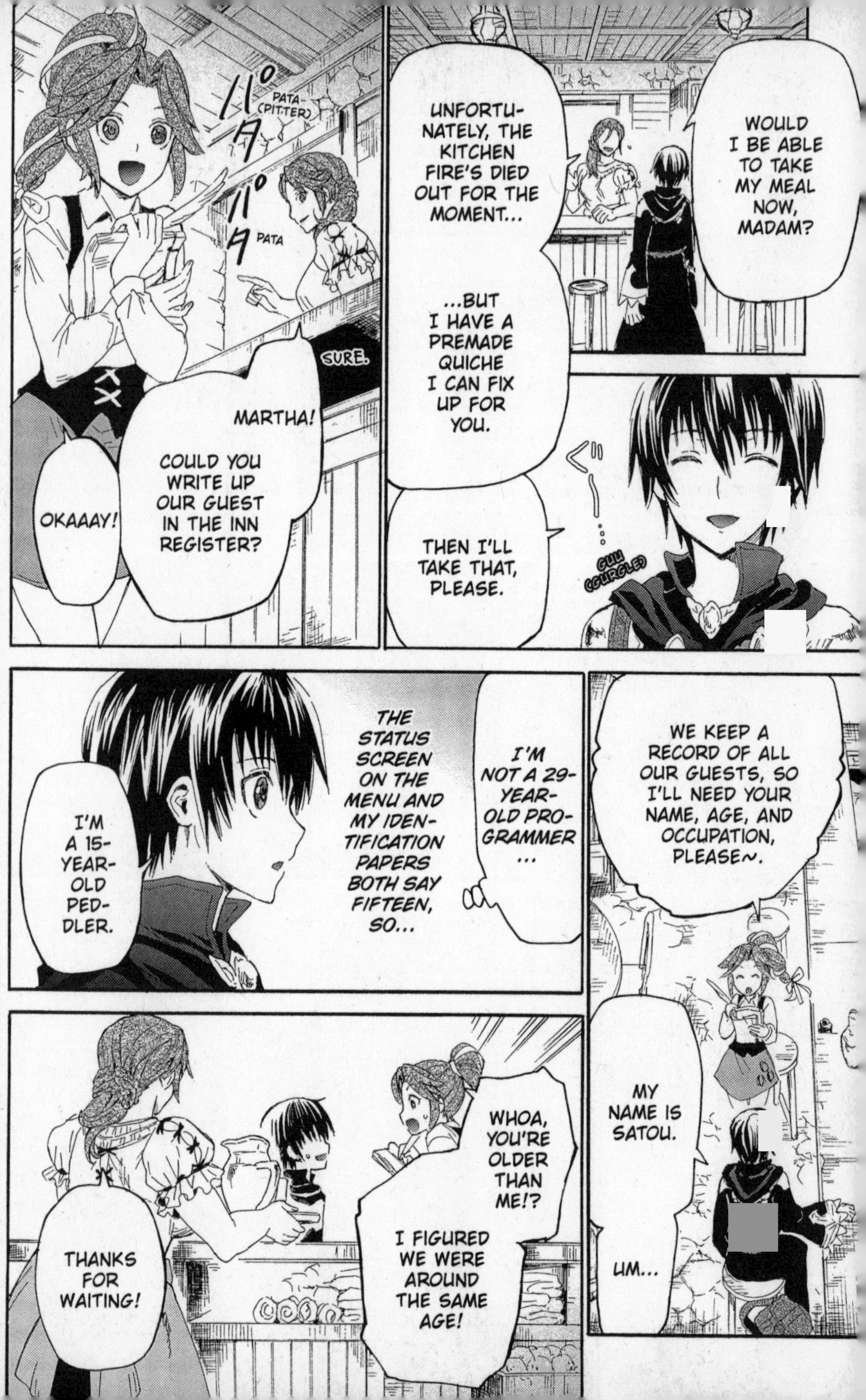
WOULD I BE ABLE TO TAKE MY MEAL NOW, MADAM?
UNFORTUNATELY, THE KITCHEN FIRE'S DIED OUT FOR THE MOMENT...
...BUT I HAVE A PREMADE QUICHE I CAN FIX UP FOR YOU.
GUU (GURGLE)
THEN I'LL TAKE THAT, PLEASE.
SURE.
MARTHA!
COULD YOU WRITE UP OUR GUEST IN THE INN REGISTER?
OKAAAY!
PATA (PITTER)
PATA
WE KEEP A RECORD OF ALL OUR GUESTS, SO I'LL NEED YOUR NAME, AGE, AND OCCUPATION, PLEASE~.
MY NAME IS SATOU.
UM...
I'M NOT A 29-YEAR-OLD PROGRAMMER...
THE STATUS SCREEN ON THE MENU AND MY IDENTIFICATION PAPERS BOTH SAY FIFTEEN, SO...
I'M A 15-YEAR-OLD PEDDLER.
WHOA, YOU'RE OLDER THAN ME!?
I FIGURED WE WERE AROUND THE SAME AGE!
THANKS FOR WAITING!

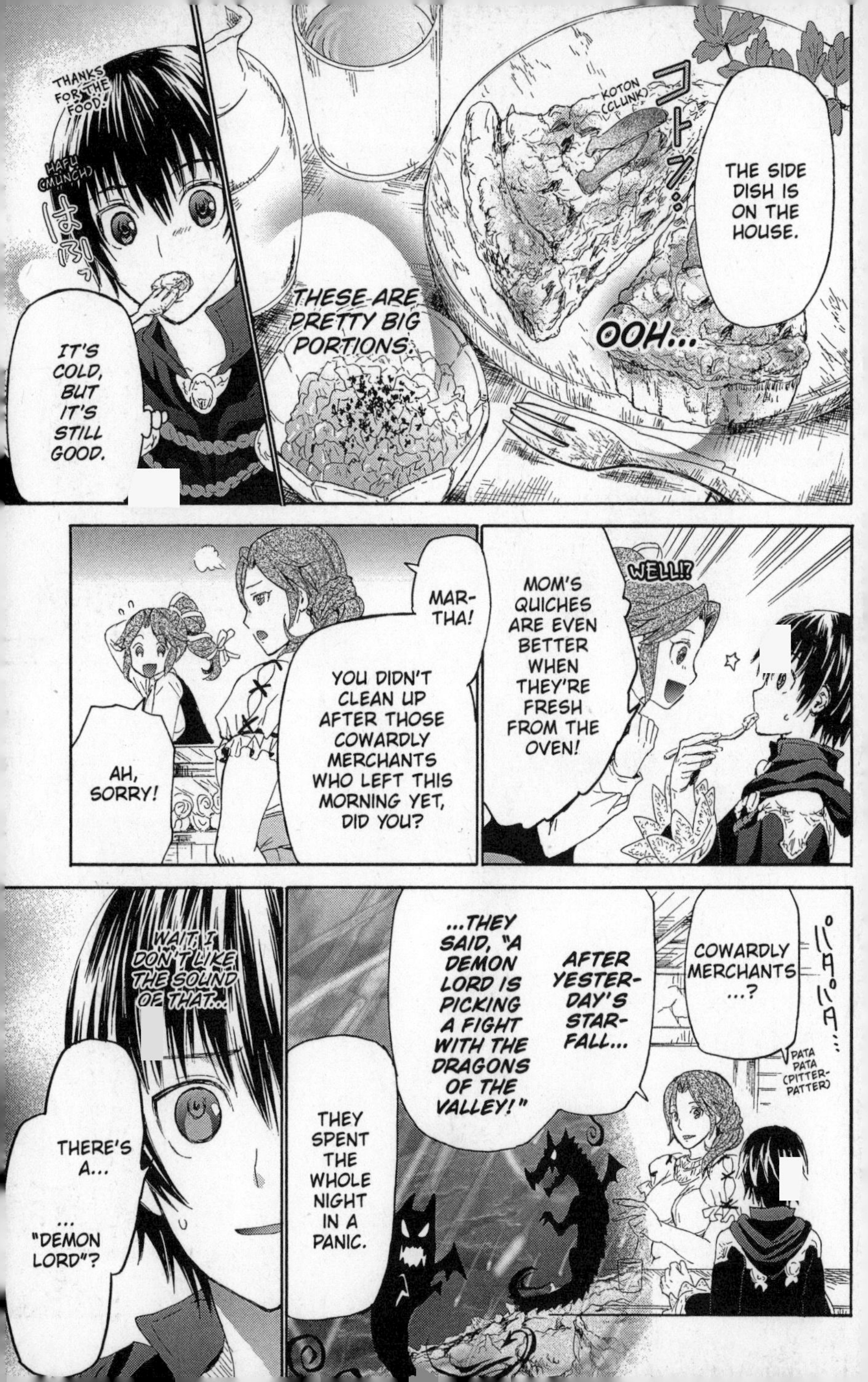
THE SIDE DISH IS ON THE HOUSE.
KOTON (CLUNK)
コトン。
OOH...
THESE ARE PRETTY BIG PORTIONS.
THANKS FOR THE FOOD!
HAFU (MUNCH)
はふ
IT'S COLD, BUT IT'S STILL GOOD.
WELL!?
MOM'S QUICHES ARE EVEN BETTER WHEN THEY'RE FRESH FROM THE OVEN!
MAR-THA!
YOU DIDN'T CLEAN UP AFTER THOSE COWARDLY MERCHANTS WHO LEFT THIS MORNING YET, DID YOU?
AH, SORRY!
パタパタ…
COWARDLY MERCHANTS ...?
PATA PATA (PITTER-PATTER)
AFTER YESTER-DAY'S STAR-FALL...
...THEY SAID, "A DEMON LORD IS PICKING A FIGHT WITH THE DRAGONS OF THE VALLEY!"
THEY SPENT THE WHOLE NIGHT IN A PANIC.
WAIT, I DON'T LIKE THE SOUND OF THAT...
THERE'S A...
..."DEMON LORD"?

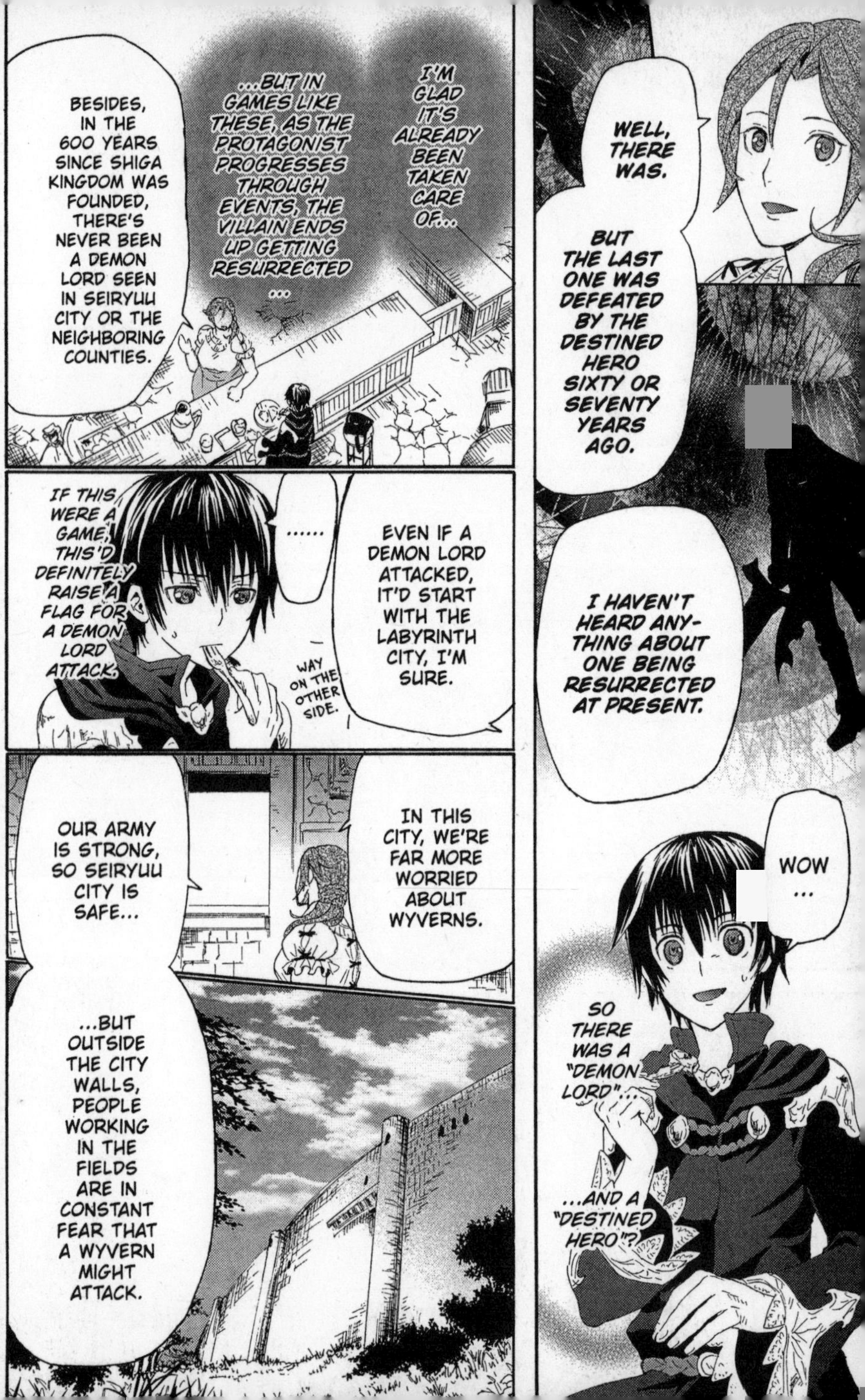
WELL, THERE WAS.
BUT THE LAST ONE WAS DEFEATED BY THE DESTINED HERO SIXTY OR SEVENTY YEARS AGO.
I HAVEN'T HEARD ANYTHING ABOUT ONE BEING RESURRECTED AT PRESENT.
WOW...
SO THERE WAS A "DEMON LORD"...
...AND A "DESTINED HERO"?
I'M GLAD IT'S ALREADY BEEN TAKEN CARE OF...
...BUT IN GAMES LIKE THESE, AS THE PROTAGONIST PROGRESSES THROUGH EVENTS, THE VILLAIN ENDS UP GETTING RESURRECTED...
BESIDES, IN THE 600 YEARS SINCE SHIGA KINGDOM WAS FOUNDED, THERE'S NEVER BEEN A DEMON LORD SEEN IN SEIRYUU CITY OR THE NEIGHBORING COUNTIES.
EVEN IF A DEMON LORD ATTACKED, IT'D START WITH THE LABYRINTH CITY, I'M SURE.
WAY ON THE OTHER SIDE.
......
IF THIS WERE A GAME, THIS'D DEFINITELY RAISE A FLAG FOR A DEMON LORD ATTACK.
IN THIS CITY, WE'RE FAR MORE WORRIED ABOUT WYVERNS.
OUR ARMY IS STRONG, SO SEIRYUU CITY IS SAFE...
...BUT OUTSIDE THE CITY WALLS, PEOPLE WORKING IN THE FIELDS ARE IN CONSTANT FEAR THAT A WYVERN MIGHT ATTACK.

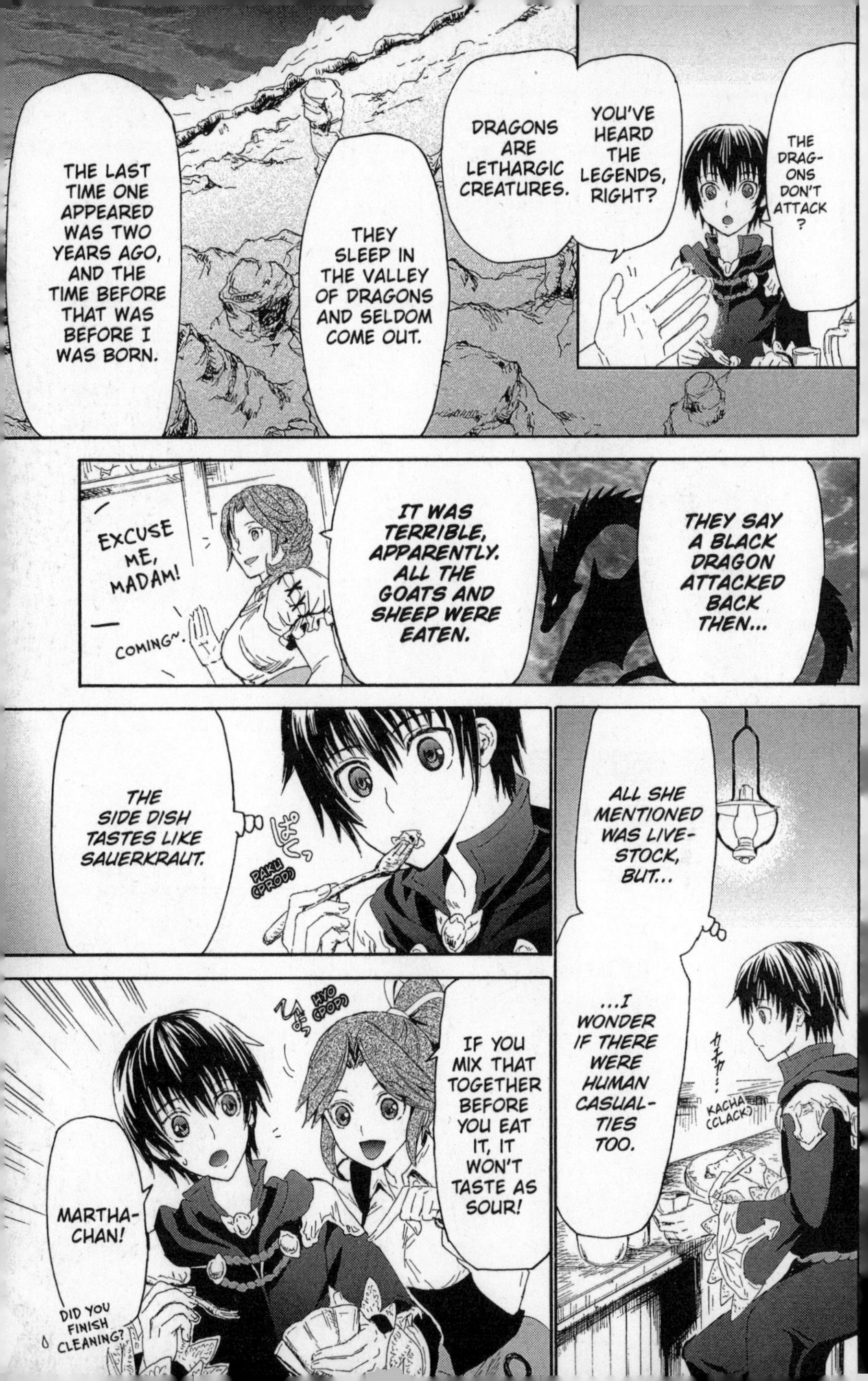
THE DRAG-ONS DON'T ATTACK?
YOU'VE HEARD THE LEGENDS, RIGHT?
DRAGONS ARE LETHARGIC CREATURES.
THEY SLEEP IN THE VALLEY OF DRAGONS AND SELDOM COME OUT.
THE LAST TIME ONE APPEARED WAS TWO YEARS AGO, AND THE TIME BEFORE THAT WAS BEFORE I WAS BORN.
THEY SAY A BLACK DRAGON ATTACKED BACK THEN...
IT WAS TERRIBLE, APPARENTLY. ALL THE GOATS AND SHEEP WERE EATEN.
EXCUSE ME, MADAM!
COMING~.
ALL SHE MENTIONED WAS LIVE-STOCK, BUT...
...I WONDER IF THERE WERE HUMAN CASUAL-TIES TOO.
KACHA (CLACK)
THE SIDE DISH TASTES LIKE SAUERKRAUT.
PAKU (PROD)
IF YOU MIX THAT TOGETHER BEFORE YOU EAT IT, IT WON'T TASTE AS SOUR!
HYO (POP)
MARTHA-CHAN!
DID YOU FINISH CLEANING?

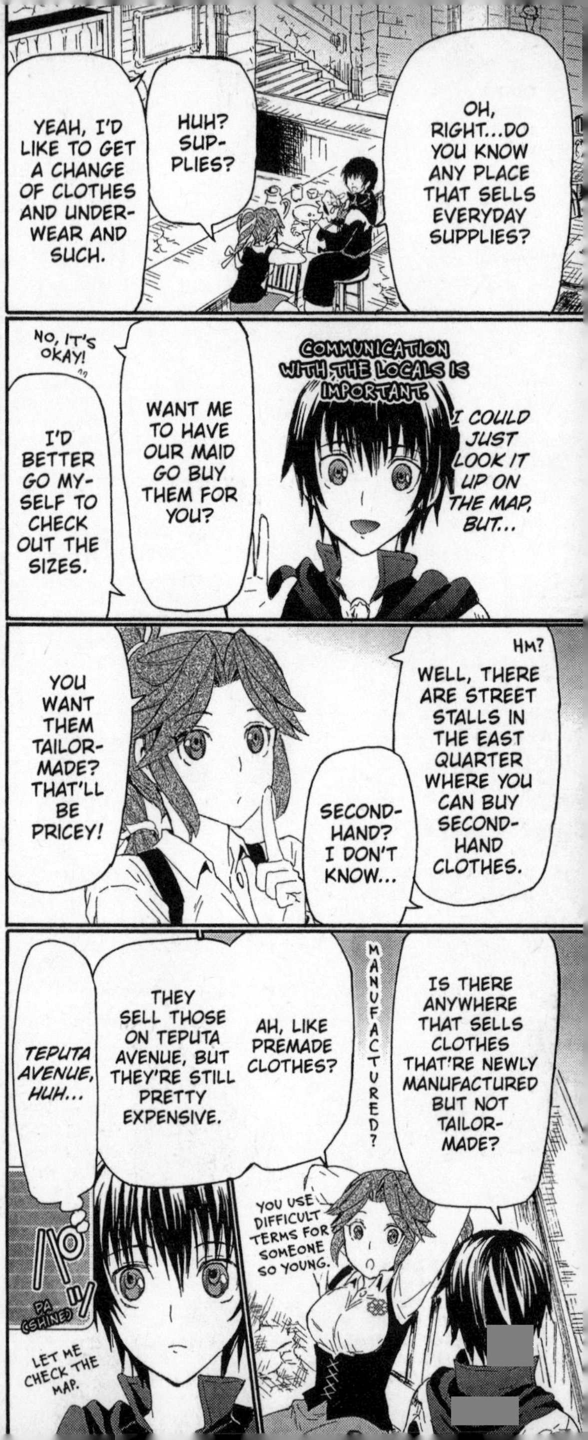
OH, RIGHT...DO YOU KNOW ANY PLACE THAT SELLS EVERYDAY SUPPLIES?
HUH? SUP-PLIES?
YEAH, I'D LIKE TO GET A CHANGE OF CLOTHES AND UNDER-WEAR AND SUCH.
COMMUNICATION WITH THE LOCALS IS IMPORTANT.
I COULD JUST LOOK IT UP ON THE MAP, BUT...
WANT ME TO HAVE OUR MAID GO BUY THEM FOR YOU?
NO, IT'S OKAY!
I'D BETTER GO MY-SELF TO CHECK OUT THE SIZES.
HM? WELL, THERE ARE STREET STALLS IN THE EAST QUARTER WHERE YOU CAN BUY SECOND-HAND CLOTHES.
SECOND-HAND? I DON'T KNOW...
YOU WANT THEM TAILOR-MADE? THAT'LL BE PRICEY!
IS THERE ANYWHERE THAT SELLS CLOTHES THAT'RE NEWLY MANUFACTURED BUT NOT TAILOR-MADE?
MANUFACTURED?
AH, LIKE PREMADE CLOTHES?
THEY SELL THOSE ON TEPUTA AVENUE, BUT THEY'RE STILL PRETTY EXPENSIVE.
YOU USE DIFFICULT TERMS FOR SOMEONE SO YOUNG.
TEPUTA AVENUE, HUH...
PA (SHINE)
LET ME CHECK THE MAP.
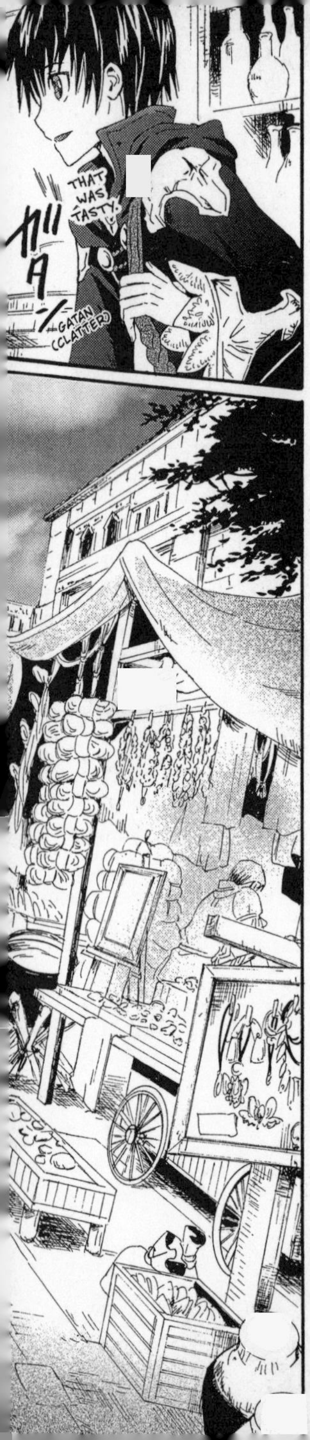
THAT WAS TASTY.
GATAN (CLATTER)

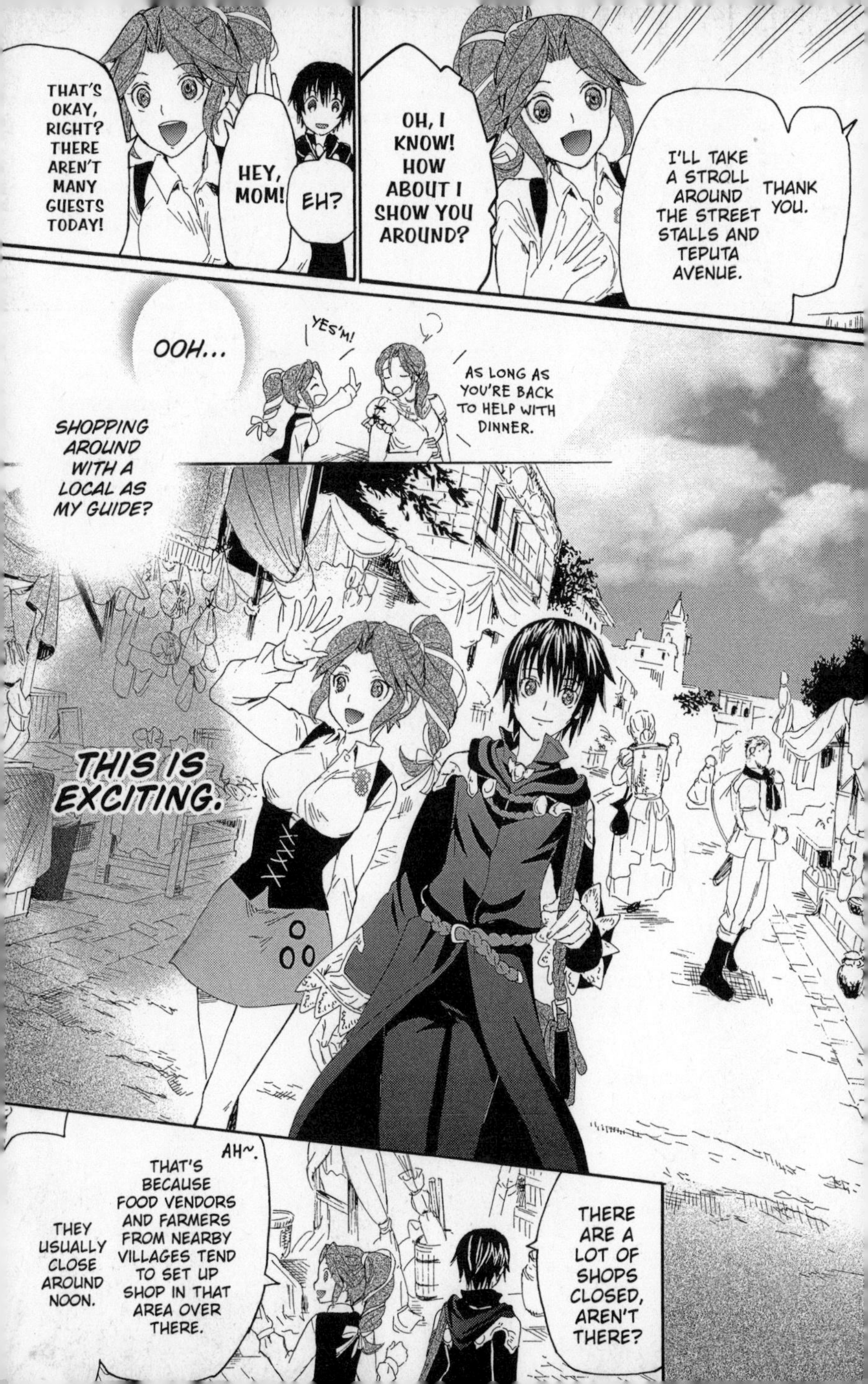
THANK YOU.
I'LL TAKE A STROLL AROUND THE STREET STALLS AND TEPUTA AVENUE.
OH, I KNOW! HOW ABOUT I SHOW YOU AROUND?
EH?
HEY, MOM!
THAT'S OKAY, RIGHT? THERE AREN'T MANY GUESTS TODAY!
AS LONG AS YOU'RE BACK TO HELP WITH DINNER.
YES'M!
OOH...
SHOPPING AROUND WITH A LOCAL AS MY GUIDE?
THIS IS EXCITING.
THERE ARE A LOT OF SHOPS CLOSED, AREN'T THERE?
AH~.
THAT'S BECAUSE FOOD VENDORS AND FARMERS FROM NEARBY VILLAGES TEND TO SET UP SHOP IN THAT AREA OVER THERE.
THEY USUALLY CLOSE AROUND NOON.

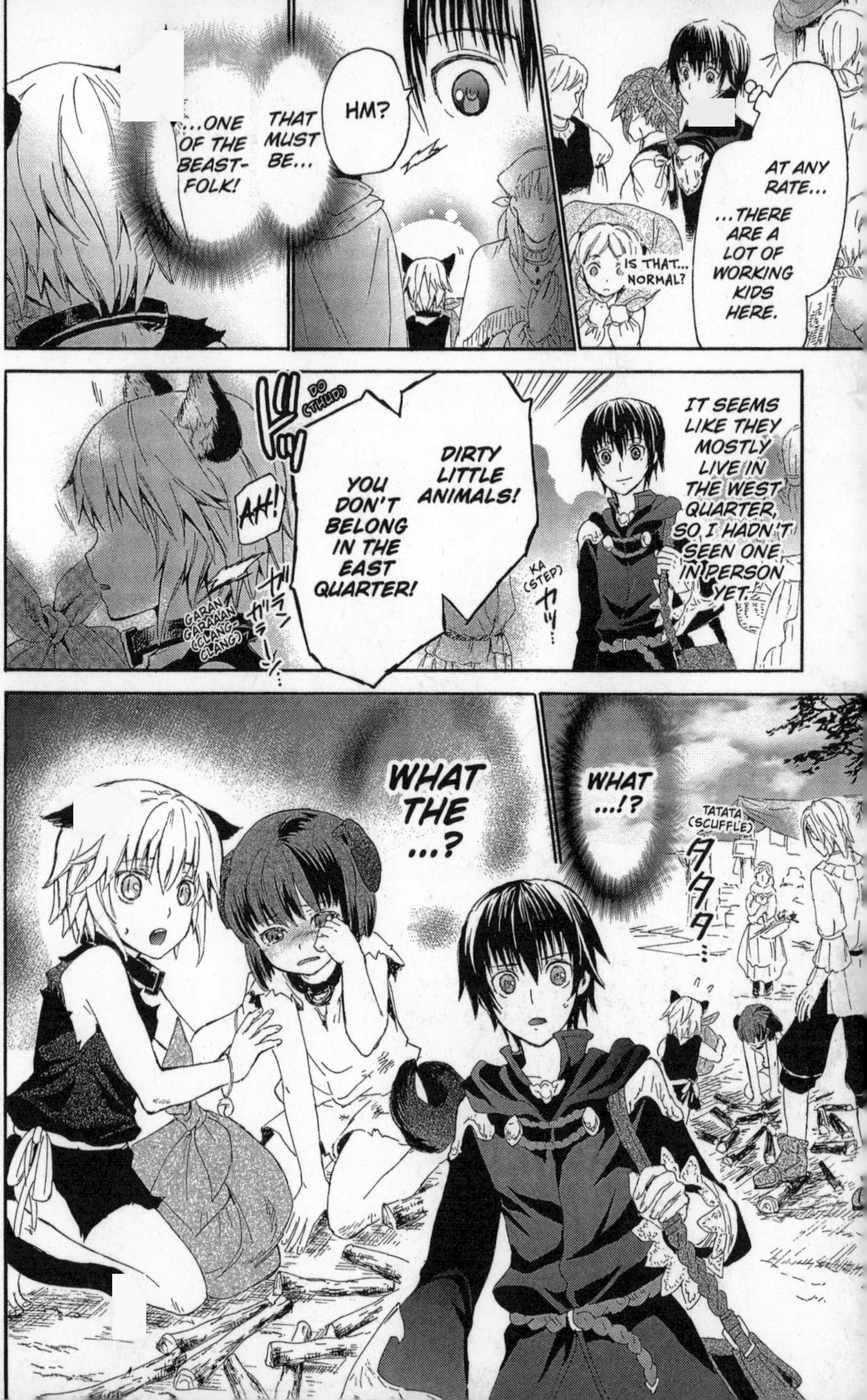
AT ANY RATE...
...THERE ARE A LOT OF WORKING KIDS HERE.
IS THAT... NORMAL?
HM?
THAT MUST BE...
...ONE OF THE BEAST-FOLK!
IT SEEMS LIKE THEY MOSTLY LIVE IN THE WEST QUARTER, SO I HADN'T SEEN ONE IN PERSON YET.
KA (STEP)
DIRTY LITTLE ANIMALS!
YOU DON'T BELONG IN THE EAST QUARTER!
DO (THUDD)
AH!
GARAN GARAAAN (CLANG CLANG)
WHAT ...!?
TATATA (SCUFFLE)
WHAT THE ...?

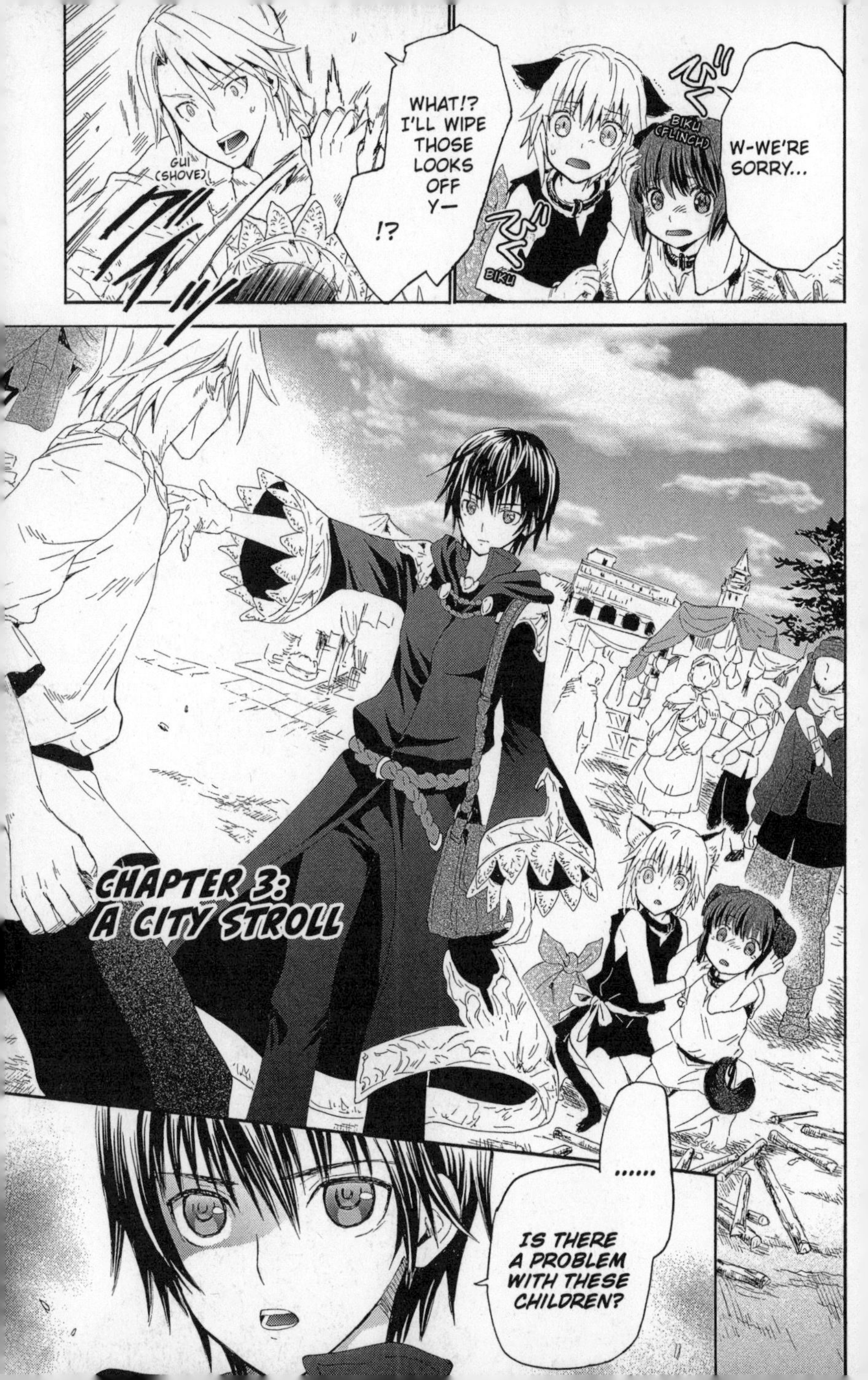
BIKU (FLINCH)
W-WE'RE SORRY...
BIKU
WHAT!? I'LL WIPE THOSE LOOKS OFF Y—
!?
GUI (SHOVE)
CHAPTER 3: A CITY STROLL
......
IS THERE A PROBLEM WITH THESE CHILDREN?

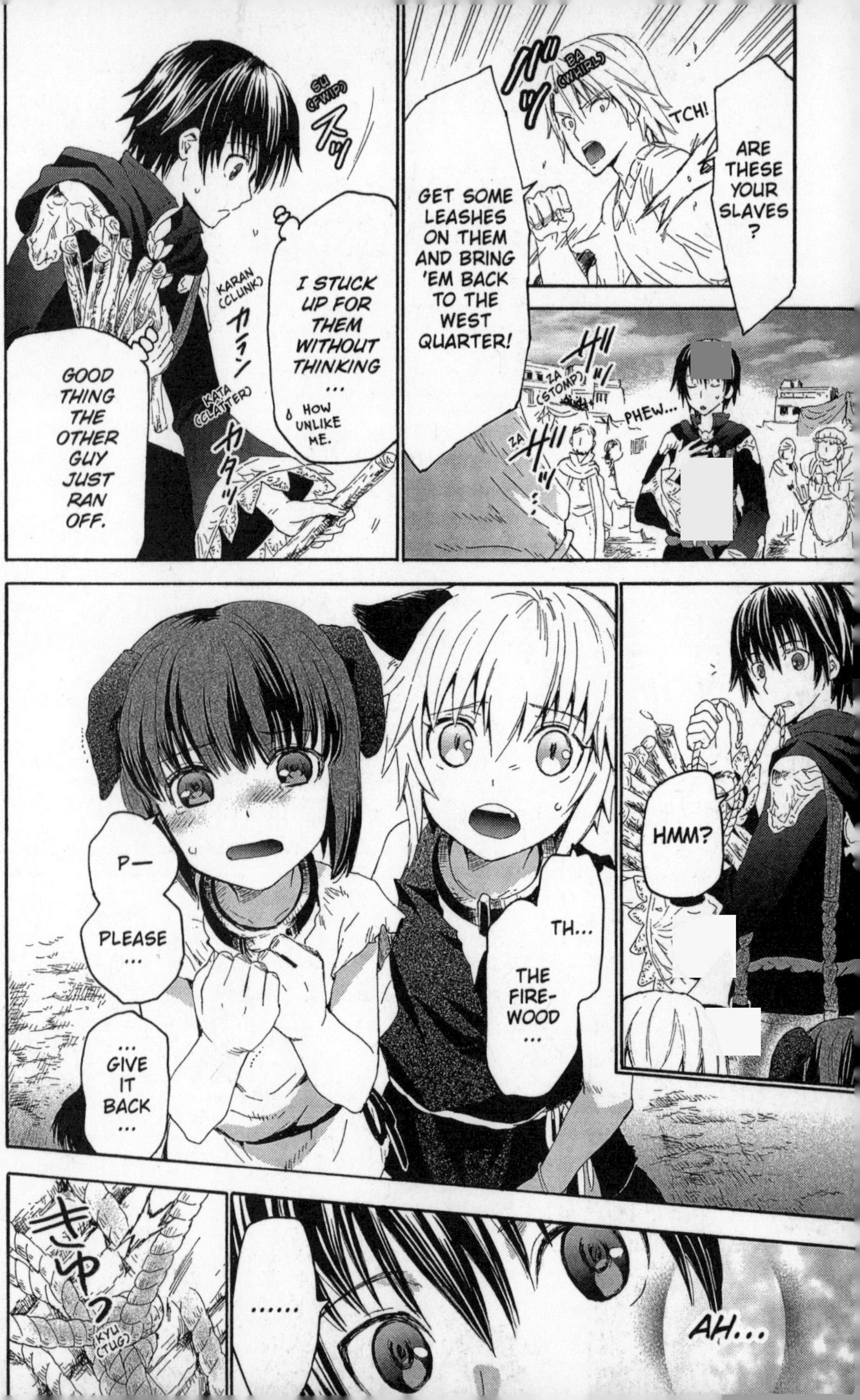
ARE THESE YOUR SLAVES?
TCH!
BA (WHIRL)
GET SOME LEASHES ON THEM AND BRING 'EM BACK TO THE WEST QUARTER!
ZA (STOMP)
ZA
PHEW...
SU (FWIP)
I STUCK UP FOR THEM WITHOUT THINKING...
HOW UNLIKE ME.
KARAN (CLUNK)
KATA (CLATTER)
GOOD THING THE OTHER GUY JUST RAN OFF.
HMM?
TH...
THE FIRE-WOOD...
P—
PLEASE...
...GIVE IT BACK...
AH...
......
KYU (TUG)

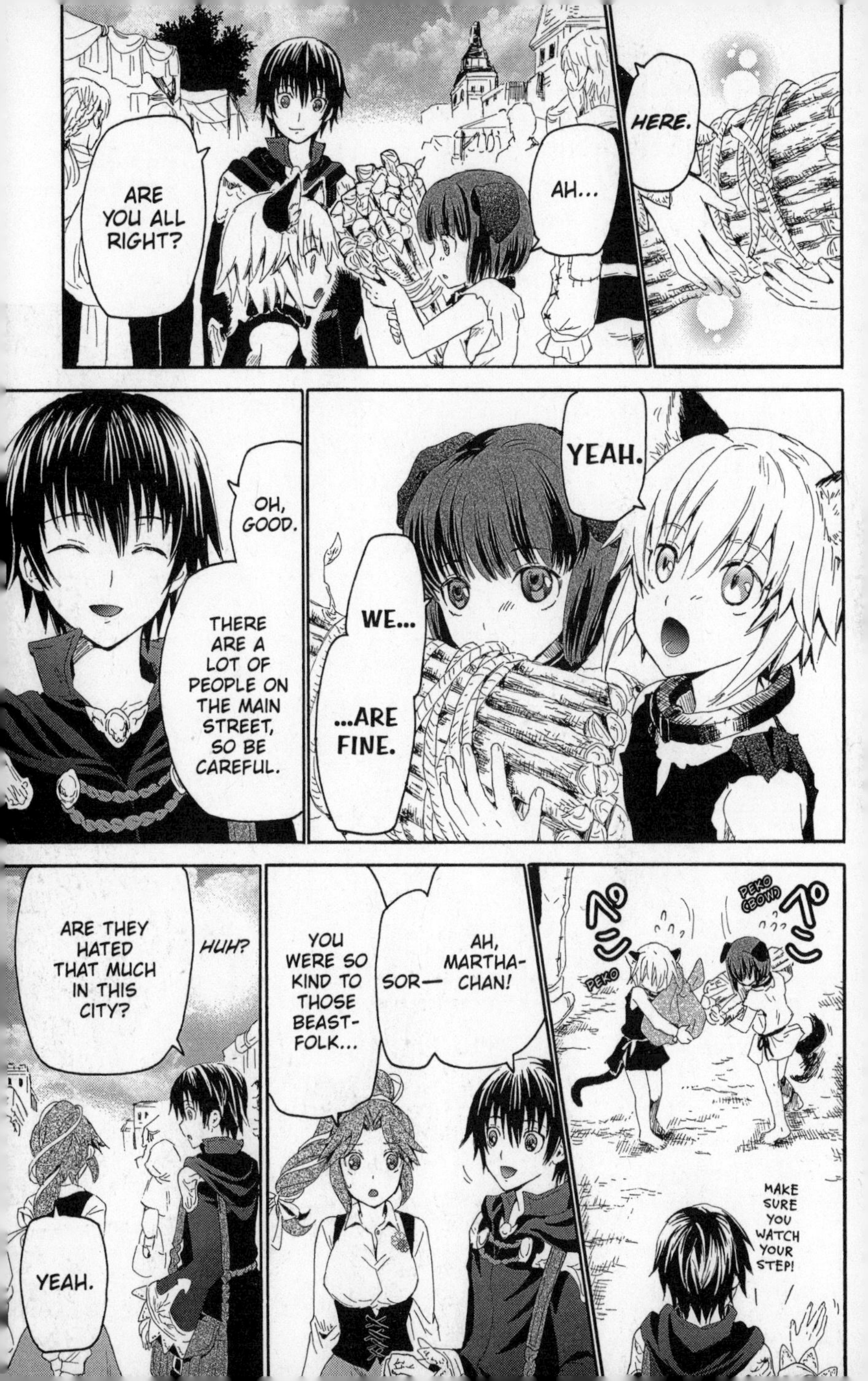
HERE.
AH...
ARE YOU ALL RIGHT?
YEAH.
WE...
...ARE FINE.
OH, GOOD.
THERE ARE A LOT OF PEOPLE ON THE MAIN STREET, SO BE CAREFUL.
PEKO (BOW)
ぺこ
ぺこ
PEKO
MAKE SURE YOU WATCH YOUR STEP!
AH, MARTHA-CHAN!
SOR—
YOU WERE SO KIND TO THOSE BEAST-FOLK...
HUH?
ARE THEY HATED THAT MUCH IN THIS CITY?
YEAH.

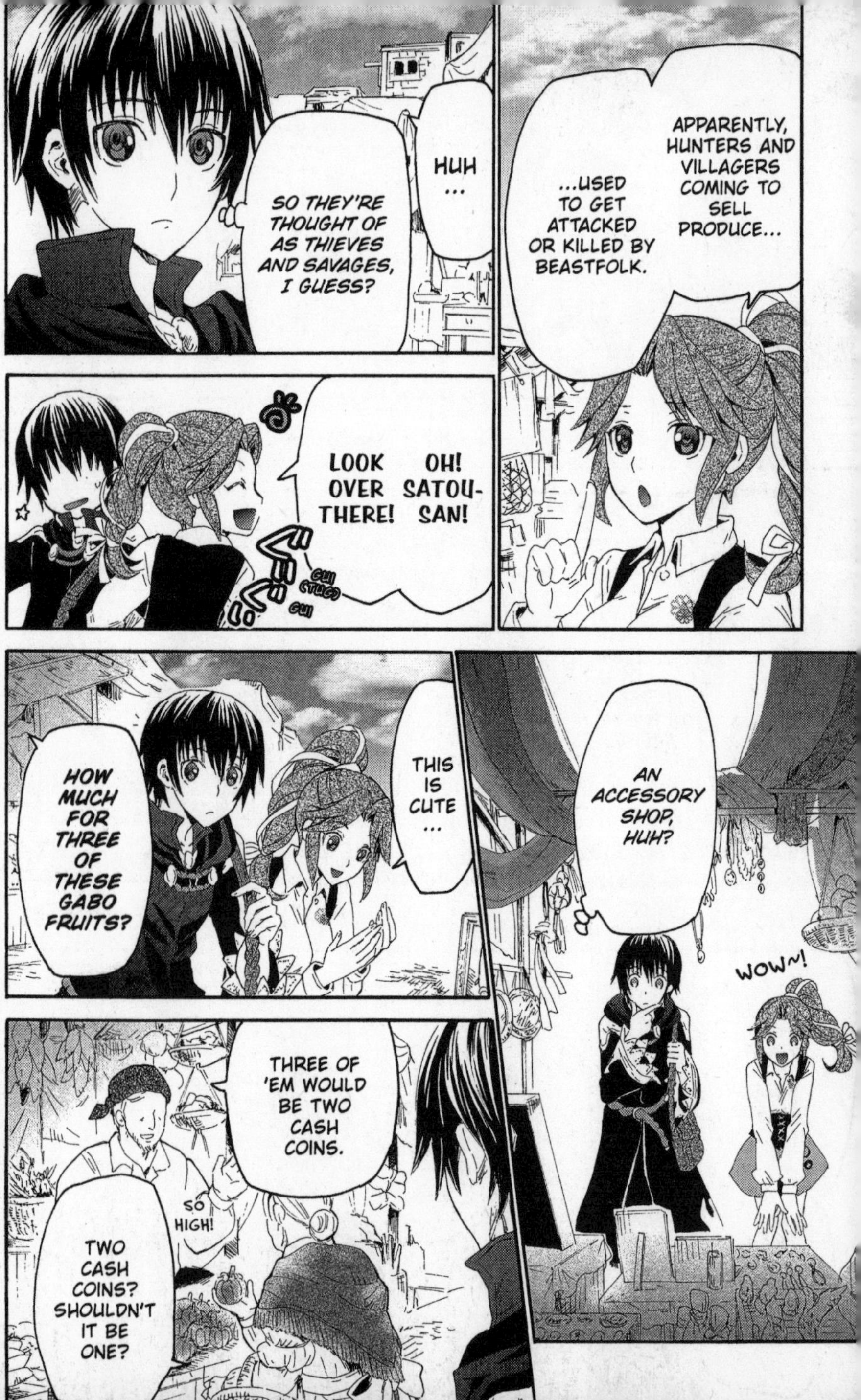
APPARENTLY, HUNTERS AND VILLAGERS COMING TO SELL PRODUCE...
...USED TO GET ATTACKED OR KILLED BY BEASTFOLK.
HUH...
SO THEY'RE THOUGHT OF AS THIEVES AND SAVAGES, I GUESS?
OH! SATOU-SAN!
LOOK OVER THERE!
GUI (TUG) GUI
AN ACCESSORY SHOP, HUH?
WOW~!
THIS IS CUTE...
HOW MUCH FOR THREE OF THESE GABO FRUITS?
THREE OF 'EM WOULD BE TWO CASH COINS.
SO HIGH!
TWO CASH COINS? SHOULDN'T IT BE ONE?

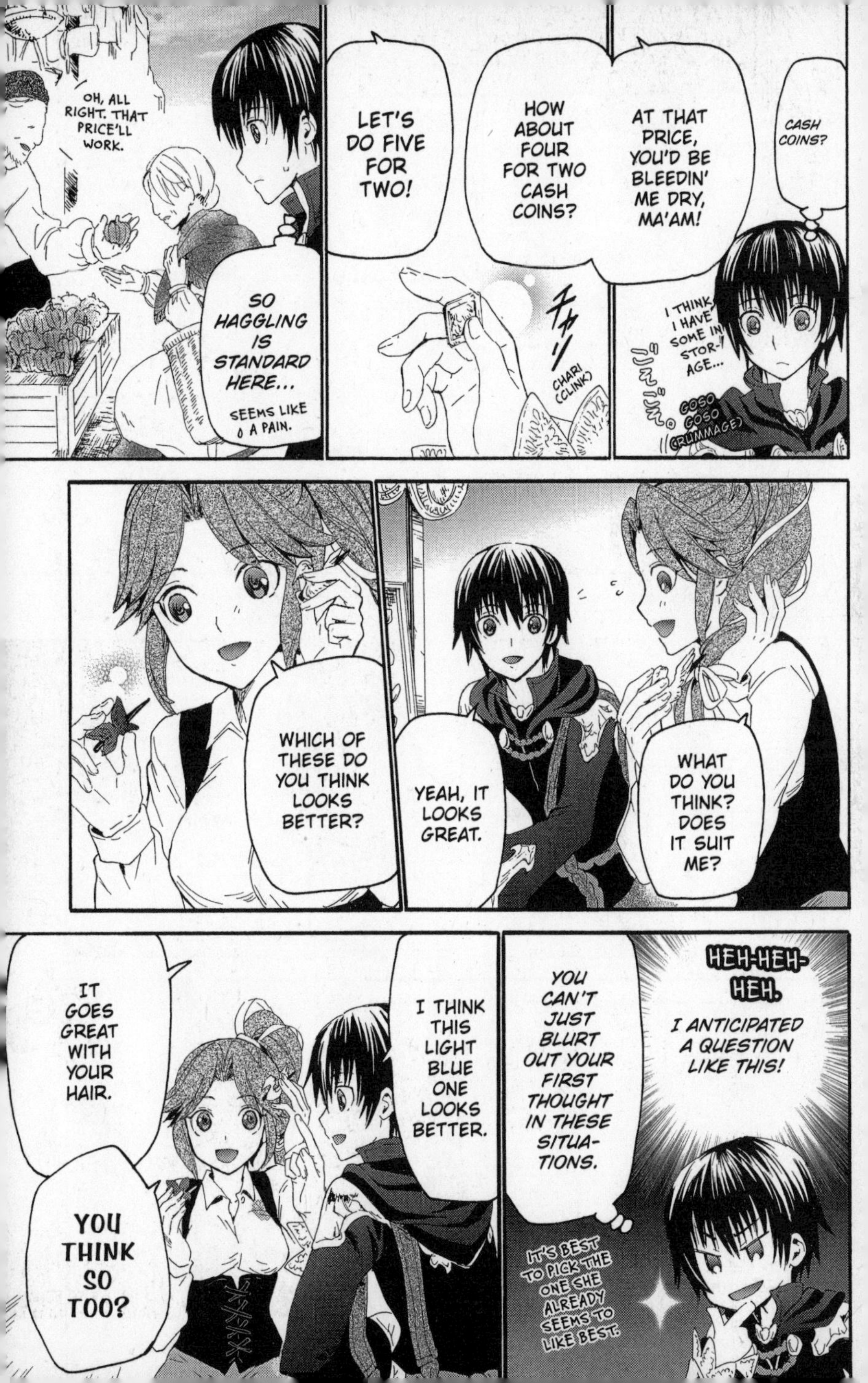
CASH COINS?
I THINK I HAVE SOME IN STORAGE...
GOSO GOSO (RUMMAGE)
AT THAT PRICE, YOU'D BE BLEEDIN' ME DRY, MA'AM!
HOW ABOUT FOUR FOR TWO CASH COINS?
LET'S DO FIVE FOR TWO!
CHARI (CLINK)
OH, ALL RIGHT. THAT PRICE'LL WORK.
SO HAGGLING IS STANDARD HERE...
SEEMS LIKE A PAIN.
WHAT DO YOU THINK? DOES IT SUIT ME?
YEAH, IT LOOKS GREAT.
WHICH OF THESE DO YOU THINK LOOKS BETTER?
HEH-HEH-HEH.
I ANTICIPATED A QUESTION LIKE THIS!
YOU CAN'T JUST BLURT OUT YOUR FIRST THOUGHT IN THESE SITUATIONS.
IT'S BEST TO PICK THE ONE SHE ALREADY SEEMS TO LIKE BEST.
I THINK THIS LIGHT BLUE ONE LOOKS BETTER.
IT GOES GREAT WITH YOUR HAIR.
YOU THINK SO TOO?

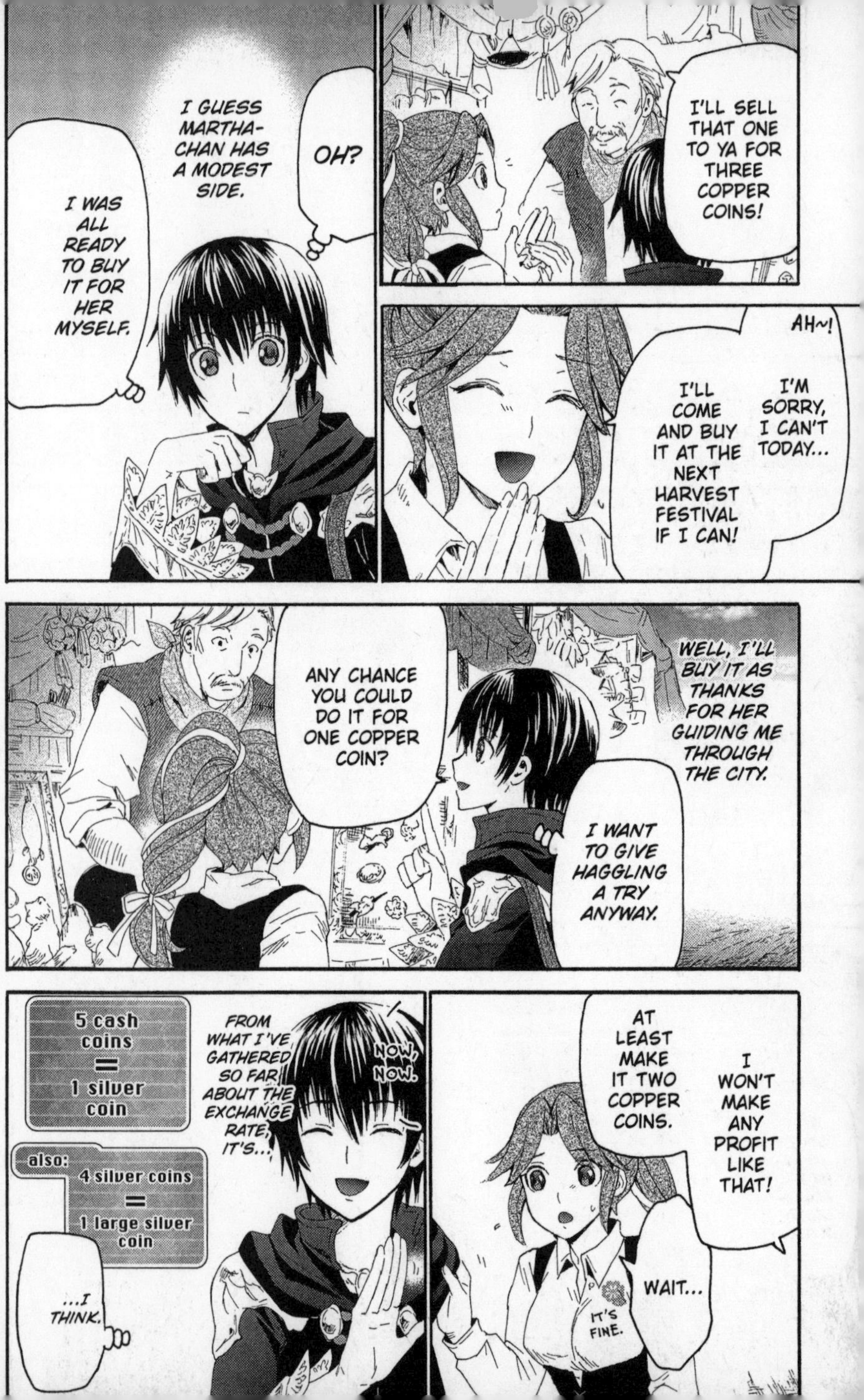

I'LL SELL THAT ONE TO YA FOR THREE COPPER COINS!
AH~!
I'M SORRY, I CAN'T TODAY...
I'LL COME AND BUY IT AT THE NEXT HARVEST FESTIVAL IF I CAN!
OH?
I GUESS MARTHA-CHAN HAS A MODEST SIDE.
I WAS ALL READY TO BUY IT FOR HER MYSELF.
WELL, I'LL BUY IT AS THANKS FOR HER GUIDING ME THROUGH THE CITY.
I WANT TO GIVE HAGGLING A TRY ANYWAY.
ANY CHANCE YOU COULD DO IT FOR ONE COPPER COIN?
I WON'T MAKE ANY PROFIT LIKE THAT!
AT LEAST MAKE IT TWO COPPER COINS.
WAIT...
IT'S FINE.
NOW, NOW.
FROM WHAT I'VE GATHERED SO FAR ABOUT THE EXCHANGE RATE, IT'S...
5 cash coins = 1 silver coin
also: 4 silver coins = 1 large silver coin
...I THINK.

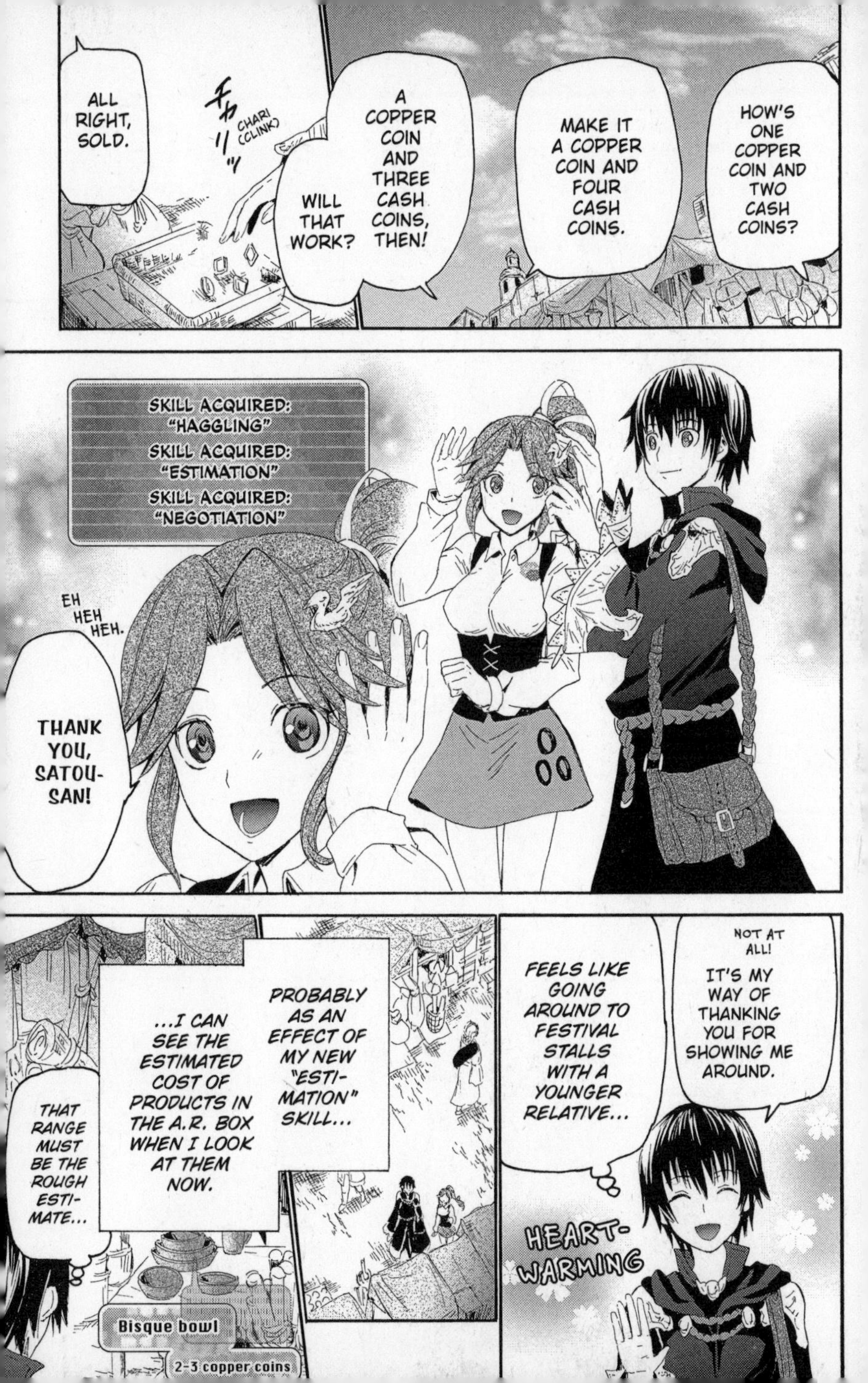
HOW'S ONE COPPER COIN AND TWO CASH COINS?
MAKE IT A COPPER COIN AND FOUR CASH COINS.
A COPPER COIN AND THREE CASH COINS, THEN!
WILL THAT WORK?
チャリッ
CHARI (CLINK)
ALL RIGHT, SOLD.
SKILL ACQUIRED: "HAGGLING"
SKILL ACQUIRED: "ESTIMATION"
SKILL ACQUIRED: "NEGOTIATION"
EH HEH HEH.
THANK YOU, SATOU-SAN!
NOT AT ALL!
IT'S MY WAY OF THANKING YOU FOR SHOWING ME AROUND.
FEELS LIKE GOING AROUND TO FESTIVAL STALLS WITH A YOUNGER RELATIVE...
HEART-WARMING
PROBABLY AS AN EFFECT OF MY NEW "ESTI-MATION" SKILL...
...I CAN SEE THE ESTIMATED COST OF PRODUCTS IN THE A.R. BOX WHEN I LOOK AT THEM NOW.
THAT RANGE MUST BE THE ROUGH ESTI-MATE...
Bisque bowl
2-3 copper coins

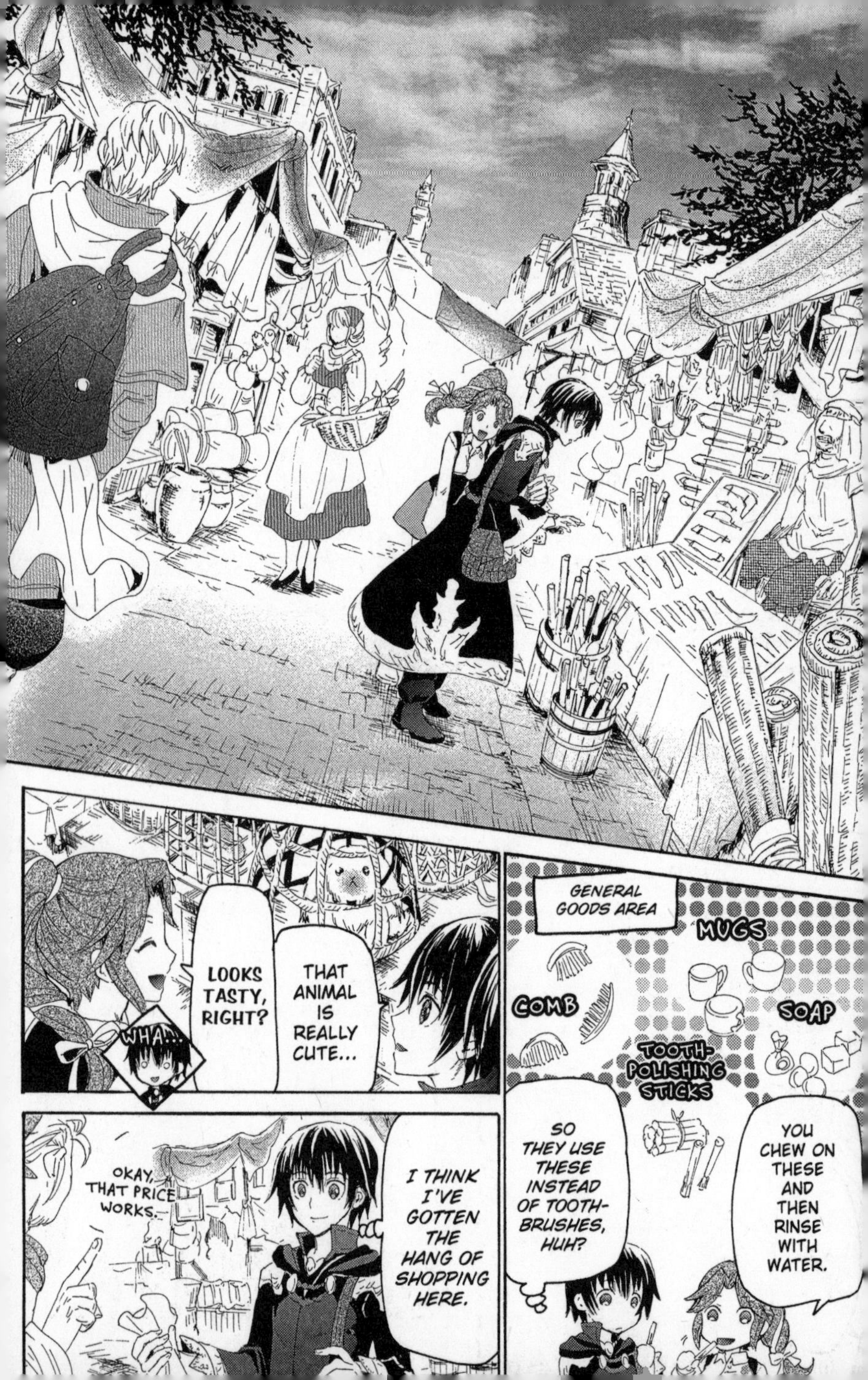
GENERAL GOODS AREA
MUGS
SOAP
COMB
TOOTH-POLISHING STICKS
YOU CHEW ON THESE AND THEN RINSE WITH WATER.
SO THEY USE THESE INSTEAD OF TOOTH-BRUSHES, HUH?
THAT ANIMAL IS REALLY CUTE...
LOOKS TASTY, RIGHT?
WHA...
I THINK I'VE GOTTEN THE HANG OF SHOPPING HERE.
OKAY, THAT PRICE WORKS.

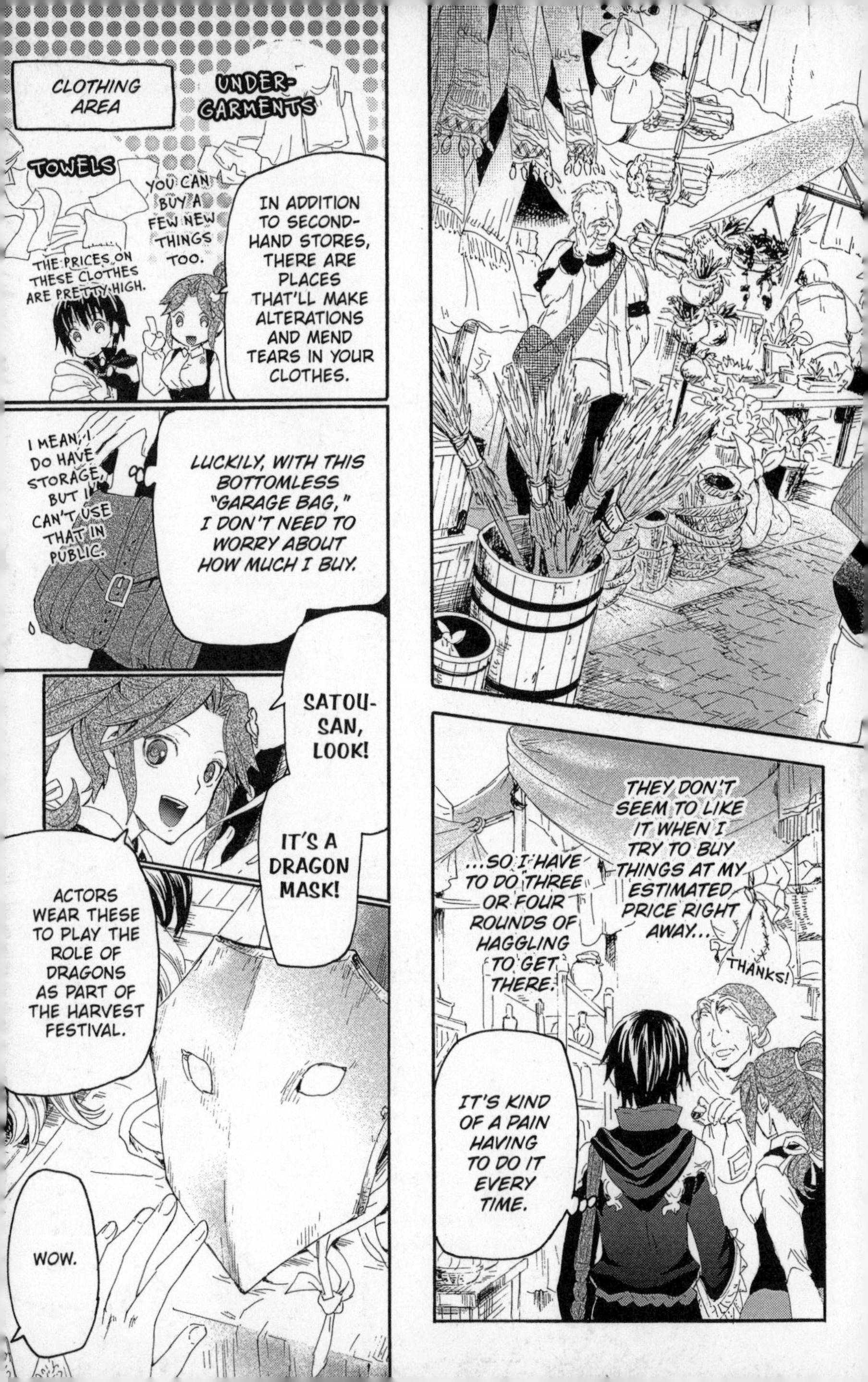
UNDER-GARMENTS
CLOTHING AREA
IN ADDITION TO SECOND-HAND STORES, THERE ARE PLACES THAT'LL MAKE ALTERATIONS AND MEND TEARS IN YOUR CLOTHES.
TOWELS
YOU CAN BUY A FEW NEW THINGS TOO.
THE PRICES ON THESE CLOTHES ARE PRETTY HIGH.
LUCKILY, WITH THIS BOTTOMLESS "GARAGE BAG," I DON'T NEED TO WORRY ABOUT HOW MUCH I BUY.
I MEAN, I DO HAVE STORAGE, BUT I CAN'T USE THAT IN PUBLIC.
THEY DON'T SEEM TO LIKE IT WHEN I TRY TO BUY THINGS AT MY ESTIMATED PRICE RIGHT AWAY...
...SO I HAVE TO DO THREE OR FOUR ROUNDS OF HAGGLING TO GET THERE.
THANKS!
IT'S KIND OF A PAIN HAVING TO DO IT EVERY TIME.
SATOU-SAN, LOOK!
IT'S A DRAGON MASK!
ACTORS WEAR THESE TO PLAY THE ROLE OF DRAGONS AS PART OF THE HARVEST FESTIVAL.
WOW.

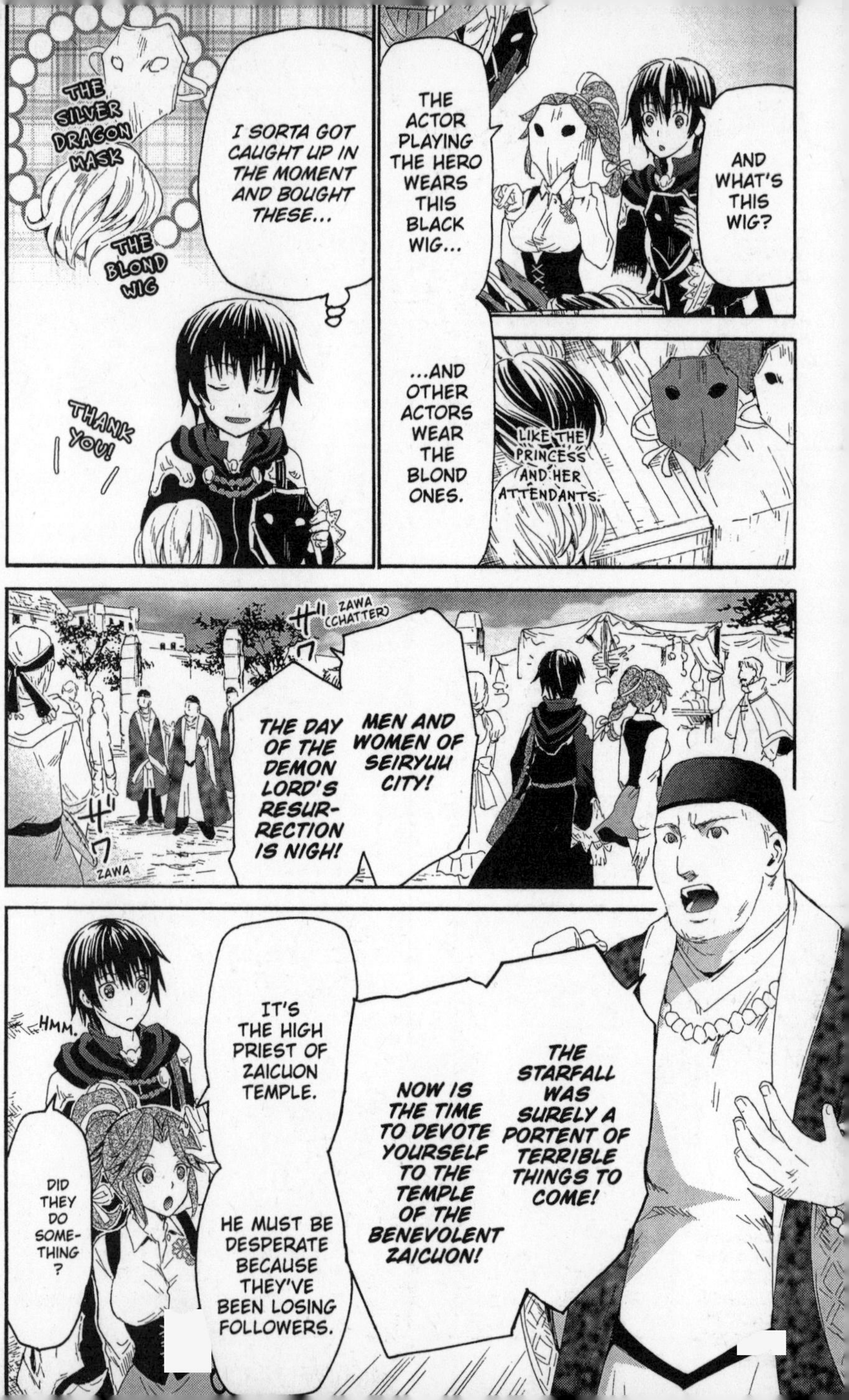
AND WHAT'S THIS WIG?
THE ACTOR PLAYING THE HERO WEARS THIS BLACK WIG...
...AND OTHER ACTORS WEAR THE BLOND ONES.
LIKE THE PRINCESS AND HER ATTENDANTS.
THE SILVER DRAGON MASK
THE BLOND WIG
I SORTA GOT CAUGHT UP IN THE MOMENT AND BOUGHT THESE...
THANK YOU!
ZAWA (CHATTER)
MEN AND WOMEN OF SEIRYUU CITY!
THE DAY OF THE DEMON LORD'S RESUR-RECTION IS NIGH!
ZAWA
THE STARFALL WAS SURELY A PORTENT OF TERRIBLE THINGS TO COME!
NOW IS THE TIME TO DEVOTE YOURSELF TO THE TEMPLE OF THE BENEVOLENT ZAICUON!
IT'S THE HIGH PRIEST OF ZAICUON TEMPLE.
HMM.
HE MUST BE DESPERATE BECAUSE THEY'VE BEEN LOSING FOLLOWERS.
DID THEY DO SOME-THING?

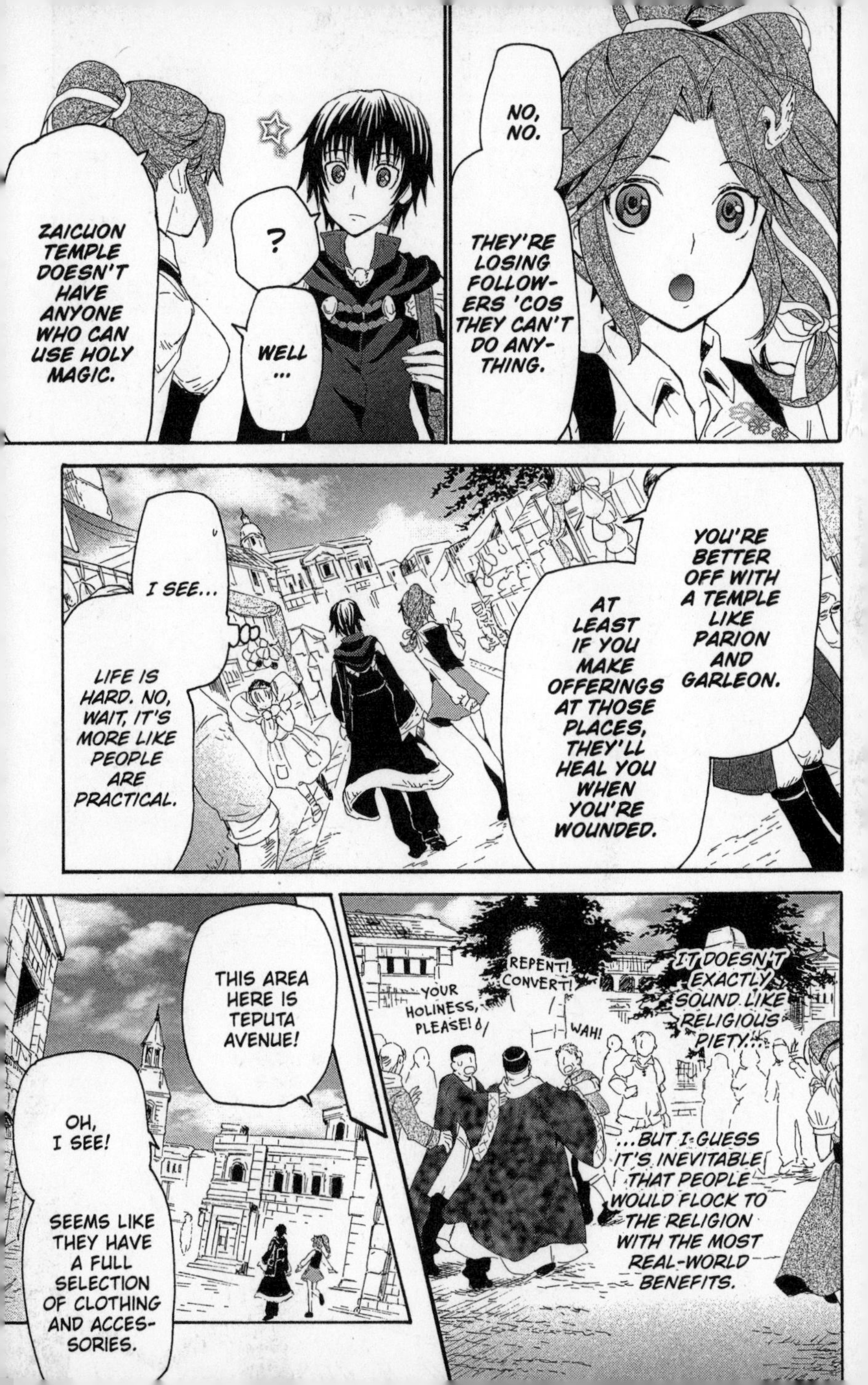
NO, NO.
THEY'RE LOSING FOLLOWERS 'COS THEY CAN'T DO ANYTHING.
?
WELL ...
ZAICUON TEMPLE DOESN'T HAVE ANYONE WHO CAN USE HOLY MAGIC.
YOU'RE BETTER OFF WITH A TEMPLE LIKE PARION AND GARLEON.
AT LEAST IF YOU MAKE OFFERINGS AT THOSE PLACES, THEY'LL HEAL YOU WHEN YOU'RE WOUNDED.
I SEE...
LIFE IS HARD. NO, WAIT, IT'S MORE LIKE PEOPLE ARE PRACTICAL.
IT DOESN'T EXACTLY SOUND LIKE RELIGIOUS PIETY...
REPENT! CONVERT!
YOUR HOLINESS, PLEASE!
WAH!
...BUT I GUESS IT'S INEVITABLE THAT PEOPLE WOULD FLOCK TO THE RELIGION WITH THE MOST REAL-WORLD BENEFITS.
THIS AREA HERE IS TEPUTA AVENUE!
OH, I SEE!
SEEMS LIKE THEY HAVE A FULL SELECTION OF CLOTHING AND ACCESSORIES.

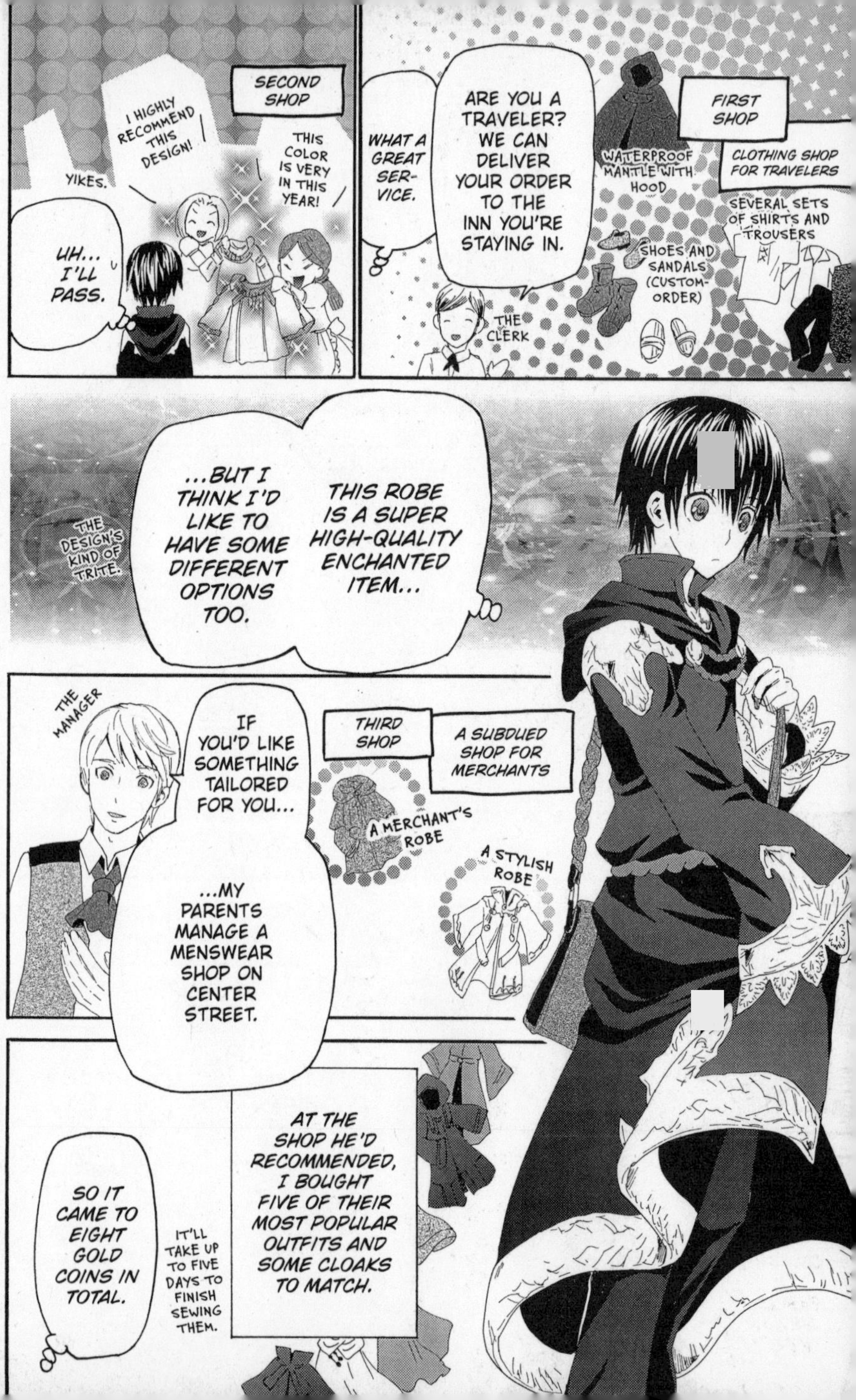
FIRST SHOP
CLOTHING SHOP FOR TRAVELERS
WATERPROOF MANTLE WITH HOOD
SEVERAL SETS OF SHIRTS AND TROUSERS
SHOES AND SANDALS (CUSTOM-ORDER)
THE CLERK
ARE YOU A TRAVELER? WE CAN DELIVER YOUR ORDER TO THE INN YOU'RE STAYING IN.
WHAT A GREAT SER-VICE.
SECOND SHOP
THIS COLOR IS VERY IN THIS YEAR!
I HIGHLY RECOMMEND THIS DESIGN!
YIKES.
UH... I'LL PASS.
THIS ROBE IS A SUPER HIGH-QUALITY ENCHANTED ITEM...
...BUT I THINK I'D LIKE TO HAVE SOME DIFFERENT OPTIONS TOO.
THE DESIGN'S KIND OF TRITE.
THIRD SHOP
A SUBDUED SHOP FOR MERCHANTS
A MERCHANT'S ROBE
A STYLISH ROBE
THE MANAGER
IF YOU'D LIKE SOMETHING TAILORED FOR YOU...
...MY PARENTS MANAGE A MENSWEAR SHOP ON CENTER STREET.
AT THE SHOP HE'D RECOMMENDED, I BOUGHT FIVE OF THEIR MOST POPULAR OUTFITS AND SOME CLOAKS TO MATCH.
IT'LL TAKE UP TO FIVE DAYS TO FINISH SEWING THEM.
SO IT CAME TO EIGHT GOLD COINS IN TOTAL.

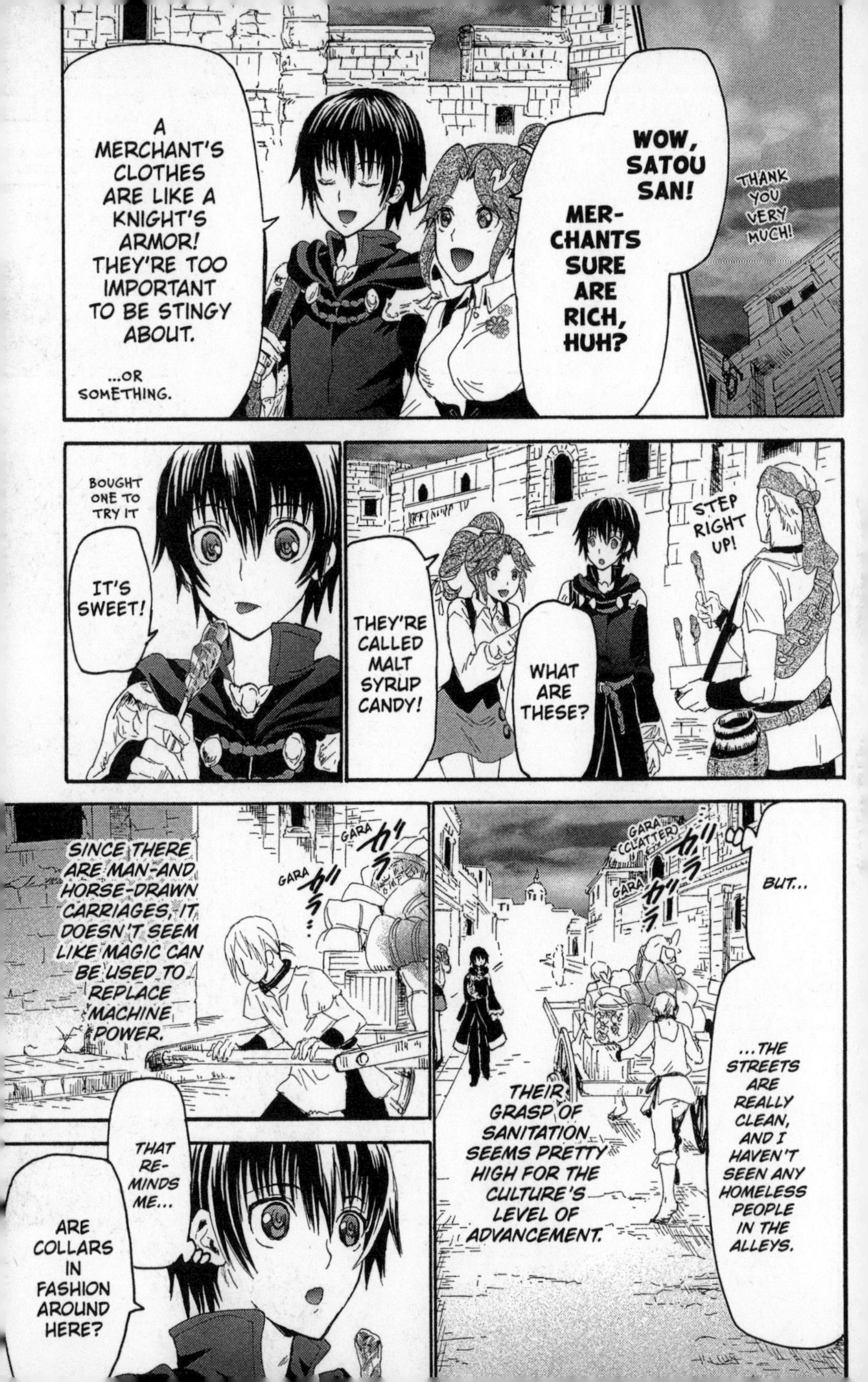
THANK YOU VERY MUCH!
WOW, SATOU SAN!
MER-CHANTS SURE ARE RICH, HUH?
A MERCHANT'S CLOTHES ARE LIKE A KNIGHT'S ARMOR! THEY'RE TOO IMPORTANT TO BE STINGY ABOUT.
...OR SOMETHING.
STEP RIGHT UP!
WHAT ARE THESE?
THEY'RE CALLED MALT SYRUP CANDY!
BOUGHT ONE TO TRY IT
IT'S SWEET!
GARA (CLATTER)
GARA
BUT...
...THE STREETS ARE REALLY CLEAN, AND I HAVEN'T SEEN ANY HOMELESS PEOPLE IN THE ALLEYS.
THEIR GRASP OF SANITATION SEEMS PRETTY HIGH FOR THE CULTURE'S LEVEL OF ADVANCEMENT.
GARA
GARA
SINCE THERE ARE MAN-AND HORSE-DRAWN CARRIAGES, IT DOESN'T SEEM LIKE MAGIC CAN BE USED TO REPLACE MACHINE POWER.
THAT RE-MINDS ME...
ARE COLLARS IN FASHION AROUND HERE?

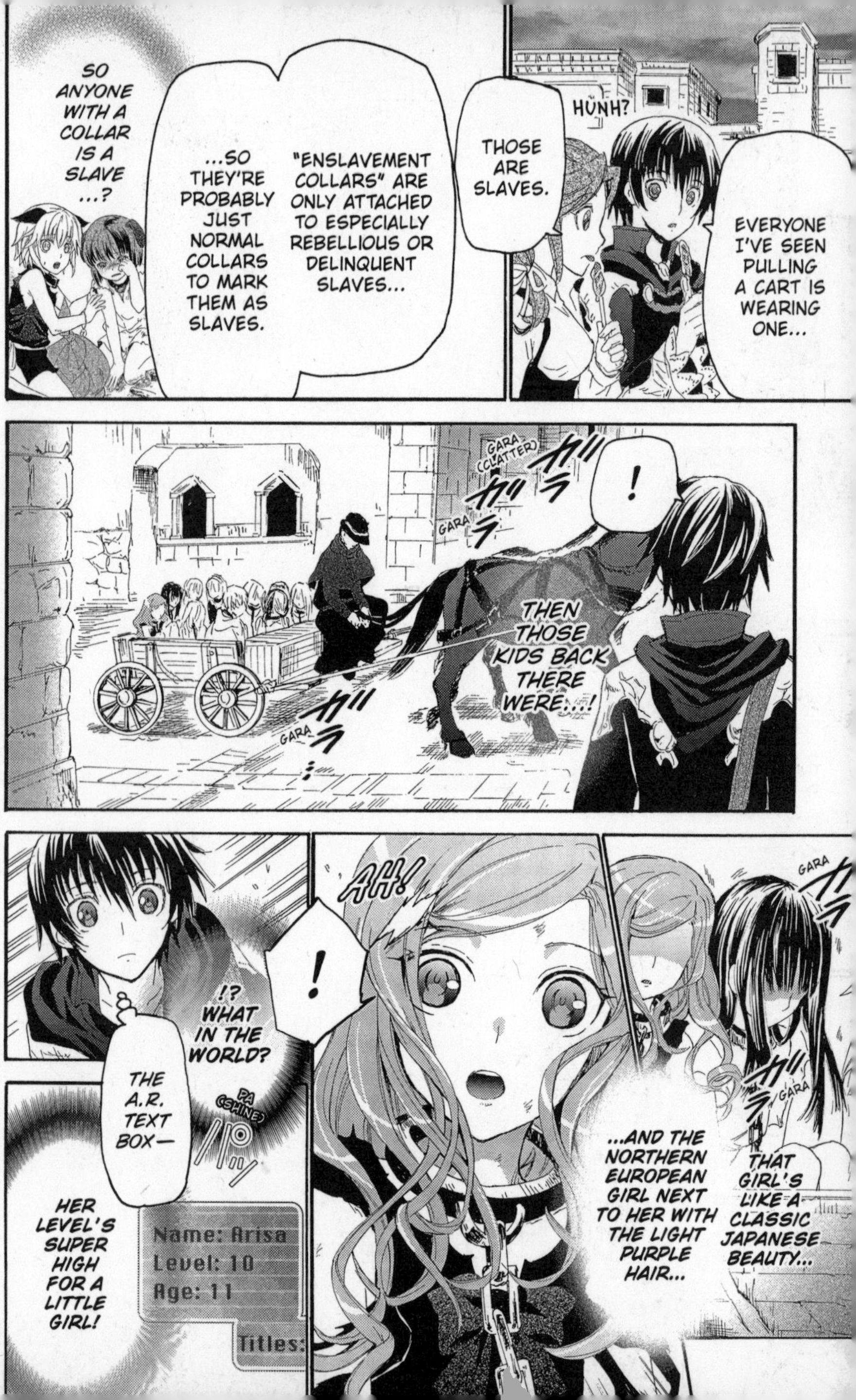
HÜNH?
EVERYONE I'VE SEEN PULLING A CART IS WEARING ONE...
THOSE ARE SLAVES.
"ENSLAVEMENT COLLARS" ARE ONLY ATTACHED TO ESPECIALLY REBELLIOUS OR DELINQUENT SLAVES...
...SO THEY'RE PROBABLY JUST NORMAL COLLARS TO MARK THEM AS SLAVES.
SO ANYONE WITH A COLLAR IS A SLAVE ...?
GARA (CLATTER)
GARA
!
THEN THOSE KIDS BACK THERE WERE...!
GARA
GARA
GARA
THAT GIRL'S LIKE A CLASSIC JAPANESE BEAUTY...
...AND THE NORTHERN EUROPEAN GIRL NEXT TO HER WITH THE LIGHT PURPLE HAIR...
AH!
!
!? WHAT IN THE WORLD?
THE A.R. TEXT BOX—
PA (SHINE)
Name: Arisa
Level: 10
Age: 11
Titles:
HER LEVEL'S SUPER HIGH FOR A LITTLE GIRL!

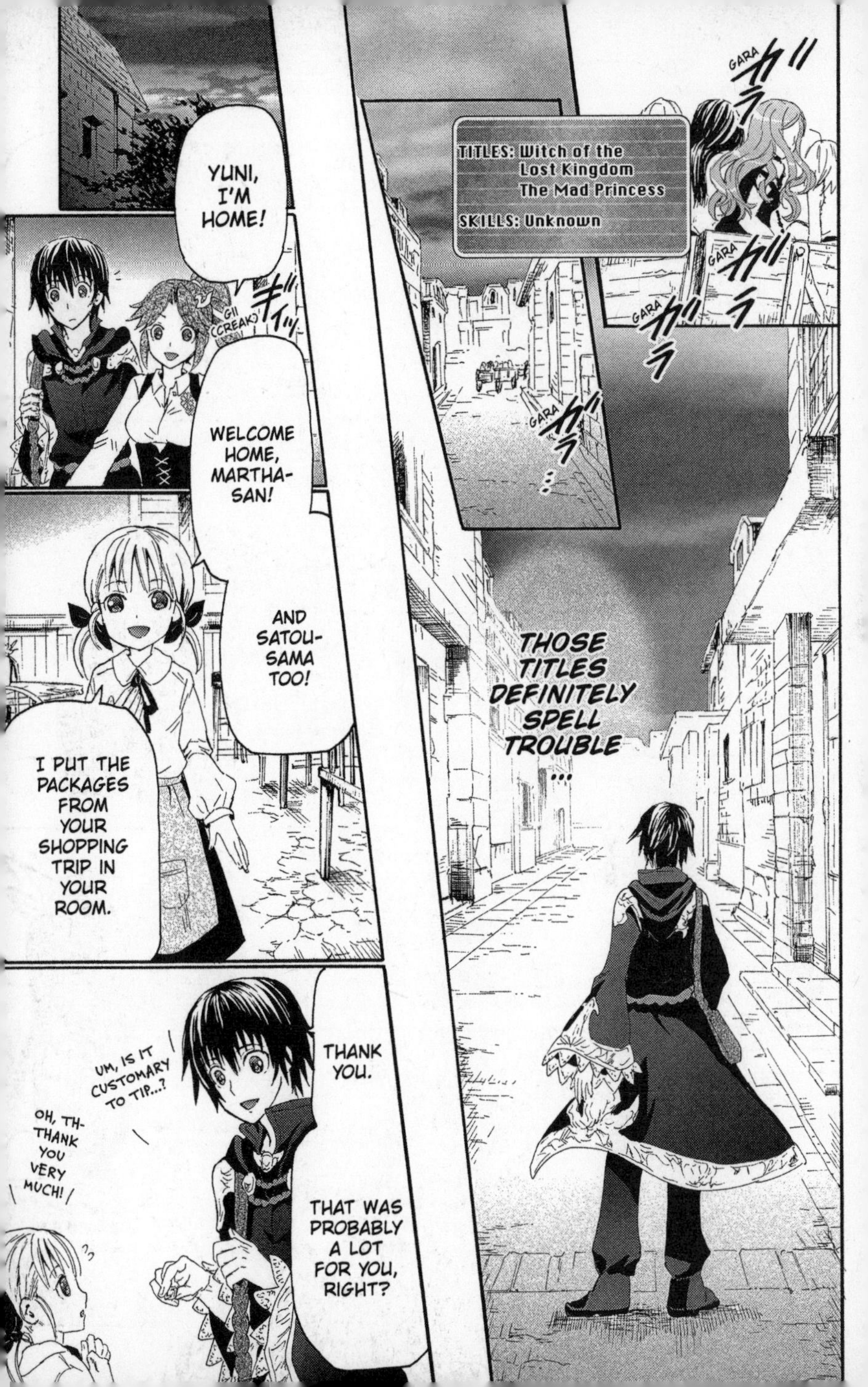
GARA
TITLES: Witch of the Lost Kingdom The Mad Princess
SKILLS: Unknown
GARA
GARA
GARA
THOSE TITLES DEFINITELY SPELL TROUBLE...
YUNI, I'M HOME!
GII (CREAK)
WELCOME HOME, MARTHA-SAN!
AND SATOU-SAMA TOO!
I PUT THE PACKAGES FROM YOUR SHOPPING TRIP IN YOUR ROOM.
THANK YOU.
UM, IS IT CUSTOMARY TO TIP...?
THAT WAS PROBABLY A LOT FOR YOU, RIGHT?
OH, TH-THANK YOU VERY MUCH!

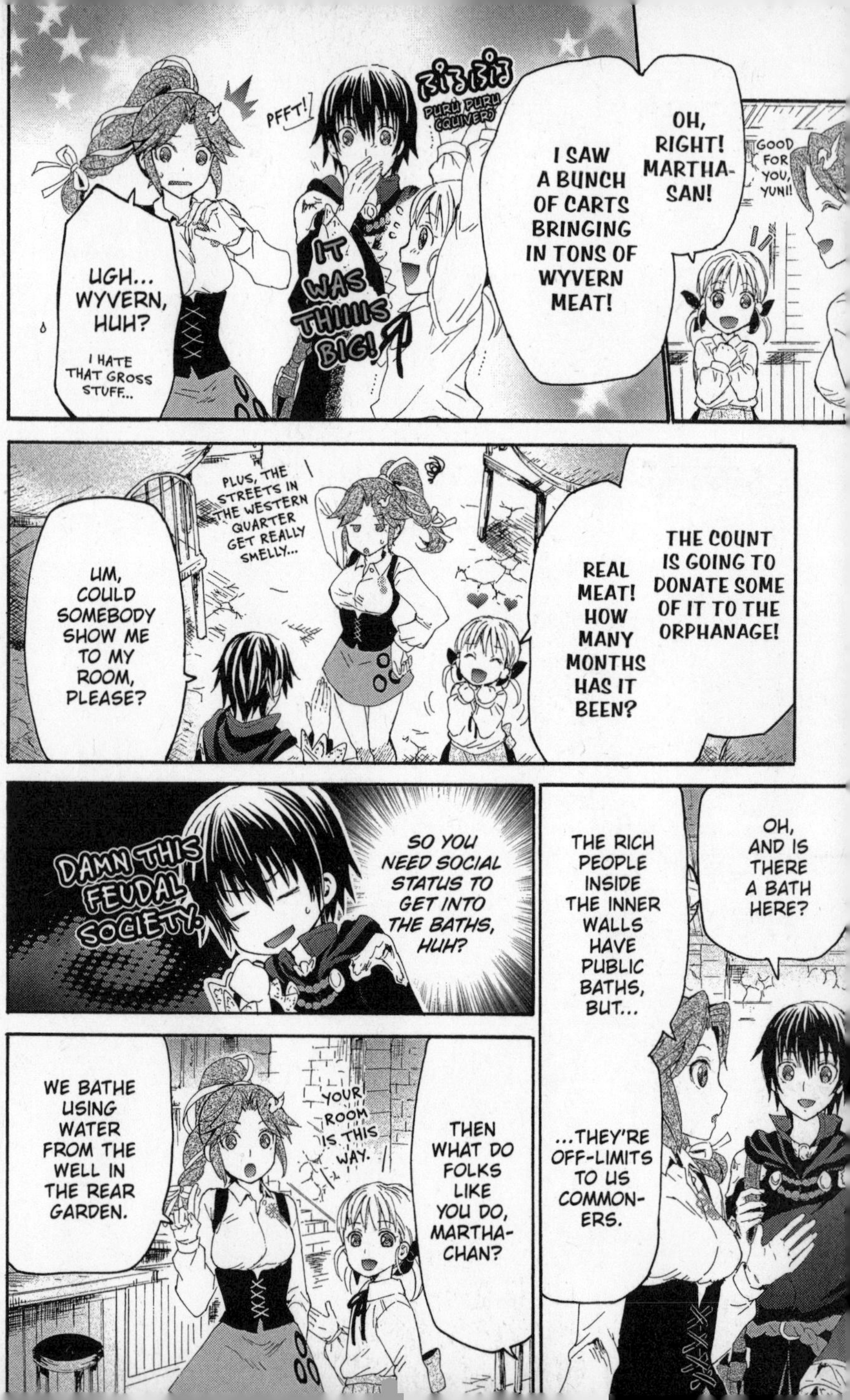
GOOD FOR YOU, YUNI!
OH, RIGHT! MARTHA-SAN!
I SAW A BUNCH OF CARTS BRINGING IN TONS OF WYVERN MEAT!
ぷるぷる PURU PURU (QUIVER)
PFFT!
IT WAS THIIIIS BIG!
UGH... WYVERN, HUH?
I HATE THAT GROSS STUFF...
THE COUNT IS GOING TO DONATE SOME OF IT TO THE ORPHANAGE!
REAL MEAT! HOW MANY MONTHS HAS IT BEEN?
PLUS, THE STREETS IN THE WESTERN QUARTER GET REALLY SMELLY...
UM, COULD SOMEBODY SHOW ME TO MY ROOM, PLEASE?
OH, AND IS THERE A BATH HERE?
THE RICH PEOPLE INSIDE THE INNER WALLS HAVE PUBLIC BATHS, BUT...
...THEY'RE OFF-LIMITS TO US COMMONERS.
SO YOU NEED SOCIAL STATUS TO GET INTO THE BATHS, HUH?
DAMN THIS FEUDAL SOCIETY.
THEN WHAT DO FOLKS LIKE YOU DO, MARTHA-CHAN?
YOUR ROOM IS THIS WAY.
WE BATHE USING WATER FROM THE WELL IN THE REAR GARDEN.

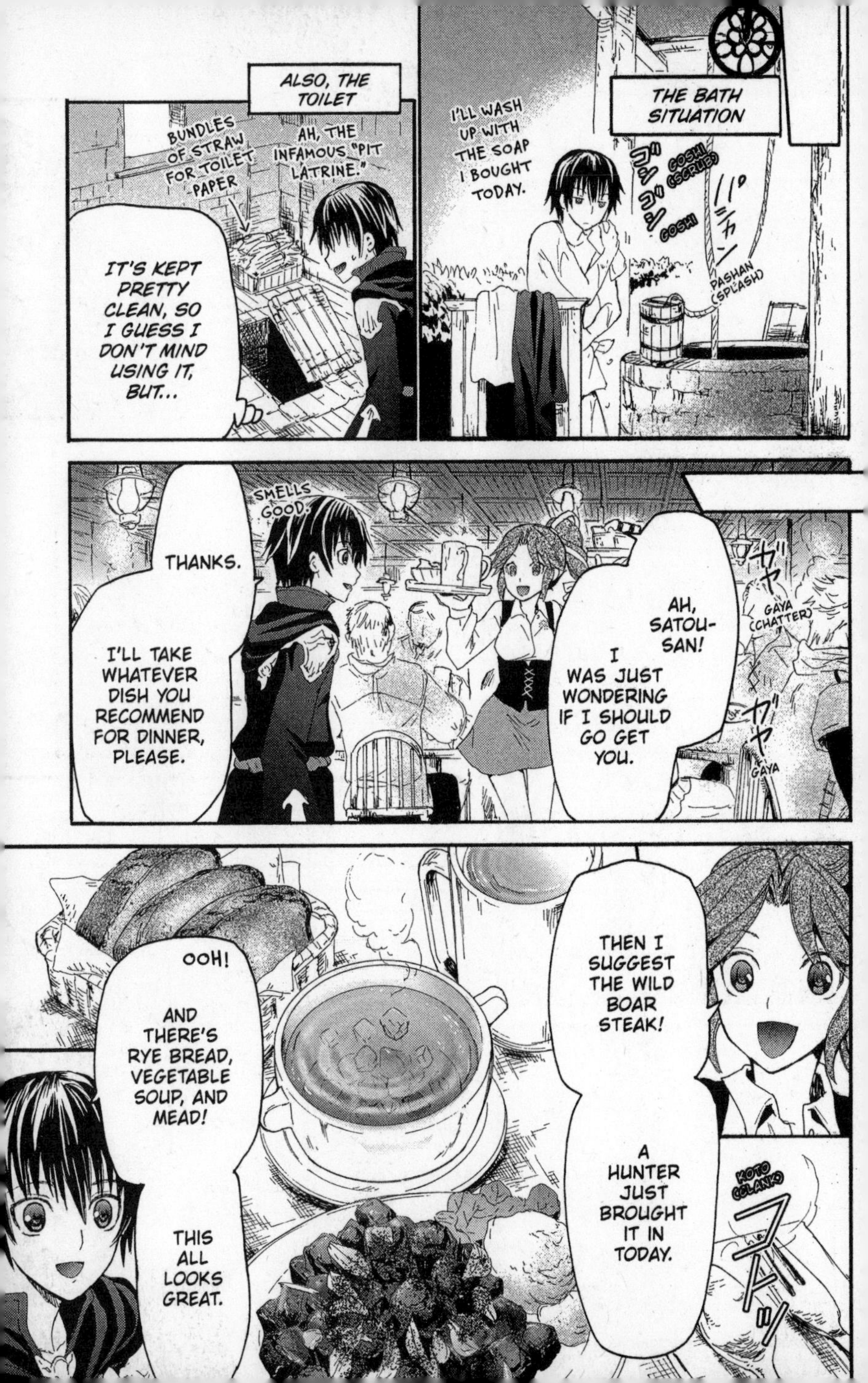
THE BATH SITUATION
I'LL WASH UP WITH THE SOAP I BOUGHT TODAY.
ゴシゴシ
GOSHI (SCRUB) GOSHI
パシャン
PASHAN (SPLASH)
ALSO, THE TOILET
AH, THE INFAMOUS "PIT LATRINE."
BUNDLES OF STRAW FOR TOILET PAPER
IT'S KEPT PRETTY CLEAN, SO I GUESS I DON'T MIND USING IT, BUT...
AH, SATOU-SAN!
I WAS JUST WONDERING IF I SHOULD GO GET YOU.
ガヤガヤ
GAYA (CHATTER) GAYA
SMELLS GOOD.
THANKS.
I'LL TAKE WHATEVER DISH YOU RECOMMEND FOR DINNER, PLEASE.
THEN I SUGGEST THE WILD BOAR STEAK!
A HUNTER JUST BROUGHT IT IN TODAY.
KOTO (CLANK)
OOH!
AND THERE'S RYE BREAD, VEGETABLE SOUP, AND MEAD!
THIS ALL LOOKS GREAT.

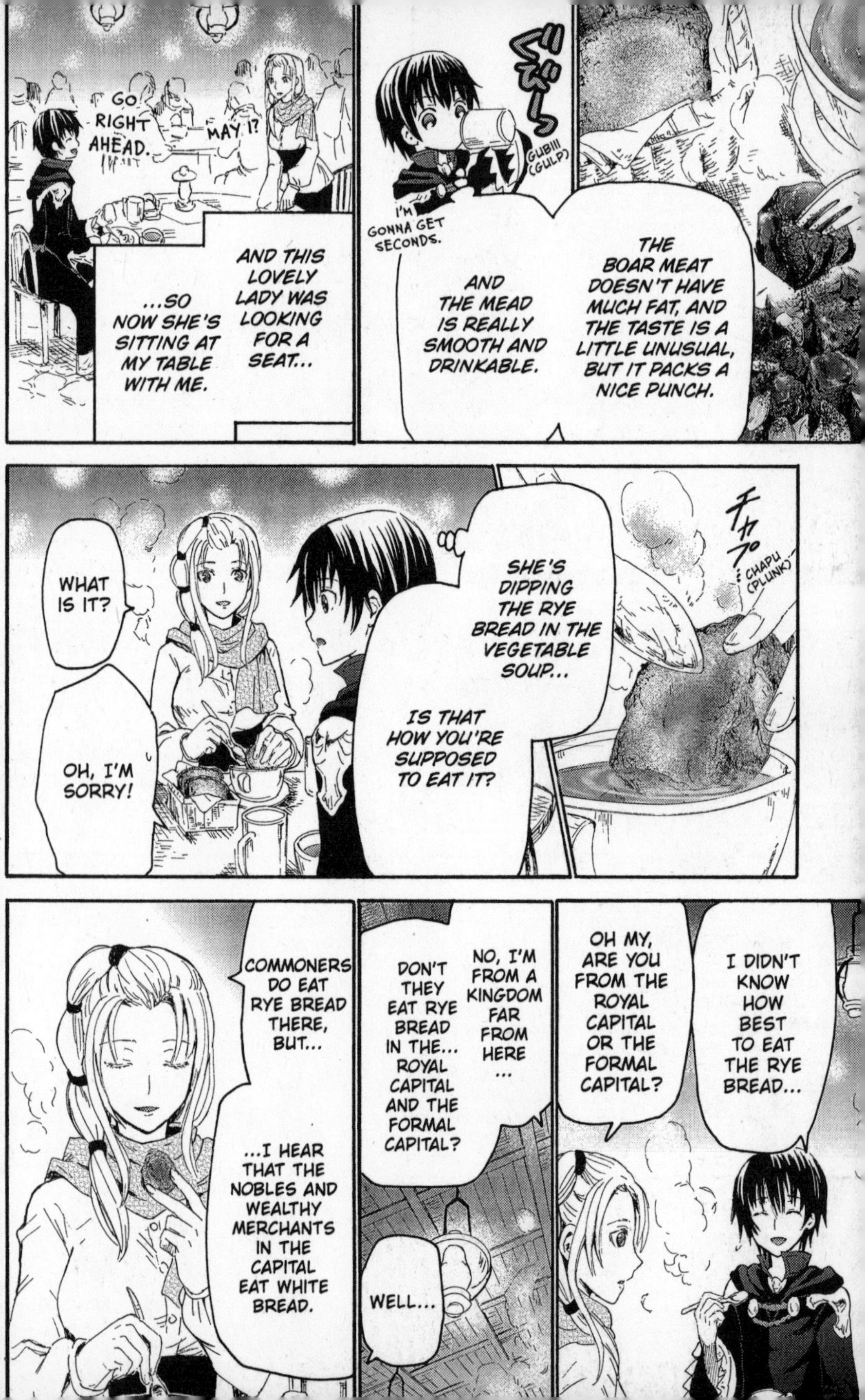
THE BOAR MEAT DOESN'T HAVE MUCH FAT, AND THE TASTE IS A LITTLE UNUSUAL, BUT IT PACKS A NICE PUNCH.
AND THE MEAD IS REALLY SMOOTH AND DRINKABLE.
ぐびーっ
GUBIII (GULP)
I'M GONNA GET SECONDS.
MAY I?
GO RIGHT AHEAD.
AND THIS LOVELY LADY WAS LOOKING FOR A SEAT...
...SO NOW SHE'S SITTING AT MY TABLE WITH ME.
チャプ
CHAPU (PLUNK)
SHE'S DIPPING THE RYE BREAD IN THE VEGETABLE SOUP...
IS THAT HOW YOU'RE SUPPOSED TO EAT IT?
WHAT IS IT?
OH, I'M SORRY!
I DIDN'T KNOW HOW BEST TO EAT THE RYE BREAD...
OH MY, ARE YOU FROM THE ROYAL CAPITAL OR THE FORMAL CAPITAL?
NO, I'M FROM A KINGDOM FAR FROM HERE...
DON'T THEY EAT RYE BREAD IN THE... ROYAL CAPITAL AND THE FORMAL CAPITAL?
WELL...
COMMONERS DO EAT RYE BREAD THERE, BUT...
...I HEAR THAT THE NOBLES AND WEALTHY MERCHANTS IN THE CAPITAL EAT WHITE BREAD.

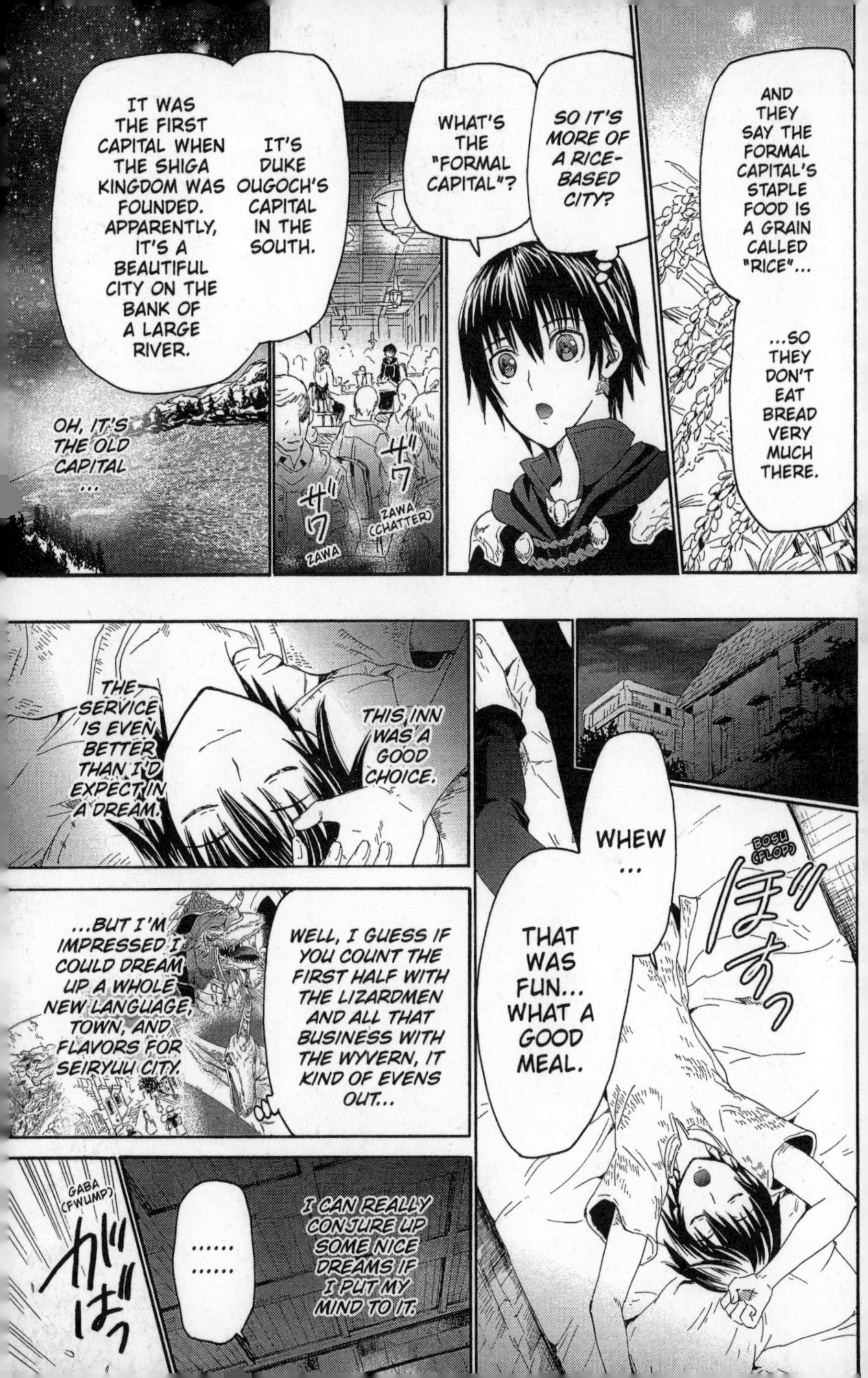
AND THEY SAY THE FORMAL CAPITAL'S STAPLE FOOD IS A GRAIN CALLED "RICE"...
...SO THEY DON'T EAT BREAD VERY MUCH THERE.
SO IT'S MORE OF A RICE-BASED CITY?
WHAT'S THE "FORMAL CAPITAL"?
IT'S DUKE OUGOCH'S CAPITAL IN THE SOUTH.
ZAWA (CHATTER)
ZAWA
IT WAS THE FIRST CAPITAL WHEN THE SHIGA KINGDOM WAS FOUNDED. APPARENTLY, IT'S A BEAUTIFUL CITY ON THE BANK OF A LARGE RIVER.
OH, IT'S THE OLD CAPITAL...
WHEW...
THAT WAS FUN... WHAT A GOOD MEAL.
BOSU (FLOP)
THIS INN WAS A GOOD CHOICE.
THE SERVICE IS EVEN BETTER THAN I'D EXPECT IN A DREAM.
WELL, I GUESS IF YOU COUNT THE FIRST HALF WITH THE LIZARDMEN AND ALL THAT BUSINESS WITH THE WYVERN, IT KIND OF EVENS OUT...
...BUT I'M IMPRESSED I COULD DREAM UP A WHOLE NEW LANGUAGE, TOWN, AND FLAVORS FOR SEIRYUU CITY.
I CAN REALLY CONJURE UP SOME NICE DREAMS IF I PUT MY MIND TO IT.
......
......
GABA (FWUMP)

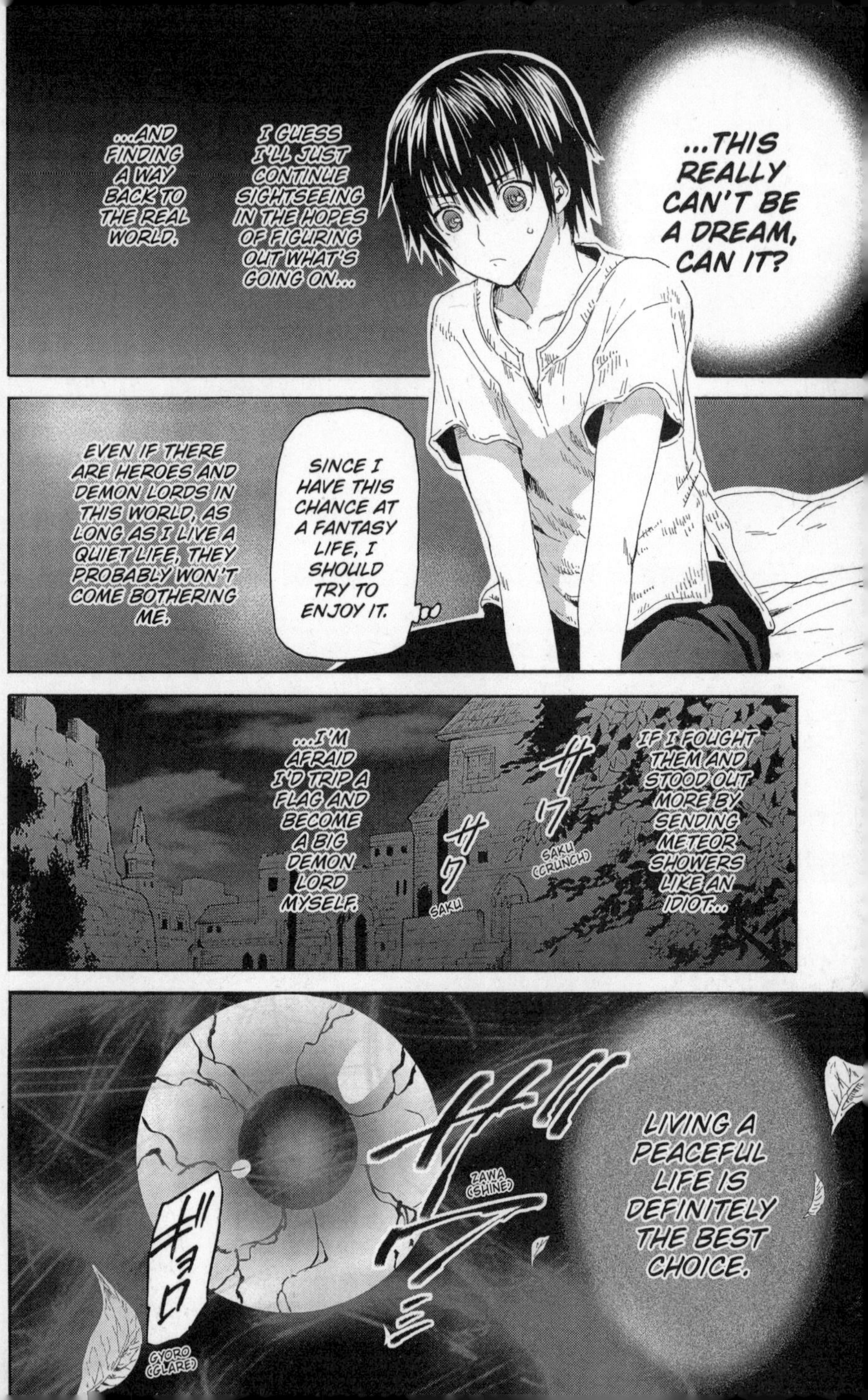
...THIS REALLY CAN'T BE A DREAM, CAN IT?
I GUESS I'LL JUST CONTINUE SIGHTSEEING IN THE HOPES OF FIGURING OUT WHAT'S GOING ON...
...AND FINDING A WAY BACK TO THE REAL WORLD.
SINCE I HAVE THIS CHANCE AT A FANTASY LIFE, I SHOULD TRY TO ENJOY IT.
EVEN IF THERE ARE HEROES AND DEMON LORDS IN THIS WORLD, AS LONG AS I LIVE A QUIET LIFE, THEY PROBABLY WON'T COME BOTHERING ME.
IF I FOUGHT THEM AND STOOD OUT MORE BY SENDING METEOR SHOWERS LIKE AN IDIOT...
SAKU (CRUNCH)
SAKU
...I'M AFRAID I'D TRIP A FLAG AND BECOME A BIG DEMON LORD MYSELF.
LIVING A PEACEFUL LIFE IS DEFINITELY THE BEST CHOICE.
ZAWA (SHINE)
GYORO (GLARE)

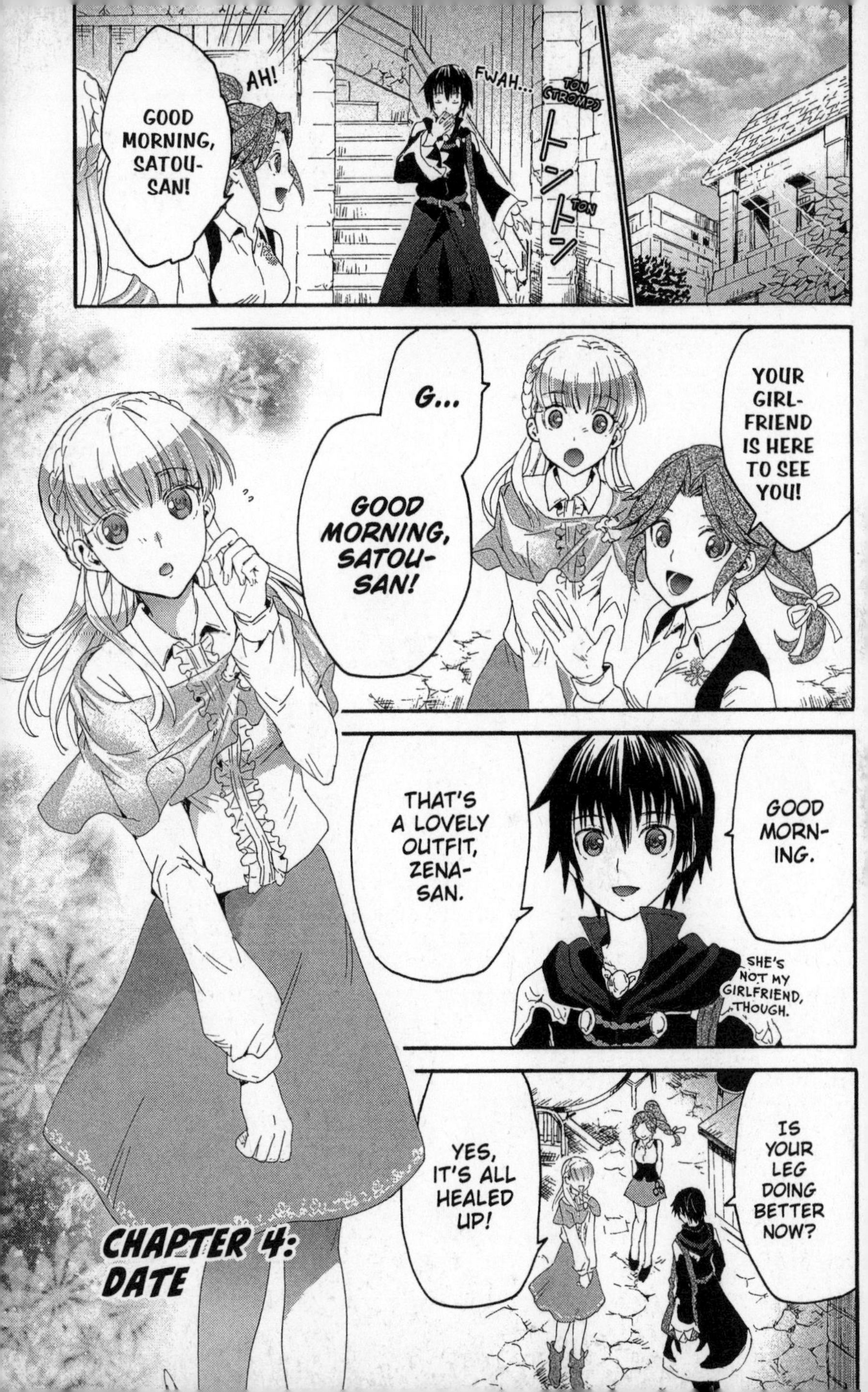
TON (STROMP)
トーン
TON
トーン
FWAH...
AH!
GOOD MORNING, SATOU-SAN!
YOUR GIRLFRIEND IS HERE TO SEE YOU!
G...
GOOD MORNING, SATOU-SAN!
GOOD MORNING.
SHE'S NOT MY GIRLFRIEND, THOUGH.
THAT'S A LOVELY OUTFIT, ZENA-SAN.
IS YOUR LEG DOING BETTER NOW?
YES, IT'S ALL HEALED UP!
CHAPTER 4: DATE

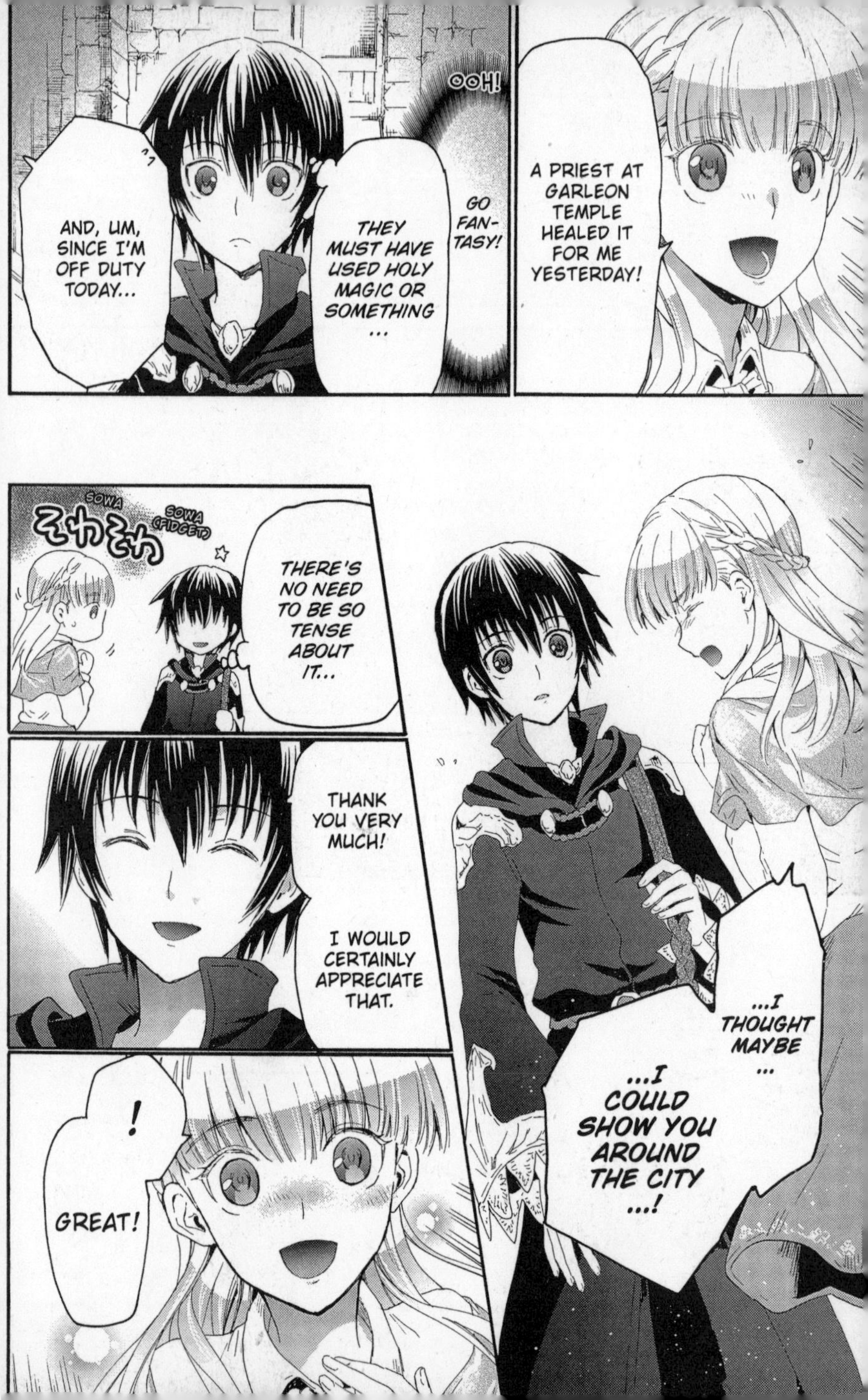
A PRIEST AT GARLEON TEMPLE HEALED IT FOR ME YESTERDAY!
OOH!
GO FAN-TASY!
THEY MUST HAVE USED HOLY MAGIC OR SOMETHING...
AND, UM, SINCE I'M OFF DUTY TODAY...
...I THOUGHT MAYBE...
...I COULD SHOW YOU AROUND THE CITY...!
SOWA
そわそわ
SOWA (FIDGET)
THERE'S NO NEED TO BE SO TENSE ABOUT IT...
THANK YOU VERY MUCH!
I WOULD CERTAINLY APPRECIATE THAT.
!
GREAT!

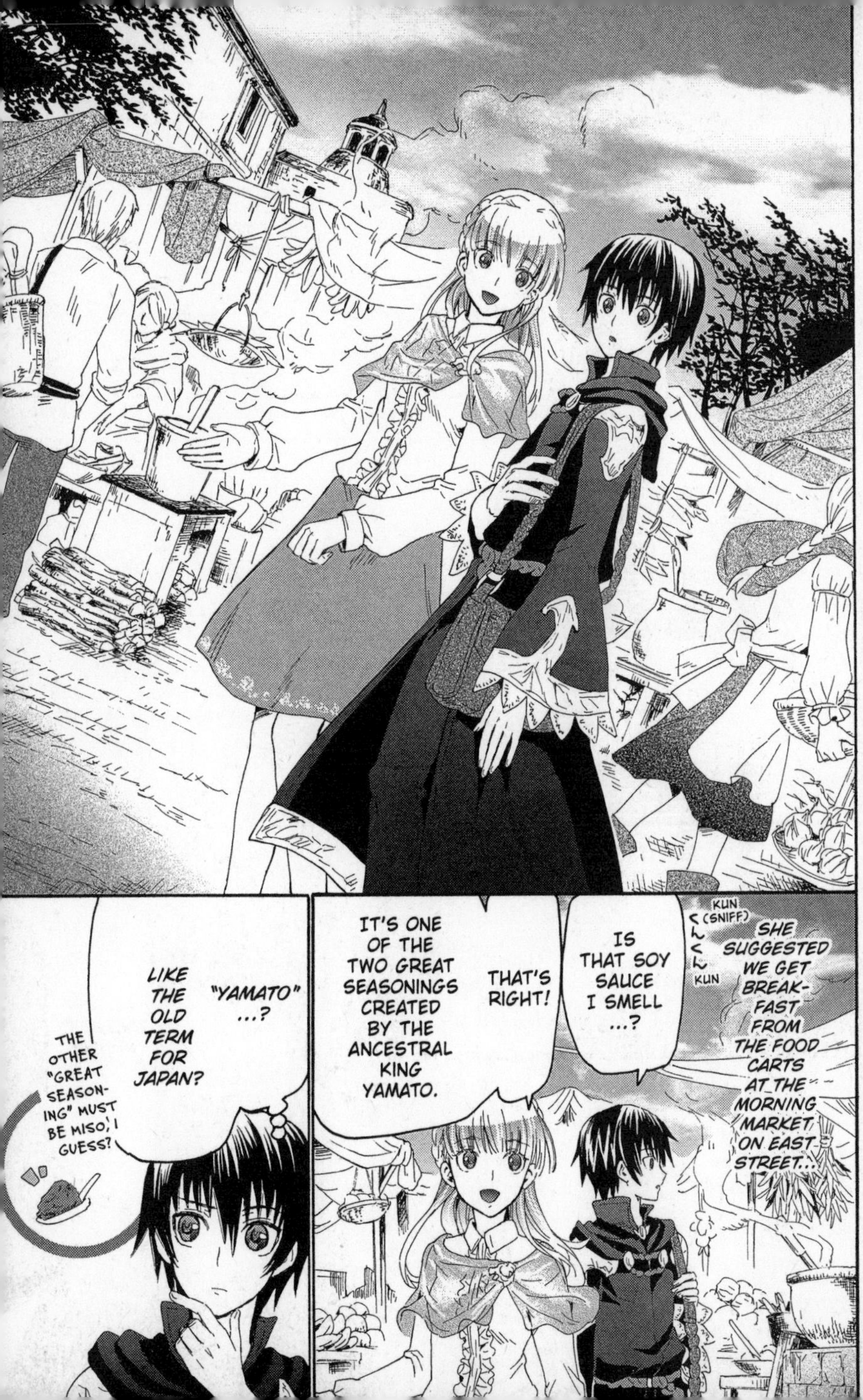
SHE SUGGESTED WE GET BREAK-FAST FROM THE FOOD CARTS AT THE MORNING MARKET ON EAST STREET...
くんくん
KUN (SNIFF) KUN
IS THAT SOY SAUCE I SMELL ...?
THAT'S RIGHT!
IT'S ONE OF THE TWO GREAT SEASONINGS CREATED BY THE ANCESTRAL KING YAMATO.
"YAMATO" ...?
LIKE THE OLD TERM FOR JAPAN?
THE OTHER "GREAT SEASON-ING" MUST BE MISO, I GUESS?

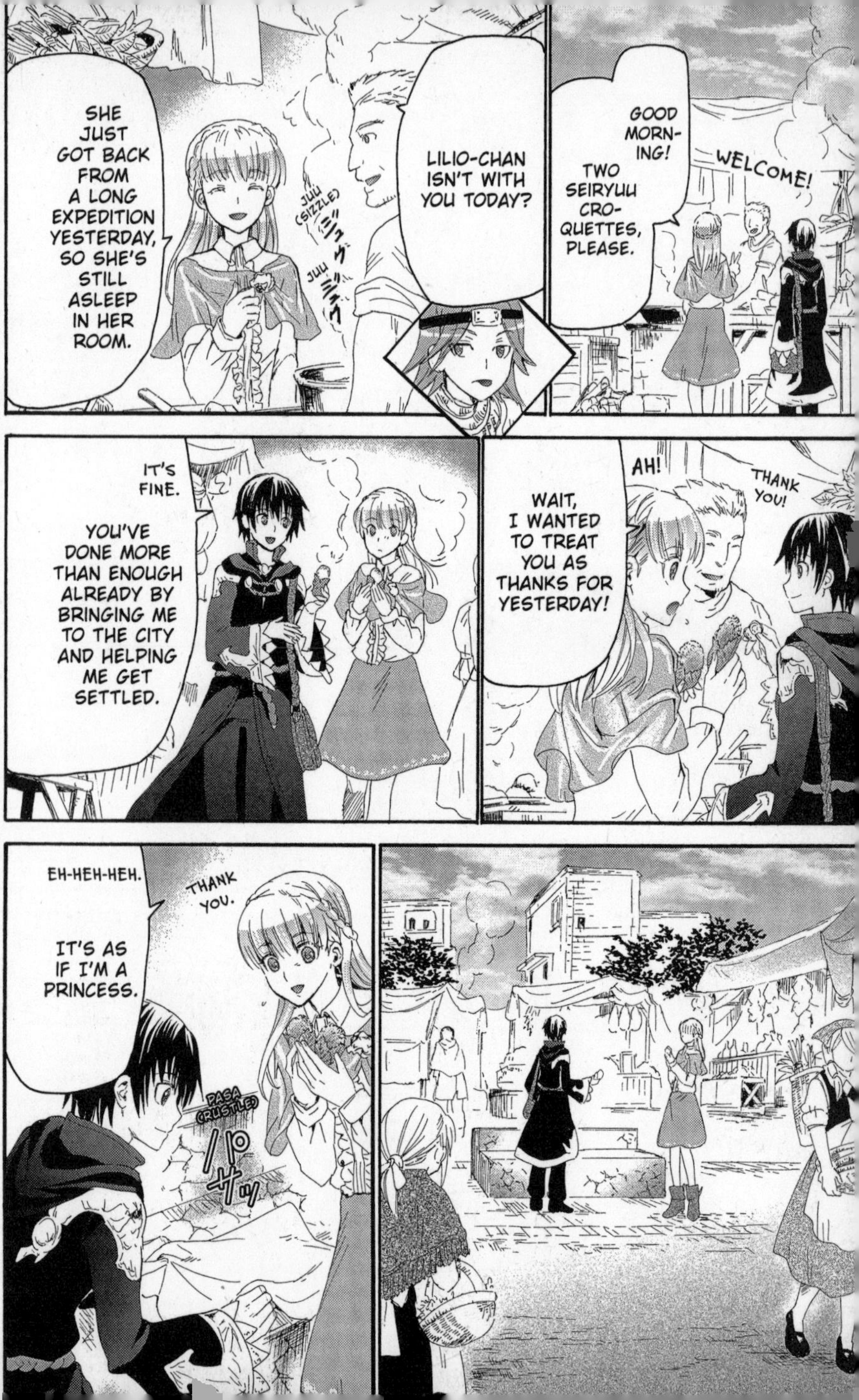
WELCOME!
GOOD MORNING! TWO SEIRYUU CROQUETTES, PLEASE.
LILIO-CHAN ISN'T WITH YOU TODAY?
JUU (SIZZLE) ジュゥ
JUU ジュゥ
SHE JUST GOT BACK FROM A LONG EXPEDITION YESTERDAY, SO SHE'S STILL ASLEEP IN HER ROOM.
THANK YOU!
AH!
WAIT, I WANTED TO TREAT YOU AS THANKS FOR YESTERDAY!
IT'S FINE.
YOU'VE DONE MORE THAN ENOUGH ALREADY BY BRINGING ME TO THE CITY AND HELPING ME GET SETTLED.
THANK YOU.
EH-HEH-HEH.
IT'S AS IF I'M A PRINCESS.
PASA (CRUSTLED) パサッ

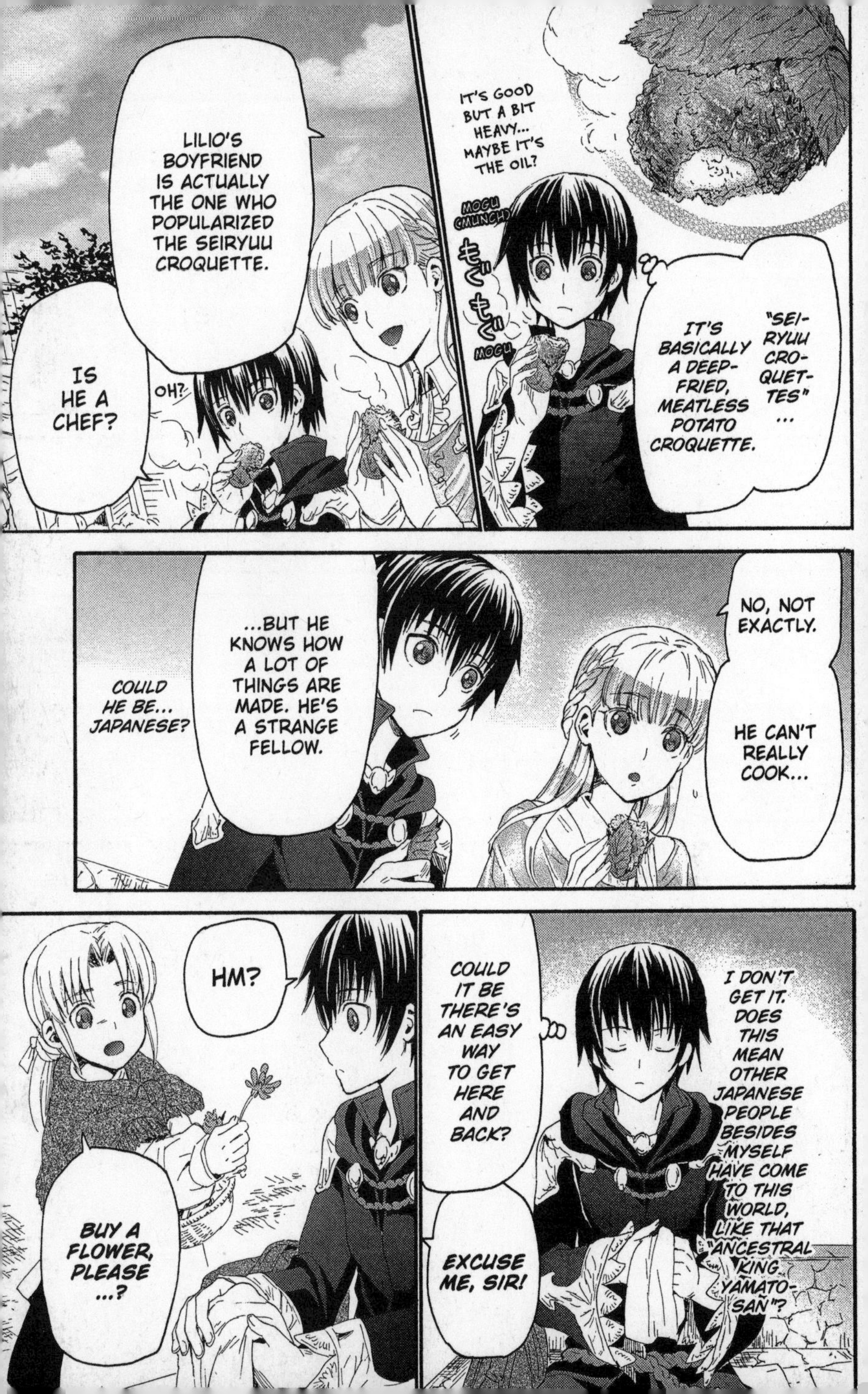
IT'S GOOD BUT A BIT HEAVY... MAYBE IT'S THE OIL?
MOGU (MUNCH) もぐもぐ MOGU
"SEI-RYUU CRO-QUET-TES"...
IT'S BASICALLY A DEEP-FRIED, MEATLESS POTATO CROQUETTE.
LILIO'S BOYFRIEND IS ACTUALLY THE ONE WHO POPULARIZED THE SEIRYUU CROQUETTE.
OH?
IS HE A CHEF?
NO, NOT EXACTLY.
HE CAN'T REALLY COOK...
...BUT HE KNOWS HOW A LOT OF THINGS ARE MADE. HE'S A STRANGE FELLOW.
COULD HE BE... JAPANESE?
I DON'T GET IT. DOES THIS MEAN OTHER JAPANESE PEOPLE BESIDES MYSELF HAVE COME TO THIS WORLD, LIKE THAT "ANCESTRAL KING YAMATO-SAN"?
COULD IT BE THERE'S AN EASY WAY TO GET HERE AND BACK?
EXCUSE ME, SIR!
HM?
BUY A FLOWER, PLEASE ...?

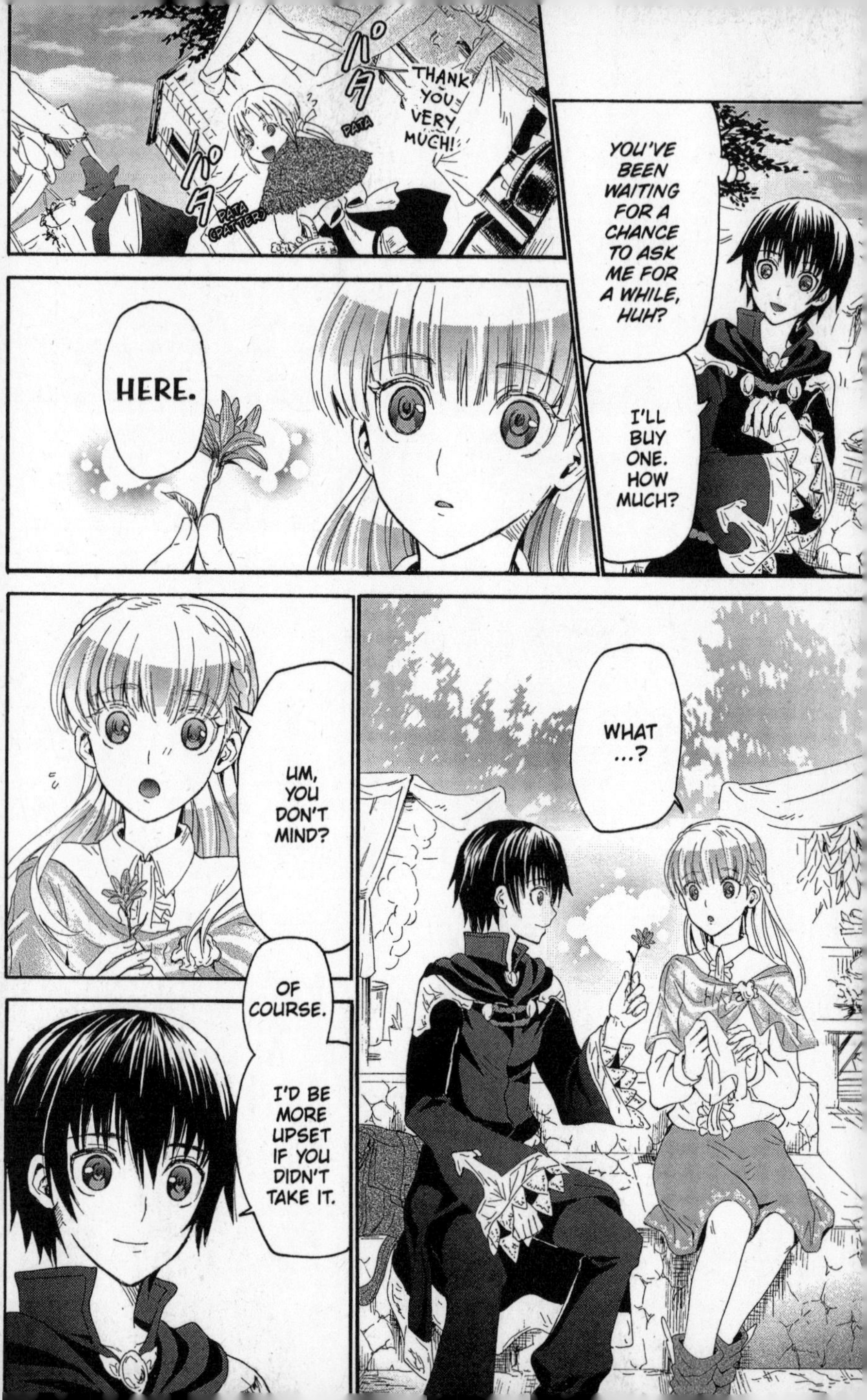
PATA PATA (PATTER)
THANK YOU VERY MUCH!
YOU'VE BEEN WAITING FOR A CHANCE TO ASK ME FOR A WHILE, HUH?
I'LL BUY ONE. HOW MUCH?
HERE.
WHAT ...?
UM, YOU DON'T MIND?
OF COURSE.
I'D BE MORE UPSET IF YOU DIDN'T TAKE IT.

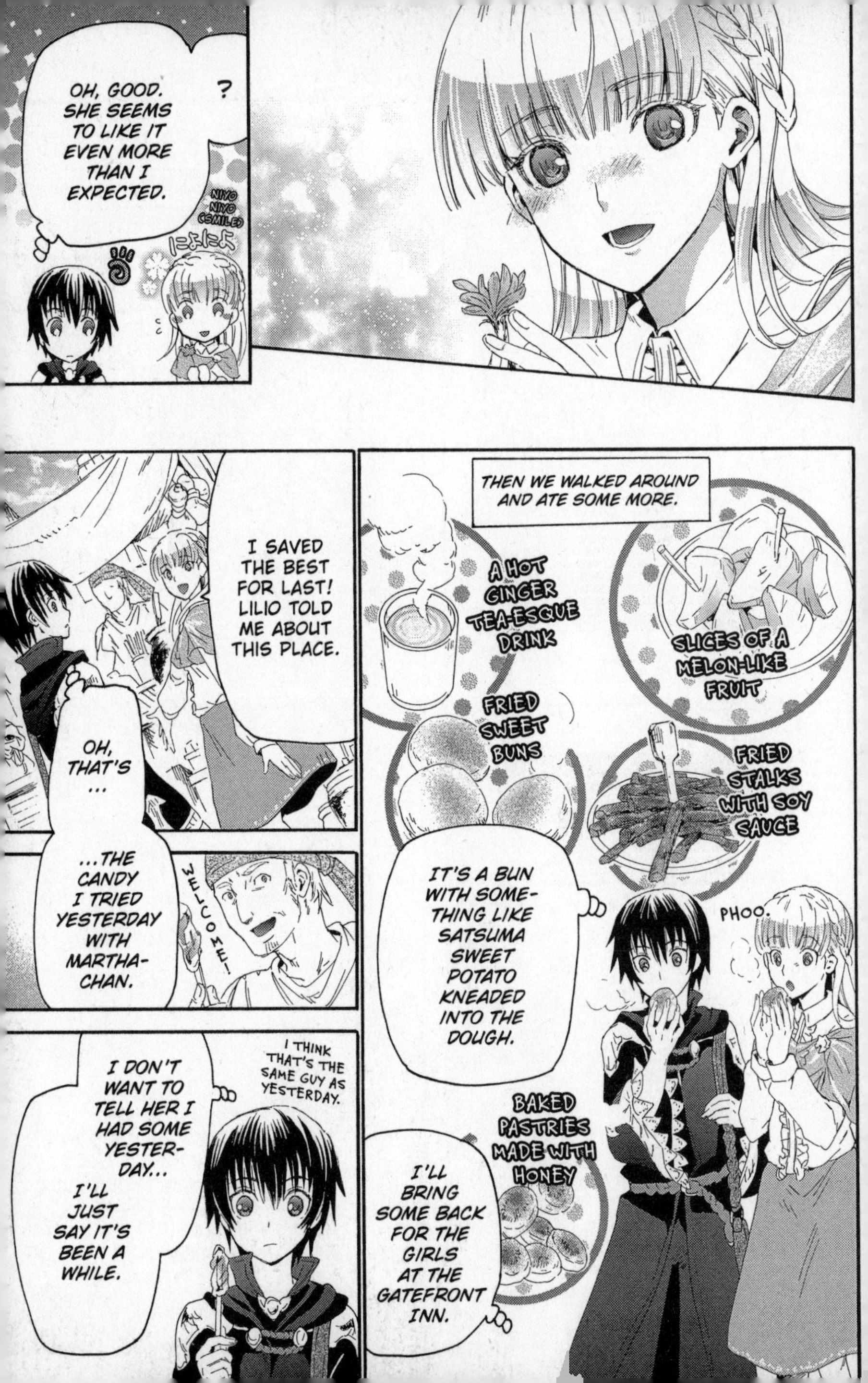
OH, GOOD. SHE SEEMS TO LIKE IT EVEN MORE THAN I EXPECTED.
?
NIYO NIYO (SMILE)
にょにょ
THEN WE WALKED AROUND AND ATE SOME MORE.
SLICES OF A MELON-LIKE FRUIT
A HOT GINGER TEA-ESQUE DRINK
FRIED STALKS WITH SOY SAUCE
FRIED SWEET BUNS
PHOO.
IT'S A BUN WITH SOMETHING LIKE SATSUMA SWEET POTATO KNEADED INTO THE DOUGH.
BAKED PASTRIES MADE WITH HONEY
I'LL BRING SOME BACK FOR THE GIRLS AT THE GATEFRONT INN.
I SAVED THE BEST FOR LAST! LILIO TOLD ME ABOUT THIS PLACE.
OH, THAT'S...
...THE CANDY I TRIED YESTERDAY WITH MARTHA-CHAN.
WELCOME!
I THINK THAT'S THE SAME GUY AS YESTERDAY.
I DON'T WANT TO TELL HER I HAD SOME YESTER-DAY...
I'LL JUST SAY IT'S BEEN A WHILE.

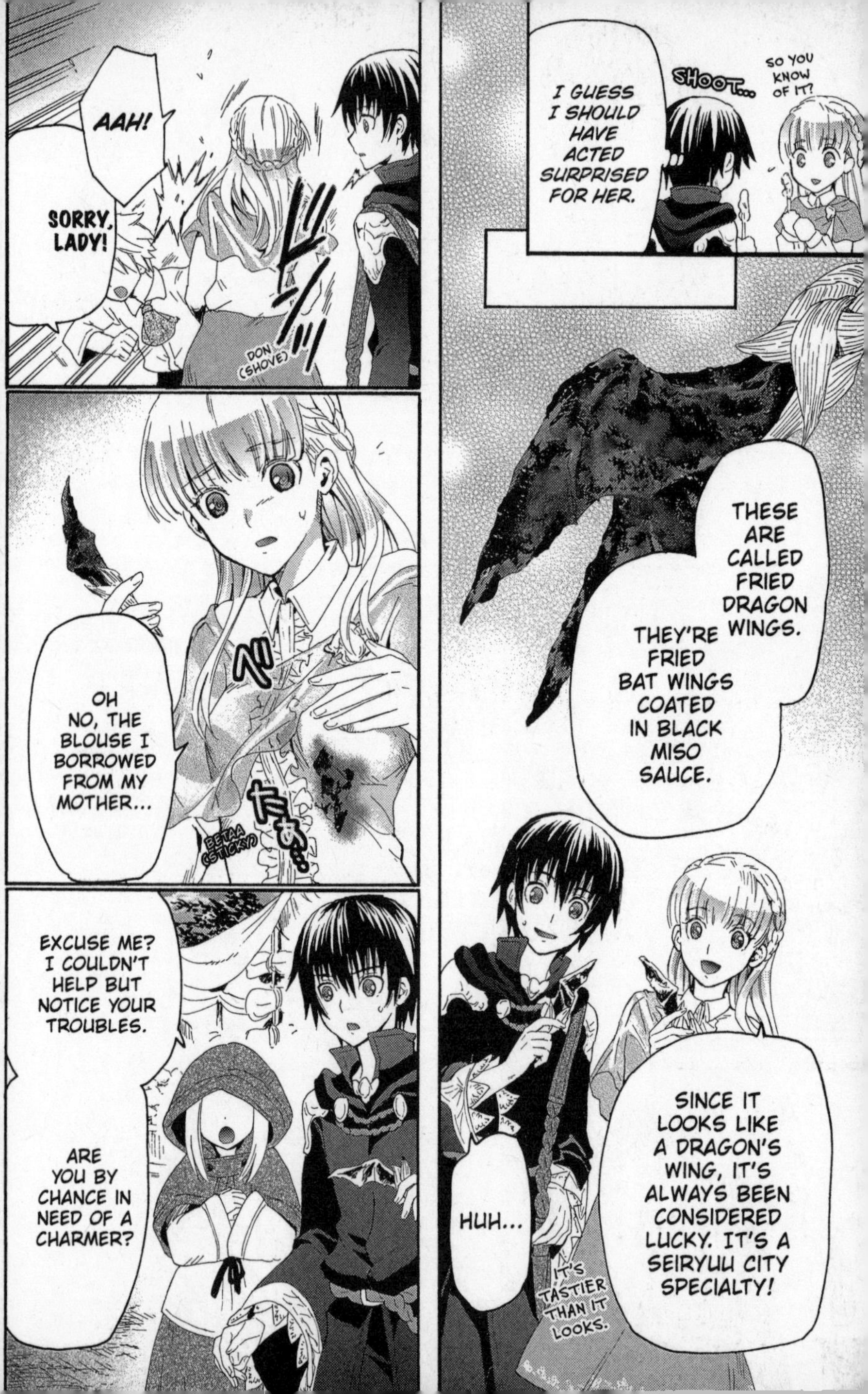

SO YOU KNOW OF IT?
SHOOT...
I GUESS I SHOULD HAVE ACTED SURPRISED FOR HER.
THESE ARE CALLED FRIED DRAGON WINGS.
THEY'RE FRIED BAT WINGS COATED IN BLACK MISO SAUCE.
SINCE IT LOOKS LIKE A DRAGON'S WING, IT'S ALWAYS BEEN CONSIDERED LUCKY. IT'S A SEIRYUU CITY SPECIALTY!
IT'S TASTIER THAN IT LOOKS.
HUH...
AAH!
SORRY, LADY!
DON (SHOVE)
OH NO, THE BLOUSE I BORROWED FROM MY MOTHER...
BETAA (STICKY)
EXCUSE ME? I COULDN'T HELP BUT NOTICE YOUR TROUBLES.
ARE YOU BY CHANCE IN NEED OF A CHARMER?

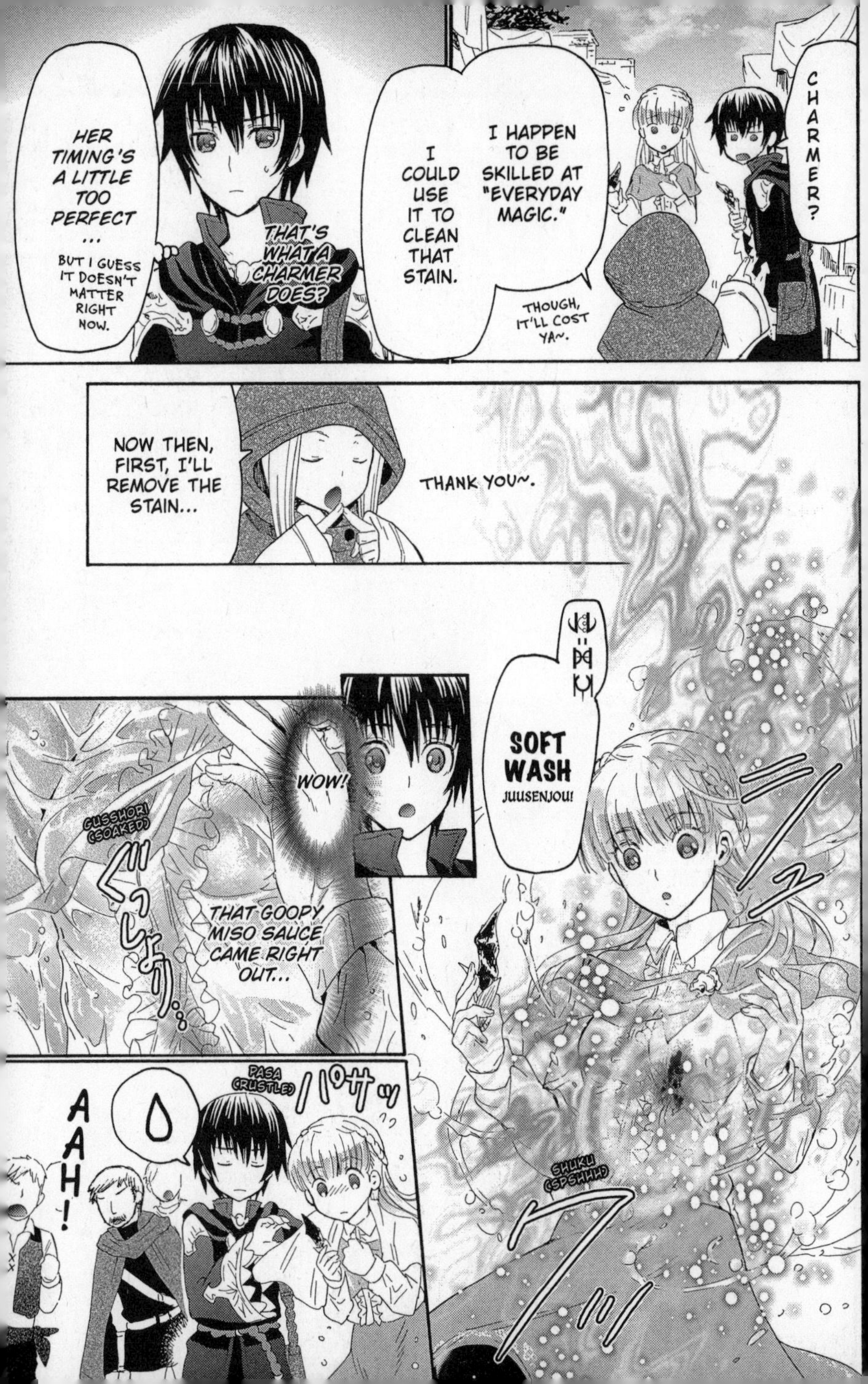
CHARMER?
I HAPPEN TO BE SKILLED AT "EVERYDAY MAGIC." I COULD USE IT TO CLEAN THAT STAIN.
THOUGH, IT'LL COST YA~.
THAT'S WHAT A CHARMER DOES?
HER TIMING'S A LITTLE TOO PERFECT... BUT I GUESS IT DOESN'T MATTER RIGHT NOW.
THANK YOU~.
NOW THEN, FIRST, I'LL REMOVE THE STAIN...
SOFT WASH JUUSENJOU!
SHUKU (SPSHHH)
WOW!
GUSSHORI (SOAKED)
THAT GOOPY MISO SAUCE CAME RIGHT OUT...
PASA (RUSTLE)
AAAH!

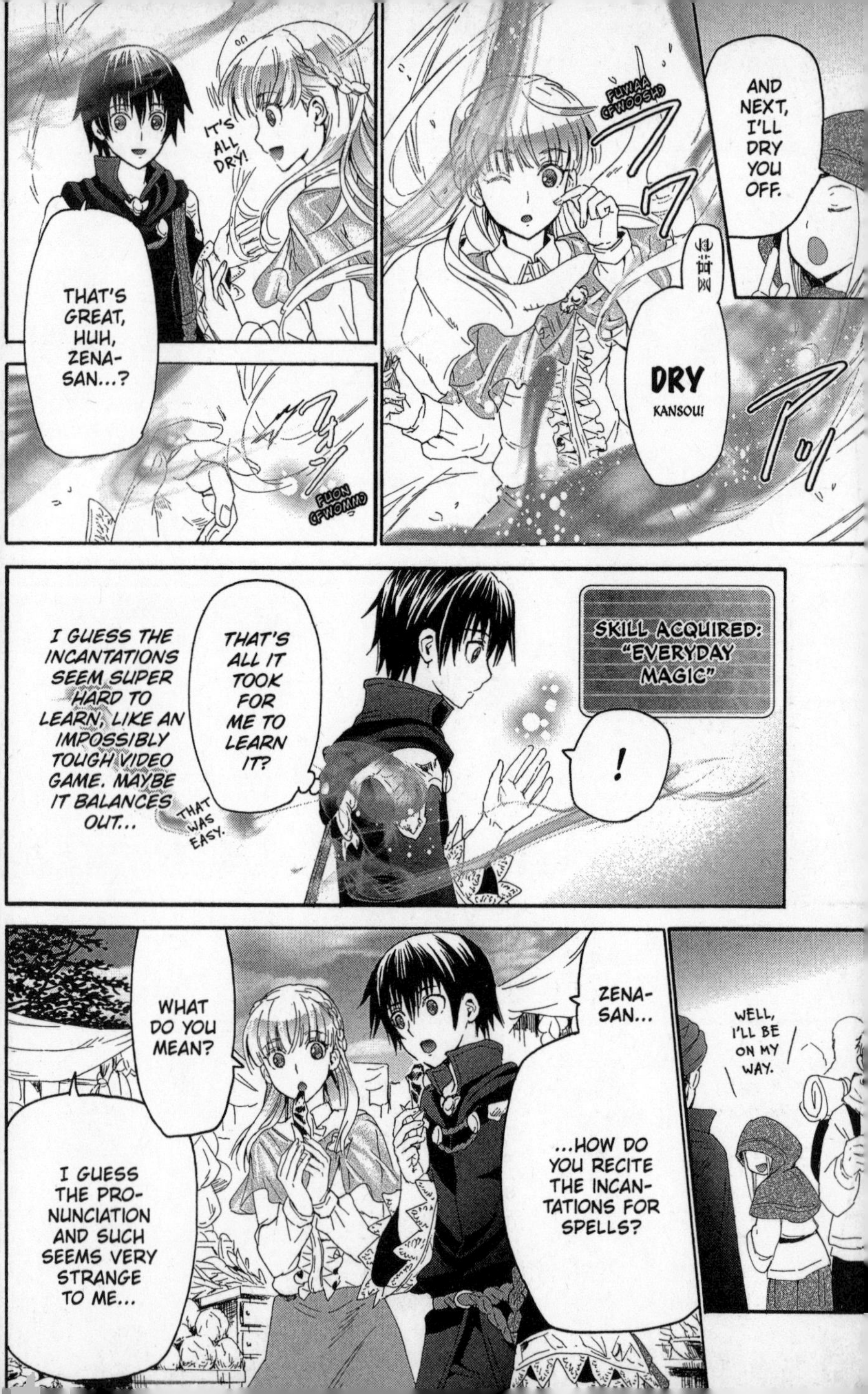
AND NEXT, I'LL DRY YOU OFF.
FUWAA (FWOOSH)
DRY
KANSOU!
IT'S ALL DRY!
THAT'S GREAT, HUH, ZENA-SAN...?
FUON (FWOMM)
SKILL ACQUIRED: "EVERYDAY MAGIC"
!
THAT'S ALL IT TOOK FOR ME TO LEARN IT?
THAT WAS EASY.
I GUESS THE INCANTATIONS SEEM SUPER HARD TO LEARN, LIKE AN IMPOSSIBLY TOUGH VIDEO GAME. MAYBE IT BALANCES OUT...
WELL, I'LL BE ON MY WAY.
ZENA-SAN...
...HOW DO YOU RECITE THE INCANTATIONS FOR SPELLS?
WHAT DO YOU MEAN?
I GUESS THE PRONUNCIATION AND SUCH SEEMS VERY STRANGE TO ME...

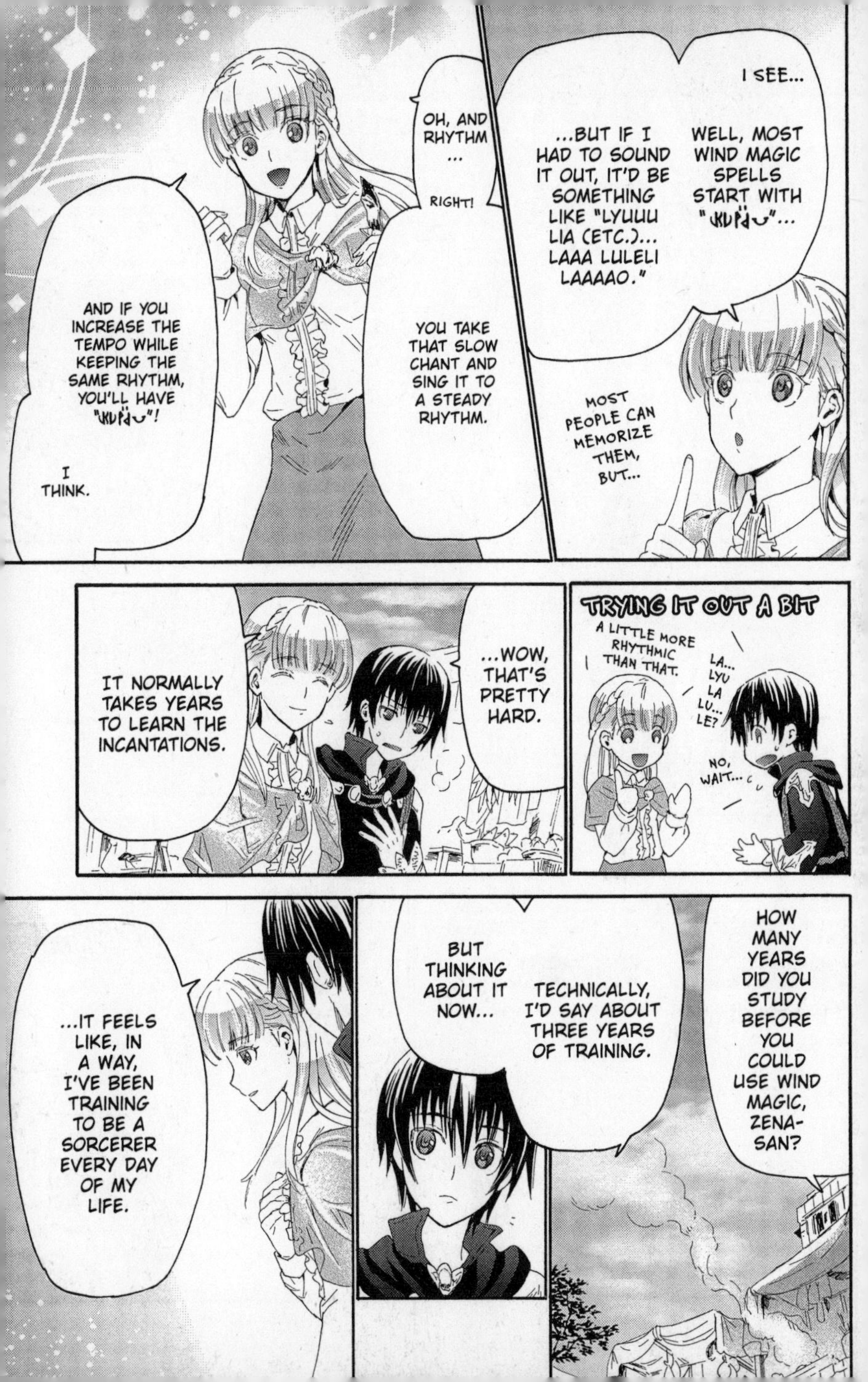
I SEE...
WELL, MOST WIND MAGIC SPELLS START WITH ""...
...BUT IF I HAD TO SOUND IT OUT, IT'D BE SOMETHING LIKE "LYUUU LIA (ETC.)... LAAA LULELI LAAAAO."
MOST PEOPLE CAN MEMORIZE THEM, BUT...
OH, AND RHYTHM ...
RIGHT!
YOU TAKE THAT SLOW CHANT AND SING IT TO A STEADY RHYTHM.
AND IF YOU INCREASE THE TEMPO WHILE KEEPING THE SAME RHYTHM, YOU'LL HAVE ""!
I THINK.
TRYING IT OUT A BIT
LA... LYU LA LU... LE?
A LITTLE MORE RHYTHMIC THAN THAT.
NO, WAIT...
...WOW, THAT'S PRETTY HARD.
IT NORMALLY TAKES YEARS TO LEARN THE INCANTATIONS.
HOW MANY YEARS DID YOU STUDY BEFORE YOU COULD USE WIND MAGIC, ZENA-SAN?
TECHNICALLY, I'D SAY ABOUT THREE YEARS OF TRAINING.
BUT THINKING ABOUT IT NOW...
...IT FEELS LIKE, IN A WAY, I'VE BEEN TRAINING TO BE A SORCERER EVERY DAY OF MY LIFE.

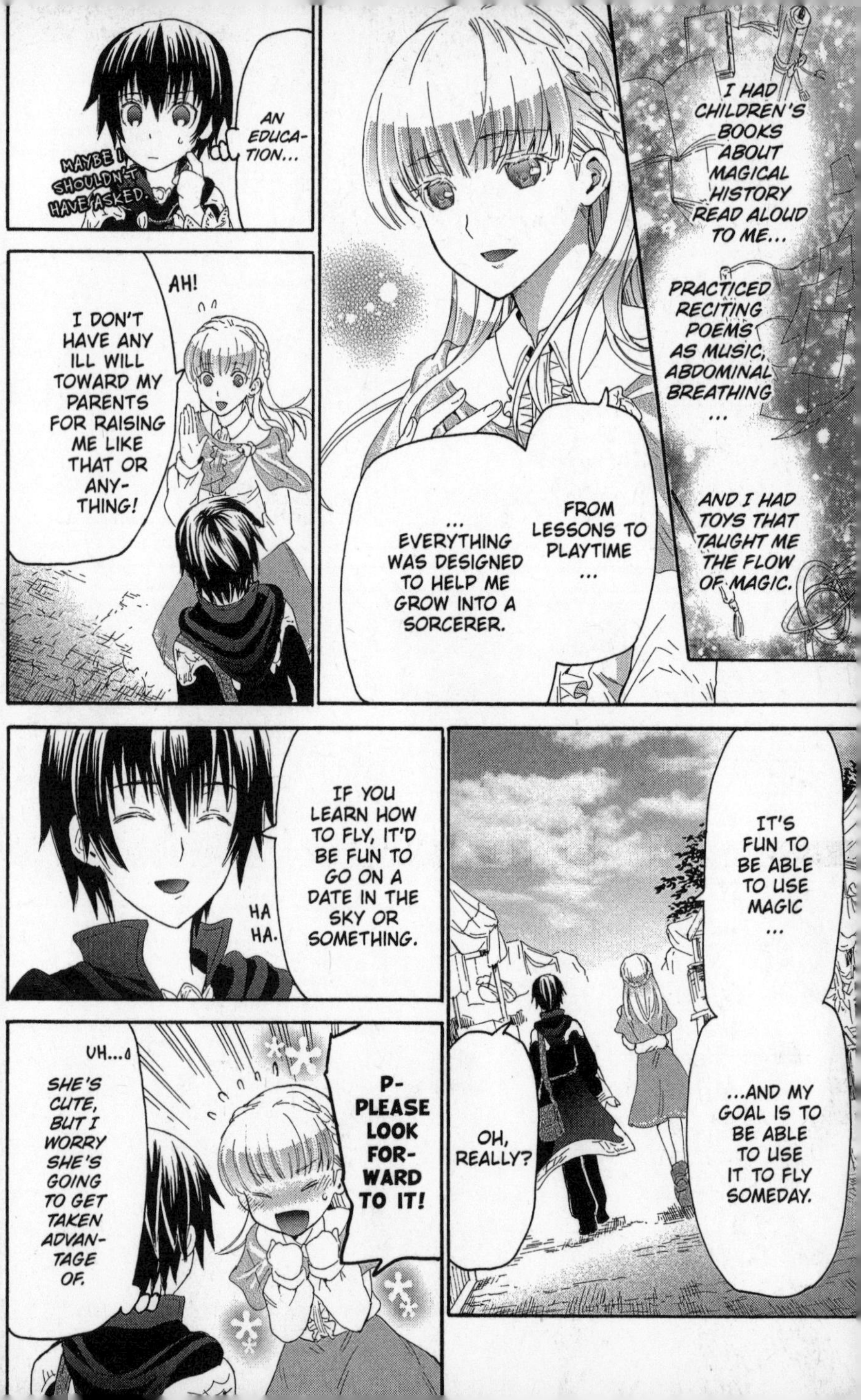
I HAD CHILDREN'S BOOKS ABOUT MAGICAL HISTORY READ ALOUD TO ME...
PRACTICED RECITING POEMS AS MUSIC, ABDOMINAL BREATHING...
AND I HAD TOYS THAT TAUGHT ME THE FLOW OF MAGIC.
FROM LESSONS TO PLAYTIME...
...EVERYTHING WAS DESIGNED TO HELP ME GROW INTO A SORCERER.
AN EDUCATION...
MAYBE I SHOULDN'T HAVE ASKED.
AH!
I DON'T HAVE ANY ILL WILL TOWARD MY PARENTS FOR RAISING ME LIKE THAT OR ANYTHING!
IT'S FUN TO BE ABLE TO USE MAGIC...
...AND MY GOAL IS TO BE ABLE TO USE IT TO FLY SOMEDAY.
OH, REALLY?
IF YOU LEARN HOW TO FLY, IT'D BE FUN TO GO ON A DATE IN THE SKY OR SOMETHING.
HA HA.
P-PLEASE LOOK FORWARD TO IT!
UH...
SHE'S CUTE, BUT I WORRY SHE'S GOING TO GET TAKEN ADVANTAGE OF.

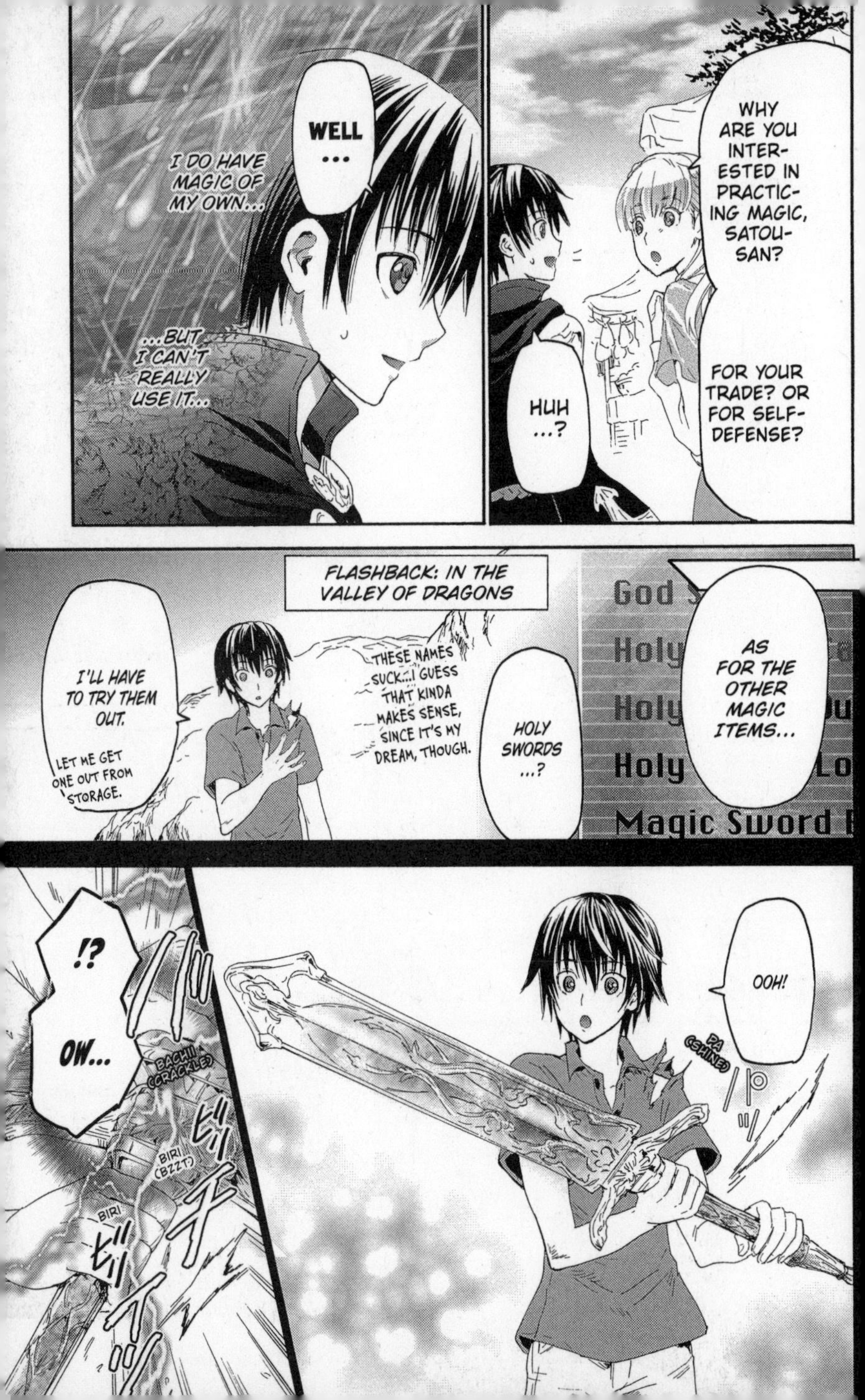
WHY ARE YOU INTER-ESTED IN PRACTIC-ING MAGIC, SATOU-SAN?
FOR YOUR TRADE? OR FOR SELF-DEFENSE?
HUH ...?
WELL ...
I DO HAVE MAGIC OF MY OWN...
...BUT I CAN'T REALLY USE IT...
FLASHBACK: IN THE VALLEY OF DRAGONS
AS FOR THE OTHER MAGIC ITEMS...
HOLY SWORDS ...?
THESE NAMES SUCK... I GUESS THAT KINDA MAKES SENSE, SINCE IT'S MY DREAM, THOUGH.
I'LL HAVE TO TRY THEM OUT.
LET ME GET ONE OUT FROM STORAGE.
OOH!
PA (SHINE)
!?
OW...
BACHI (CRACKLE)
BIRI (BZZT)
BIRI

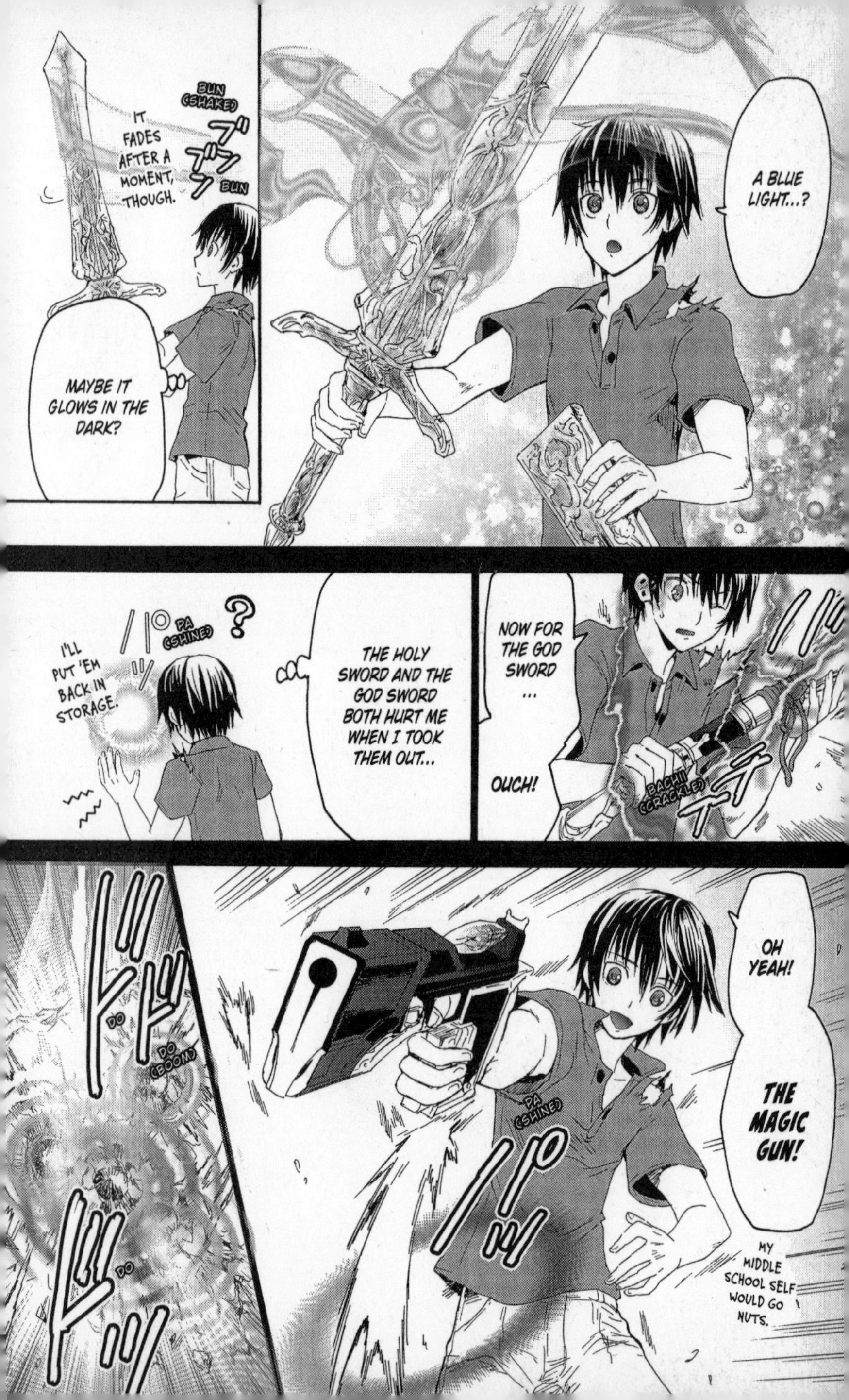
A BLUE LIGHT...?
BUN (SHAKE)
BUN
IT FADES AFTER A MOMENT, THOUGH.
MAYBE IT GLOWS IN THE DARK?
NOW FOR THE GOD SWORD ...
OUCH!
BACHI (CRACKLE)
THE HOLY SWORD AND THE GOD SWORD BOTH HURT ME WHEN I TOOK THEM OUT...
PA (SHINE)
?
I'LL PUT 'EM BACK IN STORAGE.
OH YEAH!
THE MAGIC GUN!
MY MIDDLE SCHOOL SELF WOULD GO NUTS.
PA (SHINE)
DO
DO (BOOM)
DO

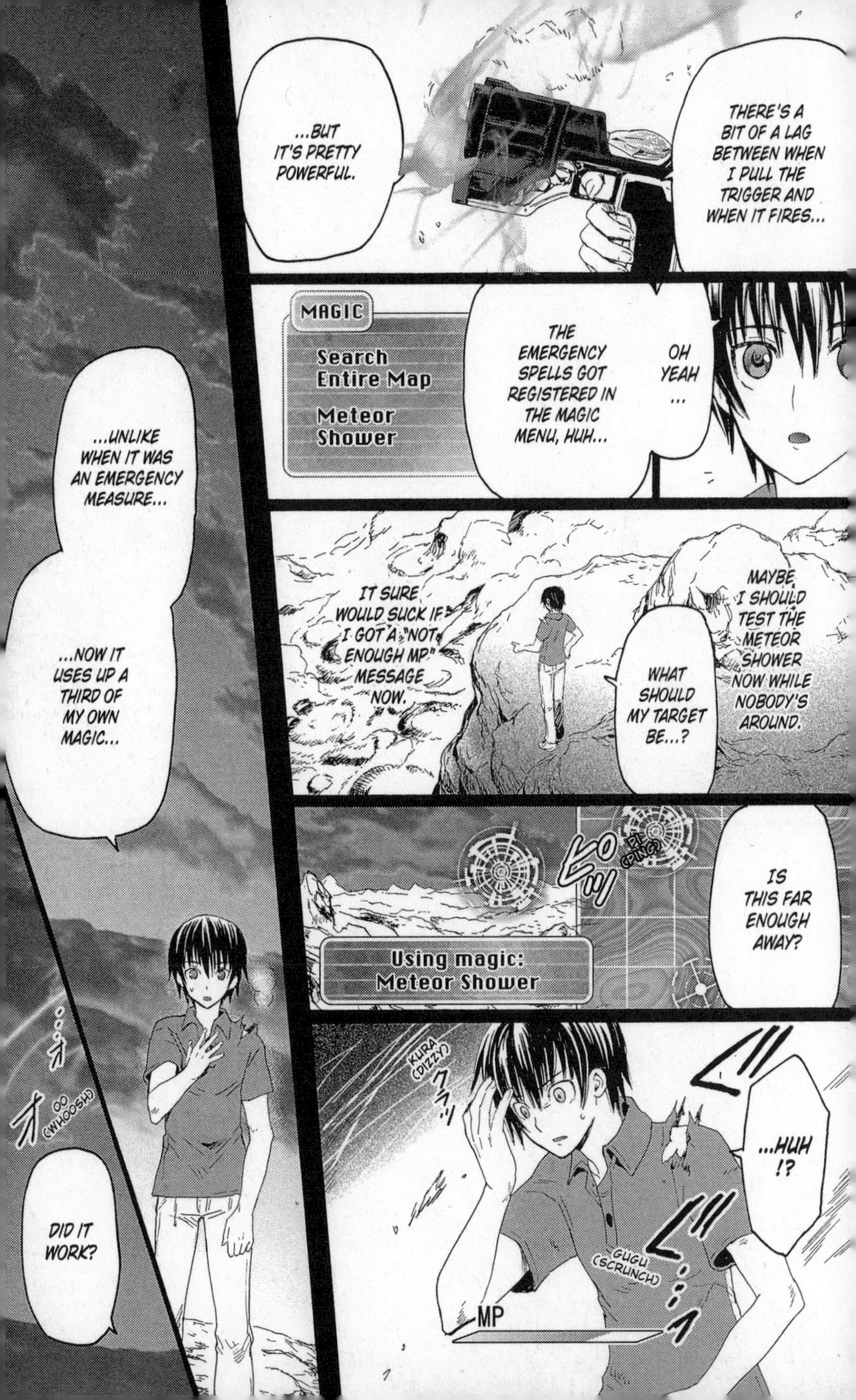
THERE'S A BIT OF A LAG BETWEEN WHEN I PULL THE TRIGGER AND WHEN IT FIRES...
...BUT IT'S PRETTY POWERFUL.
OH YEAH...
THE EMERGENCY SPELLS GOT REGISTERED IN THE MAGIC MENU, HUH...
MAGIC
Search Entire Map
Meteor Shower
MAYBE I SHOULD TEST THE METEOR SHOWER NOW WHILE NOBODY'S AROUND.
WHAT SHOULD MY TARGET BE...?
IT SURE WOULD SUCK IF I GOT A "NOT ENOUGH MP" MESSAGE NOW.
IS THIS FAR ENOUGH AWAY?
PI (PING)
Using magic: Meteor Shower
...HUH!?
GUGU (SCRUNCH)
KURA (DIZZY)
MP
...UNLIKE WHEN IT WAS AN EMERGENCY MEASURE...
...NOW IT USES UP A THIRD OF MY OWN MAGIC...
OO (WHOOSH)
DID IT WORK?

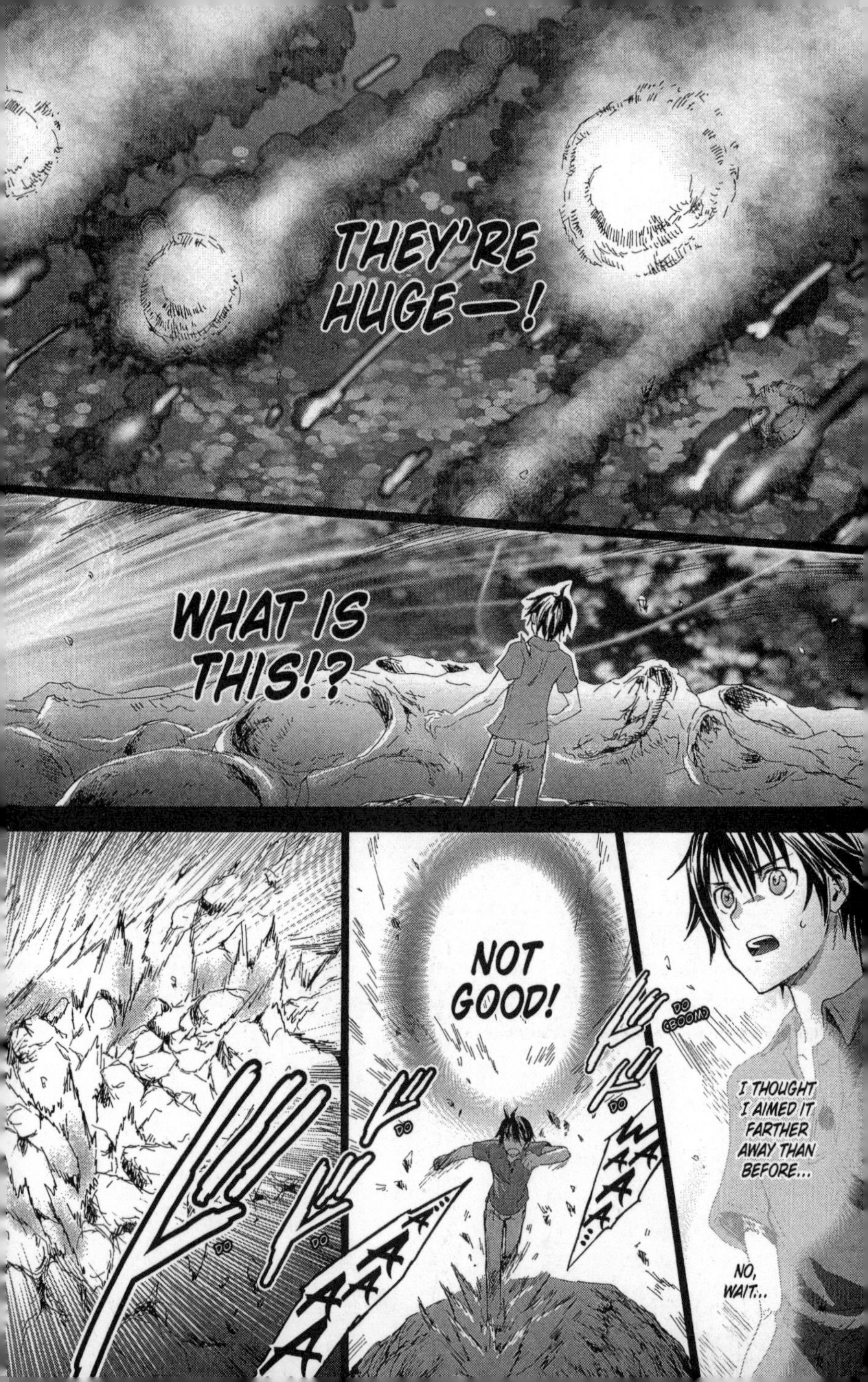
THEY'RE HUGE—!
WHAT IS THIS!?
I THOUGHT I AIMED IT FARTHER AWAY THAN BEFORE...
NO, WAIT...
DO (BOOM)
NOT GOOD!
DO
WAAAA...
DO
AAAAAA...
DO
DO

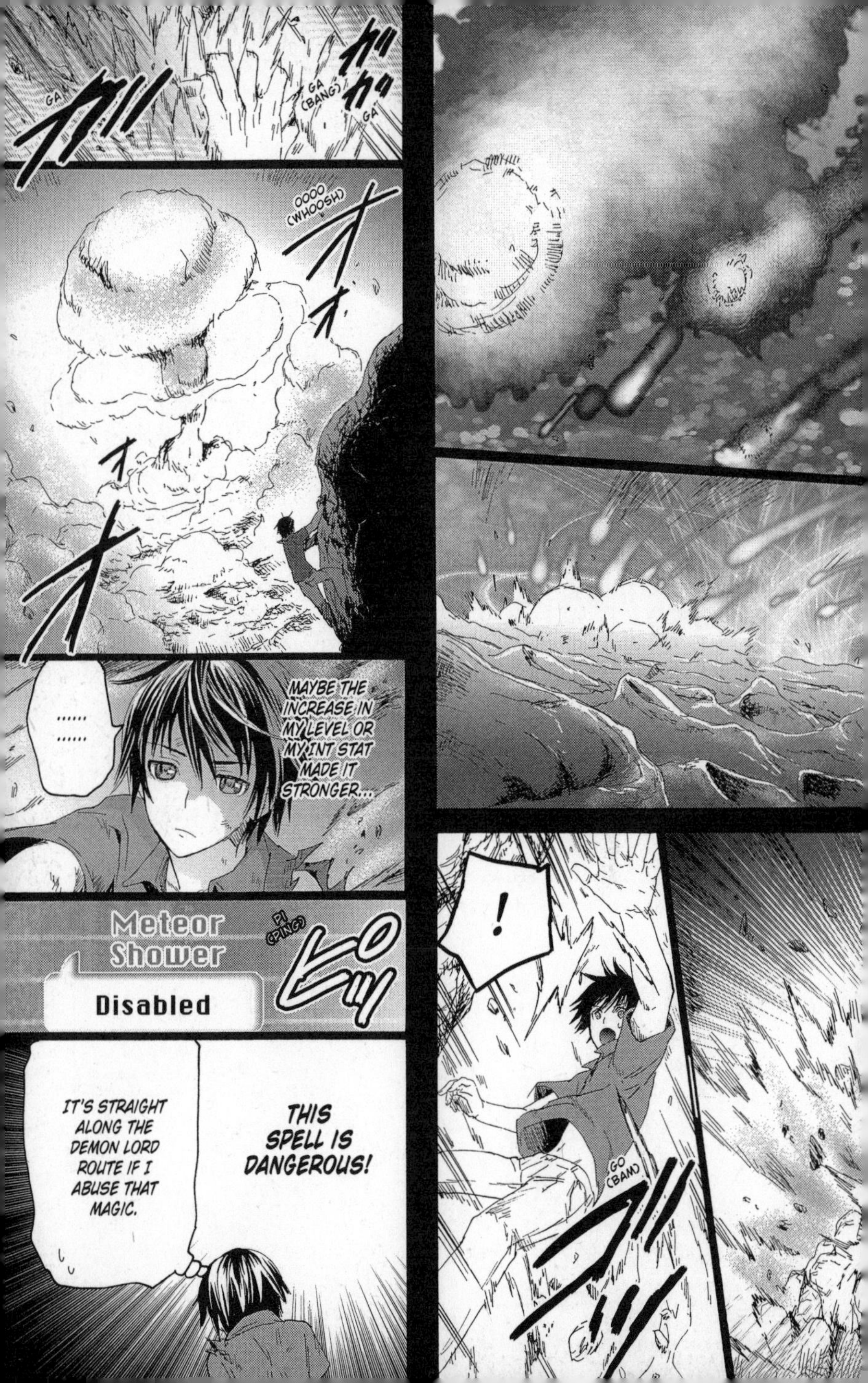
!
GO (BAM)
GA (BANG)
GA
GA
OOOO (WHOOSH)
MAYBE THE INCREASE IN MY LEVEL OR MY INT STAT MADE IT STRONGER...
....
PI (PING)
Meteor Shower
Disabled
THIS SPELL IS DANGEROUS!
IT'S STRAIGHT ALONG THE DEMON LORD ROUTE IF I ABUSE THAT MAGIC.

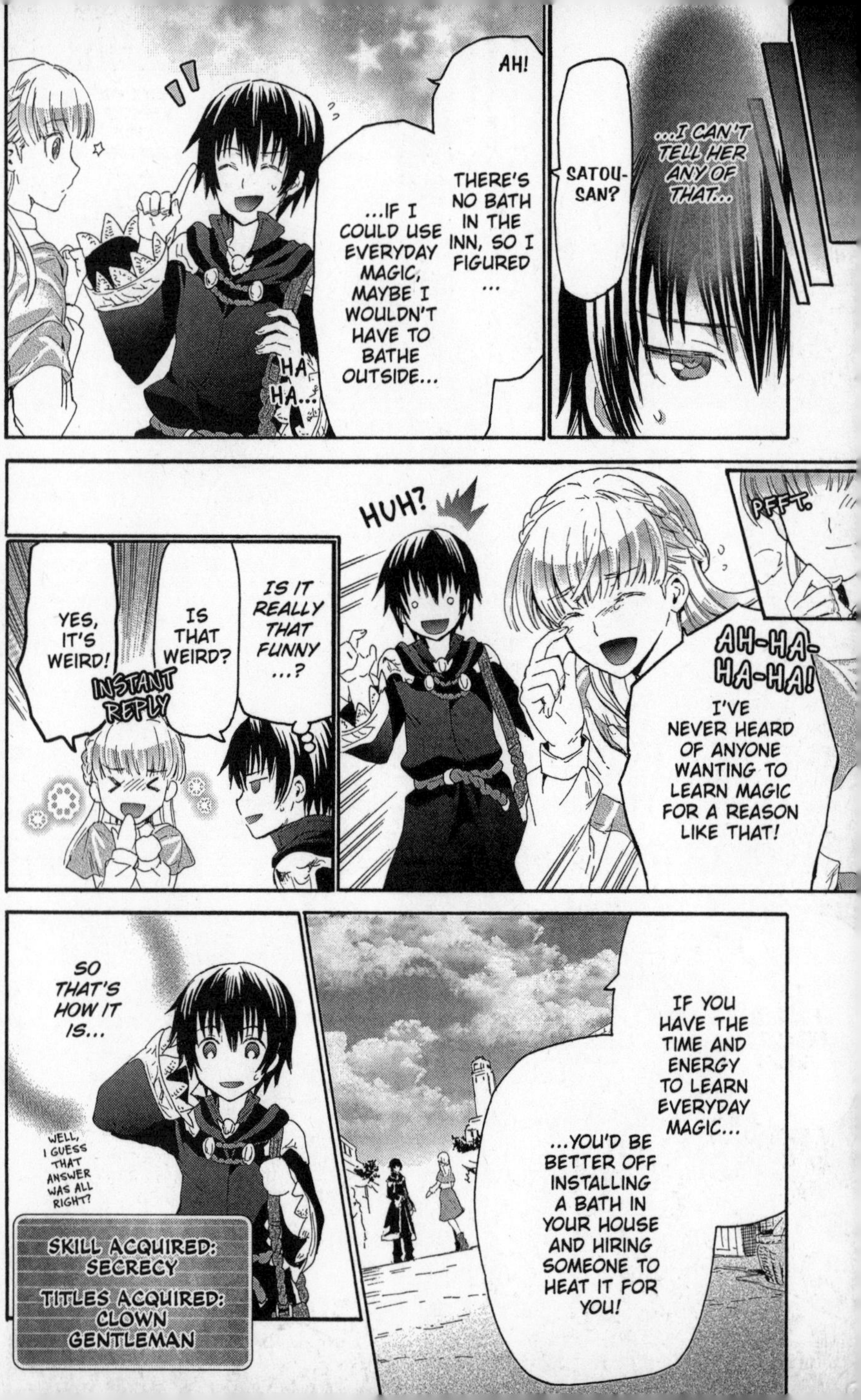

SATOU-SAN?
...I CAN'T TELL HER ANY OF THAT...
AH!
THERE'S NO BATH IN THE INN, SO I FIGURED ...
...IF I COULD USE EVERYDAY MAGIC, MAYBE I WOULDN'T HAVE TO BATHE OUTSIDE...
HA HA...
PFFT.
AH-HA-HA-HA!
I'VE NEVER HEARD OF ANYONE WANTING TO LEARN MAGIC FOR A REASON LIKE THAT!
HUH?
IS IT REALLY THAT FUNNY ...?
IS THAT WEIRD?
YES, IT'S WEIRD!
INSTANT REPLY
IF YOU HAVE THE TIME AND ENERGY TO LEARN EVERYDAY MAGIC...
...YOU'D BE BETTER OFF INSTALLING A BATH IN YOUR HOUSE AND HIRING SOMEONE TO HEAT IT FOR YOU!
SO THAT'S HOW IT IS...
WELL, I GUESS THAT ANSWER WAS ALL RIGHT?
SKILL ACQUIRED: SECRECY
TITLES ACQUIRED: CLOWN GENTLEMAN

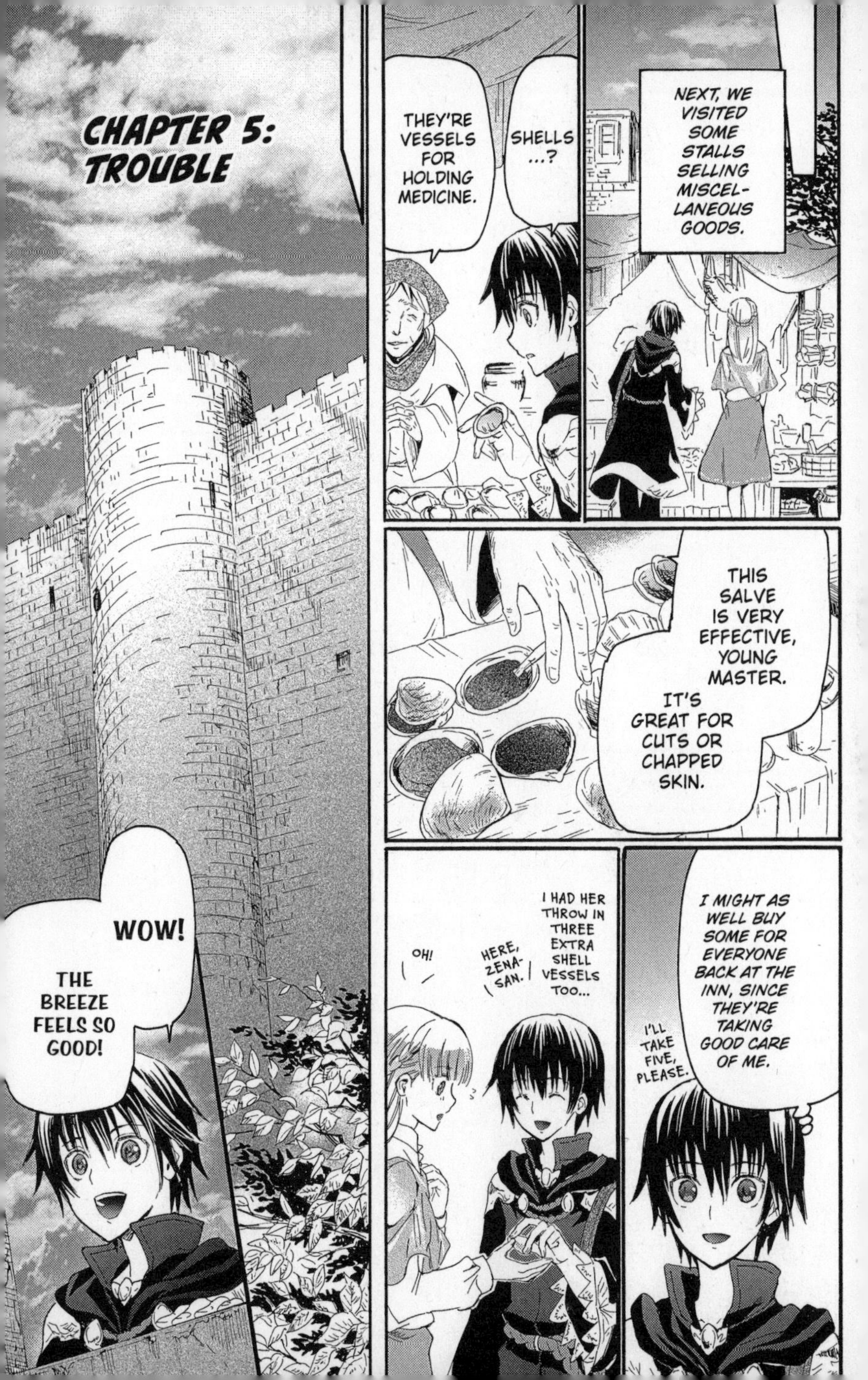

NEXT, WE VISITED SOME STALLS SELLING MISCEL-LANEOUS GOODS.
SHELLS ...?
THEY'RE VESSELS FOR HOLDING MEDICINE.
THIS SALVE IS VERY EFFECTIVE, YOUNG MASTER.
IT'S GREAT FOR CUTS OR CHAPPED SKIN.
I MIGHT AS WELL BUY SOME FOR EVERYONE BACK AT THE INN, SINCE THEY'RE TAKING GOOD CARE OF ME.
I'LL TAKE FIVE, PLEASE.
I HAD HER THROW IN THREE EXTRA SHELL VESSELS TOO...
HERE, ZENA-SAN.
OH!
CHAPTER 5: TROUBLE
WOW!
THE BREEZE FEELS SO GOOD!

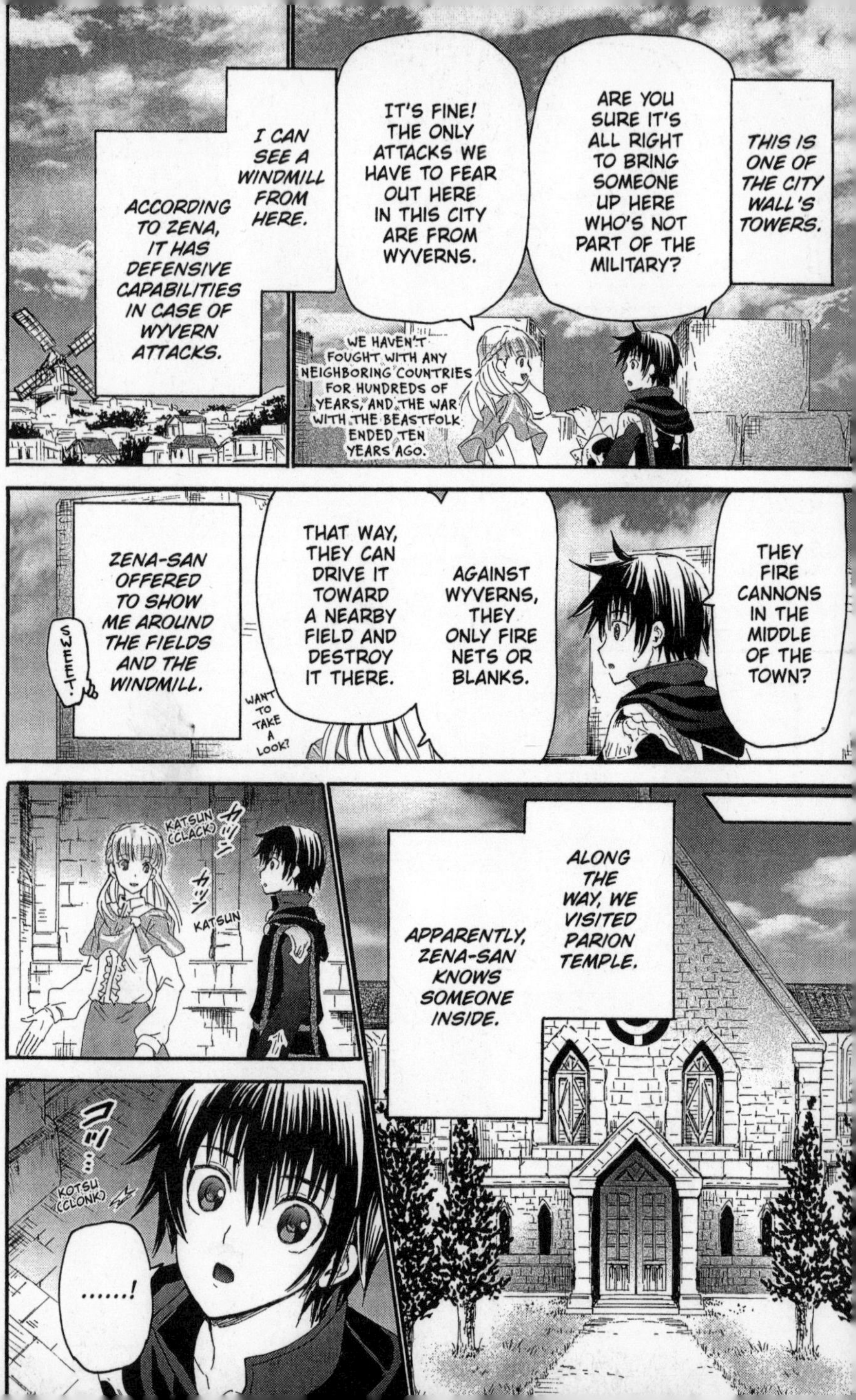
THIS IS ONE OF THE CITY WALL'S TOWERS.
ARE YOU SURE IT'S ALL RIGHT TO BRING SOMEONE UP HERE WHO'S NOT PART OF THE MILITARY?
IT'S FINE! THE ONLY ATTACKS WE HAVE TO FEAR OUT HERE IN THIS CITY ARE FROM WYVERNS.
WE HAVEN'T FOUGHT WITH ANY NEIGHBORING COUNTRIES FOR HUNDREDS OF YEARS, AND THE WAR WITH THE BEASTFOLK ENDED TEN YEARS AGO.
I CAN SEE A WINDMILL FROM HERE.
ACCORDING TO ZENA, IT HAS DEFENSIVE CAPABILITIES IN CASE OF WYVERN ATTACKS.
THEY FIRE CANNONS IN THE MIDDLE OF THE TOWN?
AGAINST WYVERNS, THEY ONLY FIRE NETS OR BLANKS.
THAT WAY, THEY CAN DRIVE IT TOWARD A NEARBY FIELD AND DESTROY IT THERE.
WANT TO TAKE A LOOK?
ZENA-SAN OFFERED TO SHOW ME AROUND THE FIELDS AND THE WINDMILL.
SWEET.
ALONG THE WAY, WE VISITED PARION TEMPLE.
APPARENTLY, ZENA-SAN KNOWS SOMEONE INSIDE.
KATSUN (CLACK)
KATSUN
KOTSU (CLONK)
......!

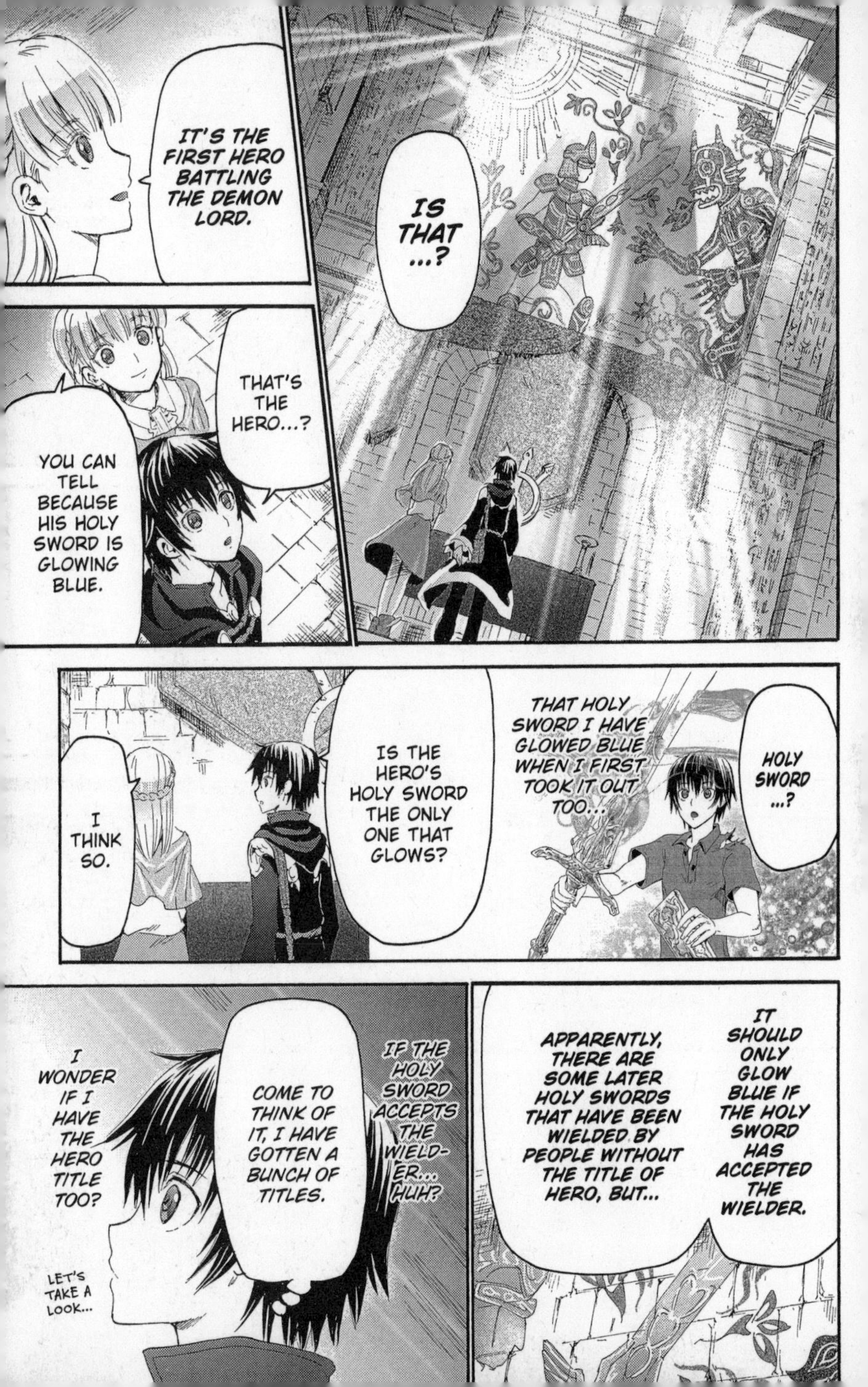
IS THAT ...?
IT'S THE FIRST HERO BATTLING THE DEMON LORD.
THAT'S THE HERO...?
YOU CAN TELL BECAUSE HIS HOLY SWORD IS GLOWING BLUE.
HOLY SWORD ...?
THAT HOLY SWORD I HAVE GLOWED BLUE WHEN I FIRST TOOK IT OUT TOO...
IS THE HERO'S HOLY SWORD THE ONLY ONE THAT GLOWS?
I THINK SO.
IT SHOULD ONLY GLOW BLUE IF THE HOLY SWORD HAS ACCEPTED THE WIELDER.
APPARENTLY, THERE ARE SOME LATER HOLY SWORDS THAT HAVE BEEN WIELDED BY PEOPLE WITHOUT THE TITLE OF HERO, BUT...
IF THE HOLY SWORD ACCEPTS THE WIELDER... HUH?
COME TO THINK OF IT, I HAVE GOTTEN A BUNCH OF TITLES.
I WONDER IF I HAVE THE HERO TITLE TOO?
LET'S TAKE A LOOK...

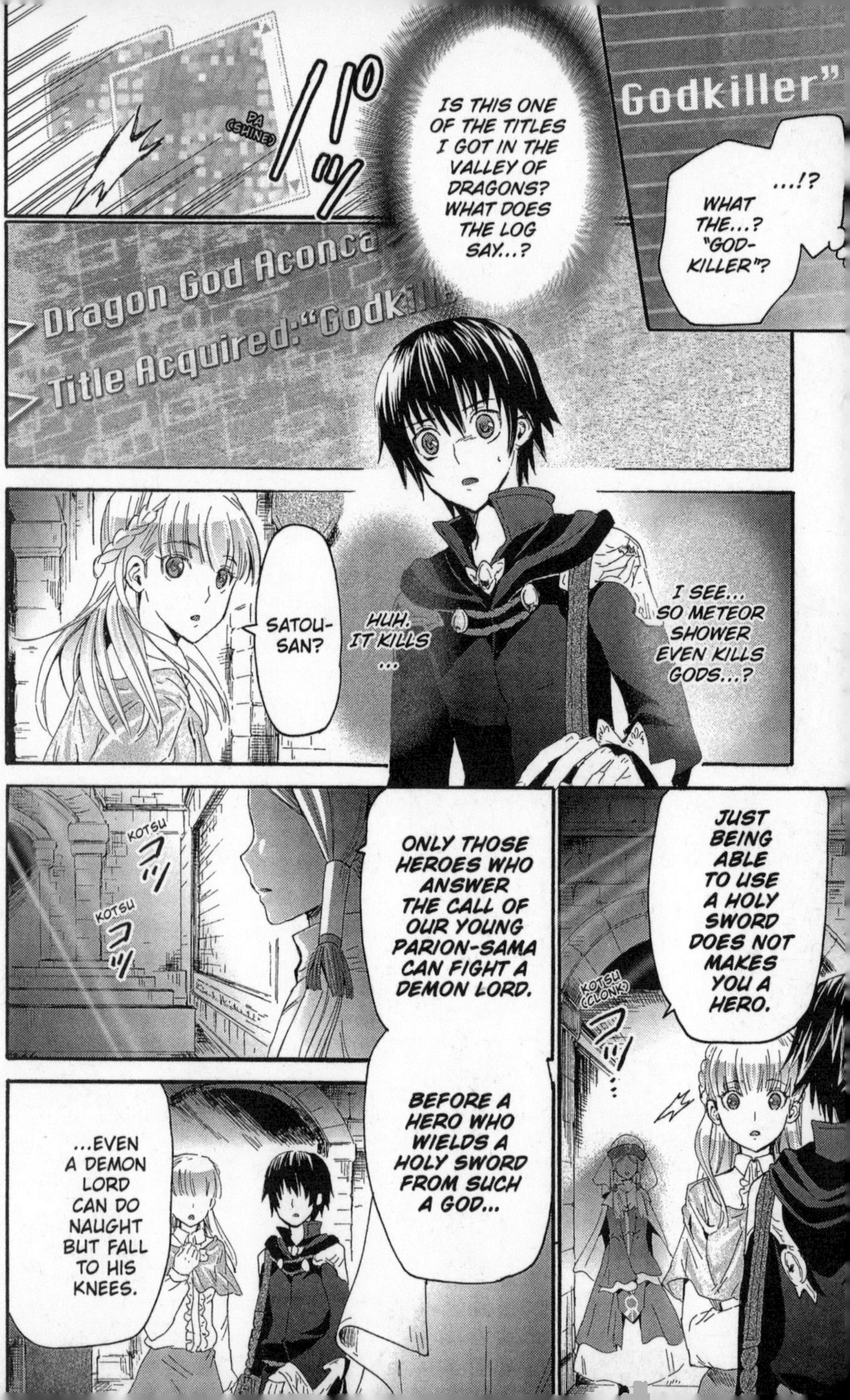

Godkiller"
...!?
WHAT THE...? "GOD-KILLER"?
IS THIS ONE OF THE TITLES I GOT IN THE VALLEY OF DRAGONS? WHAT DOES THE LOG SAY...?
PA (SHINE)
Dragon God Aconca
Title Acquired:"Godk
I SEE... SO METEOR SHOWER EVEN KILLS GODS...?
HUH. IT KILLS ...
SATOU-SAN?
KOTSU (CLONK)
JUST BEING ABLE TO USE A HOLY SWORD DOES NOT MAKES YOU A HERO.
KOTSU
KOTSU
ONLY THOSE HEROES WHO ANSWER THE CALL OF OUR YOUNG PARION-SAMA CAN FIGHT A DEMON LORD.
BEFORE A HERO WHO WIELDS A HOLY SWORD FROM SUCH A GOD...
...EVEN A DEMON LORD CAN DO NAUGHT BUT FALL TO HIS KNEES.

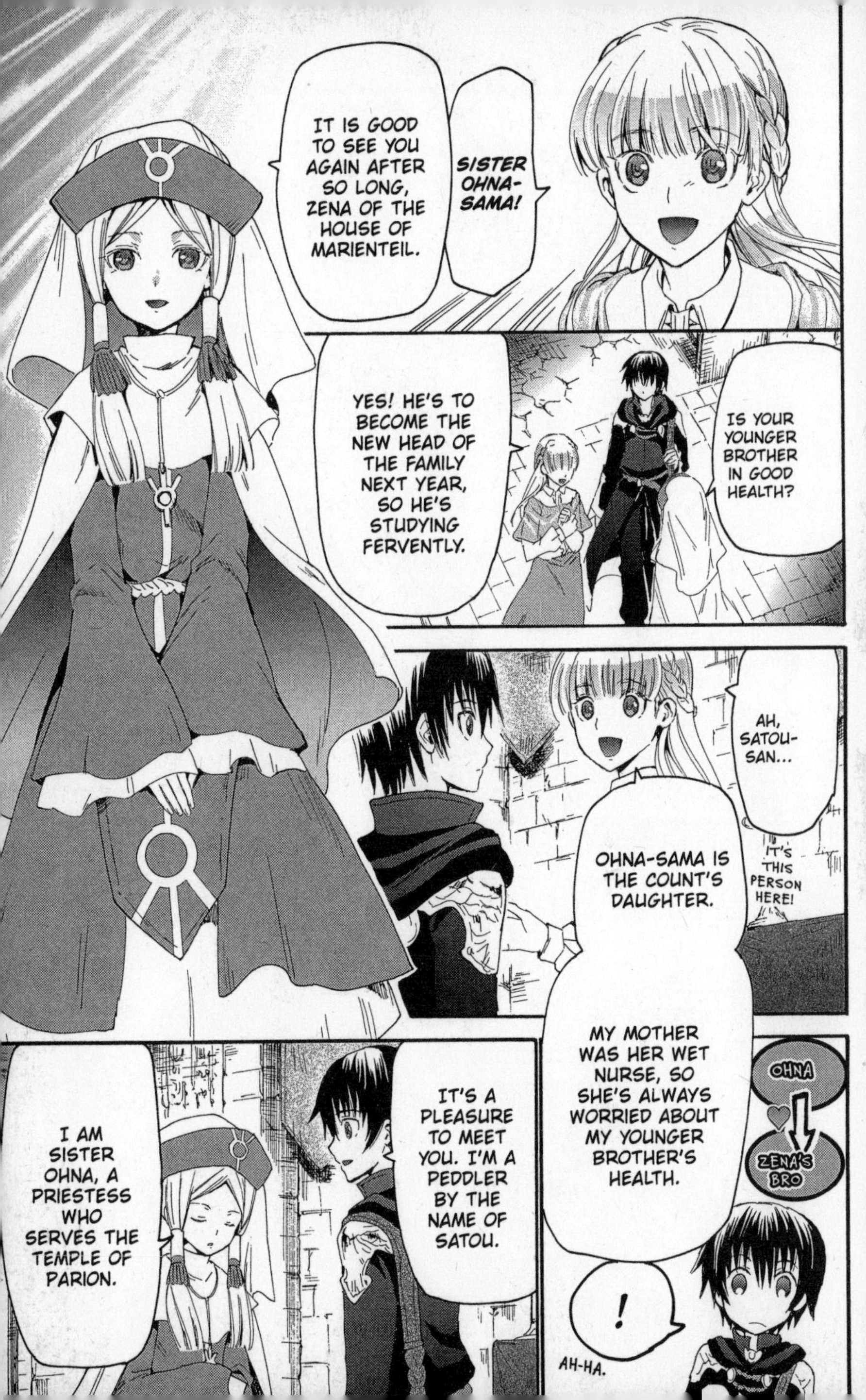
SISTER OHNA-SAMA!
IT IS GOOD TO SEE YOU AGAIN AFTER SO LONG, ZENA OF THE HOUSE OF MARIENTEIL.
IS YOUR YOUNGER BROTHER IN GOOD HEALTH?
YES! HE'S TO BECOME THE NEW HEAD OF THE FAMILY NEXT YEAR, SO HE'S STUDYING FERVENTLY.
AH, SATOU-SAN...
IT'S THIS PERSON HERE!
OHNA-SAMA IS THE COUNT'S DAUGHTER.
MY MOTHER WAS HER WET NURSE, SO SHE'S ALWAYS WORRIED ABOUT MY YOUNGER BROTHER'S HEALTH.
OHNA
ZENA'S BRO
!
AH-HA.
IT'S A PLEASURE TO MEET YOU. I'M A PEDDLER BY THE NAME OF SATOU.
I AM SISTER OHNA, A PRIESTESS WHO SERVES THE TEMPLE OF PARION.

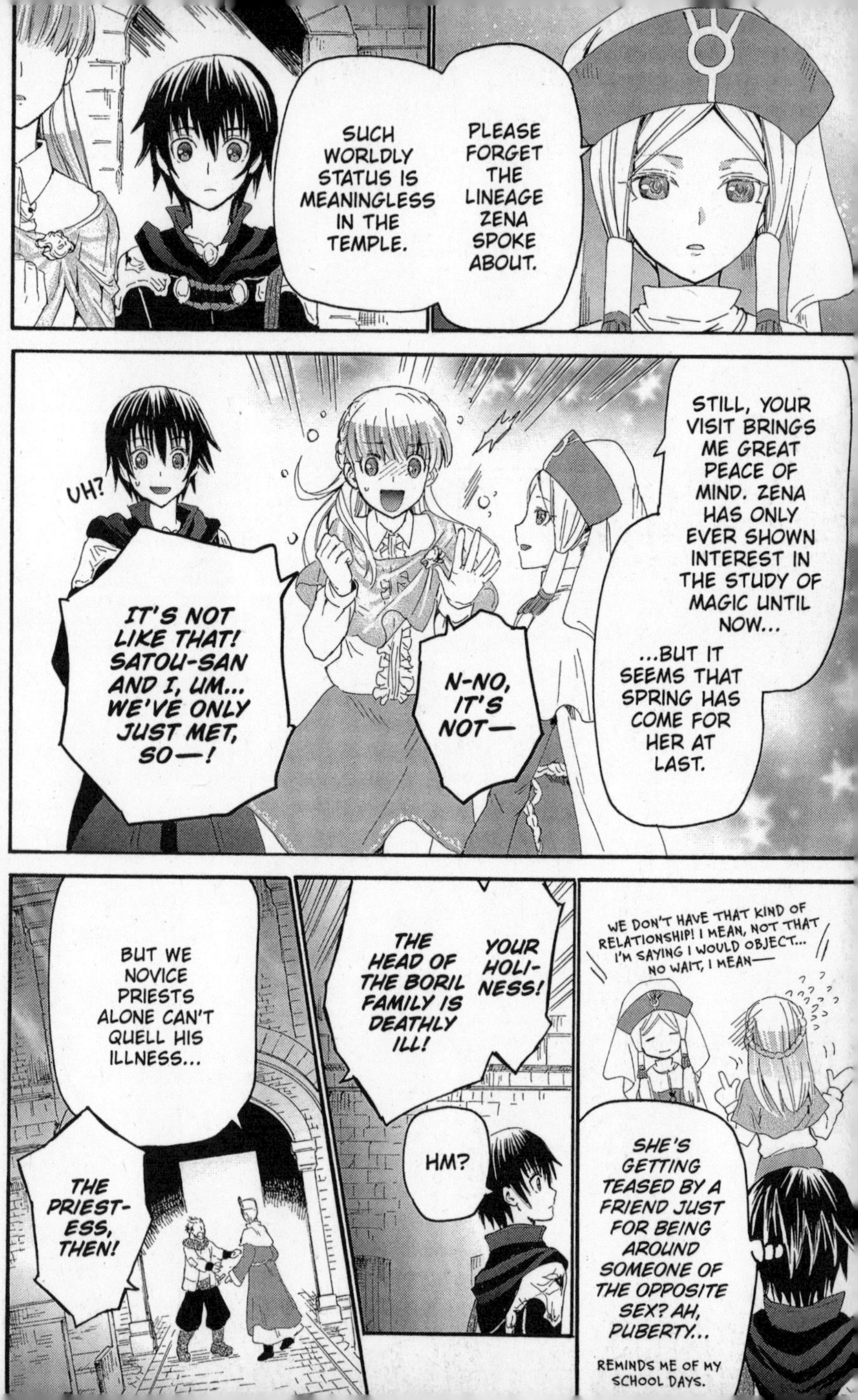

PLEASE FORGET THE LINEAGE ZENA SPOKE ABOUT.
SUCH WORLDLY STATUS IS MEANINGLESS IN THE TEMPLE.
STILL, YOUR VISIT BRINGS ME GREAT PEACE OF MIND. ZENA HAS ONLY EVER SHOWN INTEREST IN THE STUDY OF MAGIC UNTIL NOW...
...BUT IT SEEMS THAT SPRING HAS COME FOR HER AT LAST.
N-NO, IT'S NOT—
IT'S NOT LIKE THAT! SATOU-SAN AND I, UM... WE'VE ONLY JUST MET, SO—!
UH?
WE DON'T HAVE THAT KIND OF RELATIONSHIP! I MEAN, NOT THAT I'M SAYING I WOULD OBJECT... NO WAIT, I MEAN—
SHE'S GETTING TEASED BY A FRIEND JUST FOR BEING AROUND SOMEONE OF THE OPPOSITE SEX? AH, PUBERTY...
REMINDS ME OF MY SCHOOL DAYS.
YOUR HOLINESS!
THE HEAD OF THE BORIL FAMILY IS DEATHLY ILL!
HM?
BUT WE NOVICE PRIESTS ALONE CAN'T QUELL HIS ILLNESS...
THE PRIEST-ESS, THEN!

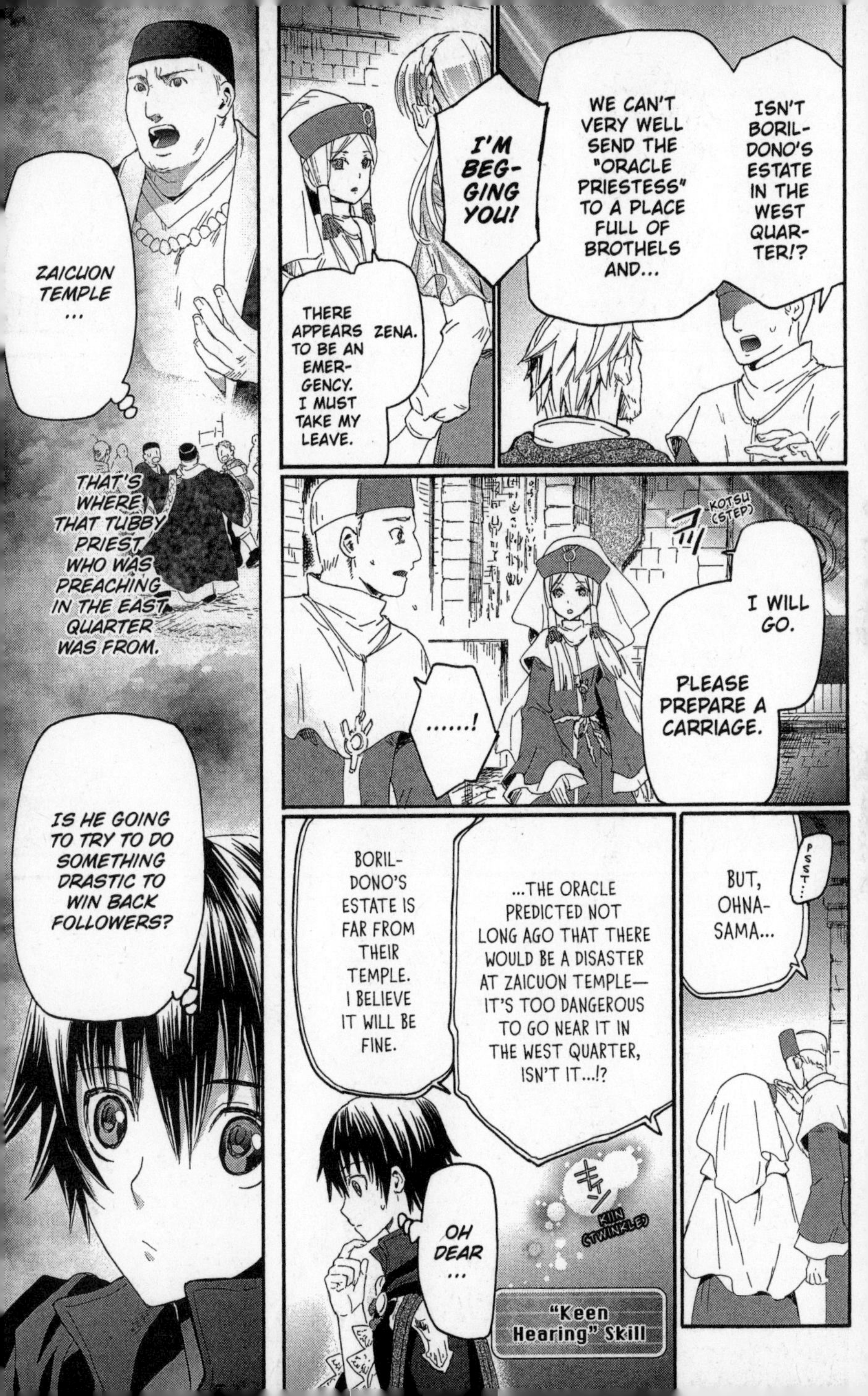
ISN'T BORIL-DONO'S ESTATE IN THE WEST QUARTER!?
WE CAN'T VERY WELL SEND THE "ORACLE PRIESTESS" TO A PLACE FULL OF BROTHELS AND...
I'M BEGGING YOU!
ZENA.
THERE APPEARS TO BE AN EMERGENCY. I MUST TAKE MY LEAVE.
KOTSU (STEP)
I WILL GO.
PLEASE PREPARE A CARRIAGE.
......!
PSST...
BUT, OHNA-SAMA...
...THE ORACLE PREDICTED NOT LONG AGO THAT THERE WOULD BE A DISASTER AT ZAICUON TEMPLE—IT'S TOO DANGEROUS TO GO NEAR IT IN THE WEST QUARTER, ISN'T IT...!?
BORIL-DONO'S ESTATE IS FAR FROM THEIR TEMPLE. I BELIEVE IT WILL BE FINE.
KIN (TWINKLE)
OH DEAR...
"Keen Hearing" Skill
ZAICUON TEMPLE...
THAT'S WHERE THAT TUBBY PRIEST WHO WAS PREACHING IN THE EAST QUARTER WAS FROM.
IS HE GOING TO TRY TO DO SOMETHING DRASTIC TO WIN BACK FOLLOWERS?

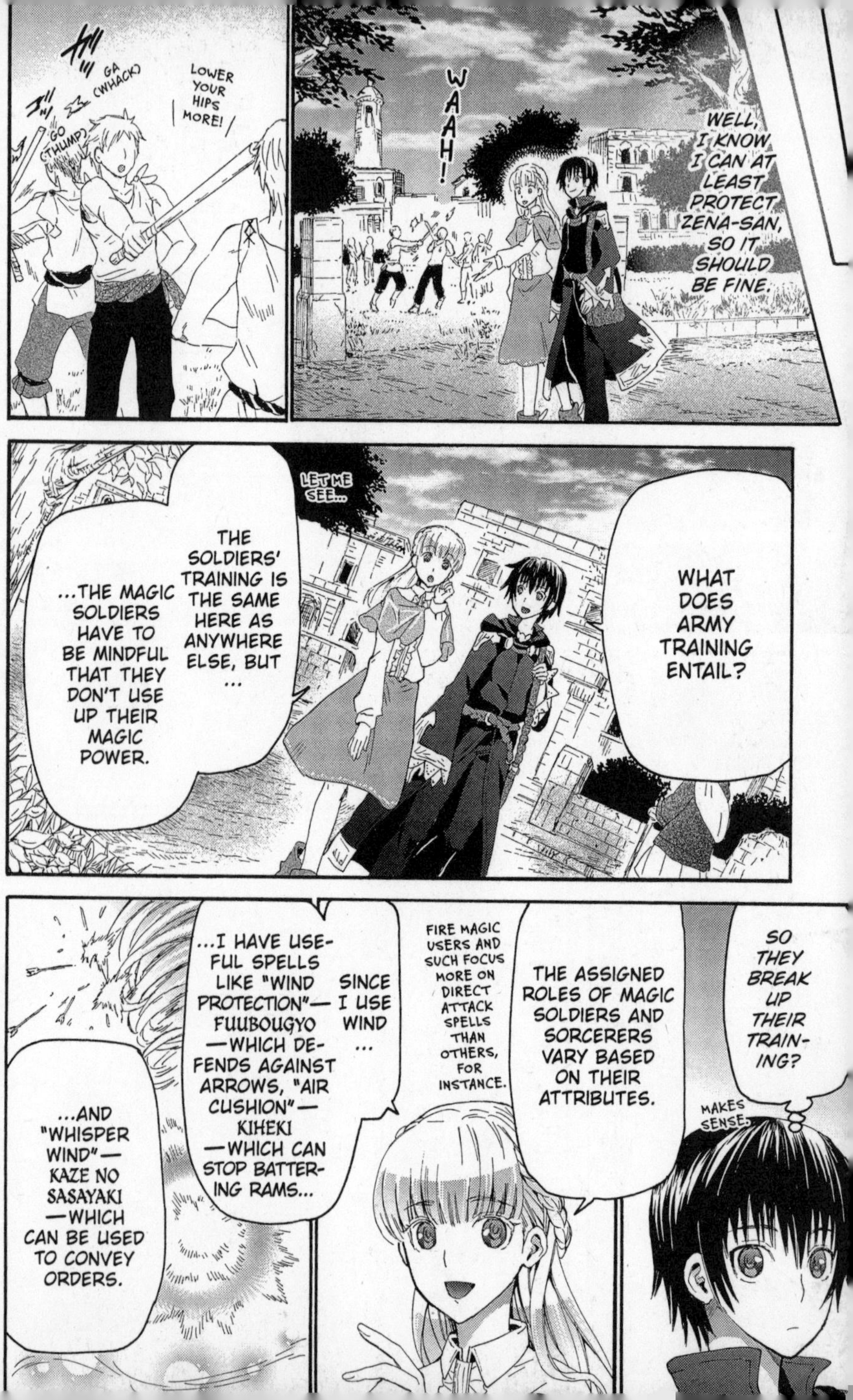
WAAAH!
WELL, I KNOW I CAN AT LEAST PROTECT ZENA-SAN, SO IT SHOULD BE FINE.
LOWER YOUR HIPS MORE!
GA (WHACK)
GO (THUMP)
WHAT DOES ARMY TRAINING ENTAIL?
LET ME SEE...
THE SOLDIERS' TRAINING IS THE SAME HERE AS ANYWHERE ELSE, BUT ...
...THE MAGIC SOLDIERS HAVE TO BE MINDFUL THAT THEY DON'T USE UP THEIR MAGIC POWER.
SO THEY BREAK UP THEIR TRAINING?
MAKES SENSE.
THE ASSIGNED ROLES OF MAGIC SOLDIERS AND SORCERERS VARY BASED ON THEIR ATTRIBUTES.
FIRE MAGIC USERS AND SUCH FOCUS MORE ON DIRECT ATTACK SPELLS THAN OTHERS, FOR INSTANCE.
SINCE I USE WIND ...
...I HAVE USEFUL SPELLS LIKE "WIND PROTECTION"—FUUBOUGYO—WHICH DEFENDS AGAINST ARROWS, "AIR CUSHION"—KIHEKI—WHICH CAN STOP BATTERING RAMS...
...AND "WHISPER WIND"—KAZE NO SASAYAKI—WHICH CAN BE USED TO CONVEY ORDERS.

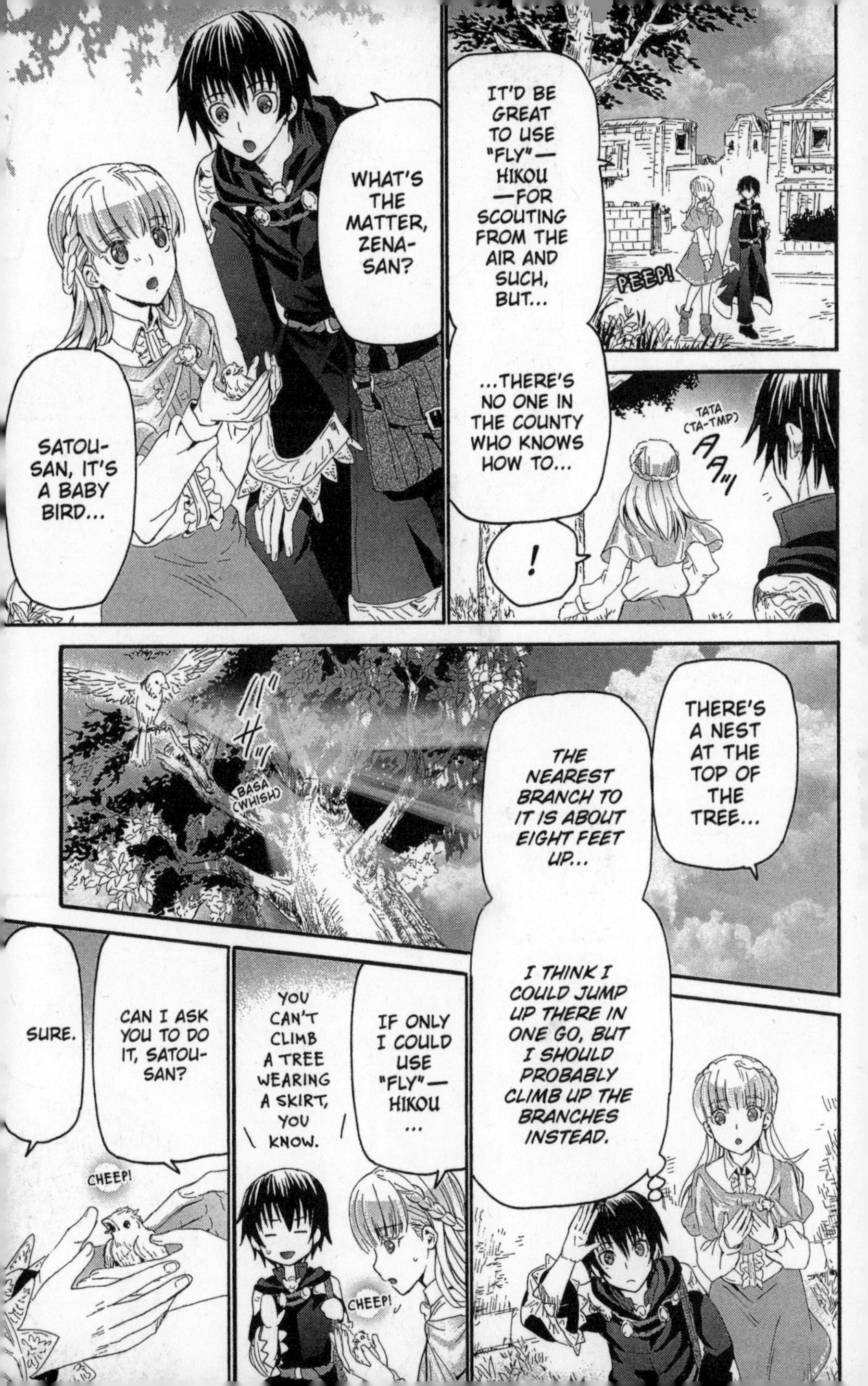
IT'D BE GREAT TO USE "FLY"—HIKOU—FOR SCOUTING FROM THE AIR AND SUCH, BUT...
PEEP!
...THERE'S NO ONE IN THE COUNTY WHO KNOWS HOW TO...
TATA (TA-TMP)
!
WHAT'S THE MATTER, ZENA-SAN?
SATOU-SAN, IT'S A BABY BIRD...
THERE'S A NEST AT THE TOP OF THE TREE...
THE NEAREST BRANCH TO IT IS ABOUT EIGHT FEET UP...
BASA (WHISH)
I THINK I COULD JUMP UP THERE IN ONE GO, BUT I SHOULD PROBABLY CLIMB UP THE BRANCHES INSTEAD.
IF ONLY I COULD USE "FLY"—HIKOU...
YOU CAN'T CLIMB A TREE WEARING A SKIRT, YOU KNOW.
CHEEP!
CAN I ASK YOU TO DO IT, SATOU-SAN?
SURE.
CHEEP!

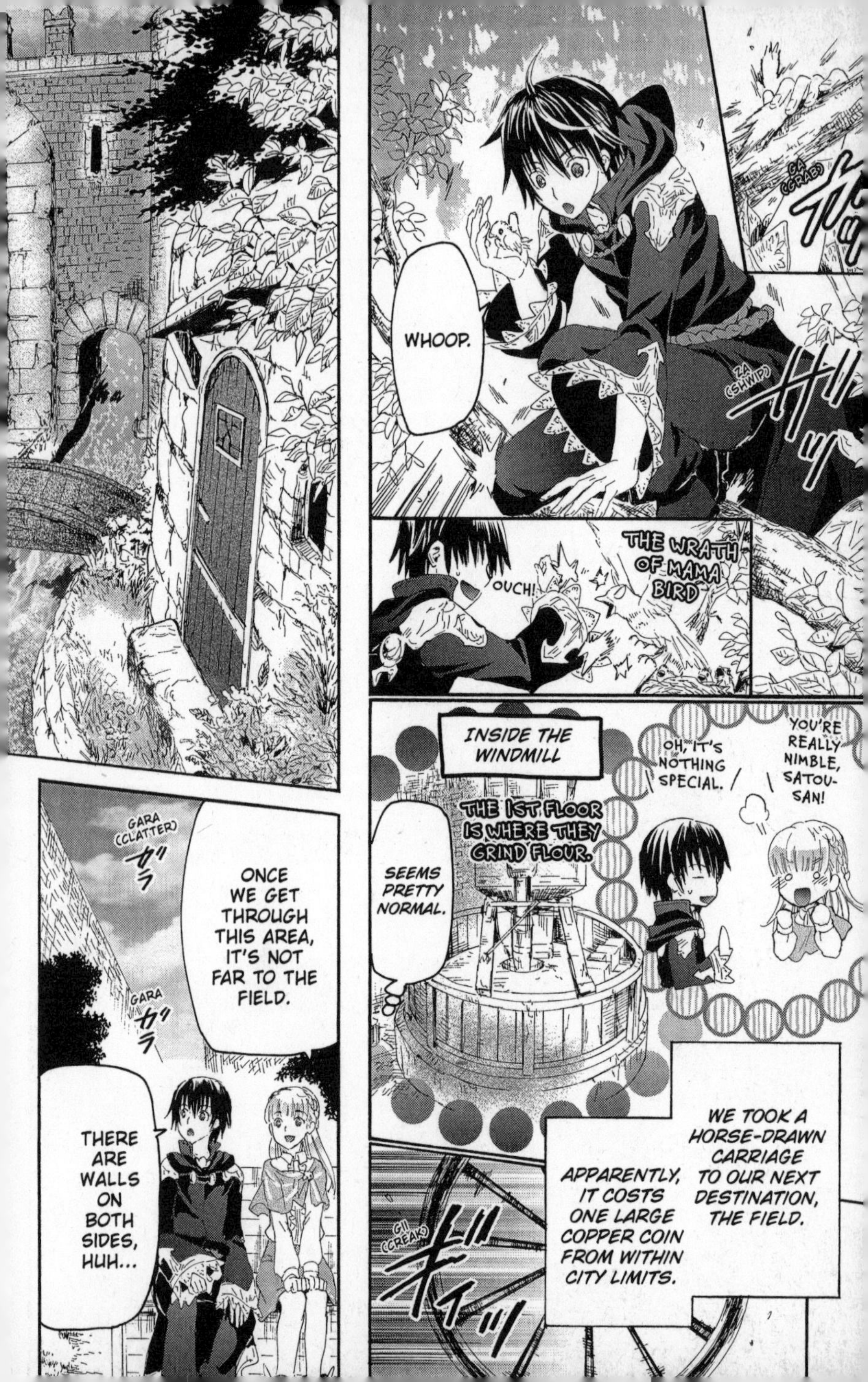
GA (GRAB)
ZA (SHWIP)
WHOOP.
THE WRATH OF MAMA BIRD
OUCH!
INSIDE THE WINDMILL
YOU'RE REALLY NIMBLE, SATOU-SAN!
OH, IT'S NOTHING SPECIAL.
THE 1ST FLOOR IS WHERE THEY GRIND FLOUR.
SEEMS PRETTY NORMAL.
WE TOOK A HORSE-DRAWN CARRIAGE TO OUR NEXT DESTINATION, THE FIELD.
APPARENTLY, IT COSTS ONE LARGE COPPER COIN FROM WITHIN CITY LIMITS.
GII (CREAK)
GARA (CLATTER)
ONCE WE GET THROUGH THIS AREA, IT'S NOT FAR TO THE FIELD.
GARA
THERE ARE WALLS ON BOTH SIDES, HUH...

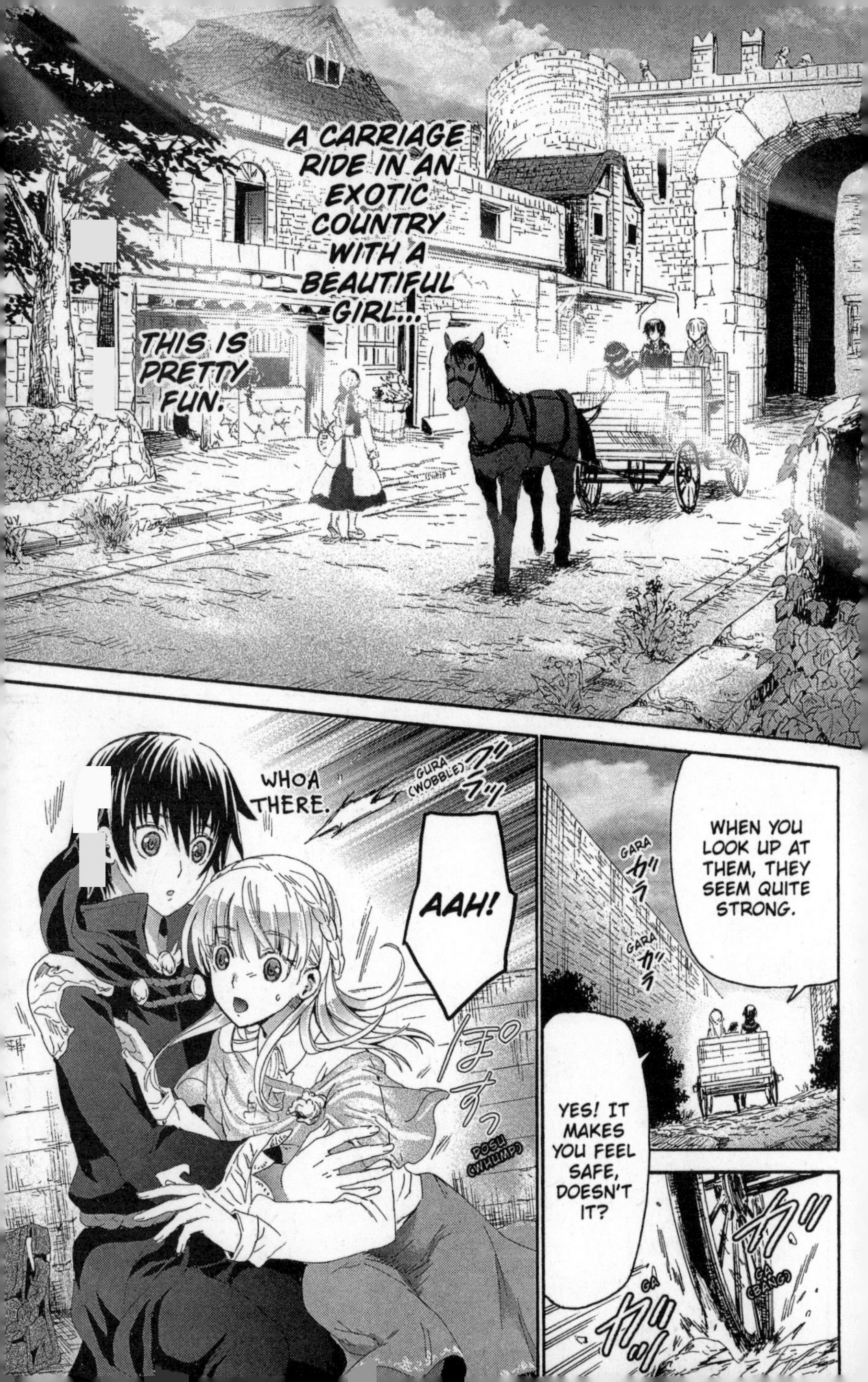
A CARRIAGE RIDE IN AN EXOTIC COUNTRY WITH A BEAUTIFUL GIRL...
THIS IS PRETTY FUN.
WHEN YOU LOOK UP AT THEM, THEY SEEM QUITE STRONG.
GARA
GARA
YES! IT MAKES YOU FEEL SAFE, DOESN'T IT?
GA (BANG)
GA
GURA (WOBBLE)
WHOA THERE.
AAH!
POSU (WHUMP)

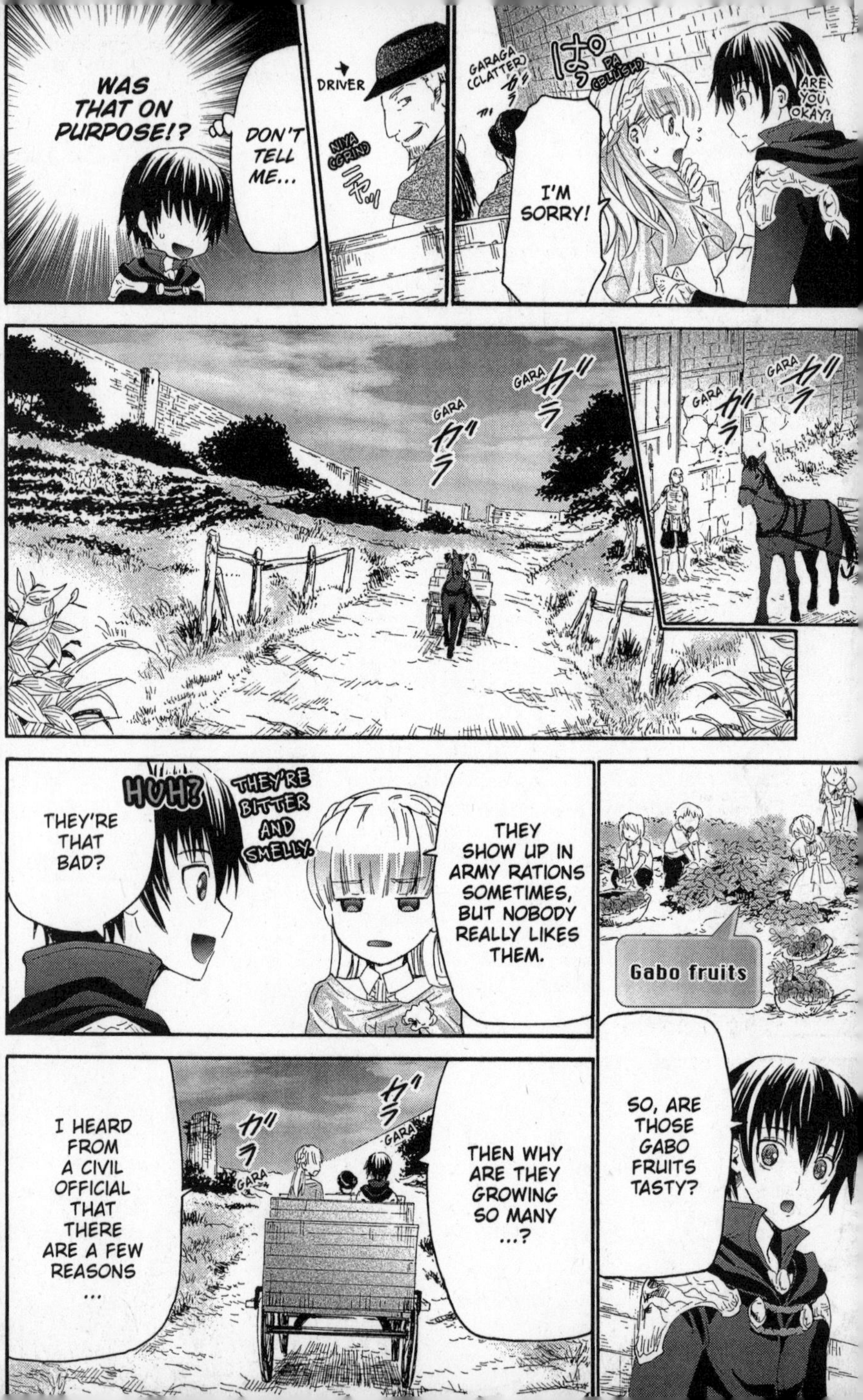
ARE YOU OKAY?
ぱっ PA (BLUSH)
GARAGA (CLATTER)
I'M SORRY!
DRIVER
NIYA (GRIN)
DON'T TELL ME...
WAS THAT ON PURPOSE!?
GARA
GARA
GARA
GARA
Gabo fruits
SO, ARE THOSE GABO FRUITS TASTY?
THEY SHOW UP IN ARMY RATIONS SOMETIMES, BUT NOBODY REALLY LIKES THEM.
THEY'RE BITTER AND SMELLY.
HUH?
THEY'RE THAT BAD?
THEN WHY ARE THEY GROWING SO MANY ...?
GARA
GARA
I HEARD FROM A CIVIL OFFICIAL THAT THERE ARE A FEW REASONS ...

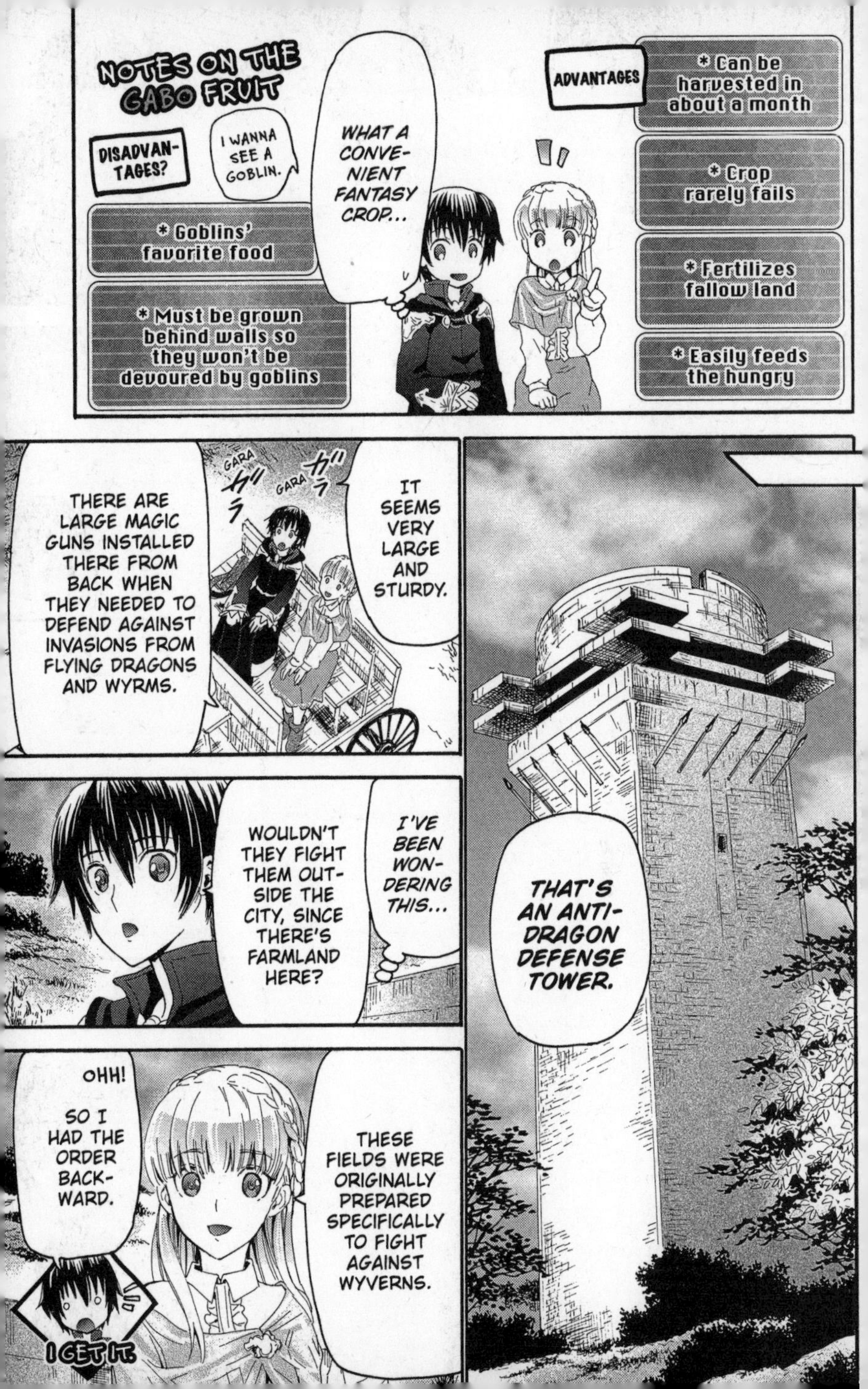
ADVANTAGES
* Can be harvested in about a month
* Crop rarely fails
* Fertilizes fallow land
* Easily feeds the hungry
!!
WHAT A CONVENIENT FANTASY CROP...
NOTES ON THE GABO FRUIT
I WANNA SEE A GOBLIN.
DISADVANTAGES?
* Goblins' favorite food
* Must be grown behind walls so they won't be devoured by goblins
THAT'S AN ANTI-DRAGON DEFENSE TOWER.
IT SEEMS VERY LARGE AND STURDY.
GARA
GARA
THERE ARE LARGE MAGIC GUNS INSTALLED THERE FROM BACK WHEN THEY NEEDED TO DEFEND AGAINST INVASIONS FROM FLYING DRAGONS AND WYRMS.
I'VE BEEN WONDERING THIS...
WOULDN'T THEY FIGHT THEM OUTSIDE THE CITY, SINCE THERE'S FARMLAND HERE?
THESE FIELDS WERE ORIGINALLY PREPARED SPECIFICALLY TO FIGHT AGAINST WYVERNS.
OHH!
SO I HAD THE ORDER BACKWARD.
I GET IT.

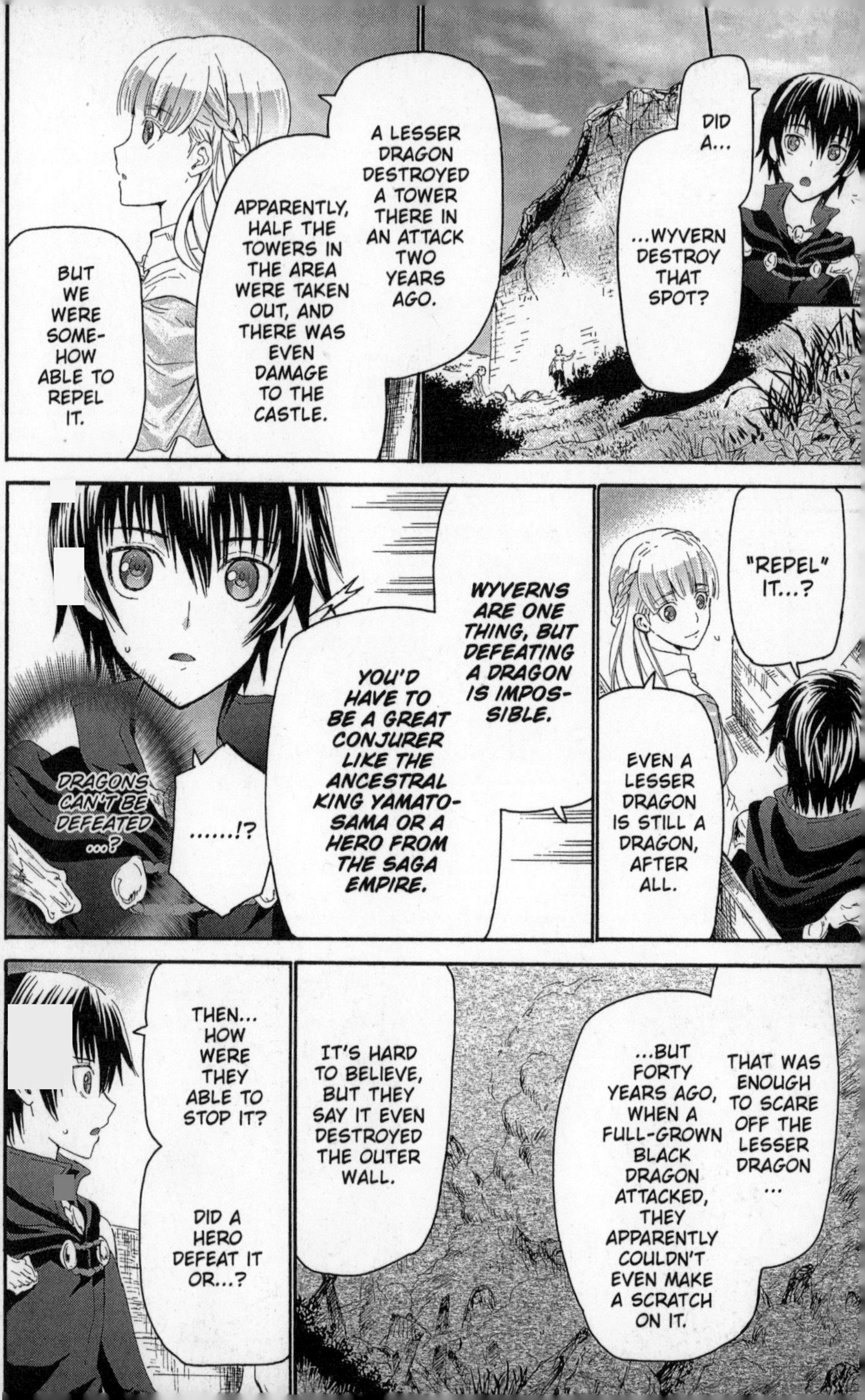
DID A...
...WYVERN DESTROY THAT SPOT?
A LESSER DRAGON DESTROYED A TOWER THERE IN AN ATTACK TWO YEARS AGO.
APPARENTLY, HALF THE TOWERS IN THE AREA WERE TAKEN OUT, AND THERE WAS EVEN DAMAGE TO THE CASTLE.
BUT WE WERE SOME-HOW ABLE TO REPEL IT.
"REPEL" IT...?
EVEN A LESSER DRAGON IS STILL A DRAGON, AFTER ALL.
WYVERNS ARE ONE THING, BUT DEFEATING A DRAGON IS IMPOS-SIBLE.
YOU'D HAVE TO BE A GREAT CONJURER LIKE THE ANCESTRAL KING YAMATO-SAMA OR A HERO FROM THE SAGA EMPIRE.
......!?
DRAGONS CAN'T BE DEFEATED ...?
THAT WAS ENOUGH TO SCARE OFF THE LESSER DRAGON ...
...BUT FORTY YEARS AGO, WHEN A FULL-GROWN BLACK DRAGON ATTACKED, THEY APPARENTLY COULDN'T EVEN MAKE A SCRATCH ON IT.
IT'S HARD TO BELIEVE, BUT THEY SAY IT EVEN DESTROYED THE OUTER WALL.
THEN... HOW WERE THEY ABLE TO STOP IT?
DID A HERO DEFEAT IT OR...?

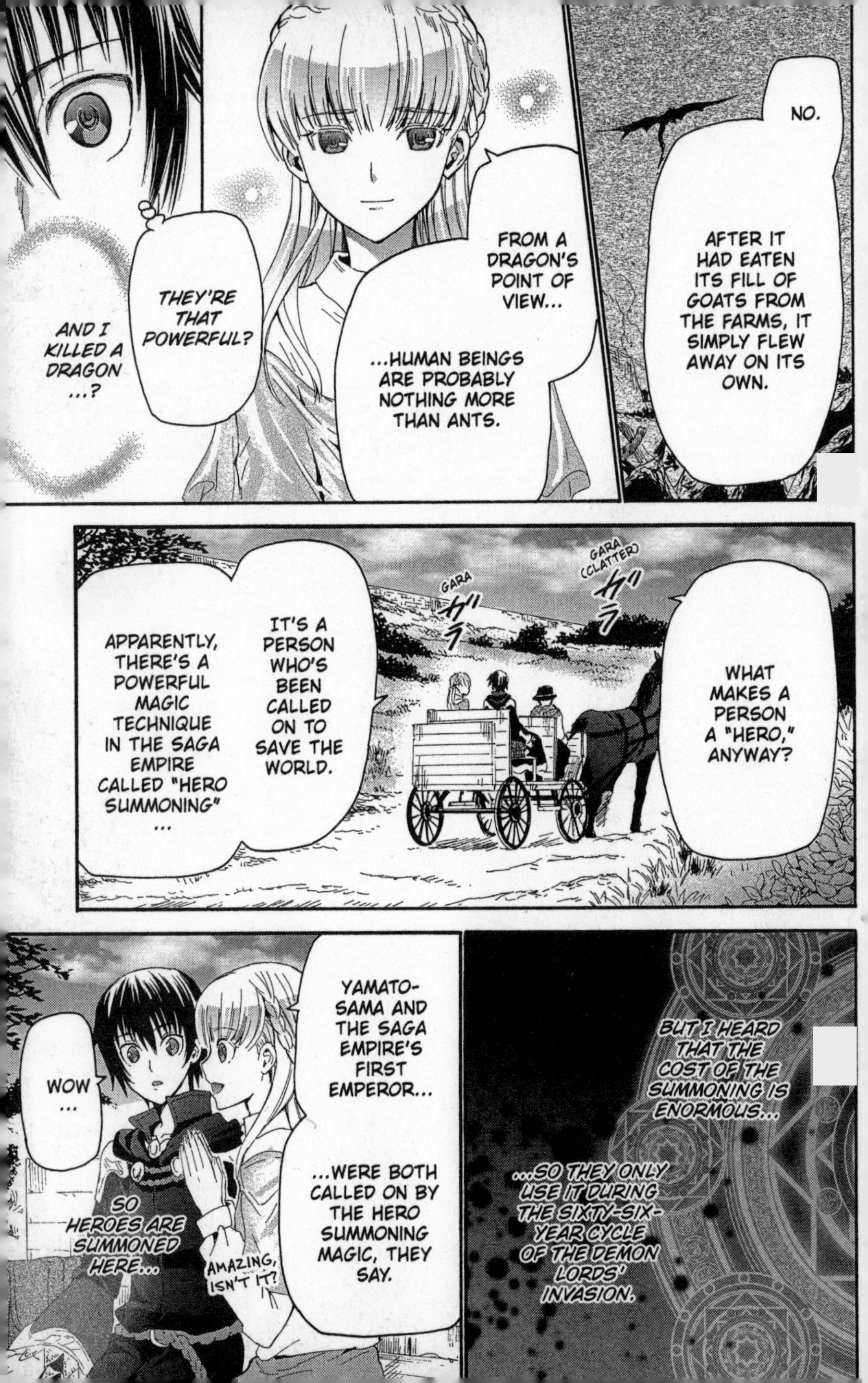
NO.
AFTER IT HAD EATEN ITS FILL OF GOATS FROM THE FARMS, IT SIMPLY FLEW AWAY ON ITS OWN.
FROM A DRAGON'S POINT OF VIEW...
...HUMAN BEINGS ARE PROBABLY NOTHING MORE THAN ANTS.
THEY'RE THAT POWERFUL?
AND I KILLED A DRAGON ...?
GARA (CLATTER)
GARA
WHAT MAKES A PERSON A "HERO," ANYWAY?
IT'S A PERSON WHO'S BEEN CALLED ON TO SAVE THE WORLD.
APPARENTLY, THERE'S A POWERFUL MAGIC TECHNIQUE IN THE SAGA EMPIRE CALLED "HERO SUMMONING" ...
BUT I HEARD THAT THE COST OF THE SUMMONING IS ENORMOUS...
...SO THEY ONLY USE IT DURING THE SIXTY-SIX-YEAR CYCLE OF THE DEMON LORDS' INVASION.
YAMATO-SAMA AND THE SAGA EMPIRE'S FIRST EMPEROR...
...WERE BOTH CALLED ON BY THE HERO SUMMONING MAGIC, THEY SAY.
WOW ...
AMAZING, ISN'T IT?
SO HEROES ARE SUMMONED HERE...

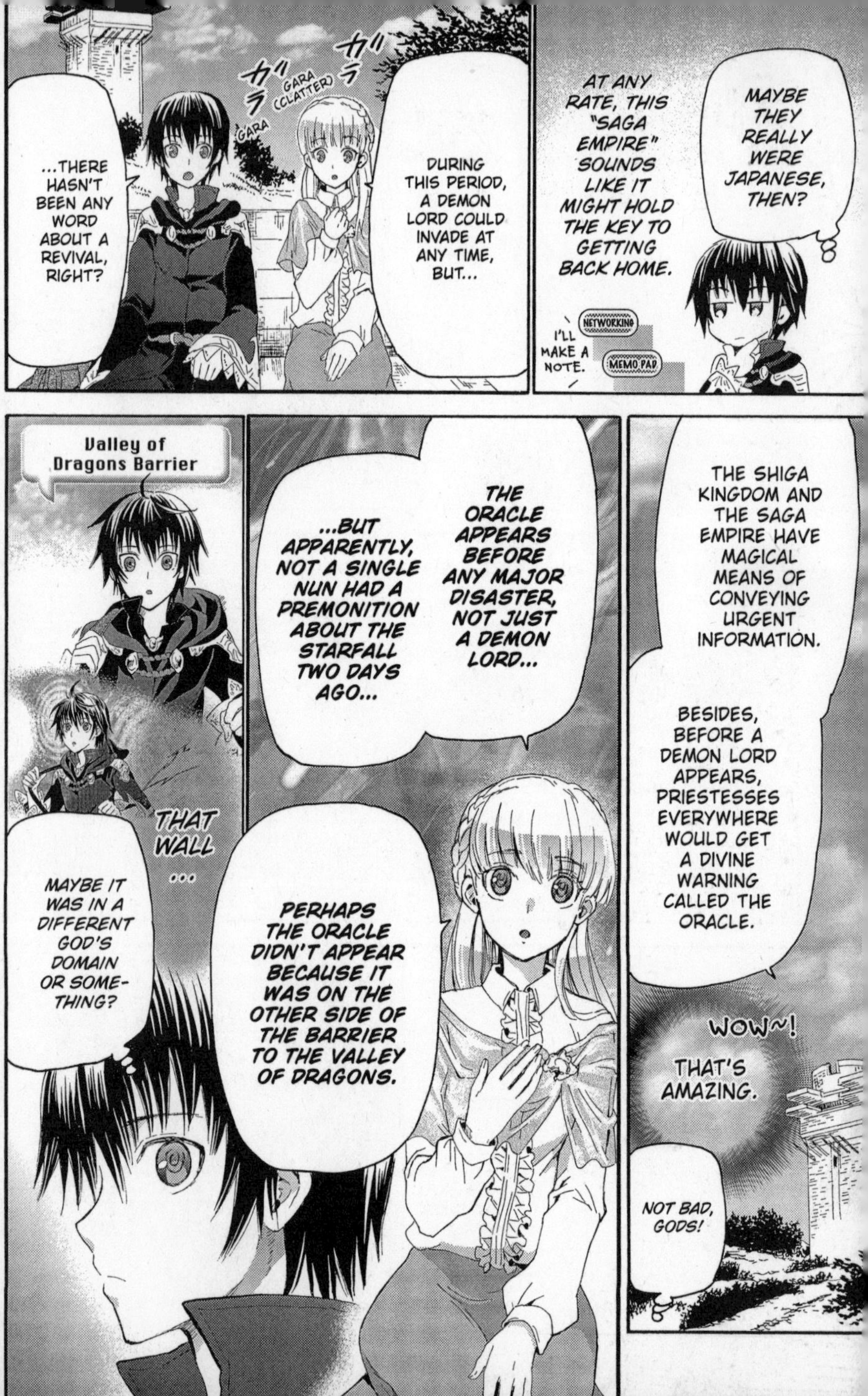
MAYBE THEY REALLY WERE JAPANESE, THEN?
AT ANY RATE, THIS "SAGA EMPIRE" SOUNDS LIKE IT MIGHT HOLD THE KEY TO GETTING BACK HOME.
NETWORKING
MEMO PAD
I'LL MAKE A NOTE.
ガラ
GARA (CLATTER)
ガラ
GARA
DURING THIS PERIOD, A DEMON LORD COULD INVADE AT ANY TIME, BUT...
...THERE HASN'T BEEN ANY WORD ABOUT A REVIVAL, RIGHT?
THE SHIGA KINGDOM AND THE SAGA EMPIRE HAVE MAGICAL MEANS OF CONVEYING URGENT INFORMATION.
BESIDES, BEFORE A DEMON LORD APPEARS, PRIESTESSES EVERYWHERE WOULD GET A DIVINE WARNING CALLED THE ORACLE.
WOW~! THAT'S AMAZING.
NOT BAD, GODS!
THE ORACLE APPEARS BEFORE ANY MAJOR DISASTER, NOT JUST A DEMON LORD...
...BUT APPARENTLY, NOT A SINGLE NUN HAD A PREMONITION ABOUT THE STARFALL TWO DAYS AGO...
PERHAPS THE ORACLE DIDN'T APPEAR BECAUSE IT WAS ON THE OTHER SIDE OF THE BARRIER TO THE VALLEY OF DRAGONS.
Valley of Dragons Barrier
THAT WALL...
MAYBE IT WAS IN A DIFFERENT GOD'S DOMAIN OR SOMETHING?

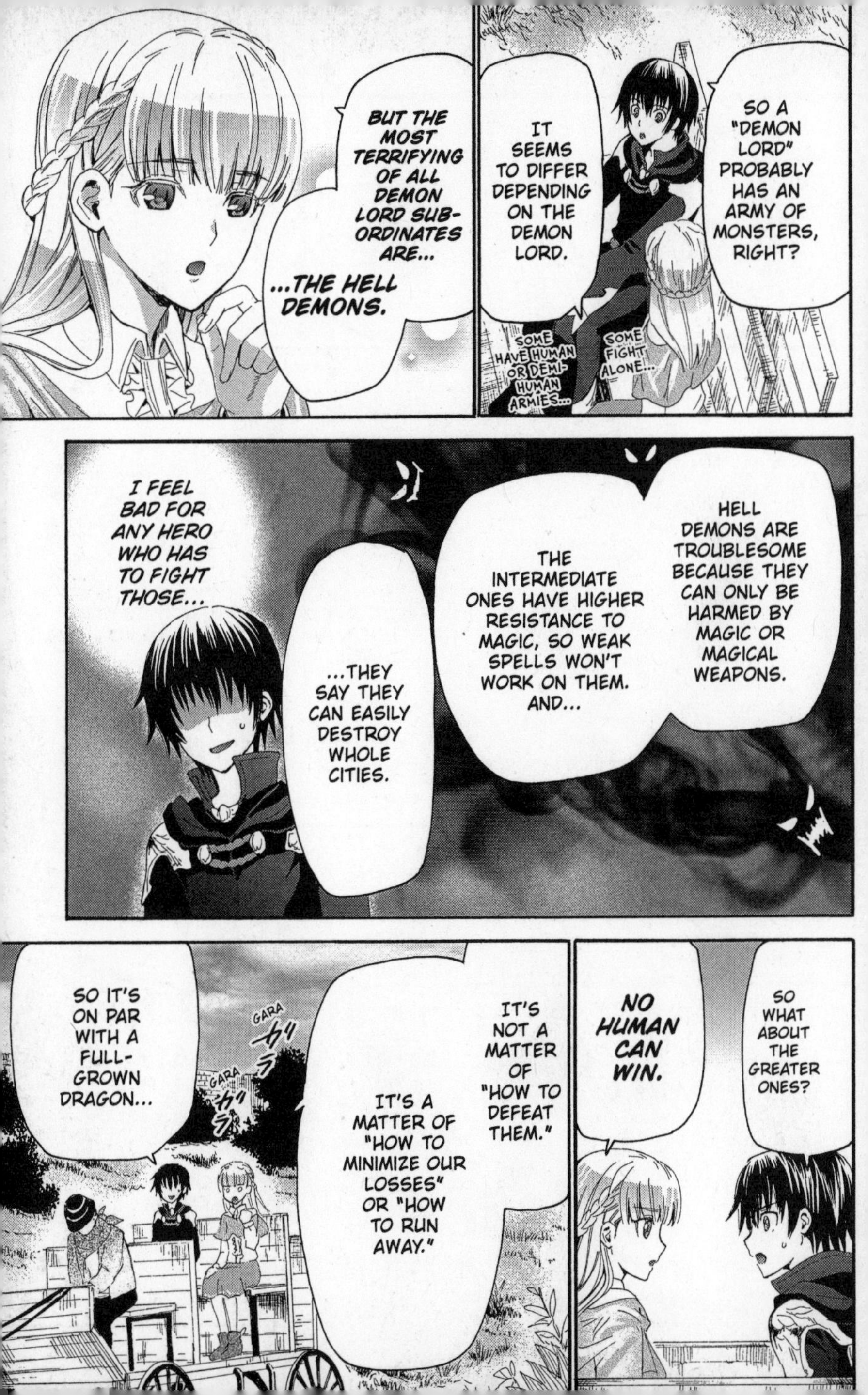

SO A "DEMON LORD" PROBABLY HAS AN ARMY OF MONSTERS, RIGHT?
IT SEEMS TO DIFFER DEPENDING ON THE DEMON LORD.
SOME FIGHT ALONE...
SOME HAVE HUMAN OR DEMI-HUMAN ARMIES...
BUT THE MOST TERRIFYING OF ALL DEMON LORD SUB-ORDINATES ARE...
...THE HELL DEMONS.
HELL DEMONS ARE TROUBLESOME BECAUSE THEY CAN ONLY BE HARMED BY MAGIC OR MAGICAL WEAPONS.
THE INTERMEDIATE ONES HAVE HIGHER RESISTANCE TO MAGIC, SO WEAK SPELLS WON'T WORK ON THEM. AND...
...THEY SAY THEY CAN EASILY DESTROY WHOLE CITIES.
I FEEL BAD FOR ANY HERO WHO HAS TO FIGHT THOSE...
SO WHAT ABOUT THE GREATER ONES?
NO HUMAN CAN WIN.
IT'S NOT A MATTER OF "HOW TO DEFEAT THEM."
IT'S A MATTER OF "HOW TO MINIMIZE OUR LOSSES" OR "HOW TO RUN AWAY."
GARA ガラ
GARA ガラ
SO IT'S ON PAR WITH A FULL-GROWN DRAGON...

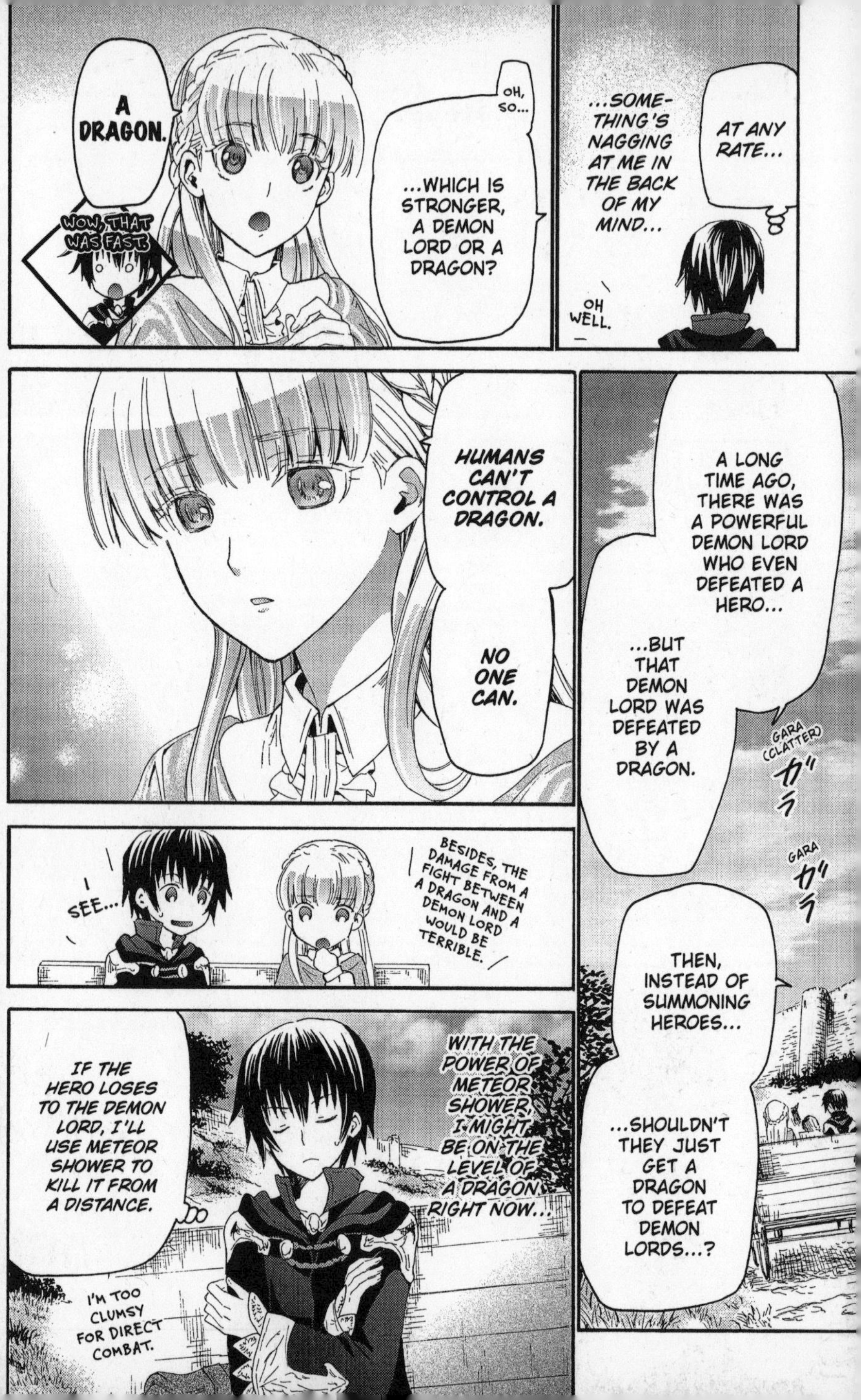
AT ANY RATE...
...SOMETHING'S NAGGING AT ME IN THE BACK OF MY MIND...
OH WELL.
OH, SO...
...WHICH IS STRONGER, A DEMON LORD OR A DRAGON?
A DRAGON.
WOW, THAT WAS FAST.
A LONG TIME AGO, THERE WAS A POWERFUL DEMON LORD WHO EVEN DEFEATED A HERO...
...BUT THAT DEMON LORD WAS DEFEATED BY A DRAGON.
GARA (CLATTER)
GARA
THEN, INSTEAD OF SUMMONING HEROES...
...SHOULDN'T THEY JUST GET A DRAGON TO DEFEAT DEMON LORDS...?
HUMANS CAN'T CONTROL A DRAGON.
NO ONE CAN.
BESIDES, THE DAMAGE FROM A FIGHT BETWEEN A DRAGON AND A DEMON LORD WOULD BE TERRIBLE.
I SEE...
WITH THE POWER OF METEOR SHOWER, I MIGHT BE ON THE LEVEL OF A DRAGON RIGHT NOW...
IF THE HERO LOSES TO THE DEMON LORD, I'LL USE METEOR SHOWER TO KILL IT FROM A DISTANCE.
I'M TOO CLUMSY FOR DIRECT COMBAT.

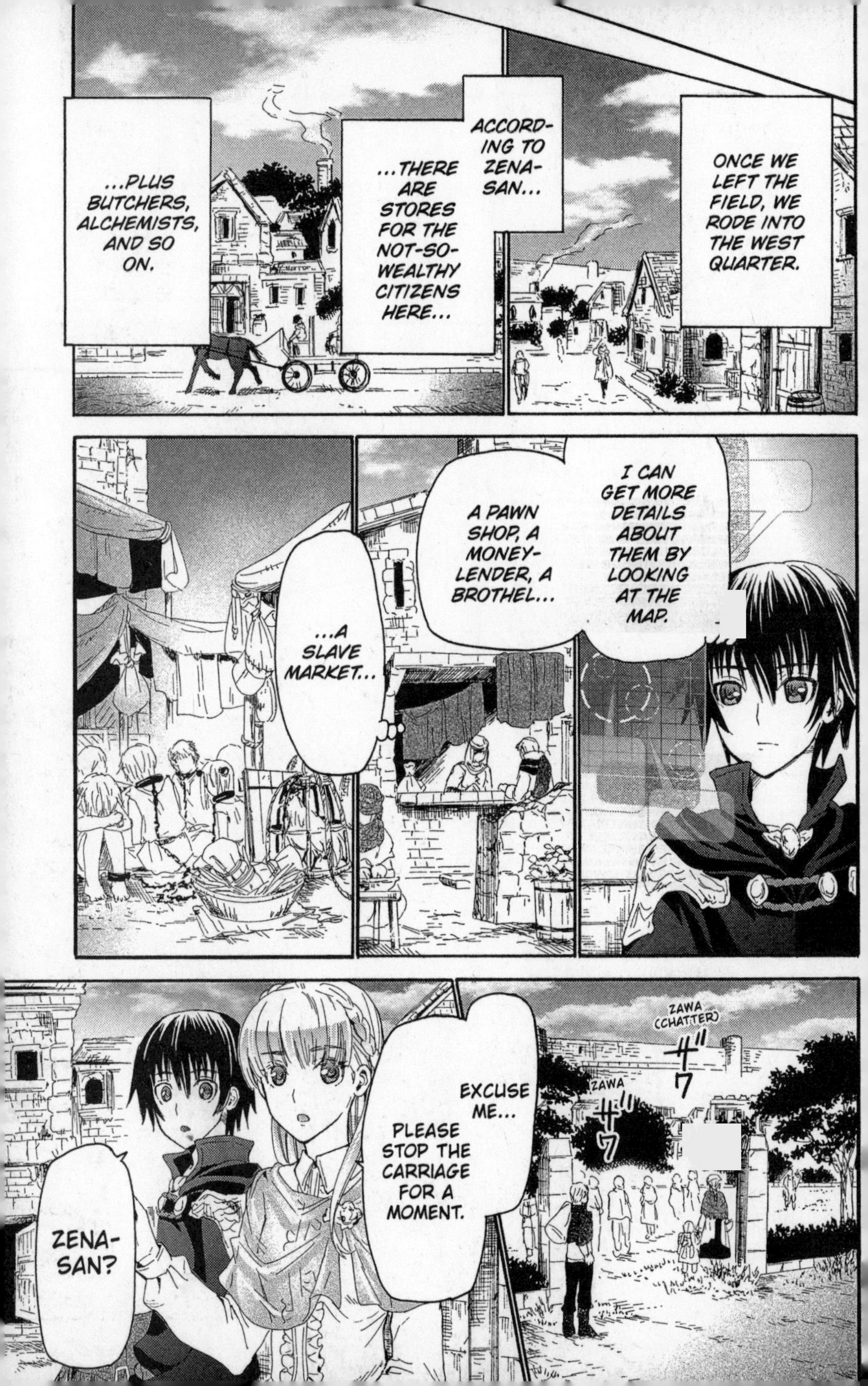
ONCE WE LEFT THE FIELD, WE RODE INTO THE WEST QUARTER.
ACCORDING TO ZENA-SAN...
...THERE ARE STORES FOR THE NOT-SO-WEALTHY CITIZENS HERE...
...PLUS BUTCHERS, ALCHEMISTS, AND SO ON.
I CAN GET MORE DETAILS ABOUT THEM BY LOOKING AT THE MAP.
A PAWN SHOP, A MONEY-LENDER, A BROTHEL...
...A SLAVE MARKET...
ZAWA (CHATTER)
ZAWA
EXCUSE ME...
PLEASE STOP THE CARRIAGE FOR A MOMENT.
ZENA-SAN?

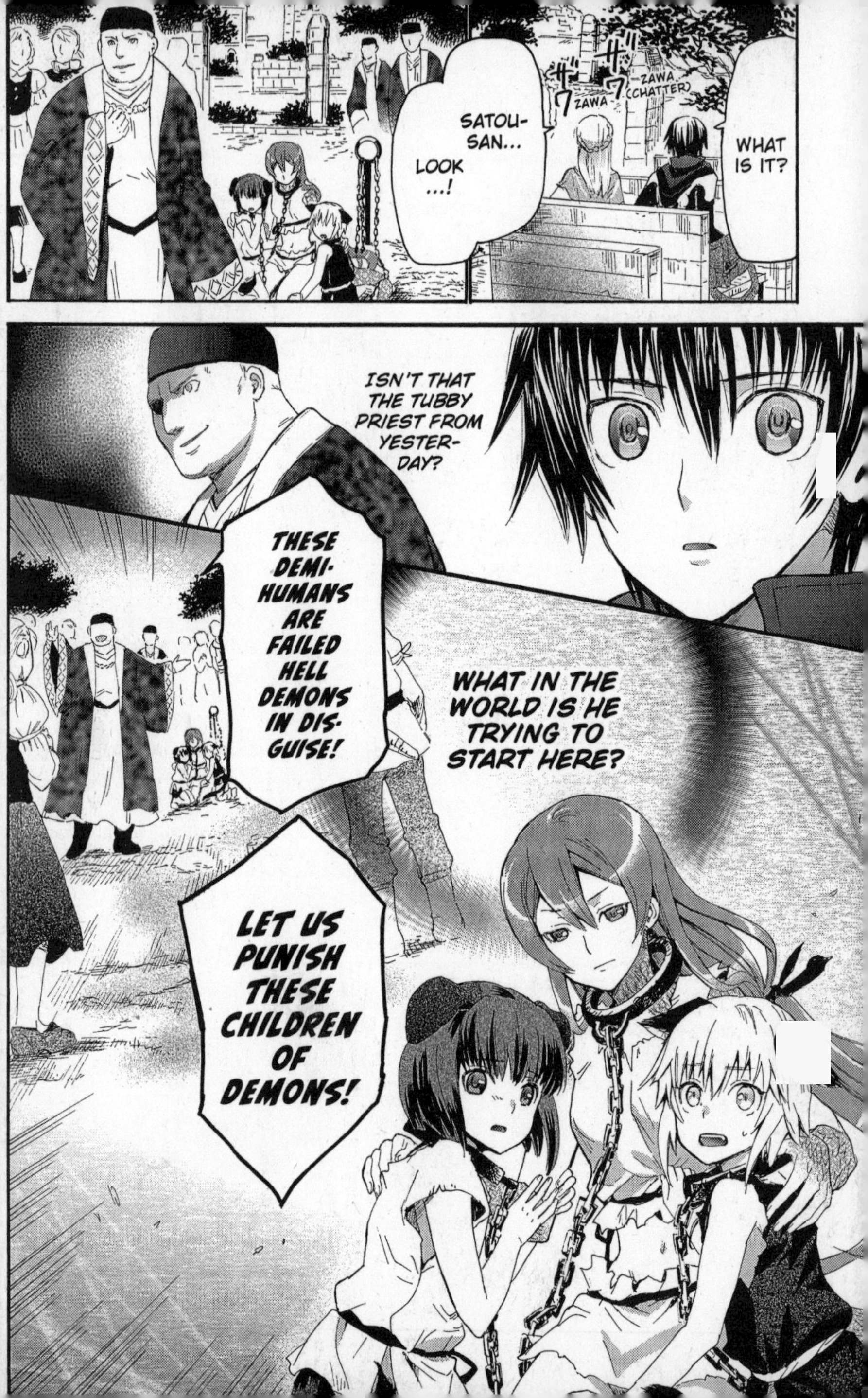

ZAWA ZAWA (CHATTER)
SATOU-SAN... LOOK ...!
WHAT IS IT?
ISN'T THAT THE TUBBY PRIEST FROM YESTERDAY?
THESE DEMI-HUMANS ARE FAILED HELL DEMONS IN DISGUISE!
WHAT IN THE WORLD IS HE TRYING TO START HERE?
LET US PUNISH THESE CHILDREN OF DEMONS!

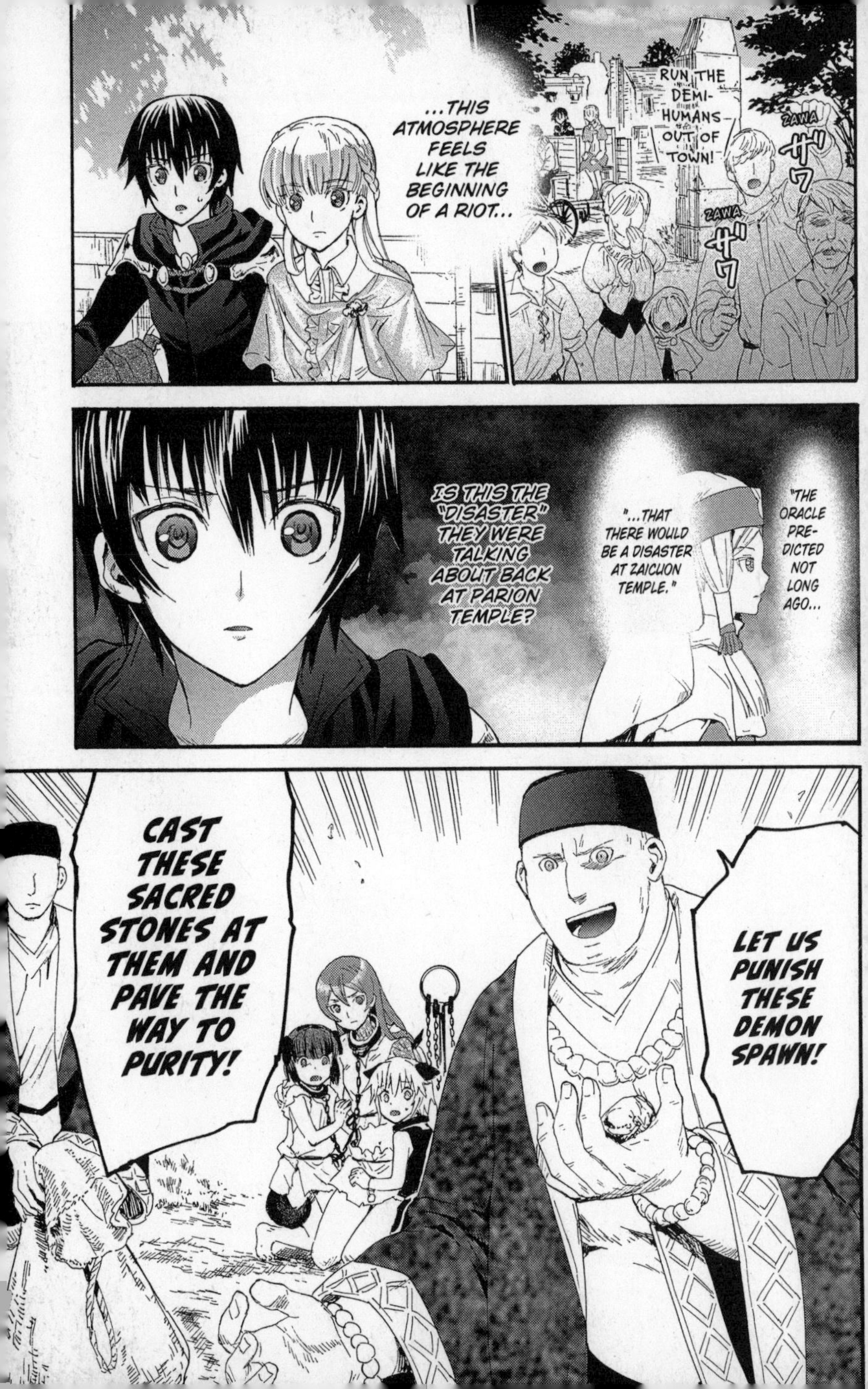
RUN THE DEMI-HUMANS OUT OF TOWN!
ZAWA ザワ
ZAWA ザワ
...THIS ATMOSPHERE FEELS LIKE THE BEGINNING OF A RIOT...
"THE ORACLE PREDICTED NOT LONG AGO...
"...THAT THERE WOULD BE A DISASTER AT ZAICUON TEMPLE."
IS THIS THE "DISASTER" THEY WERE TALKING ABOUT BACK AT PARION TEMPLE?
LET US PUNISH THESE DEMON SPAWN!
CAST THESE SACRED STONES AT THEM AND PAVE THE WAY TO PURITY!

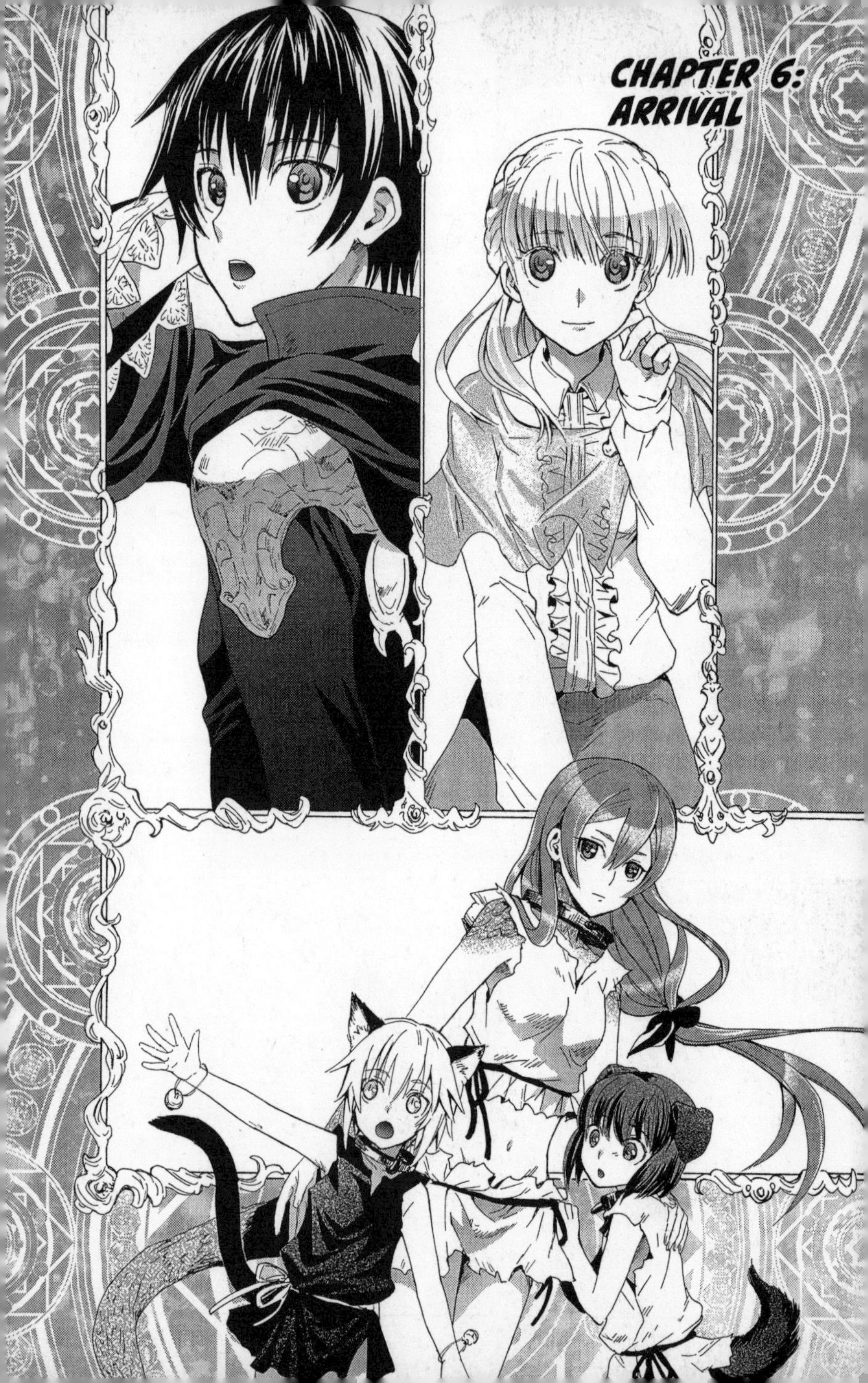
CHAPTER 6:
ARRIVAL

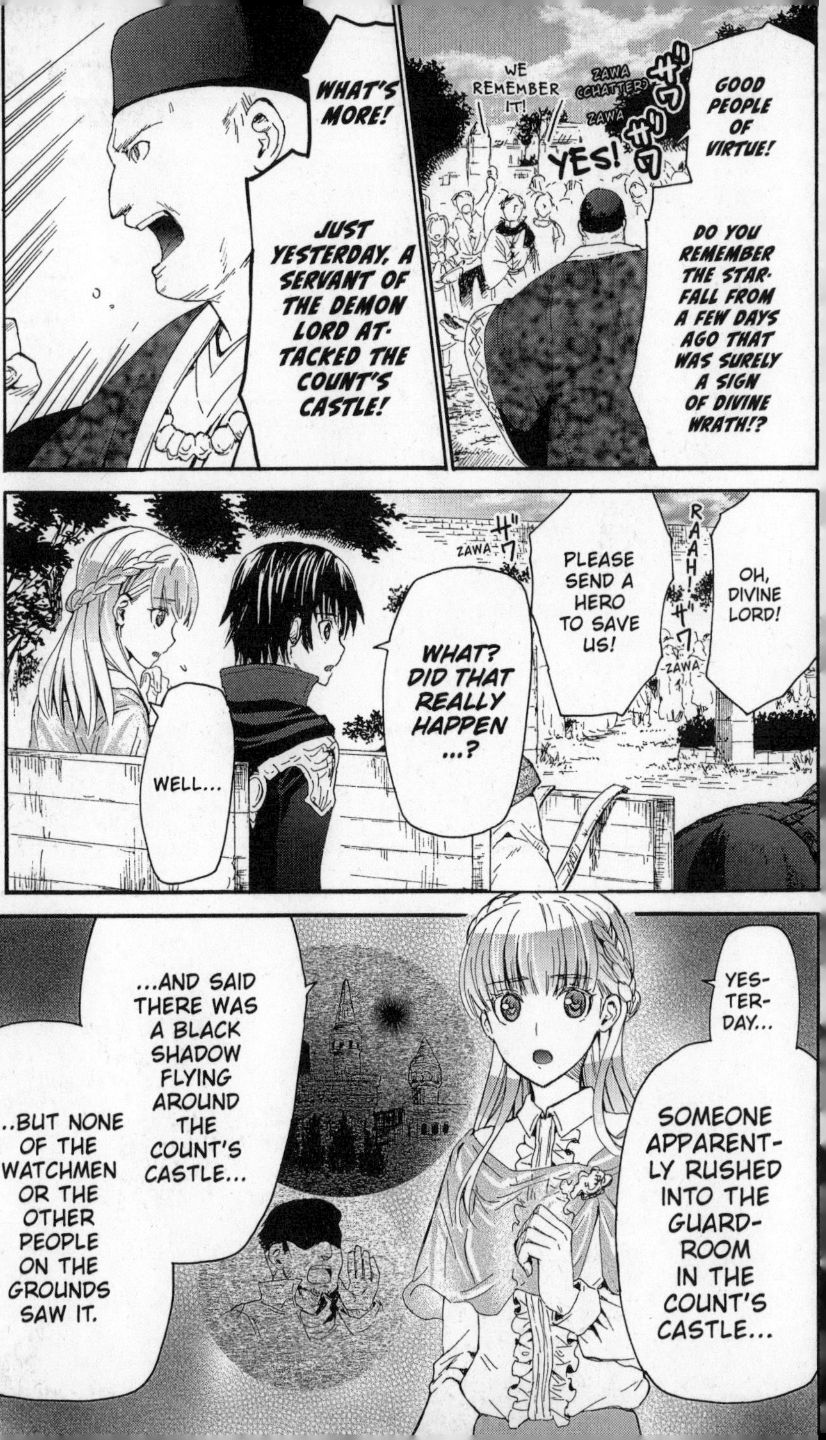
GOOD PEOPLE OF VIRTUE!
DO YOU REMEMBER THE STAR-FALL FROM A FEW DAYS AGO THAT WAS SURELY A SIGN OF DIVINE WRATH!?
ZAWA (CHATTER)
ZAWA
YES!
WE REMEMBER IT!
WHAT'S MORE!
JUST YESTERDAY, A SERVANT OF THE DEMON LORD ATTACKED THE COUNT'S CASTLE!
OH, DIVINE LORD!
RAAAH!
ZAWA
PLEASE SEND A HERO TO SAVE US!
ZAWA
WHAT? DID THAT REALLY HAPPEN...?
WELL...
YESTERDAY...
SOMEONE APPARENTLY RUSHED INTO THE GUARDROOM IN THE COUNT'S CASTLE...
...AND SAID THERE WAS A BLACK SHADOW FLYING AROUND THE COUNT'S CASTLE...
...BUT NONE OF THE WATCHMEN OR THE OTHER PEOPLE ON THE GROUNDS SAW IT.

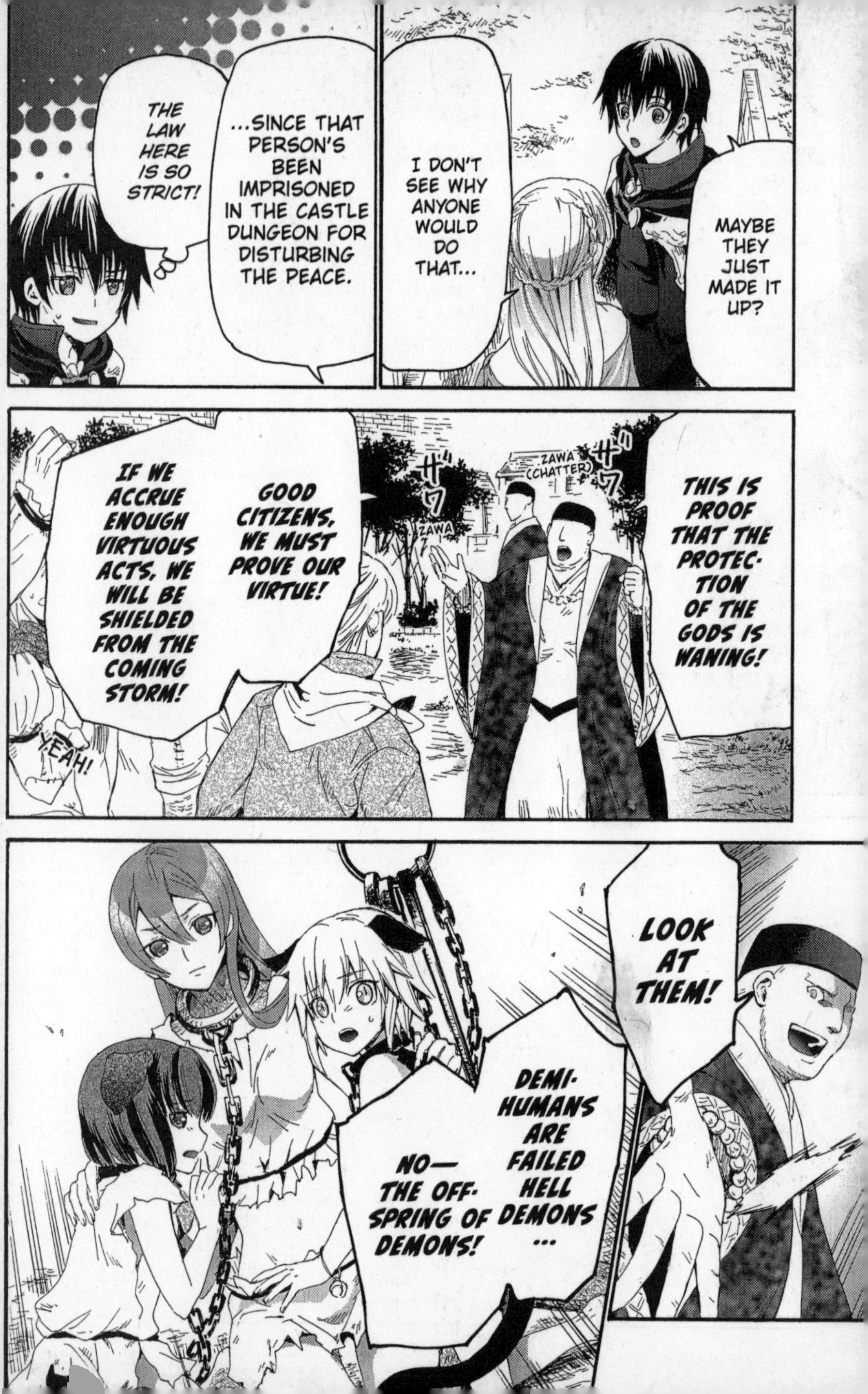
MAYBE THEY JUST MADE IT UP?
I DON'T SEE WHY ANYONE WOULD DO THAT...
...SINCE THAT PERSON'S BEEN IMPRISONED IN THE CASTLE DUNGEON FOR DISTURBING THE PEACE.
THE LAW HERE IS SO STRICT!
THIS IS PROOF THAT THE PROTECTION OF THE GODS IS WANING!
ZAWA (CHATTER)
ZAWA
GOOD CITIZENS, WE MUST PROVE OUR VIRTUE!
IF WE ACCRUE ENOUGH VIRTUOUS ACTS, WE WILL BE SHIELDED FROM THE COMING STORM!
YEAH!
LOOK AT THEM!
DEMI-HUMANS ARE FAILED HELL DEMONS...
NO— THE OFF-SPRING OF DEMONS!

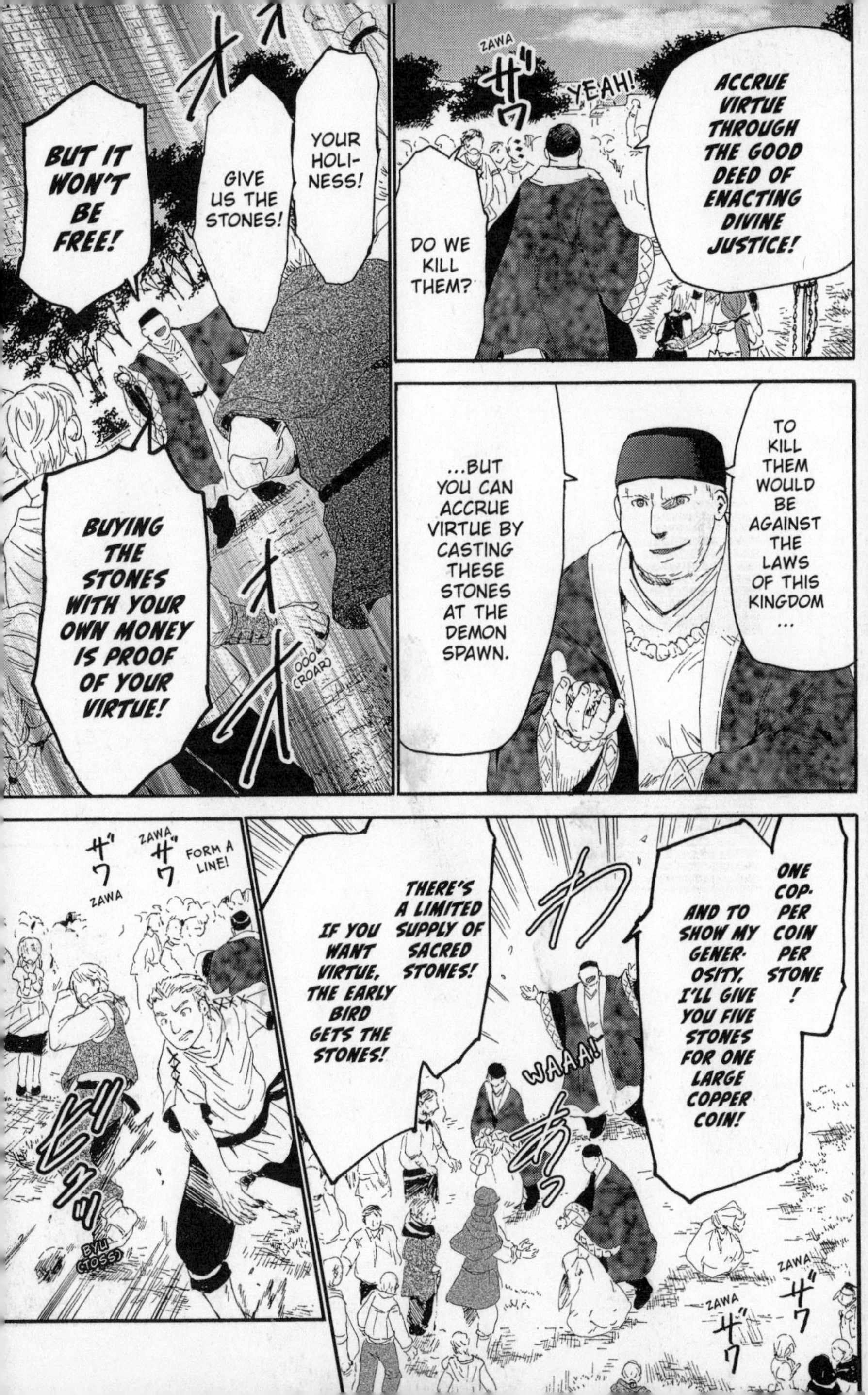
ZAWA
YEAH!
ACCRUE VIRTUE THROUGH THE GOOD DEED OF ENACTING DIVINE JUSTICE!
DO WE KILL THEM?
TO KILL THEM WOULD BE AGAINST THE LAWS OF THIS KINGDOM ...
...BUT YOU CAN ACCRUE VIRTUE BY CASTING THESE STONES AT THE DEMON SPAWN.
YOUR HOLINESS!
GIVE US THE STONES!
BUT IT WON'T BE FREE!
BUYING THE STONES WITH YOUR OWN MONEY IS PROOF OF YOUR VIRTUE!
OOO (ROAR)
ONE COPPER COIN PER STONE!
AND TO SHOW MY GENEROSITY, I'LL GIVE YOU FIVE STONES FOR ONE LARGE COPPER COIN!
THERE'S A LIMITED SUPPLY OF SACRED STONES!
IF YOU WANT VIRTUE, THE EARLY BIRD GETS THE STONES!
WAAAA!
ZAWA
ZAWA
ZAWA
FORM A LINE!
ZAWA
BYU (TOSS)

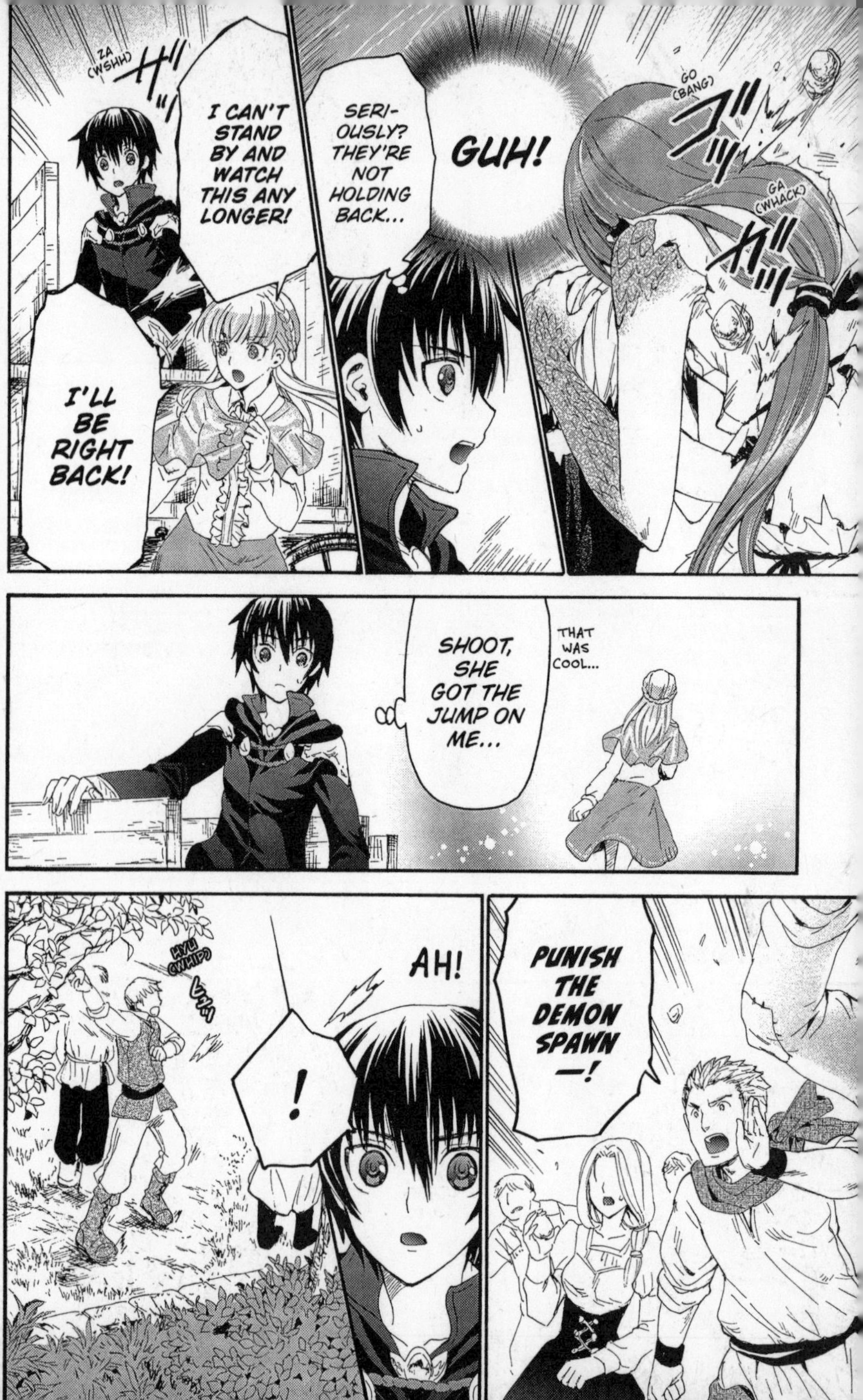
GO (BANG)
GA (WHACK)
GUH!
SERI-OUSLY? THEY'RE NOT HOLDING BACK...
I CAN'T STAND BY AND WATCH THIS ANY LONGER!
ZA (WSHH)
I'LL BE RIGHT BACK!
THAT WAS COOL...
SHOOT, SHE GOT THE JUMP ON ME...
PUNISH THE DEMON SPAWN—!
AH!
!
HYU (WHIP)

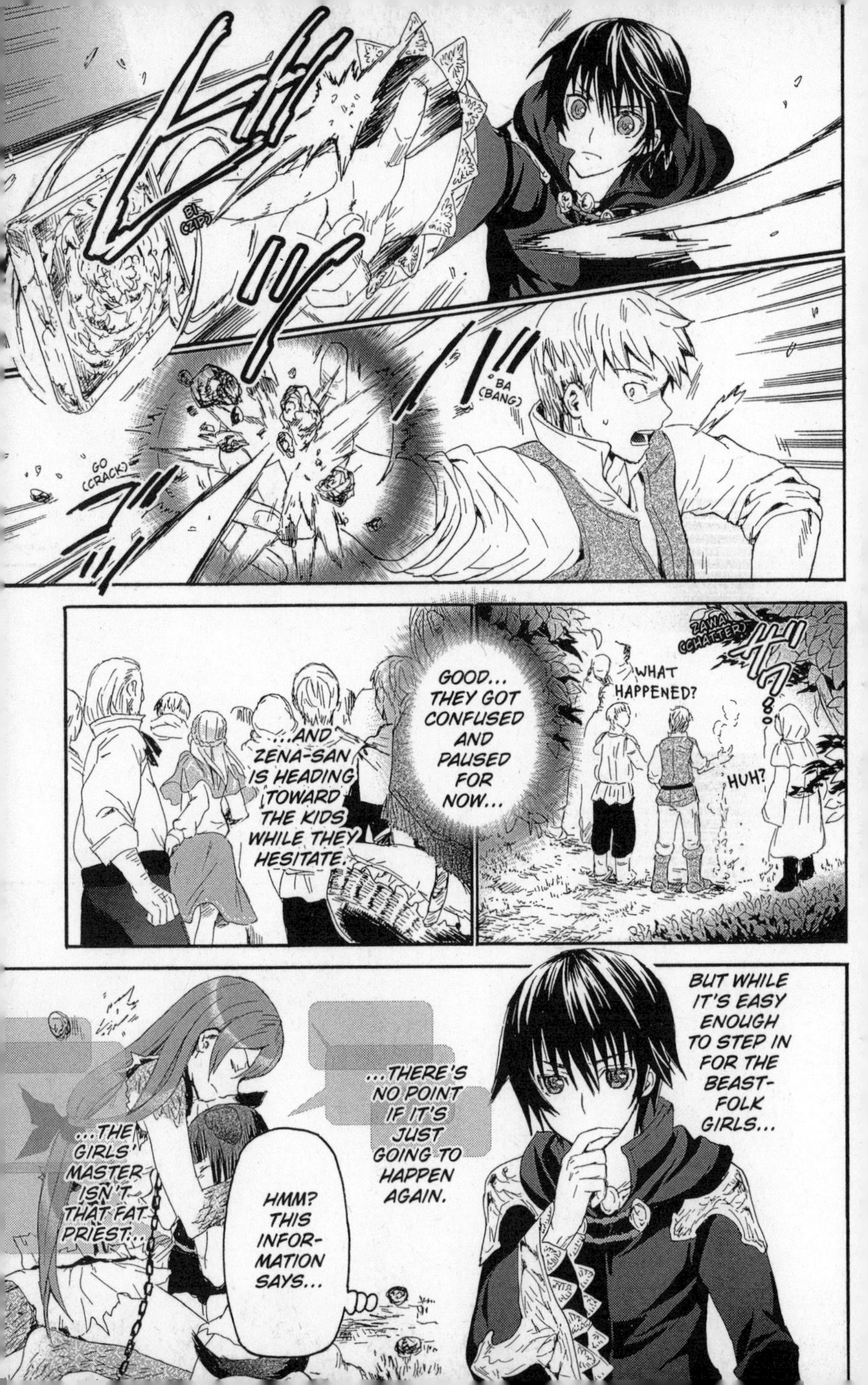
BI (ZAP)
BA (BANG)
GO (CRACK)
ZAWA (CHATTER)
WHAT HAPPENED?
HUH?
GOOD... THEY GOT CONFUSED AND PAUSED FOR NOW...
...AND ZENA-SAN IS HEADING TOWARD THE KIDS WHILE THEY HESITATE.
BUT WHILE IT'S EASY ENOUGH TO STEP IN FOR THE BEAST-FOLK GIRLS...
...THERE'S NO POINT IF IT'S JUST GOING TO HAPPEN AGAIN.
HMM? THIS INFORMATION SAYS...
...THE GIRLS' MASTER ISN'T THAT FAT PRIEST...

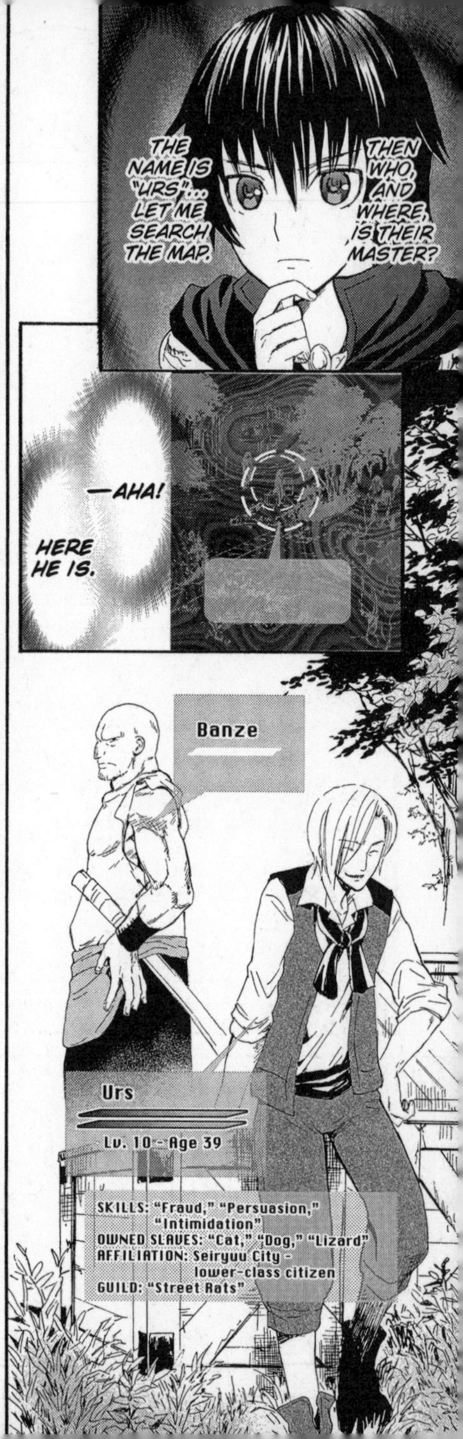
THEN WHO, AND WHERE, IS THEIR MASTER?
THE NAME IS "URS"... LET ME SEARCH THE MAP.
—AHA!
HERE HE IS.
Banze
Urs
Lv. 10 - Age 39
SKILLS: "Fraud," "Persuasion," "Intimidation"
OWNED SLAVES: "Cat," "Dog," "Lizard"
AFFILIATION: Seiryuu City - lower-class citizen
GUILD: "Street Rats"
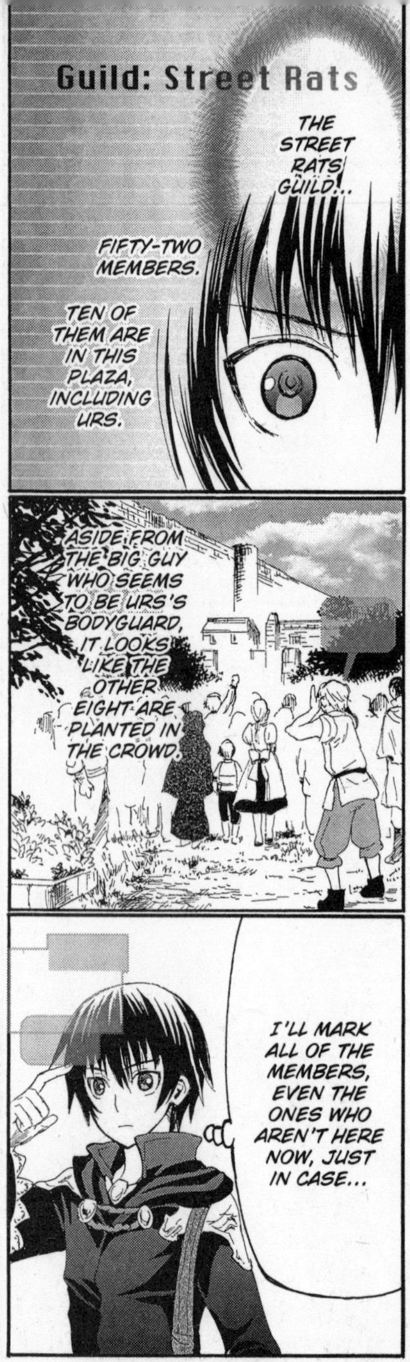
Guild: Street Rats
THE STREET RATS GUILD...
FIFTY-TWO MEMBERS.
TEN OF THEM ARE IN THIS PLAZA, INCLUDING URS.
ASIDE FROM THE BIG GUY WHO SEEMS TO BE URS'S BODYGUARD, IT LOOKS LIKE THE OTHER EIGHT ARE PLANTED IN THE CROWD.
I'LL MARK ALL OF THE MEMBERS, EVEN THE ONES WHO AREN'T HERE NOW, JUST IN CASE...

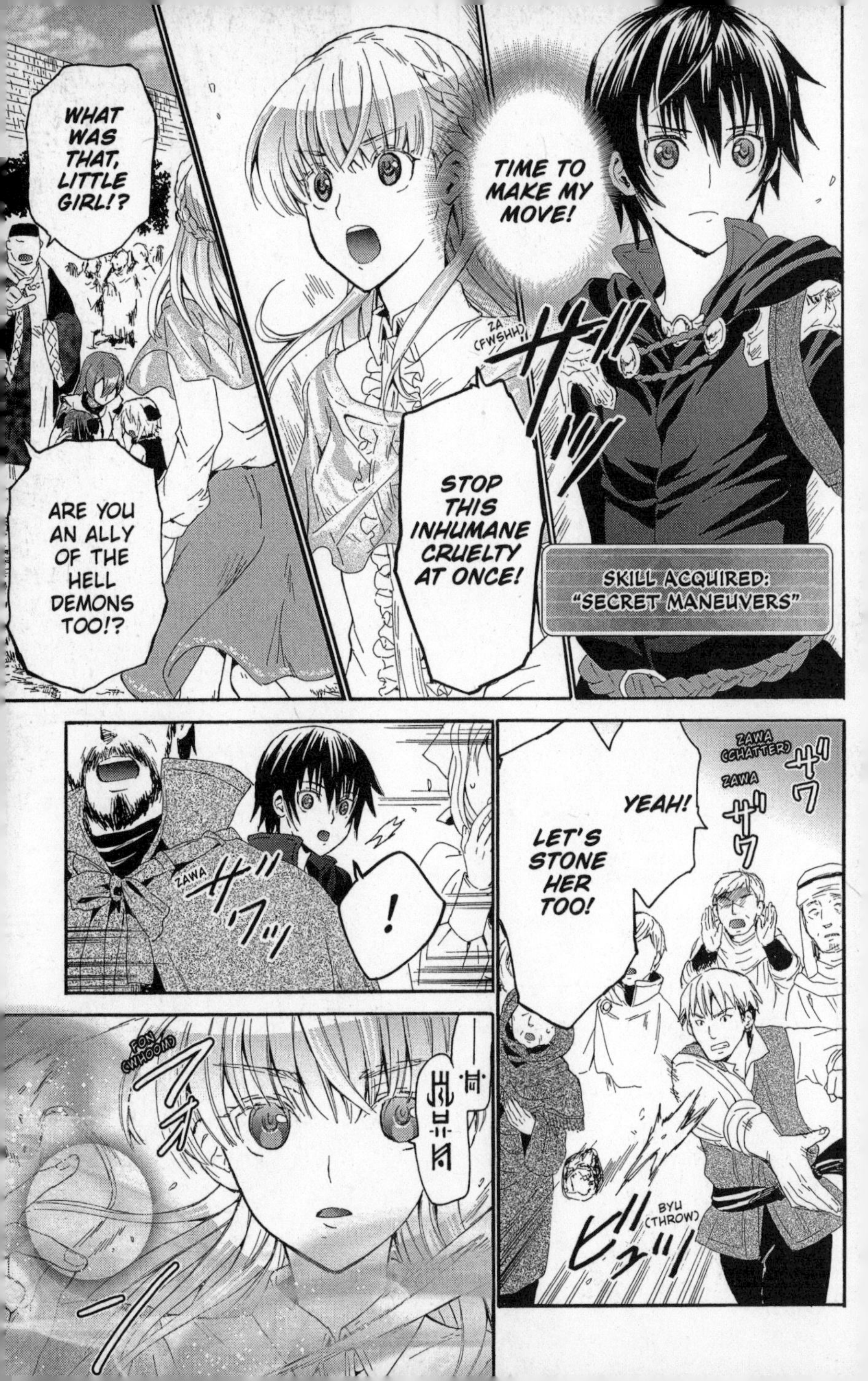

TIME TO MAKE MY MOVE!
ZA (FWSHH)
SKILL ACQUIRED: "SECRET MANEUVERS"
STOP THIS INHUMANE CRUELTY AT ONCE!
WHAT WAS THAT, LITTLE GIRL!?
ARE YOU AN ALLY OF THE HELL DEMONS TOO!?
ZAWA (CHATTER)
ZAWA
YEAH!
LET'S STONE HER TOO!
BYU (THROW)
ZAWA
!
PON (WHOOM)

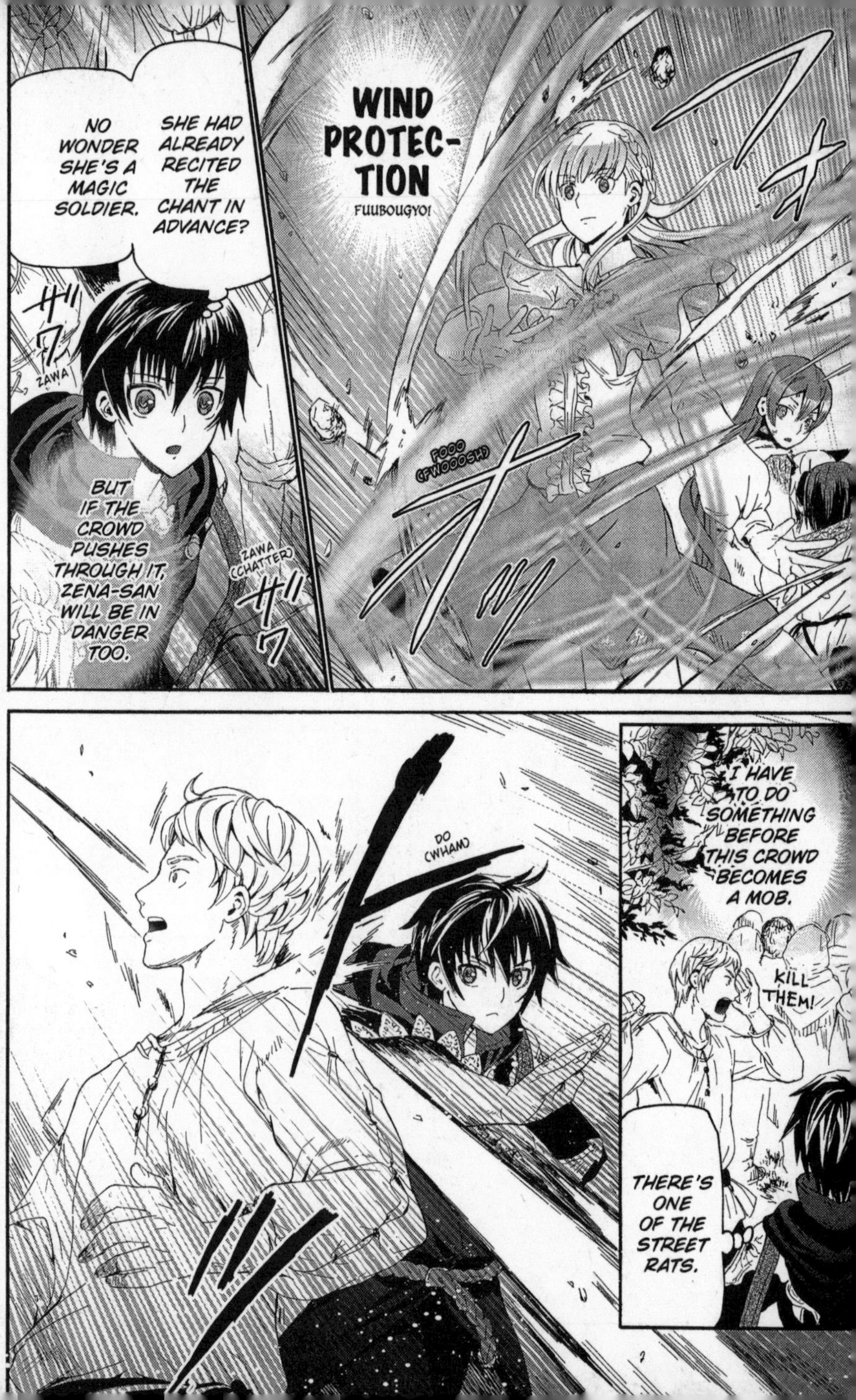
WIND PROTECTION
FUUBOUGYO!
FOOO (FWOOOSH)
SHE HAD ALREADY RECITED THE CHANT IN ADVANCE?
NO WONDER SHE'S A MAGIC SOLDIER.
ZAWA
BUT IF THE CROWD PUSHES THROUGH IT, ZENA-SAN WILL BE IN DANGER TOO.
ZAWA (CHATTER)
I HAVE TO DO SOMETHING BEFORE THIS CROWD BECOMES A MOB.
KILL THEM!
THERE'S ONE OF THE STREET RATS.
DO (WHAM)

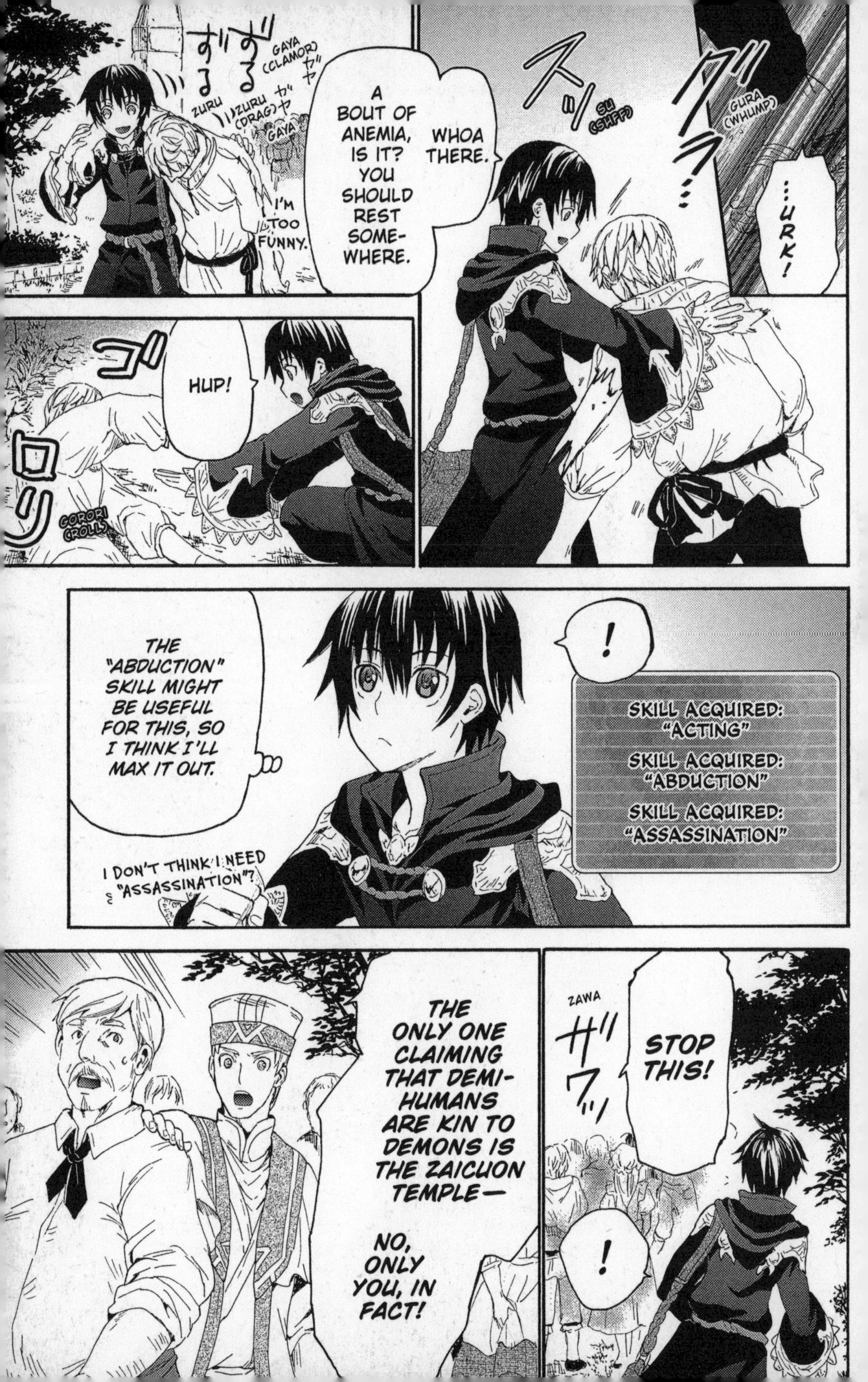
...URK!
GURA (WHUMP)
SU (SHFF)
WHOA THERE.
A BOUT OF ANEMIA, IS IT? YOU SHOULD REST SOME-WHERE.
GAYA (CLAMOR) ガヤ ガヤ GAYA
ZURU (DRAG) ずる ずる ZURU
I'M TOO FUNNY.
HUP!
GORORI (ROLL)
!
SKILL ACQUIRED: "ACTING"
SKILL ACQUIRED: "ABDUCTION"
SKILL ACQUIRED: "ASSASSINATION"
THE "ABDUCTION" SKILL MIGHT BE USEFUL FOR THIS, SO I THINK I'LL MAX IT OUT.
I DON'T THINK I NEED "ASSASSINATION"?
ZAWA
STOP THIS!
!
THE ONLY ONE CLAIMING THAT DEMI-HUMANS ARE KIN TO DEMONS IS THE ZAICUON TEMPLE—
NO, ONLY YOU, IN FACT!

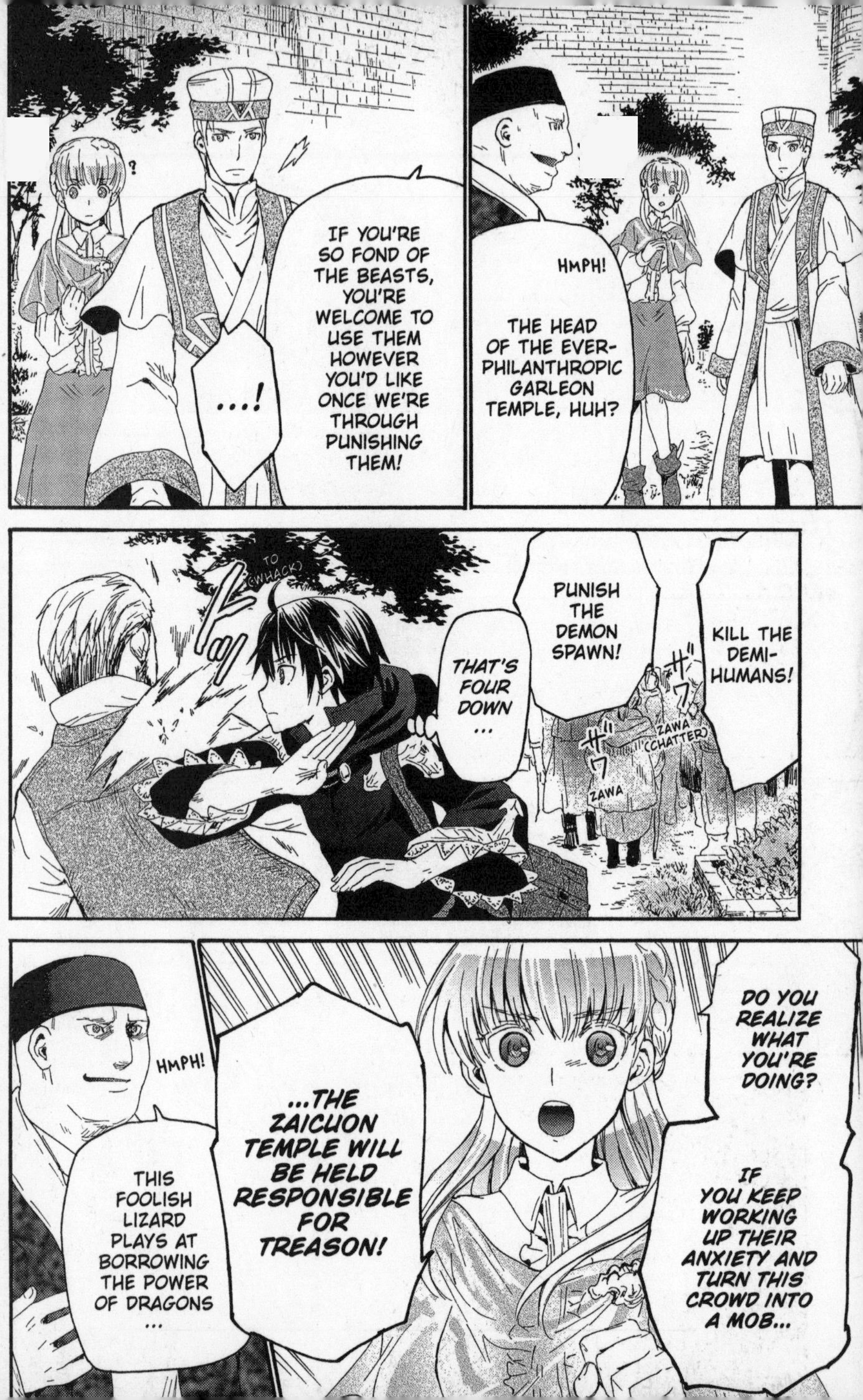
HMPH!
THE HEAD OF THE EVER-PHILANTHROPIC GARLEON TEMPLE, HUH?
IF YOU'RE SO FOND OF THE BEASTS, YOU'RE WELCOME TO USE THEM HOWEVER YOU'D LIKE ONCE WE'RE THROUGH PUNISHING THEM!
...!
KILL THE DEMI-HUMANS!
PUNISH THE DEMON SPAWN!
ZAWA (CHATTER)
ZAWA
THAT'S FOUR DOWN ...
TO (WHACK)
DO YOU REALIZE WHAT YOU'RE DOING?
IF YOU KEEP WORKING UP THEIR ANXIETY AND TURN THIS CROWD INTO A MOB...
...THE ZAICUON TEMPLE WILL BE HELD RESPONSIBLE FOR TREASON!
HMPH!
THIS FOOLISH LIZARD PLAYS AT BORROWING THE POWER OF DRAGONS ...

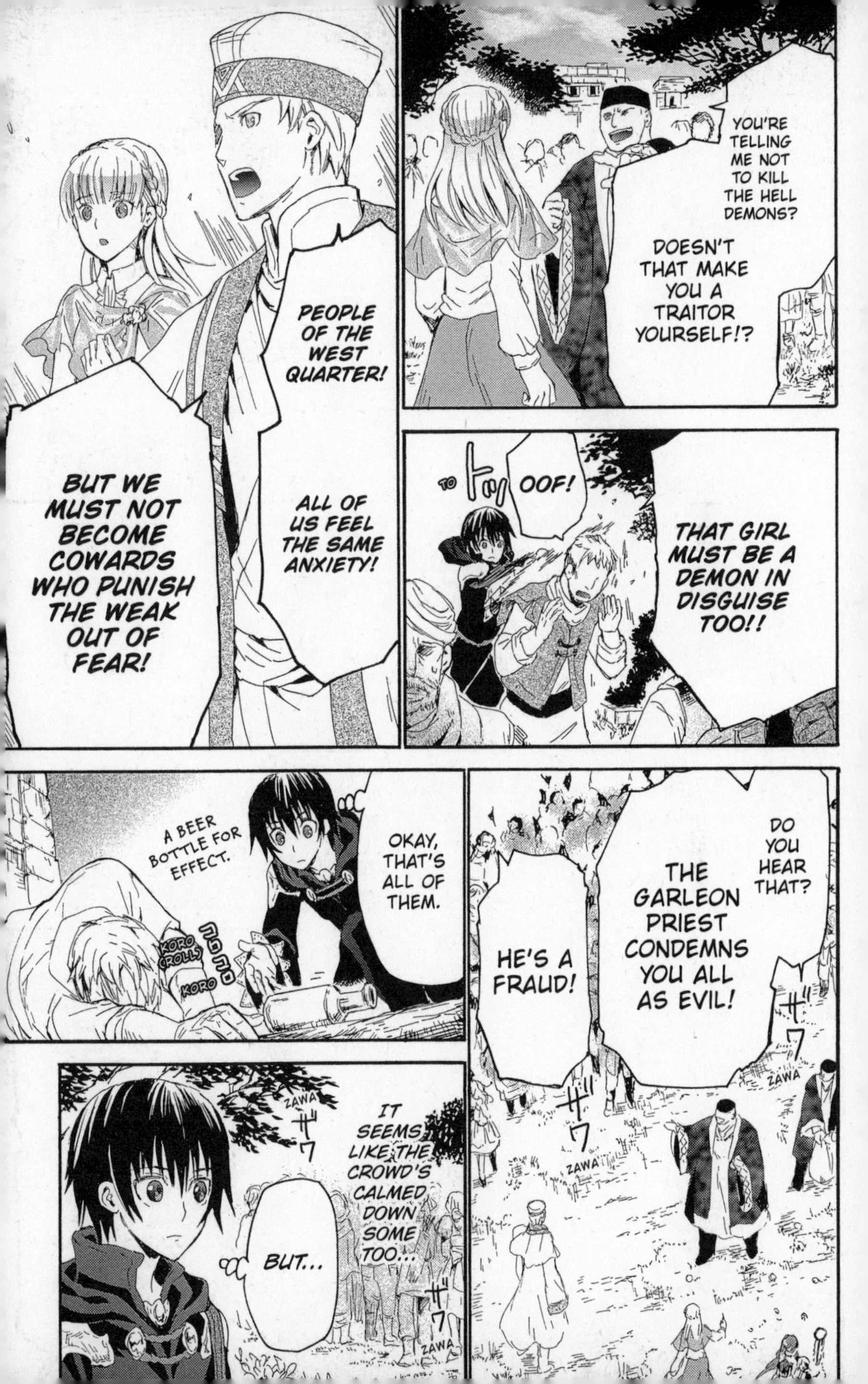
YOU'RE TELLING ME NOT TO KILL THE HELL DEMONS?
DOESN'T THAT MAKE YOU A TRAITOR YOURSELF!?
THAT GIRL MUST BE A DEMON IN DISGUISE TOO!!
OOF!
TO
PEOPLE OF THE WEST QUARTER!
ALL OF US FEEL THE SAME ANXIETY!
BUT WE MUST NOT BECOME COWARDS WHO PUNISH THE WEAK OUT OF FEAR!
DO YOU HEAR THAT?
THE GARLEON PRIEST CONDEMNS YOU ALL AS EVIL!
HE'S A FRAUD!
ZAWA
ZAWA
OKAY, THAT'S ALL OF THEM.
A BEER BOTTLE FOR EFFECT.
KORO (ROLL)
KORO
IT SEEMS LIKE THE CROWD'S CALMED DOWN SOME TOO...
BUT...
ZAWA
ZAWA

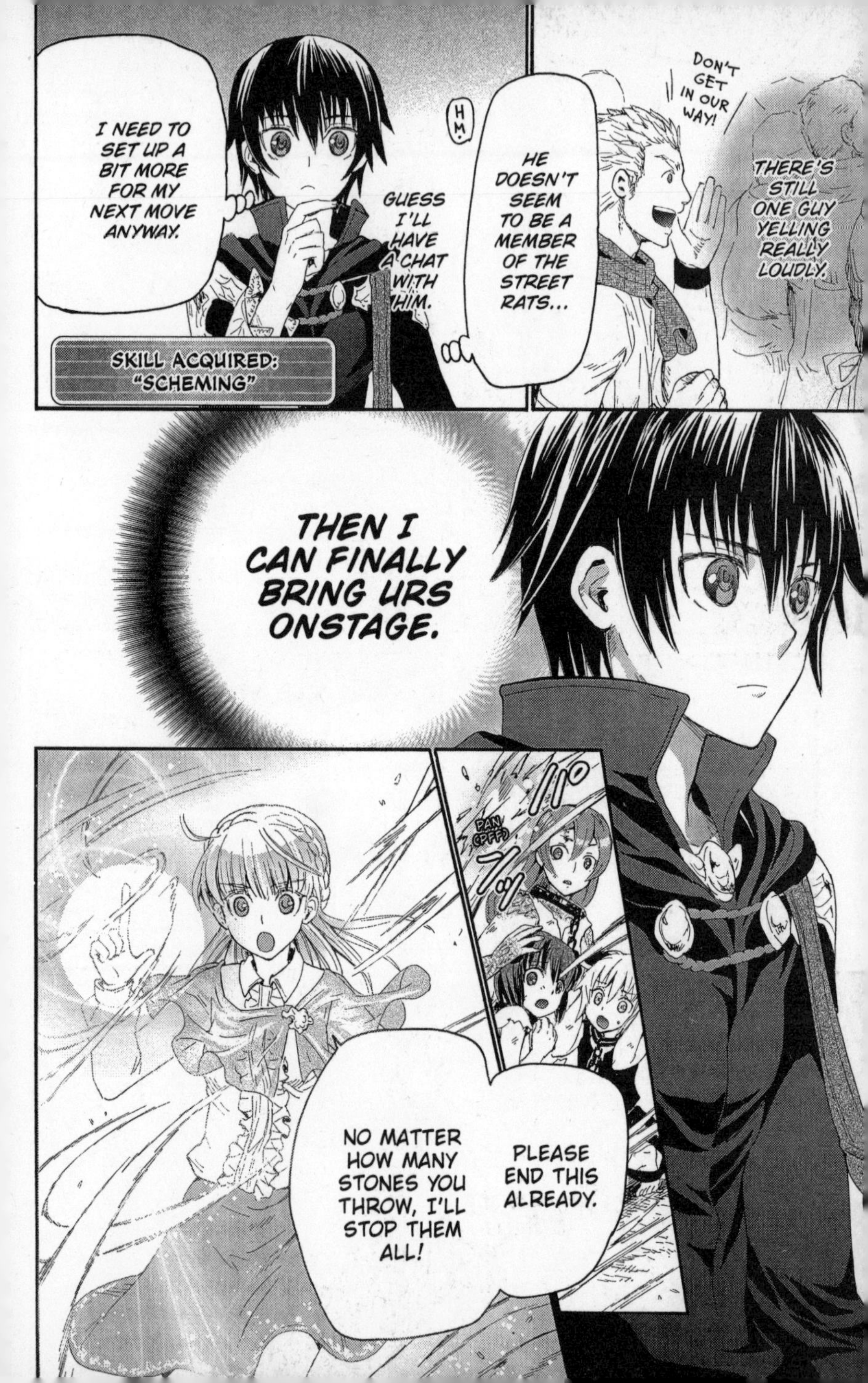
THERE'S STILL ONE GUY YELLING REALLY LOUDLY.
DON'T GET IN OUR WAY!
HE DOESN'T SEEM TO BE A MEMBER OF THE STREET RATS...
HM.
GUESS I'LL HAVE A CHAT WITH HIM.
I NEED TO SET UP A BIT MORE FOR MY NEXT MOVE ANYWAY.
SKILL ACQUIRED: "SCHEMING"
THEN I CAN FINALLY BRING URS ONSTAGE.
PAN (PFF)
PLEASE END THIS ALREADY.
NO MATTER HOW MANY STONES YOU THROW, I'LL STOP THEM ALL!

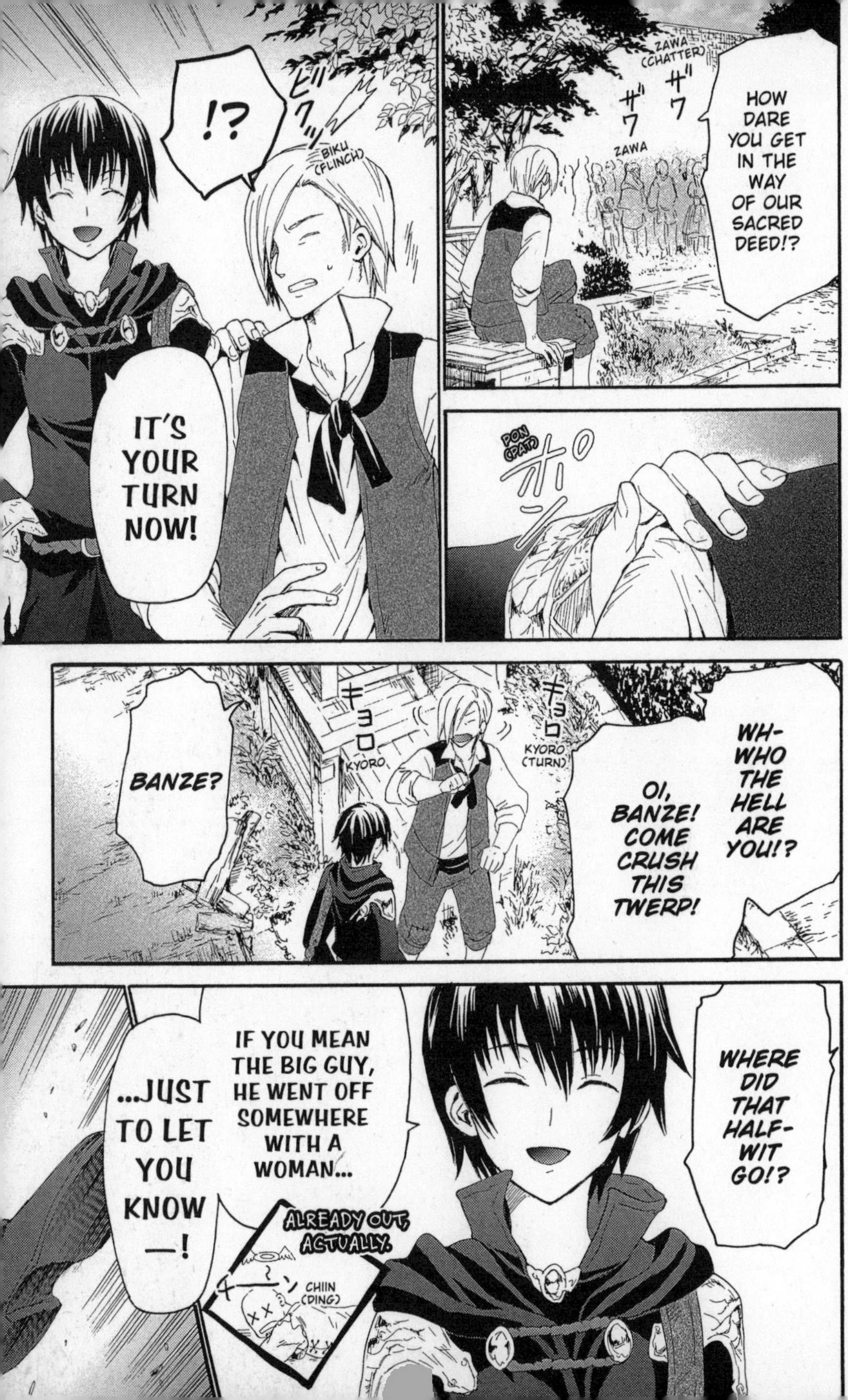

ZAWA (CHATTER)
ザワ
ザワ
ZAWA
HOW DARE YOU GET IN THE WAY OF OUR SACRED DEED!?
PON (PAT)
ポン
ビクッ
BIKU (FLINCH)
!?
IT'S YOUR TURN NOW!
WH- WHO THE HELL ARE YOU!?
OI, BANZE! COME CRUSH THIS TWERP!
キョロ
KYORO (TURN)
キョロ
KYORO
BANZE?
WHERE DID THAT HALF-WIT GO!?
IF YOU MEAN THE BIG GUY, HE WENT OFF SOMEWHERE WITH A WOMAN...
...JUST TO LET YOU KNOW—!
ALREADY OUT, ACTUALLY.
CHIIN (DING)

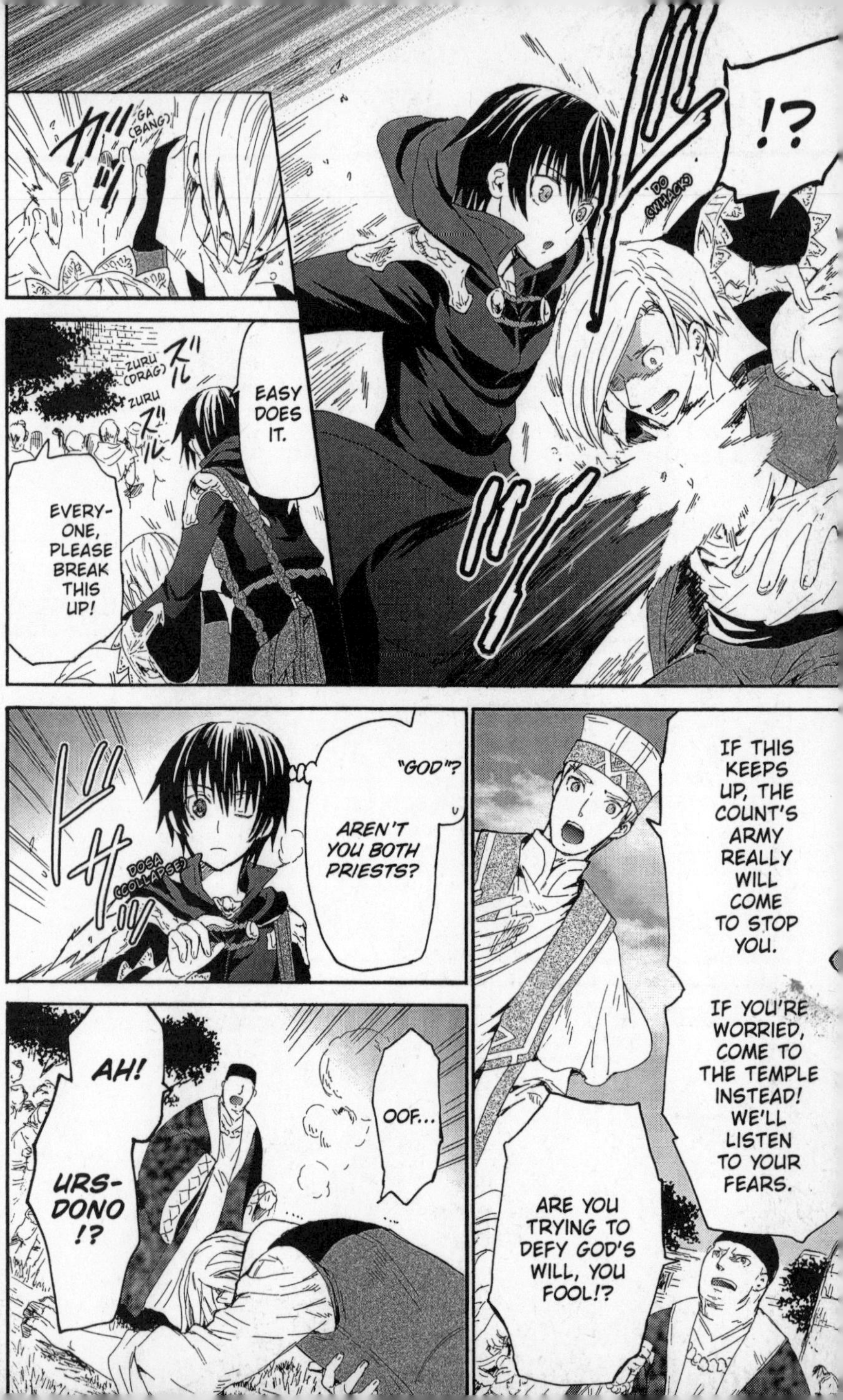
!?
DO (WHACK)
GA (BANG)
EASY DOES IT.
ZURU (DRAG)
ZURU
EVERY-ONE, PLEASE BREAK THIS UP!
IF THIS KEEPS UP, THE COUNT'S ARMY REALLY WILL COME TO STOP YOU.
IF YOU'RE WORRIED, COME TO THE TEMPLE INSTEAD! WE'LL LISTEN TO YOUR FEARS.
ARE YOU TRYING TO DEFY GOD'S WILL, YOU FOOL!?
"GOD"?
AREN'T YOU BOTH PRIESTS?
DOSA (COLLAPSE)
OOF...
...
...
AH!
URS-DONO!?

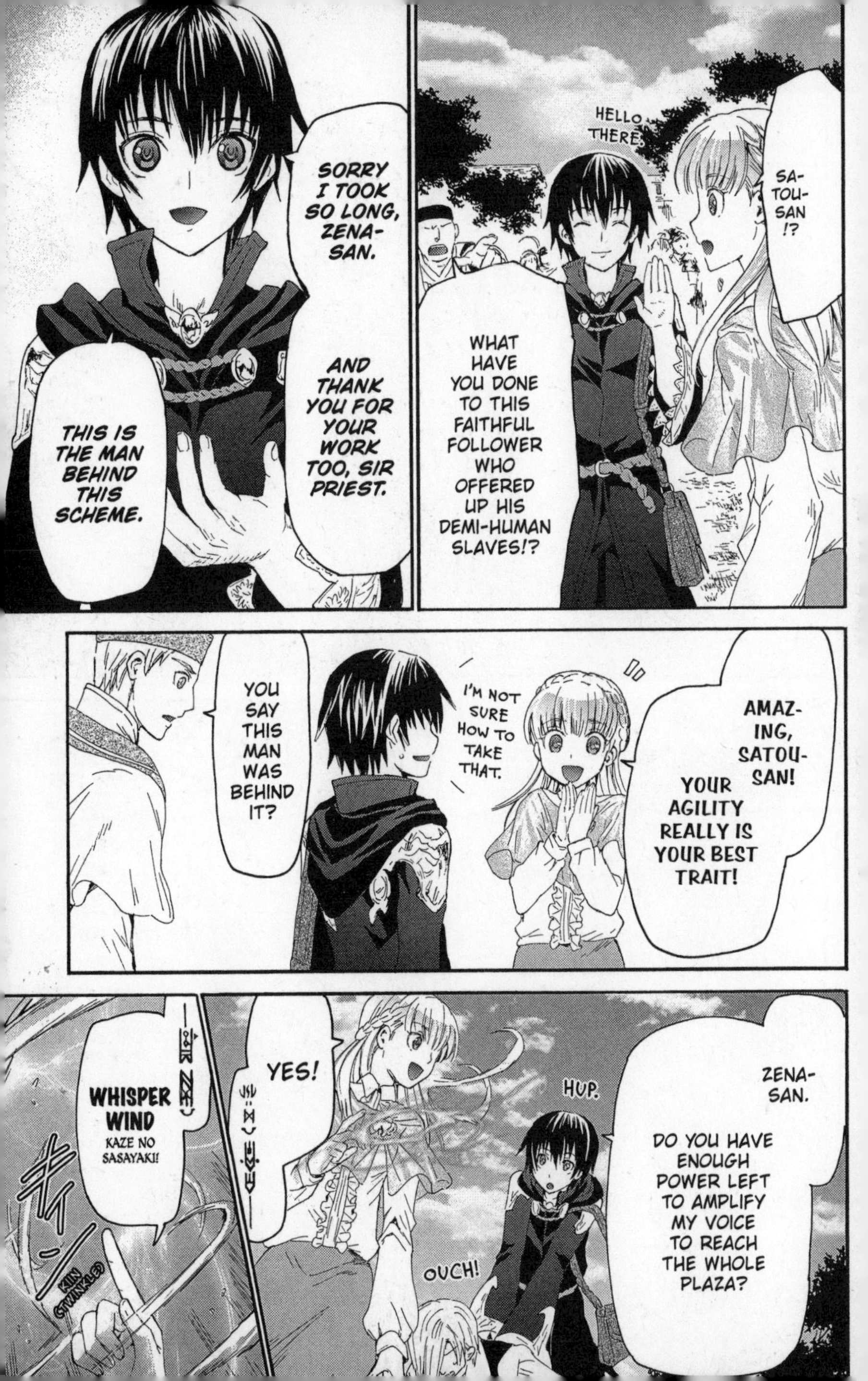
SA-TOU-SAN!?
HELLO THERE.
WHAT HAVE YOU DONE TO THIS FAITHFUL FOLLOWER WHO OFFERED UP HIS DEMI-HUMAN SLAVES!?
SORRY I TOOK SO LONG, ZENA-SAN.
AND THANK YOU FOR YOUR WORK TOO, SIR PRIEST.
THIS IS THE MAN BEHIND THIS SCHEME.
AMAZ-ING, SATOU-SAN!
YOUR AGILITY REALLY IS YOUR BEST TRAIT!
I'M NOT SURE HOW TO TAKE THAT.
YOU SAY THIS MAN WAS BEHIND IT?
ZENA-SAN.
DO YOU HAVE ENOUGH POWER LEFT TO AMPLIFY MY VOICE TO REACH THE WHOLE PLAZA?
HUP.
OUCH!
YES!
WHISPER WIND
KAZE NO SASAYAKI!
KIIN (TWINKLE)

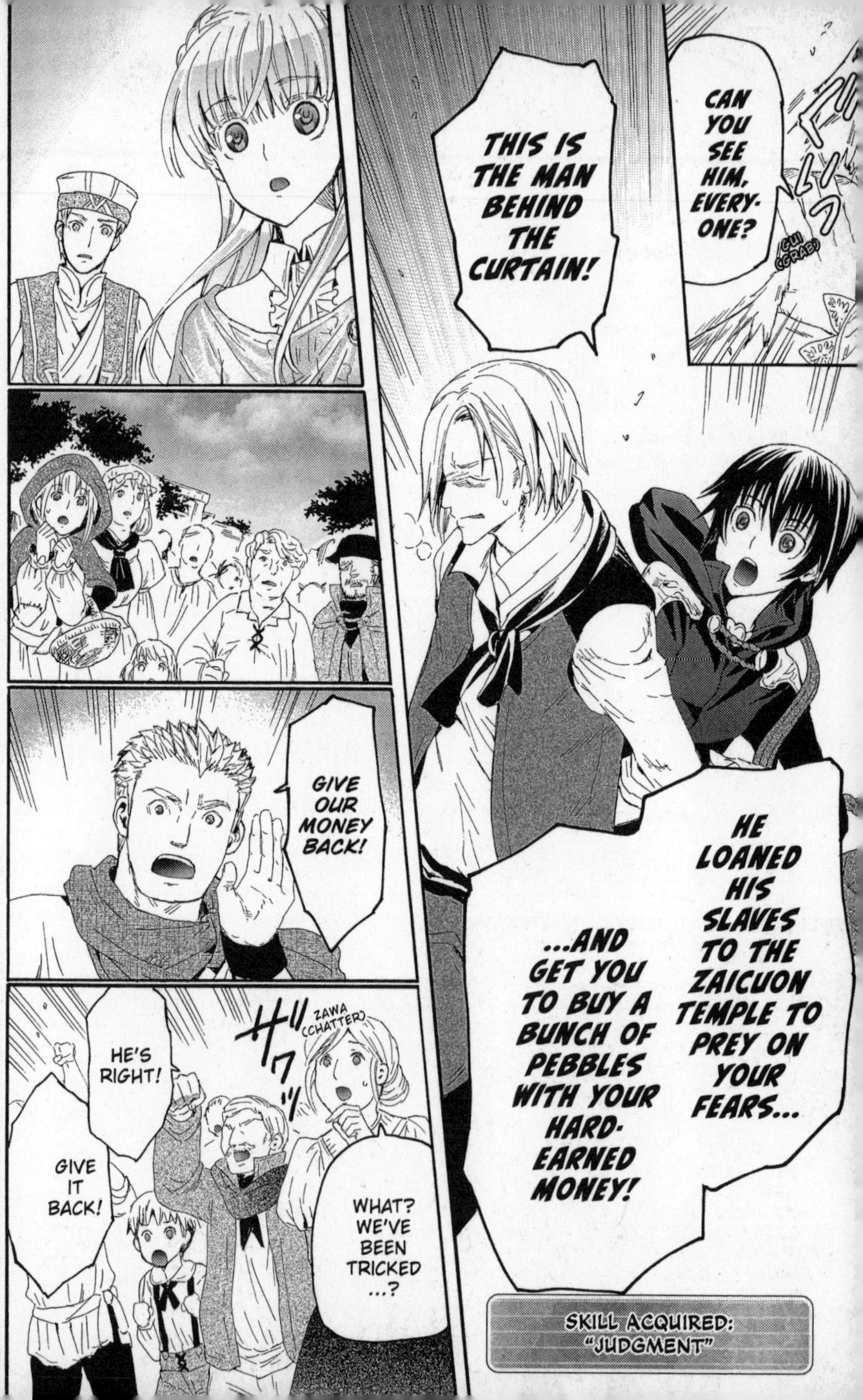
CAN YOU SEE HIM, EVERY-ONE?
GUI (GRAB)
THIS IS THE MAN BEHIND THE CURTAIN!
HE LOANED HIS SLAVES TO THE ZAICUON TEMPLE TO PREY ON YOUR FEARS...
...AND GET YOU TO BUY A BUNCH OF PEBBLES WITH YOUR HARD-EARNED MONEY!
SKILL ACQUIRED: "JUDGMENT"
GIVE OUR MONEY BACK!
ZAWA (CHATTER)
WHAT? WE'VE BEEN TRICKED ...?
HE'S RIGHT!
GIVE IT BACK!

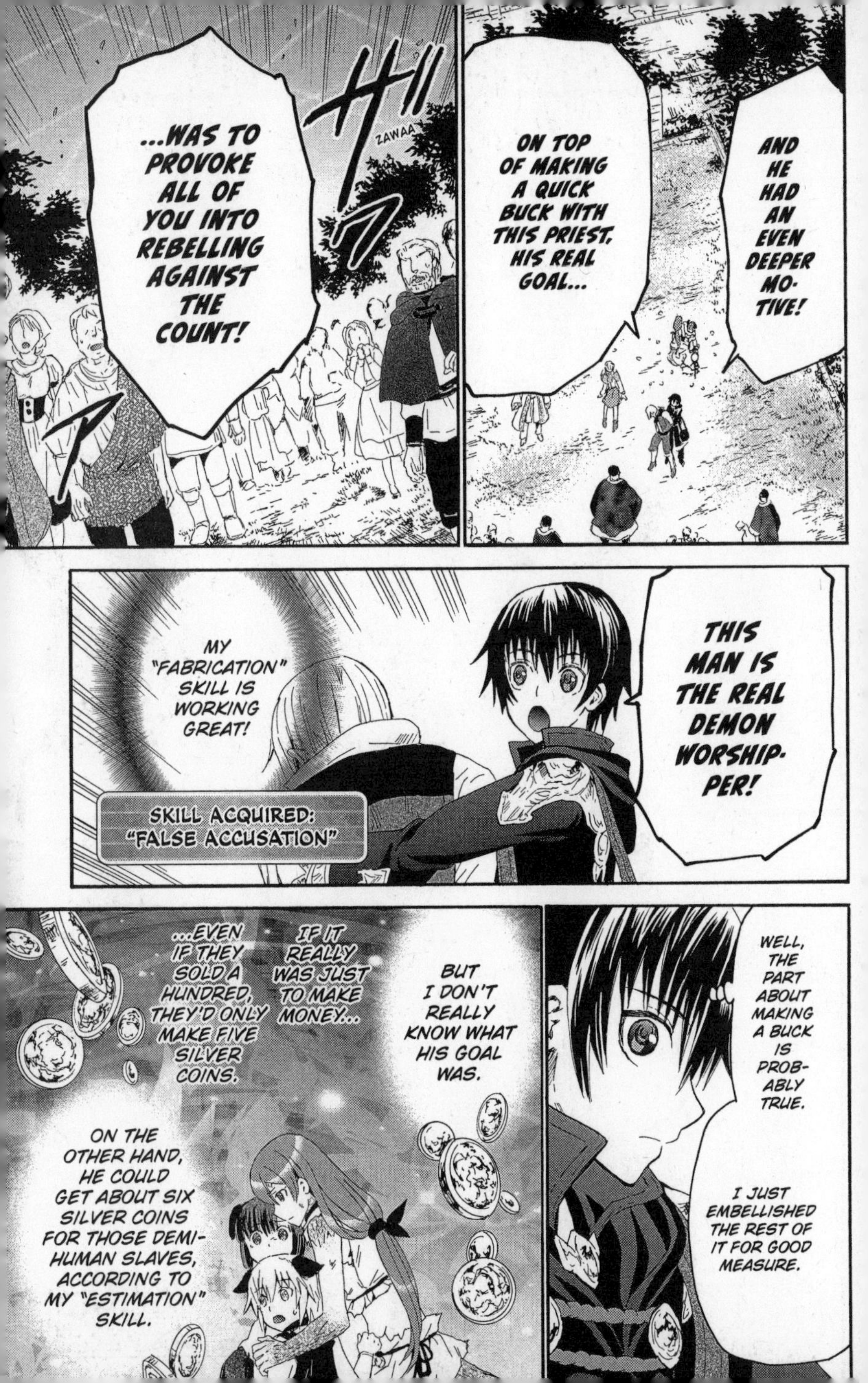
AND HE HAD AN EVEN DEEPER MOTIVE!
ON TOP OF MAKING A QUICK BUCK WITH THIS PRIEST, HIS REAL GOAL...
ZAWAA
...WAS TO PROVOKE ALL OF YOU INTO REBELLING AGAINST THE COUNT!
THIS MAN IS THE REAL DEMON WORSHIPPER!
MY "FABRICATION" SKILL IS WORKING GREAT!
SKILL ACQUIRED: "FALSE ACCUSATION"
WELL, THE PART ABOUT MAKING A BUCK IS PROBABLY TRUE.
I JUST EMBELLISHED THE REST OF IT FOR GOOD MEASURE.
BUT I DON'T REALLY KNOW WHAT HIS GOAL WAS.
IF IT REALLY WAS JUST TO MAKE MONEY...
...EVEN IF THEY SOLD A HUNDRED, THEY'D ONLY MAKE FIVE SILVER COINS.
ON THE OTHER HAND, HE COULD GET ABOUT SIX SILVER COINS FOR THOSE DEMI-HUMAN SLAVES, ACCORDING TO MY "ESTIMATION" SKILL.

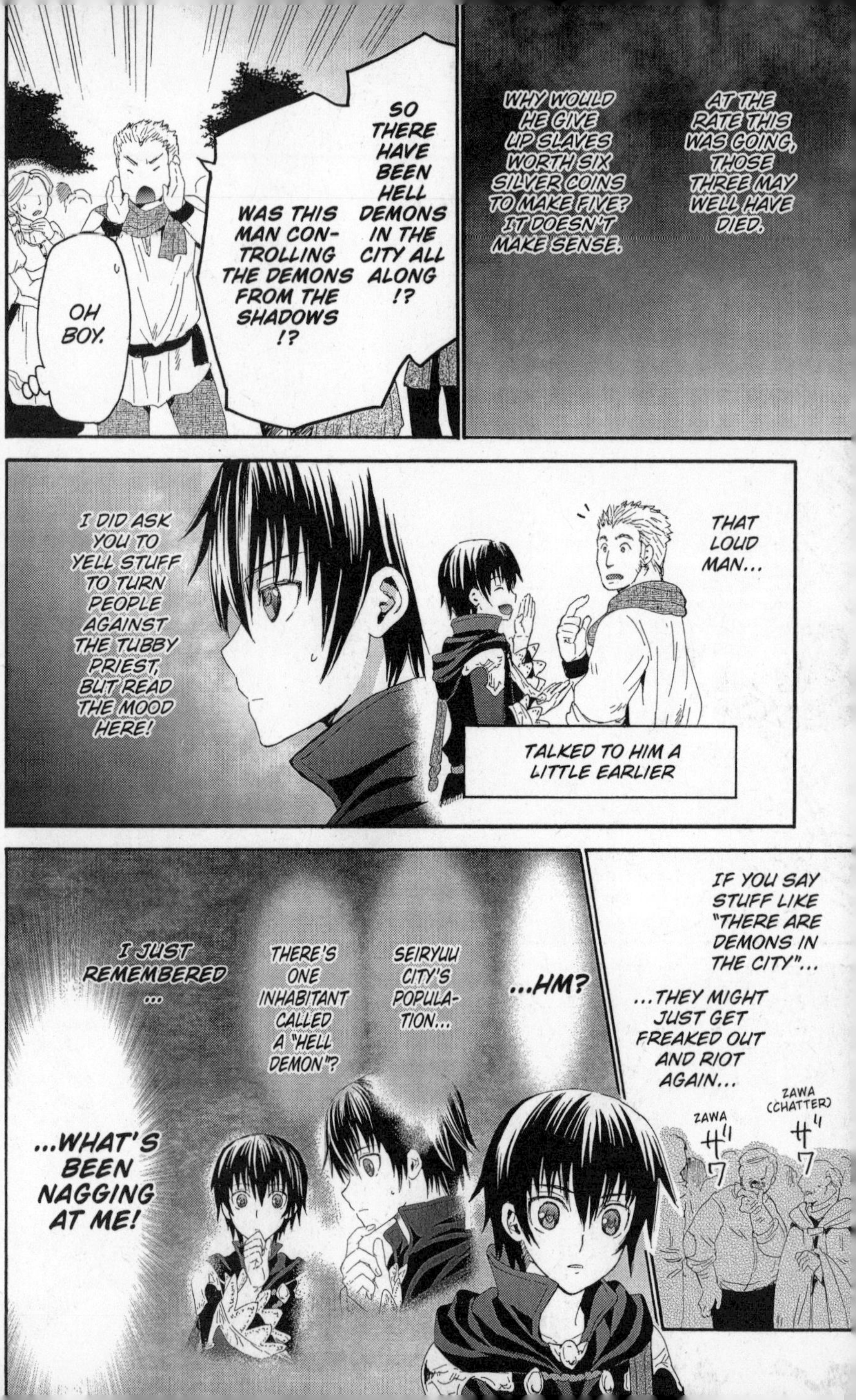
AT THE RATE THIS WAS GOING, THOSE THREE MAY WELL HAVE DIED.
WHY WOULD HE GIVE UP SLAVES WORTH SIX SILVER COINS TO MAKE FIVE? IT DOESN'T MAKE SENSE.
SO THERE HAVE BEEN HELL DEMONS IN THE CITY ALL ALONG!?
WAS THIS MAN CONTROLLING THE DEMONS FROM THE SHADOWS!?
OH BOY.
THAT LOUD MAN...
TALKED TO HIM A LITTLE EARLIER
I DID ASK YOU TO YELL STUFF TO TURN PEOPLE AGAINST THE TUBBY PRIEST, BUT READ THE MOOD HERE!
IF YOU SAY STUFF LIKE "THERE ARE DEMONS IN THE CITY"...
...THEY MIGHT JUST GET FREAKED OUT AND RIOT AGAIN...
ZAWA (CHATTER)
ザワ
ZAWA
ザワ
...HM?
SEIRYUU CITY'S POPULATION...
THERE'S ONE INHABITANT CALLED A "HELL DEMON"?
I JUST REMEMBERED...
...WHAT'S BEEN NAGGING AT ME!

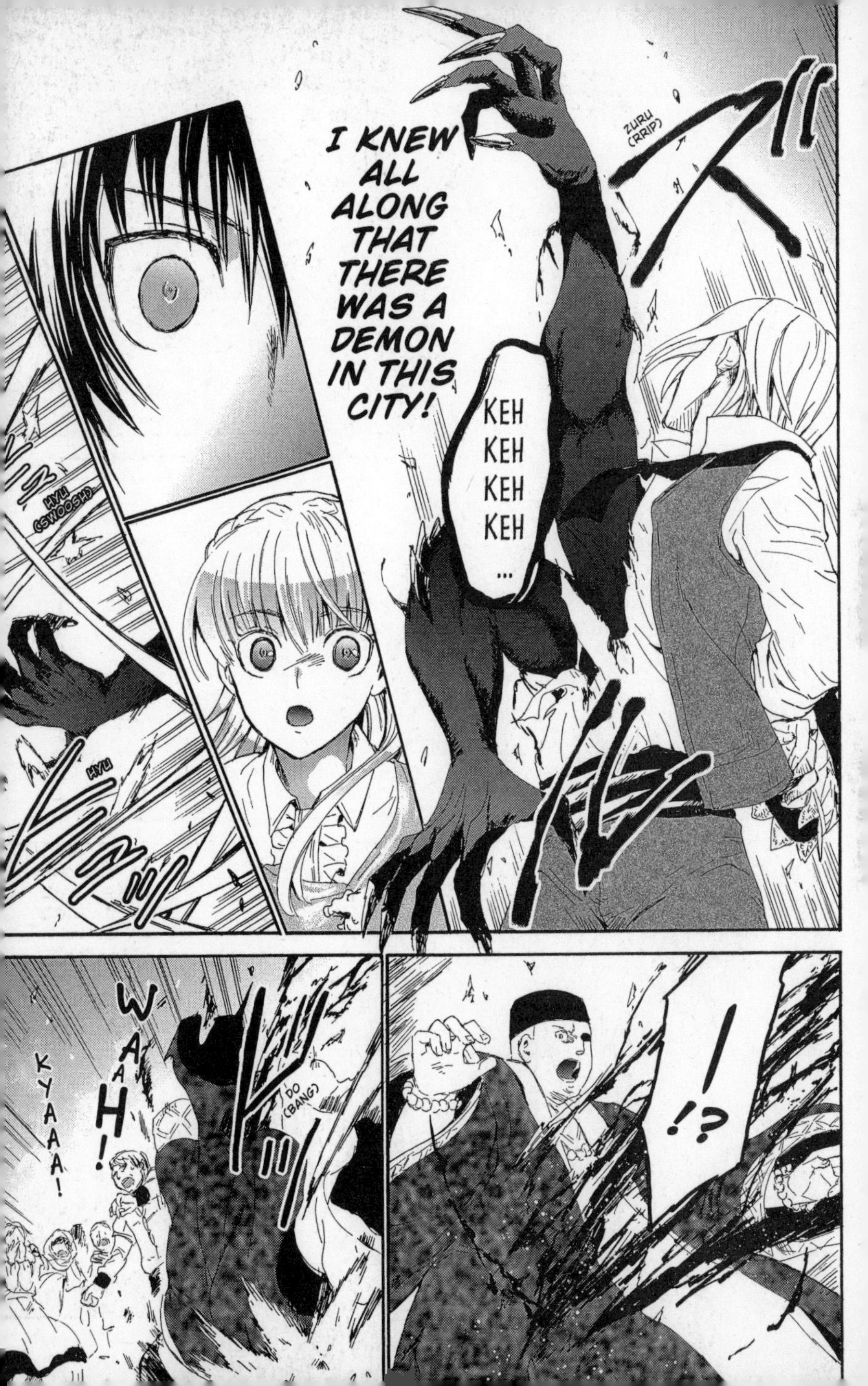
ZURU (RRIP)
I KNEW ALL ALONG THAT THERE WAS A DEMON IN THIS CITY!
KEH KEH KEH KEH ...
HYU (SWOOSH)
HYU
!?
DO (BANG)
WAAH!
KYAAAA!

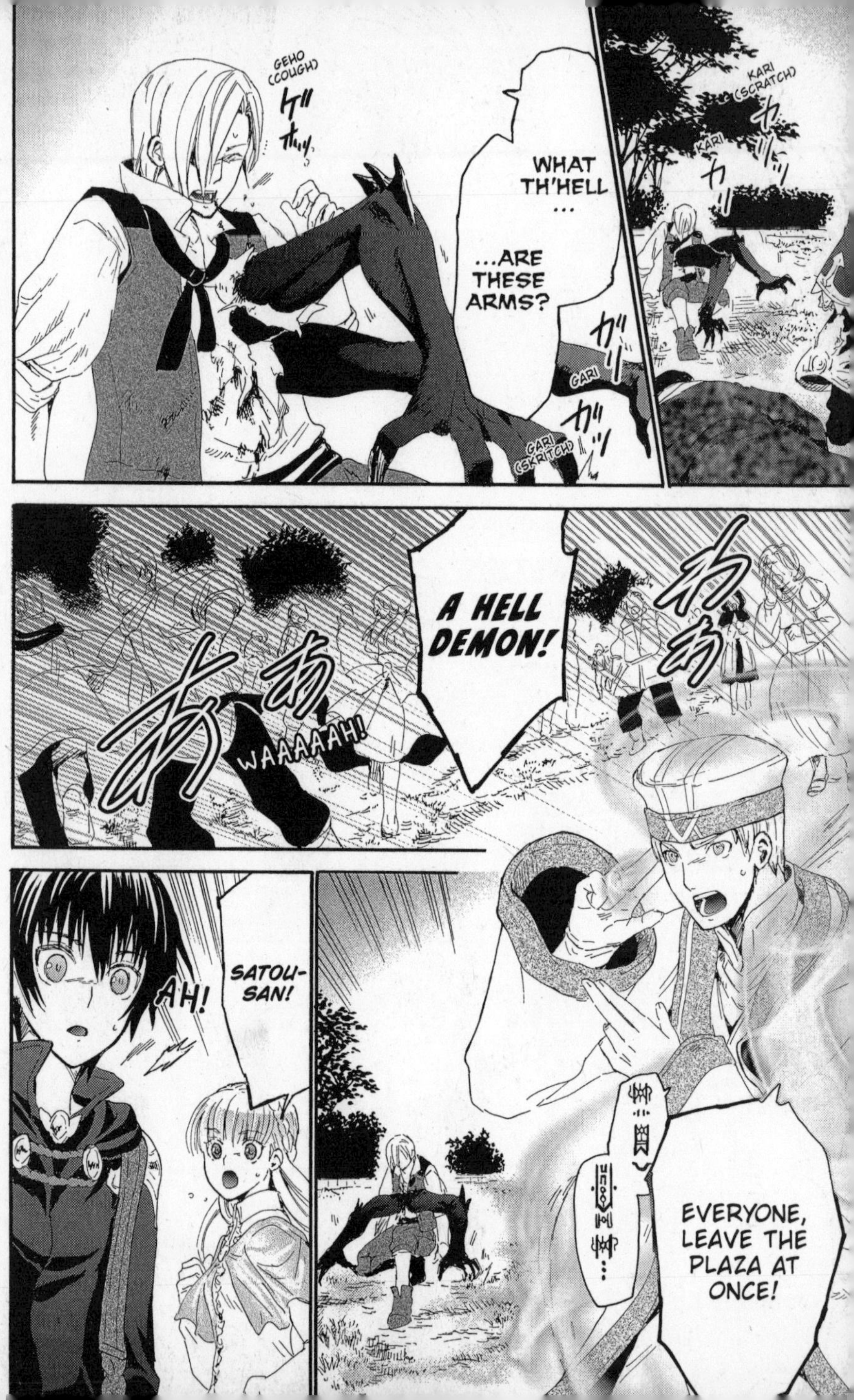
KARI (SCRATCH)
KARI
WHAT TH'HELL ...
...ARE THESE ARMS?
GARI
GARI (SKRITCH)
GEHO (COUGH)
A HELL DEMON!
WAAAAAH!
EVERYONE, LEAVE THE PLAZA AT ONCE!
SATOU-SAN!
AH!

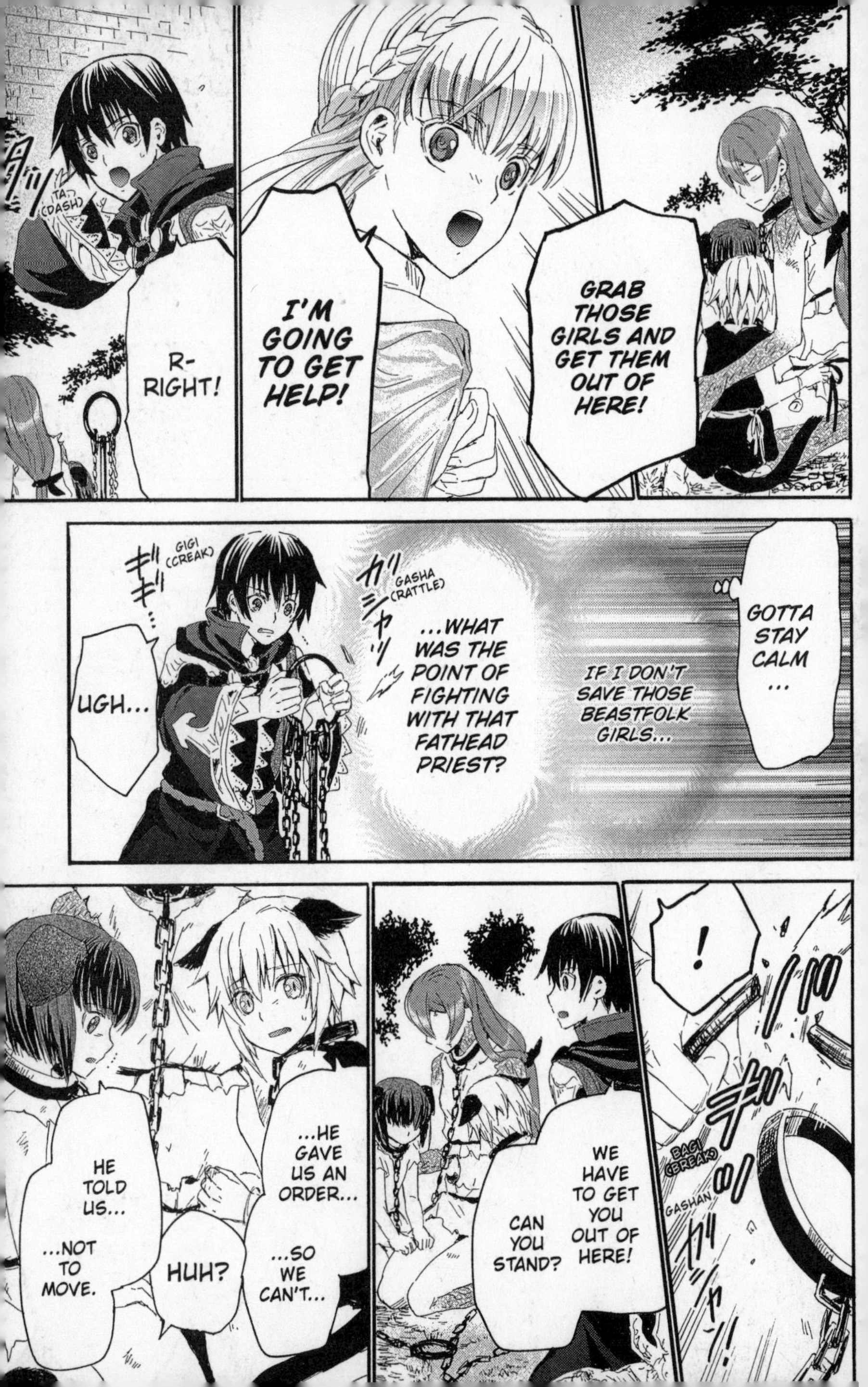
GRAB THOSE GIRLS AND GET THEM OUT OF HERE!
I'M GOING TO GET HELP!
TA (DASH)
R-RIGHT!
GOTTA STAY CALM ...
IF I DON'T SAVE THOSE BEASTFOLK GIRLS...
...WHAT WAS THE POINT OF FIGHTING WITH THAT FATHEAD PRIEST?
GASHA (RATTLE)
GIGI (CREAK)
UGH...
!
BAGI (BREAK)
GASHAN
WE HAVE TO GET YOU OUT OF HERE!
CAN YOU STAND?
...HE GAVE US AN ORDER...
...SO WE CAN'T...
HUH?
HE TOLD US...
...NOT TO MOVE.

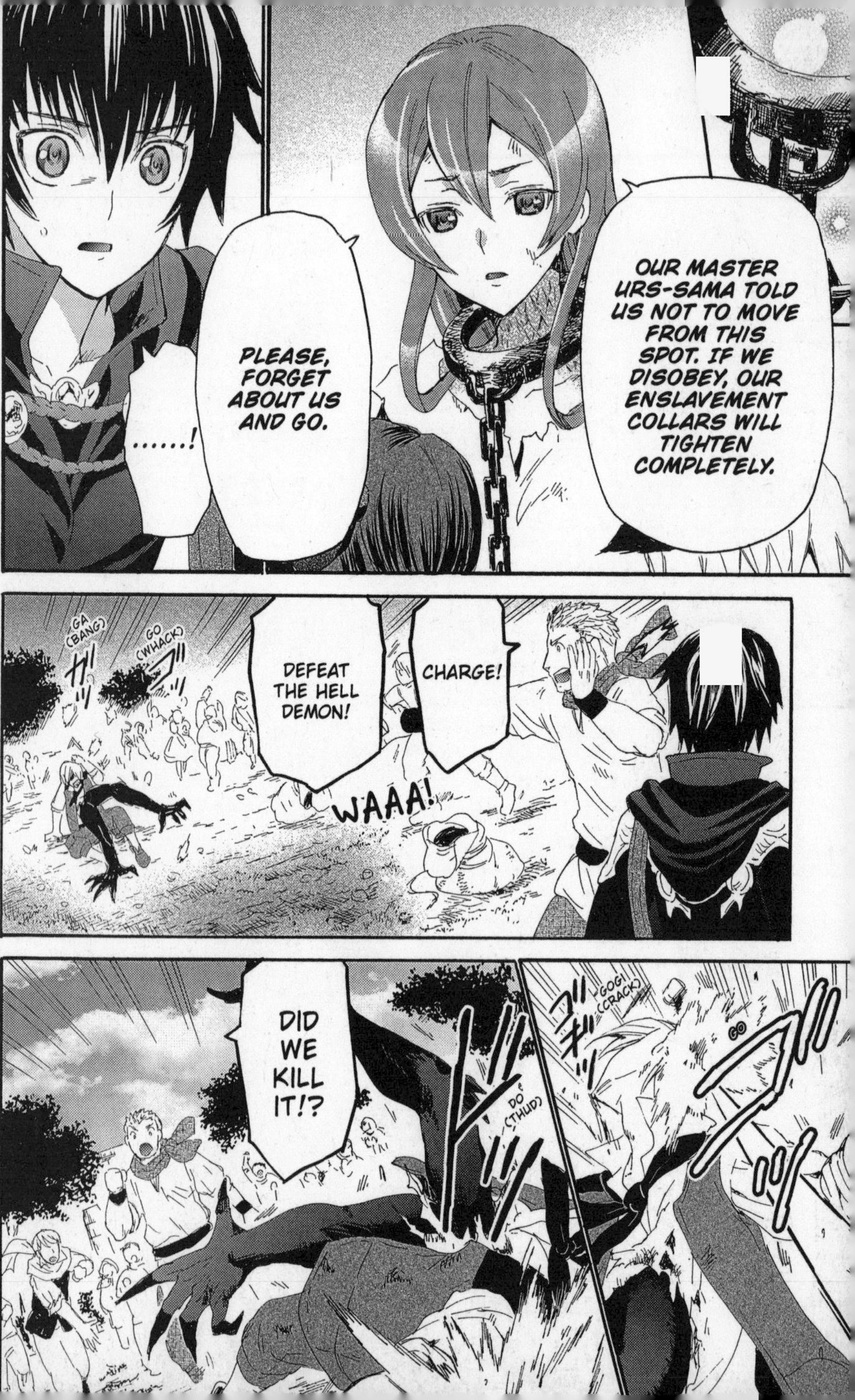
OUR MASTER URS-SAMA TOLD US NOT TO MOVE FROM THIS SPOT. IF WE DISOBEY, OUR ENSLAVEMENT COLLARS WILL TIGHTEN COMPLETELY.
PLEASE, FORGET ABOUT US AND GO.
......!
CHARGE!
DEFEAT THE HELL DEMON!
WAAA!
GO (WHACK)
GA (BANG)
GOGI (CRACK)
DO (THUD)
DID WE KILL IT!?

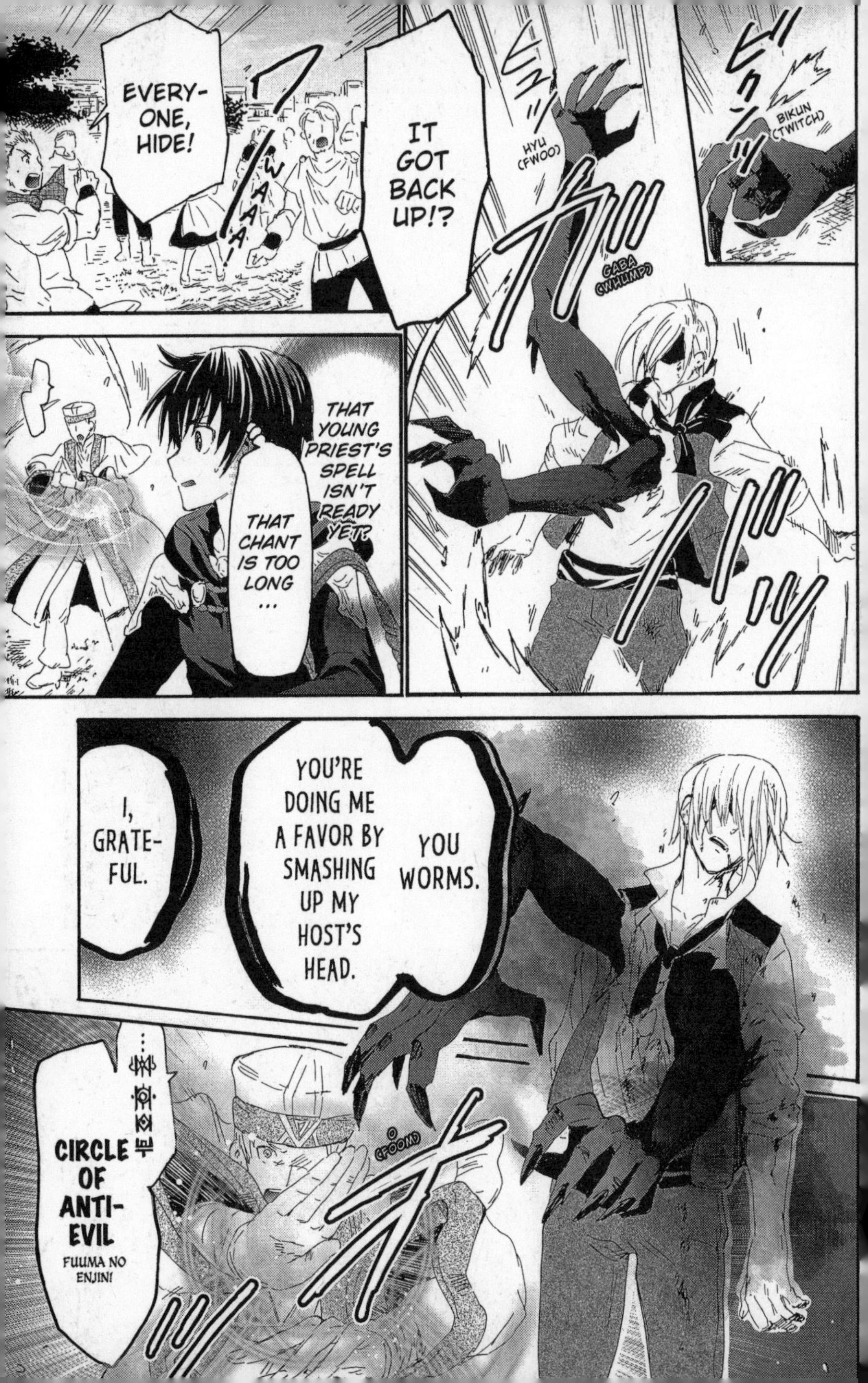
BIKUN (TWITCH)
HYU (FWOO)
GABA (WHUMP)
IT GOT BACK UP!?
WAAAA!
EVERY-ONE, HIDE!
THAT YOUNG PRIEST'S SPELL ISN'T READY YET!?
THAT CHANT IS TOO LONG...
YOU WORMS.
YOU'RE DOING ME A FAVOR BY SMASHING UP MY HOST'S HEAD.
I, GRATEFUL.
O (FOOM)
...
CIRCLE OF ANTI-EVIL
FUUMA NO ENJIN!

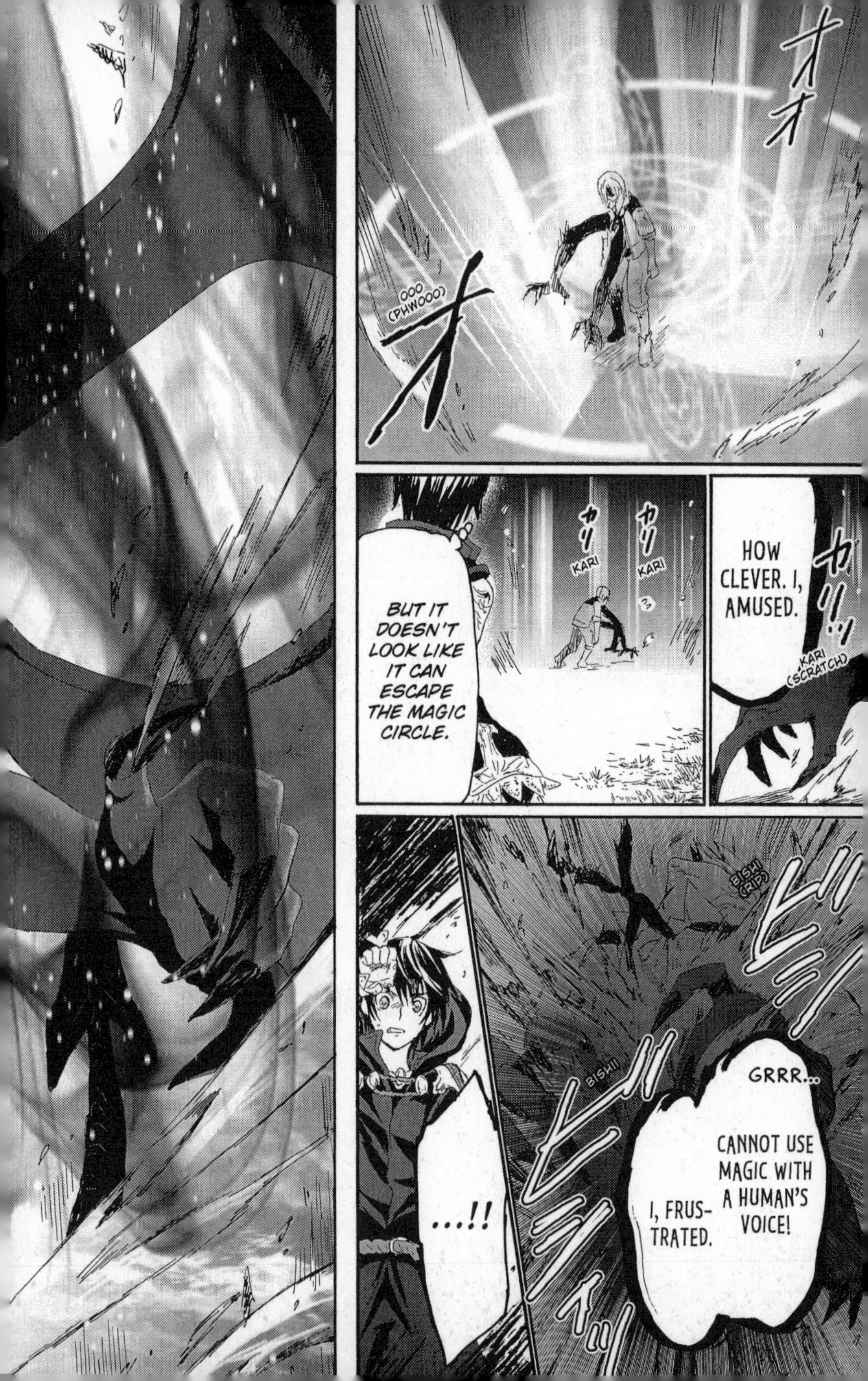
OOO (PHWOOO)
HOW CLEVER. I, AMUSED.
KARI (SCRATCH)
KARI
KARI
BUT IT DOESN'T LOOK LIKE IT CAN ESCAPE THE MAGIC CIRCLE.
BISHI (RIP)
GRRR...
CANNOT USE MAGIC WITH A HUMAN'S VOICE!
I, FRUS-TRATED.
BISHI
...!!

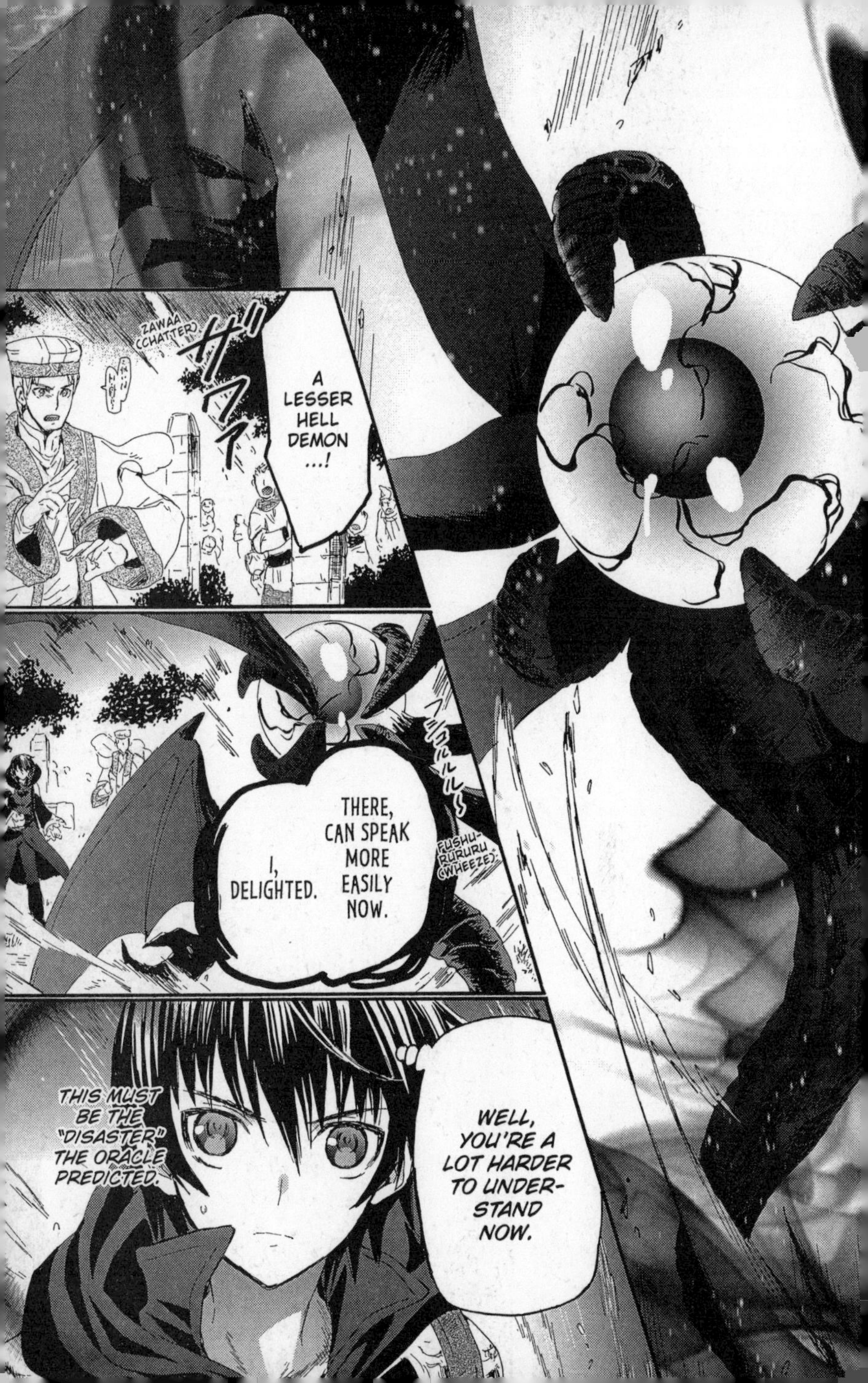
ZAWAA (CHATTER)
A LESSER HELL DEMON ...!
I, DELIGHTED.
THERE, CAN SPEAK MORE EASILY NOW.
FUSHU-RURURU (WHEEZE)
WELL, YOU'RE A LOT HARDER TO UNDER-STAND NOW.
THIS MUST BE THE "DISASTER" THE ORACLE PREDICTED.

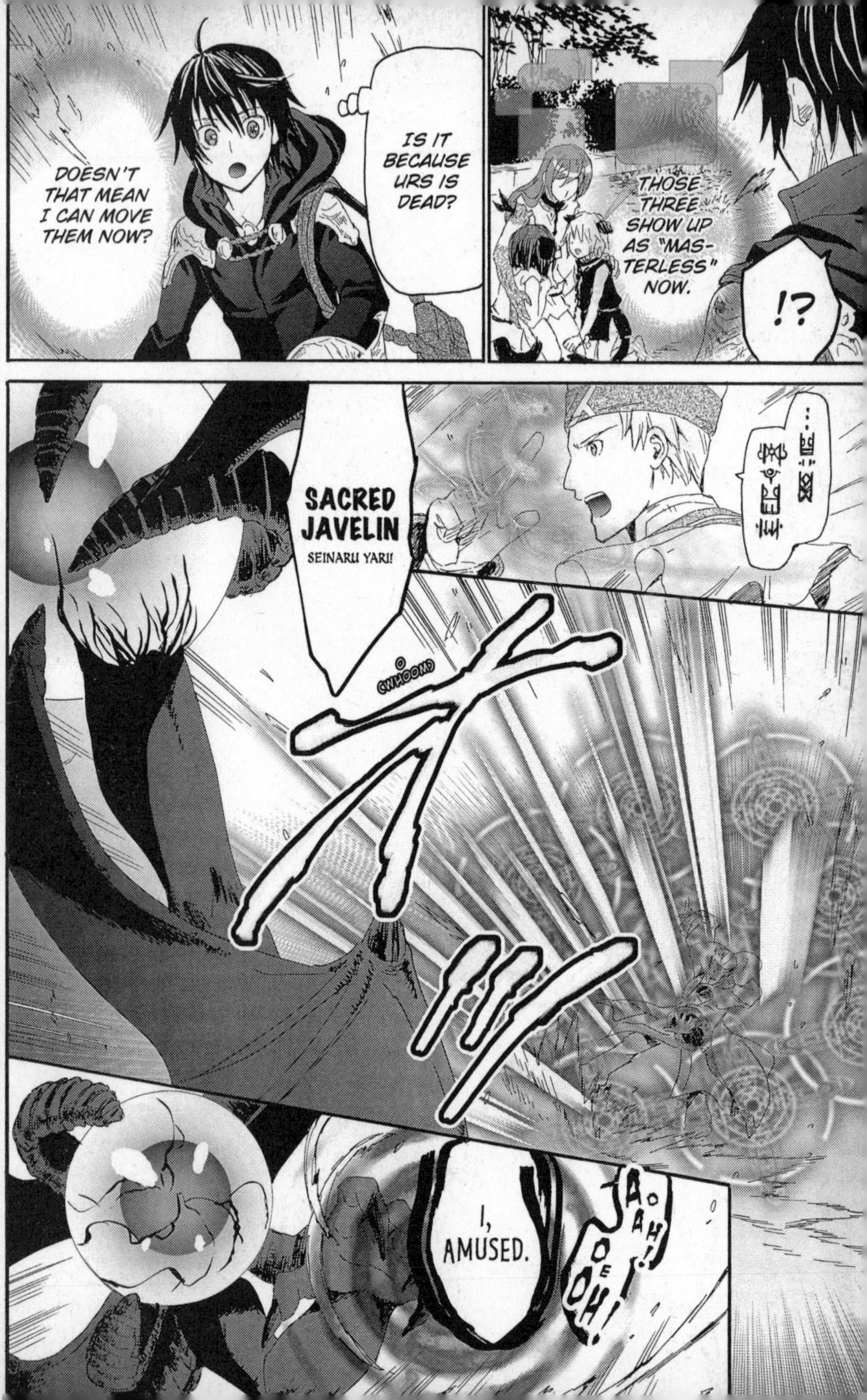
THOSE THREE SHOW UP AS "MASTERLESS" NOW.
!?
IS IT BECAUSE URS IS DEAD?
DOESN'T THAT MEAN I CAN MOVE THEM NOW?
SACRED JAVELIN
SEINARU YARI!
(WHOOM)
AAH!
OH!
I, AMUSED.

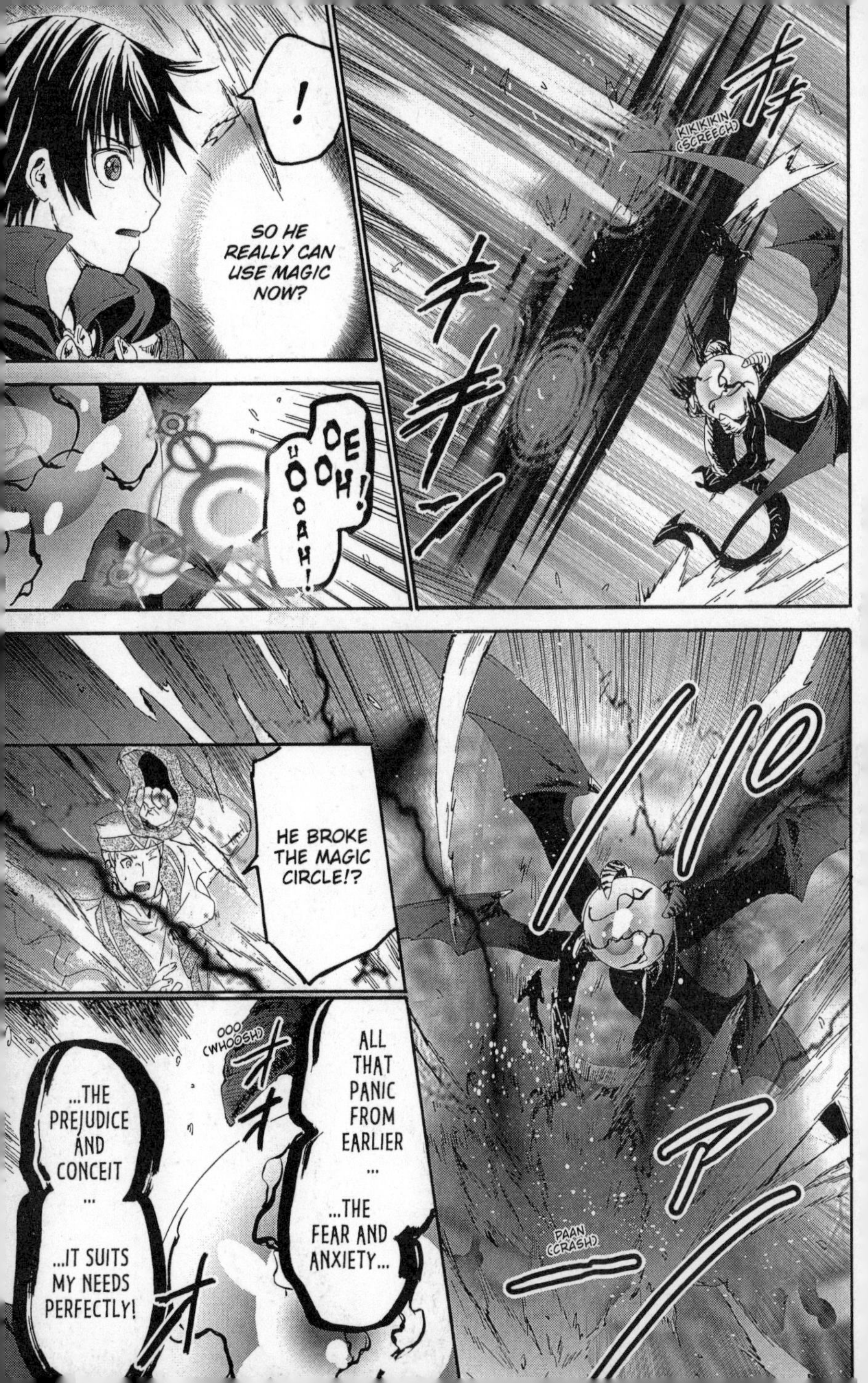
KIKIKIKIN (SCREECH)
!
SO HE REALLY CAN USE MAGIC NOW?
OEOH!
UOOOAH!
PAAN (CRASH)
HE BROKE THE MAGIC CIRCLE!?
OOO (WHOOSH)
ALL THAT PANIC FROM EARLIER ... ...THE FEAR AND ANXIETY...
...THE PREJUDICE AND CONCEIT ... ...IT SUITS MY NEEDS PERFECTLY!

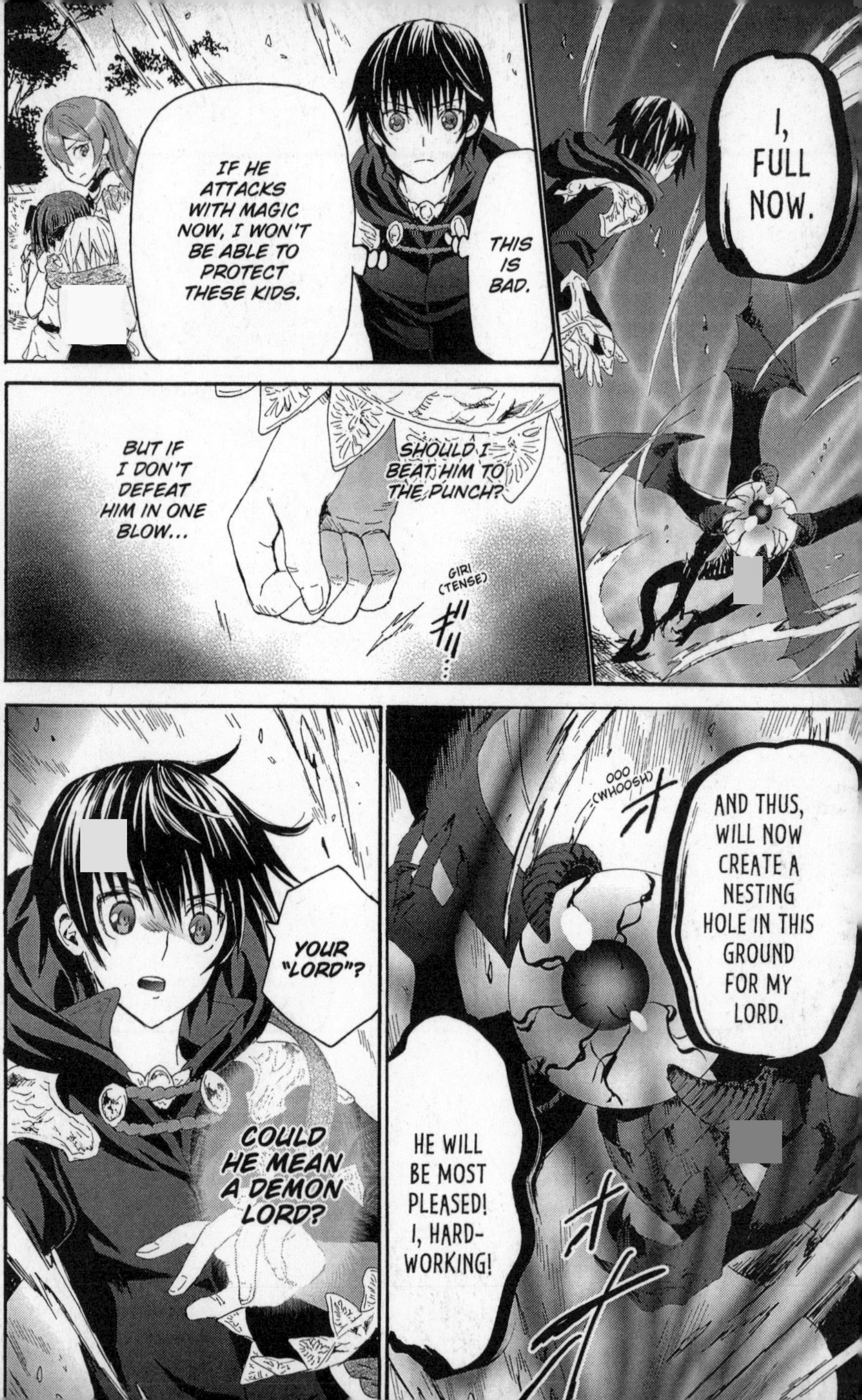
I, FULL NOW.
THIS IS BAD.
IF HE ATTACKS WITH MAGIC NOW, I WON'T BE ABLE TO PROTECT THESE KIDS.
SHOULD I BEAT HIM TO THE PUNCH?
GIRI (TENSE)
BUT IF I DON'T DEFEAT HIM IN ONE BLOW...
OOO (WHOOSH)
AND THUS, WILL NOW CREATE A NESTING HOLE IN THIS GROUND FOR MY LORD.
HE WILL BE MOST PLEASED! I, HARD-WORKING!
YOUR "LORD"?
COULD HE MEAN A DEMON LORD?

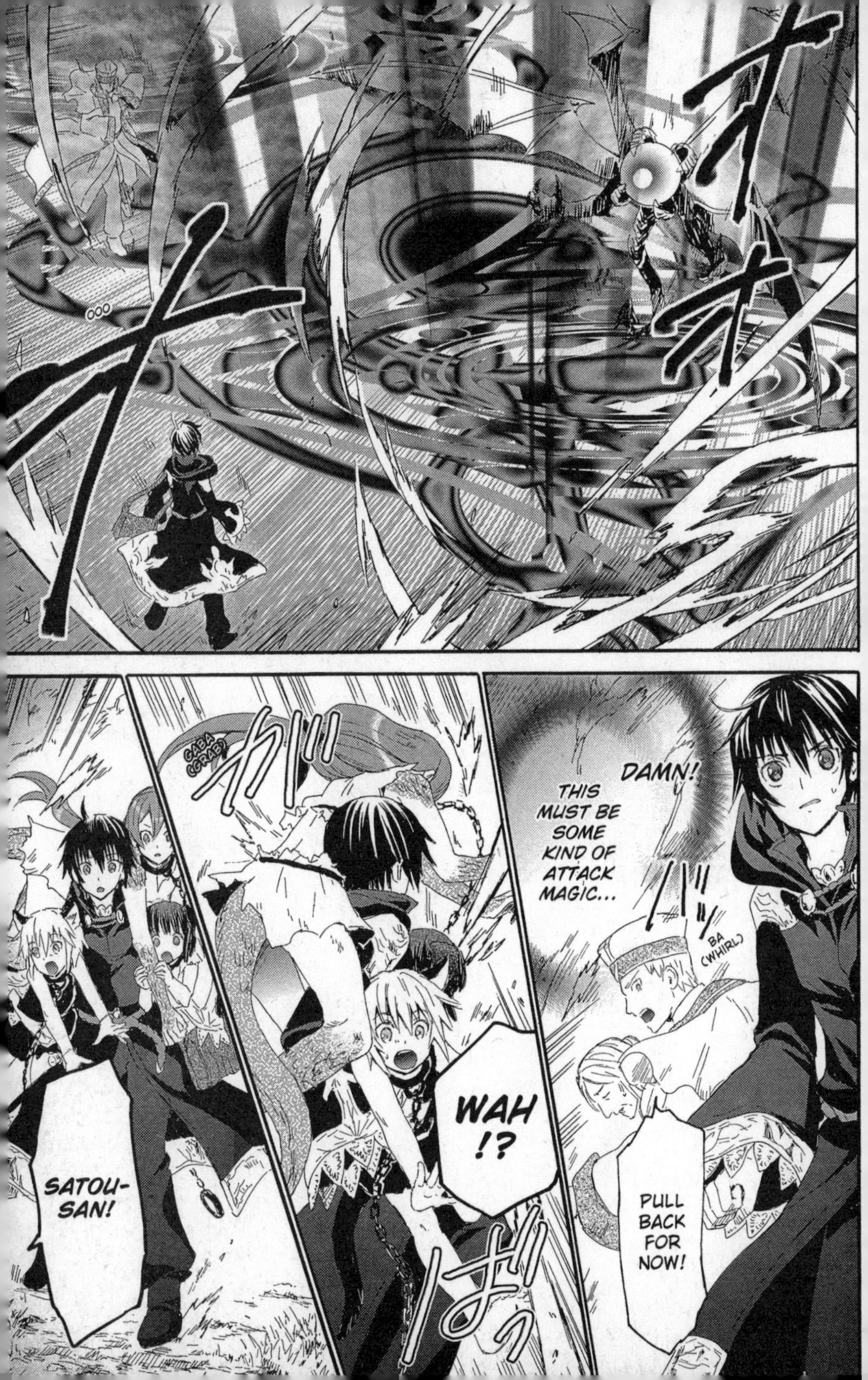
ooo
DAMN!
THIS MUST BE SOME KIND OF ATTACK MAGIC...
BA (WHIRL)
PULL BACK FOR NOW!
GABA (GRAB)
WAH!?
SATOU-SAN!

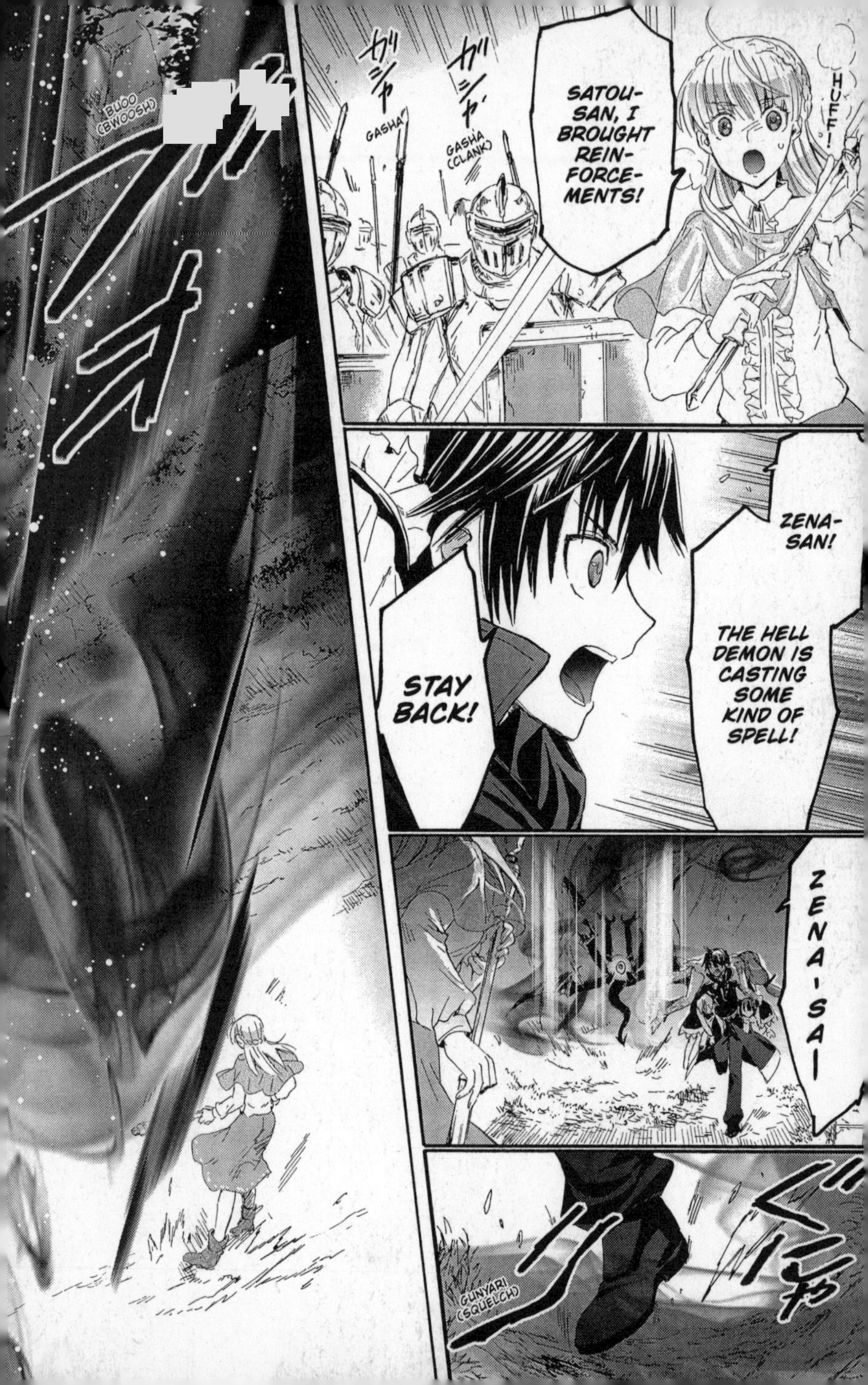
HUFF!
SATOU-SAN, I BROUGHT REIN-FORCE-MENTS!
GASHA (CLANK)
GASHA
ZENA-SAN!
THE HELL DEMON IS CASTING SOME KIND OF SPELL!
STAY BACK!
ZENA-SA!
GUNYARI (SQUELCH)
BUOO (BWOOSH)

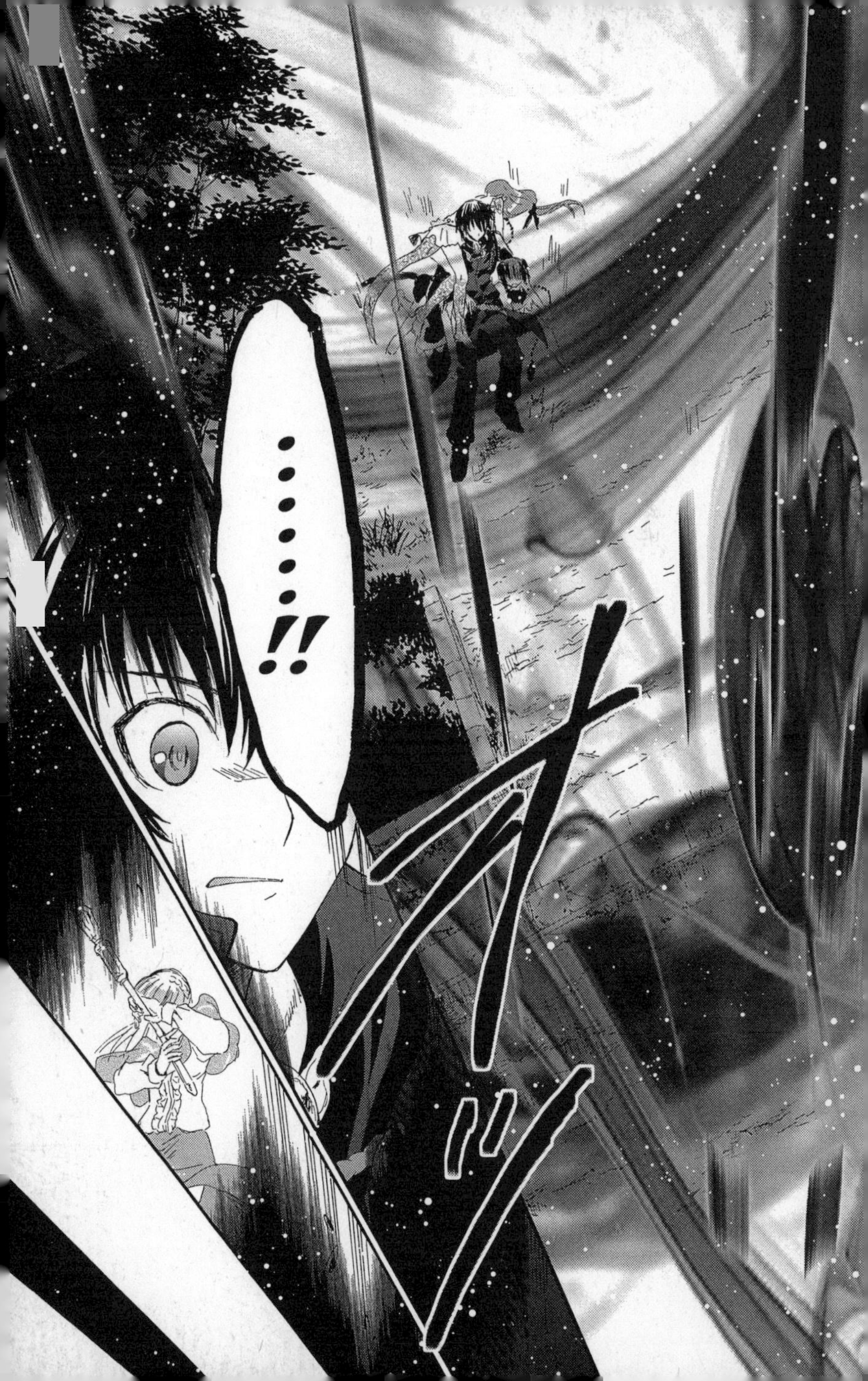

......!!

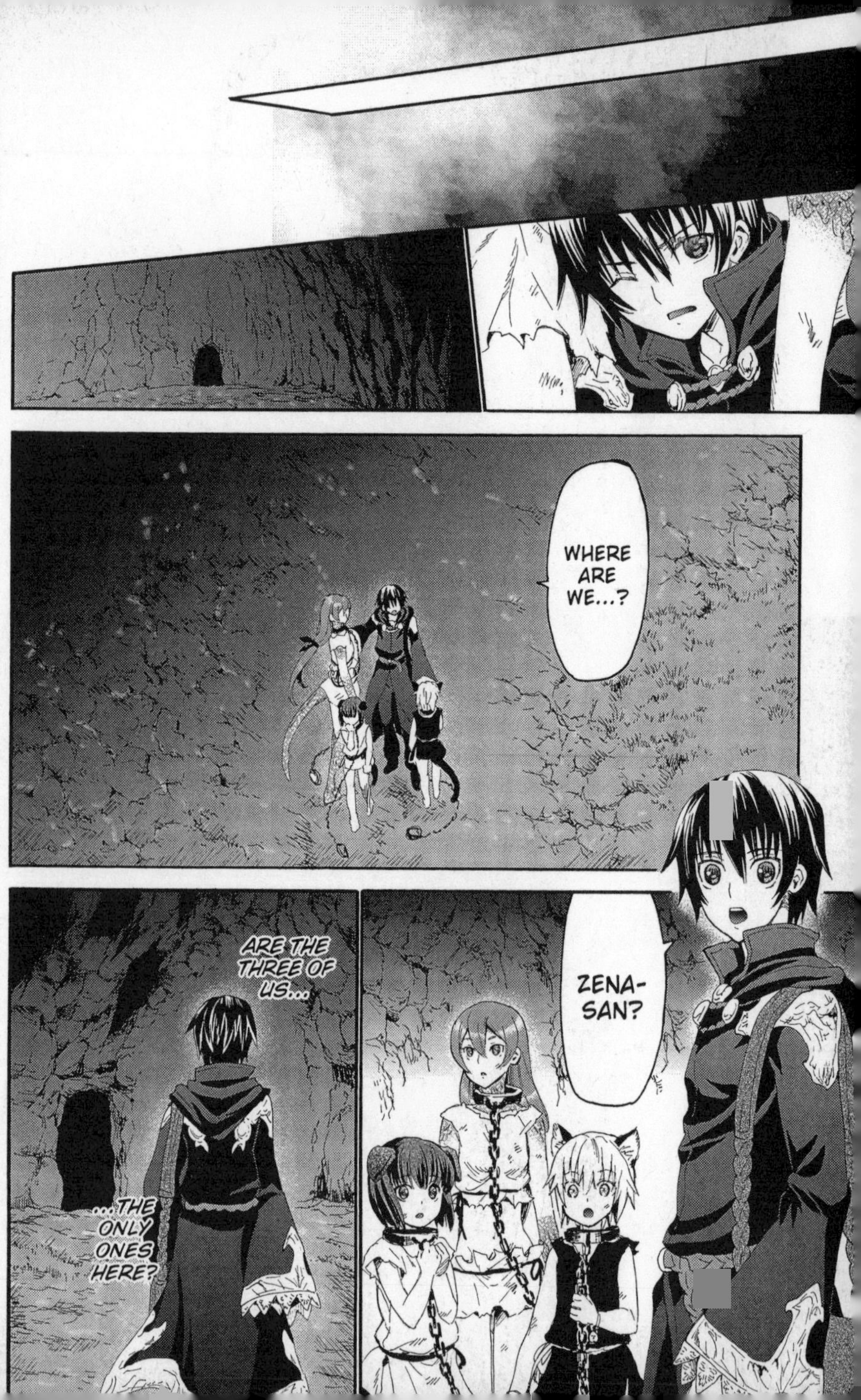
WHERE ARE WE...?
ZENA-SAN?
ARE THE THREE OF US...
...THE ONLY ONES HERE?

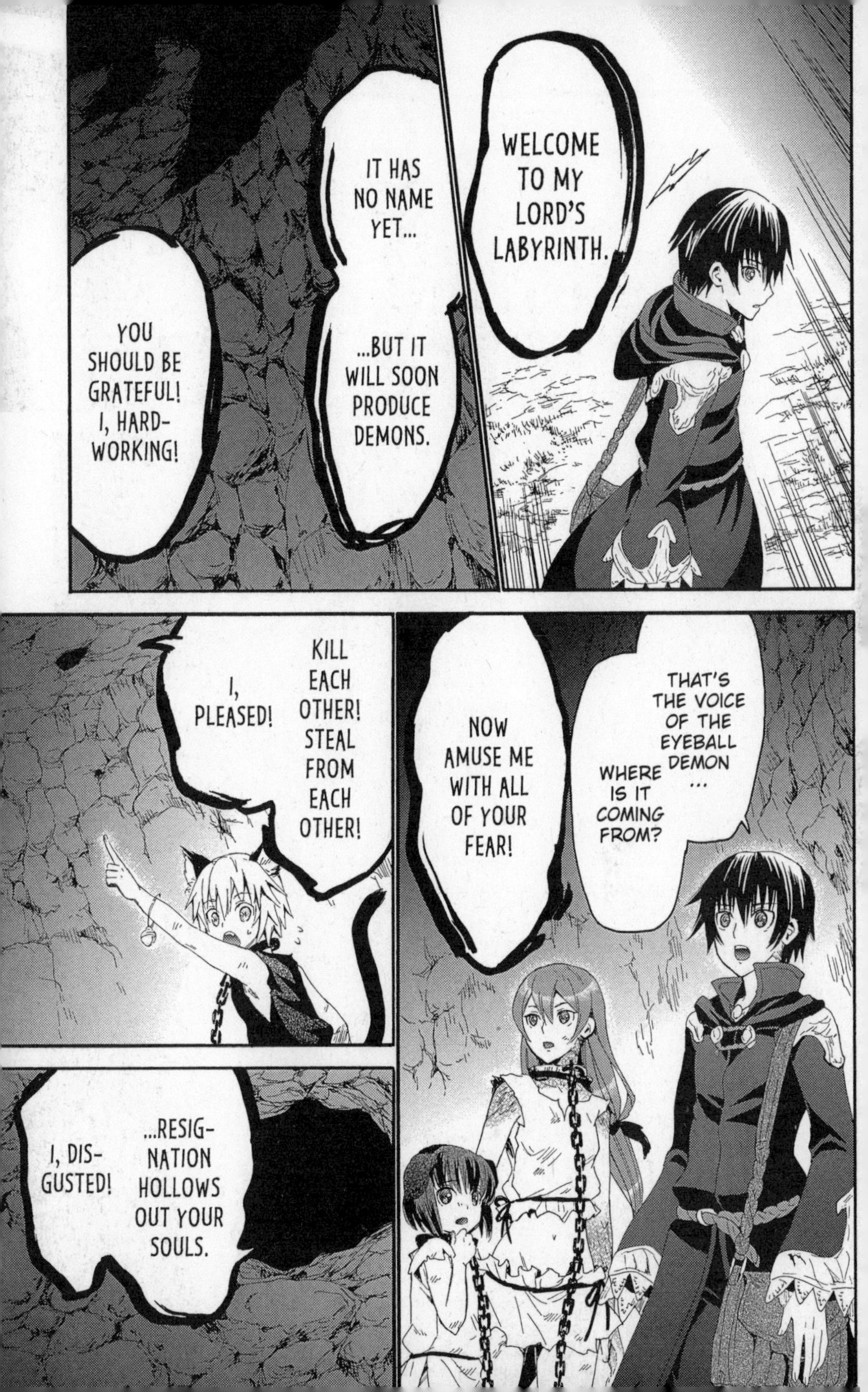
WELCOME TO MY LORD'S LABYRINTH.
IT HAS NO NAME YET...
...BUT IT WILL SOON PRODUCE DEMONS.
YOU SHOULD BE GRATEFUL! I, HARD-WORKING!
THAT'S THE VOICE OF THE EYEBALL DEMON...
WHERE IS IT COMING FROM?
NOW AMUSE ME WITH ALL OF YOUR FEAR!
KILL EACH OTHER! STEAL FROM EACH OTHER!
I, PLEASED!
...RESIGNATION HOLLOWS OUT YOUR SOULS.
I, DISGUSTED!

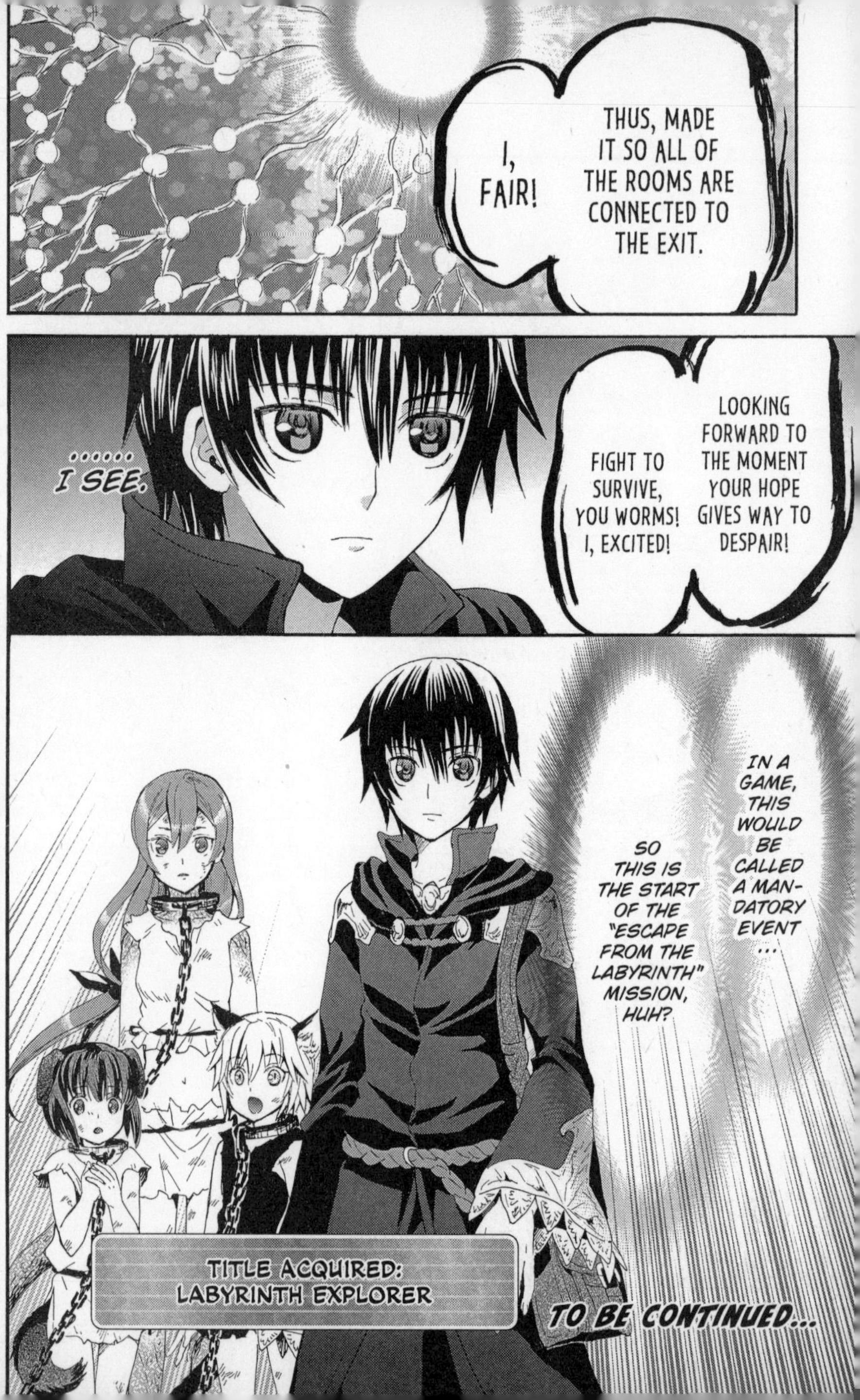
I, FAIR!
THUS, MADE IT SO ALL OF THE ROOMS ARE CONNECTED TO THE EXIT.
FIGHT TO SURVIVE, YOU WORMS! I, EXCITED!
LOOKING FORWARD TO THE MOMENT YOUR HOPE GIVES WAY TO DESPAIR!
......I SEE.
IN A GAME, THIS WOULD BE CALLED A MAN-DATORY EVENT...
SO THIS IS THE START OF THE "ESCAPE FROM THE LABYRINTH" MISSION, HUH?
TITLE ACQUIRED: LABYRINTH EXPLORER
TO BE CONTINUED...

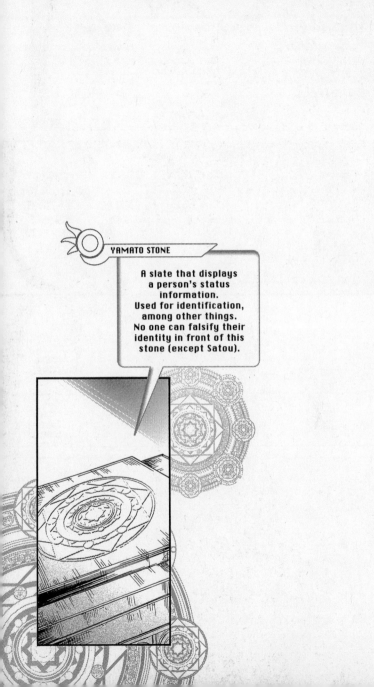

YAMATO STONE

A slate that displays
a person's status
information.
Used for identification,
among other things.
No one can falsify their
identity in front of this
stone (except Satou).

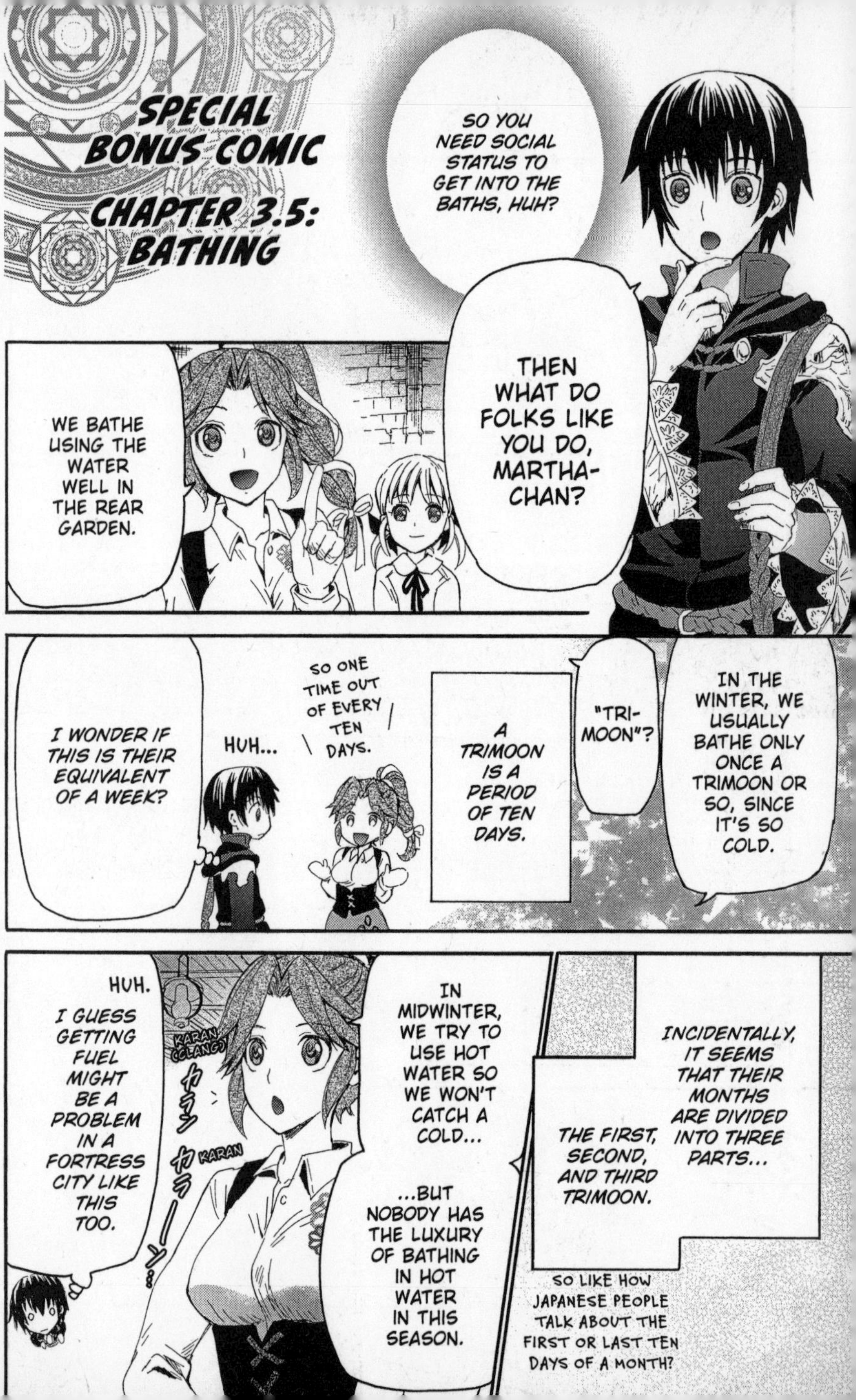
SPECIAL BONUS COMIC
CHAPTER 3.5: BATHING
SO YOU NEED SOCIAL STATUS TO GET INTO THE BATHS, HUH?
THEN WHAT DO FOLKS LIKE YOU DO, MARTHA-CHAN?
WE BATHE USING THE WATER WELL IN THE REAR GARDEN.
IN THE WINTER, WE USUALLY BATHE ONLY ONCE A TRIMOON OR SO, SINCE IT'S SO COLD.
"TRI-MOON"?
A TRIMOON IS A PERIOD OF TEN DAYS.
SO ONE TIME OUT OF EVERY TEN DAYS.
HUH...
I WONDER IF THIS IS THEIR EQUIVALENT OF A WEEK?
INCIDENTALLY, IT SEEMS THAT THEIR MONTHS ARE DIVIDED INTO THREE PARTS...
THE FIRST, SECOND, AND THIRD TRIMOON.
SO LIKE HOW JAPANESE PEOPLE TALK ABOUT THE FIRST OR LAST TEN DAYS OF A MONTH?
IN MIDWINTER, WE TRY TO USE HOT WATER SO WE WON'T CATCH A COLD...
...BUT NOBODY HAS THE LUXURY OF BATHING IN HOT WATER IN THIS SEASON.
KARAN (CLANG)
KARAN
HUH.
I GUESS GETTING FUEL MIGHT BE A PROBLEM IN A FORTRESS CITY LIKE THIS TOO.

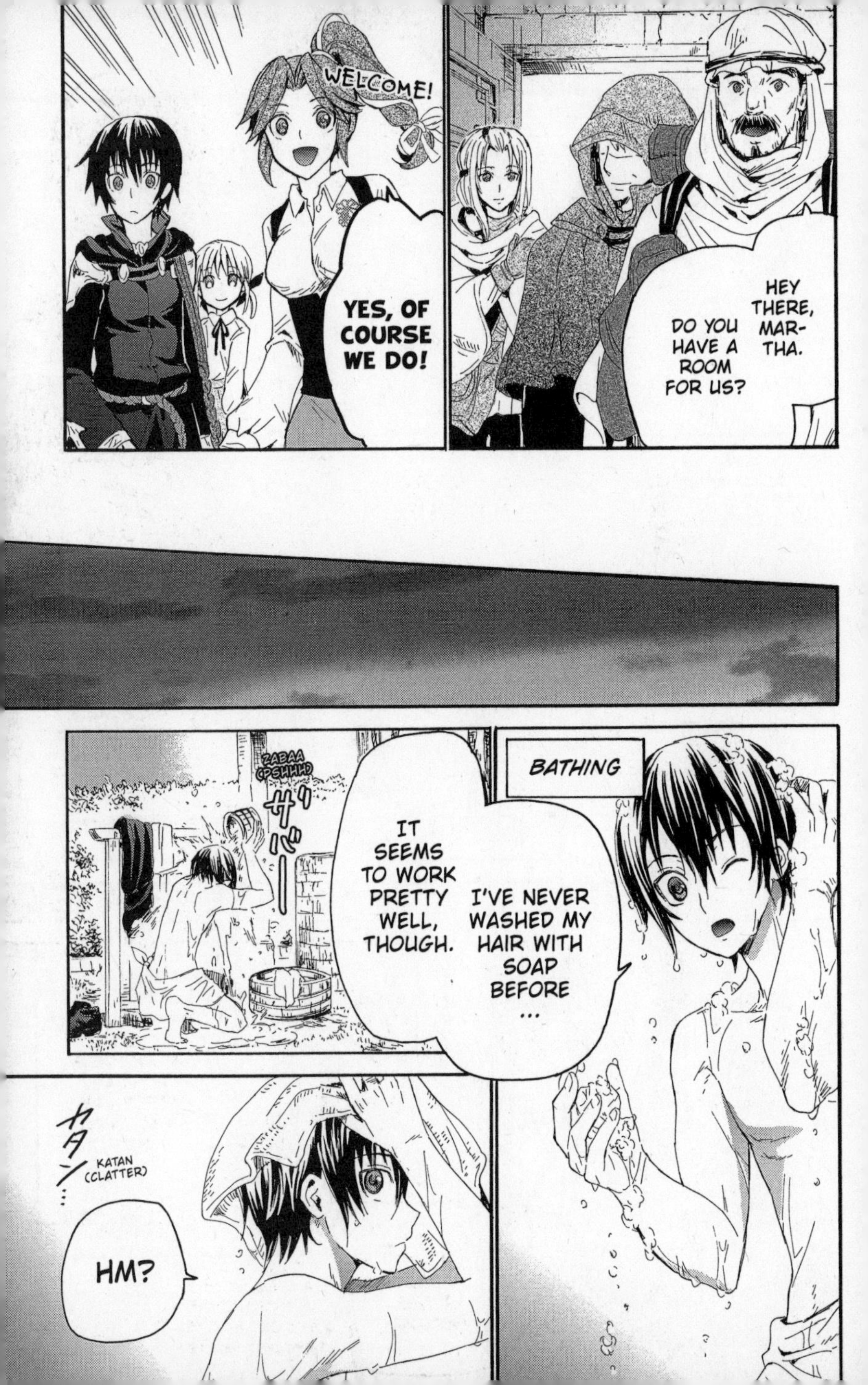
HEY THERE, MARTHA.
DO YOU HAVE A ROOM FOR US?
WELCOME!
YES, OF COURSE WE DO!
BATHING
I'VE NEVER WASHED MY HAIR WITH SOAP BEFORE ...
IT SEEMS TO WORK PRETTY WELL, THOUGH.
ザバー
ZABAA (PSHHH)
カタン…
KATAN (CLATTER)
HM?

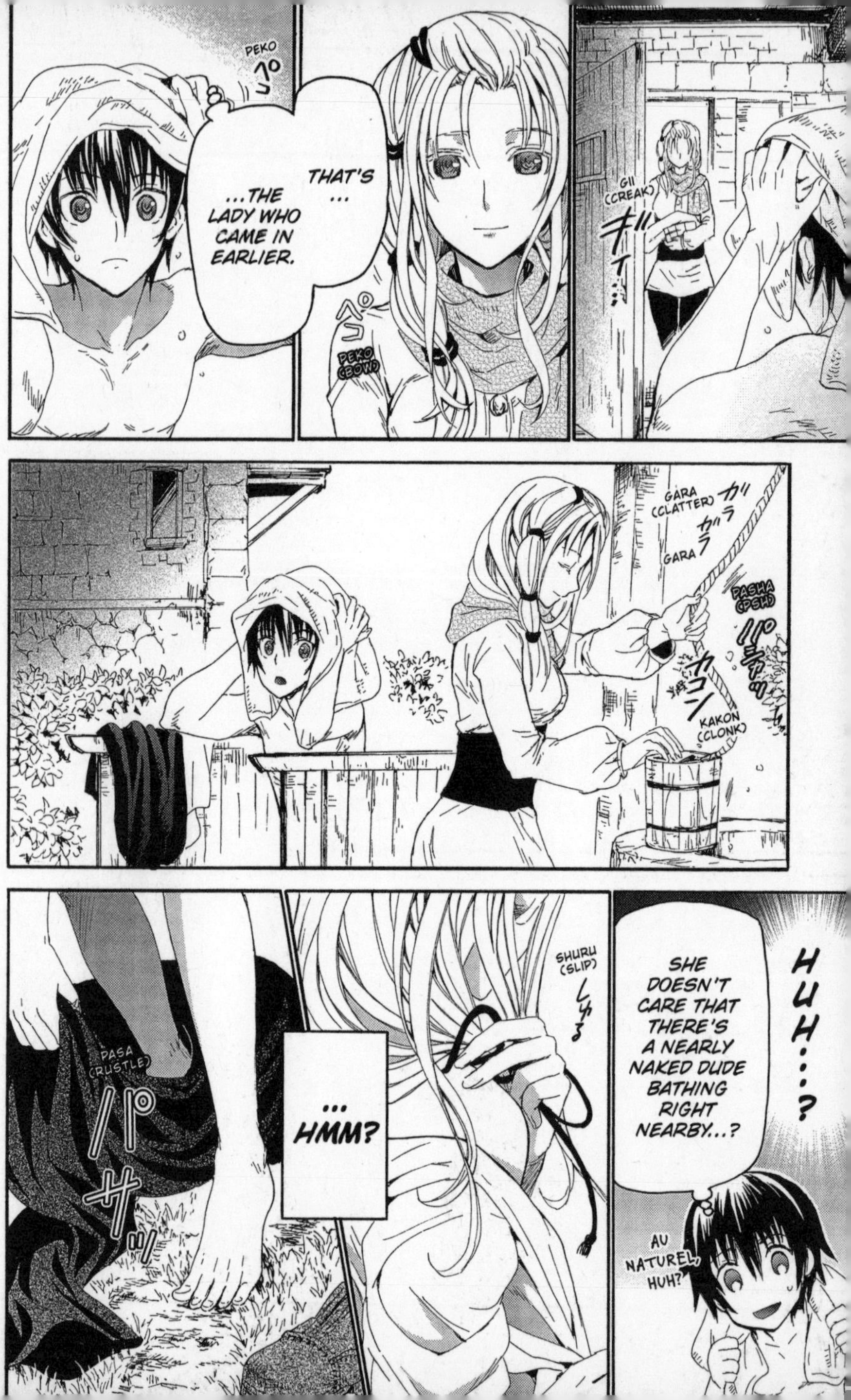
GII (CREAK)
THAT'S ...
...THE LADY WHO CAME IN EARLIER.
PEKO (BOW)
PEKO
GARA (CLATTER)
GARA
PASHA (PSH)
KAKON (CLONK)
HUH...?
SHE DOESN'T CARE THAT THERE'S A NEARLY NAKED DUDE BATHING RIGHT NEARBY...?
AU NATUREL, HUH?
SHURU (SLIP)
... HMM?
PASA (RUSTLE)

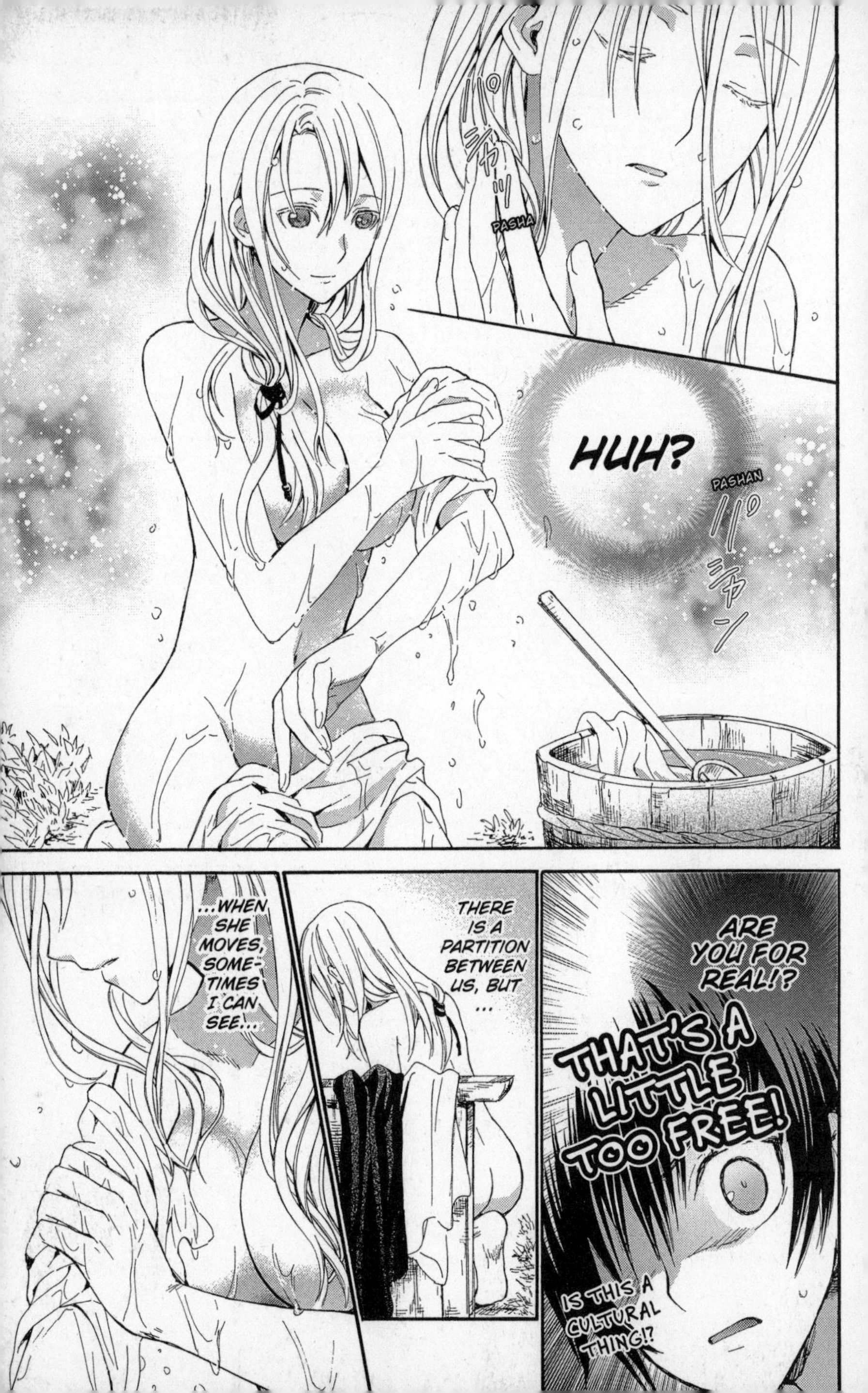
パシャッ
PASHA
HUH?
PASHAN
パシャン
ARE YOU FOR REAL!?
THAT'S A LITTLE TOO FREE!
IS THIS A CULTURAL THING!?
THERE IS A PARTITION BETWEEN US, BUT ...
...WHEN SHE MOVES, SOME-TIMES I CAN SEE...

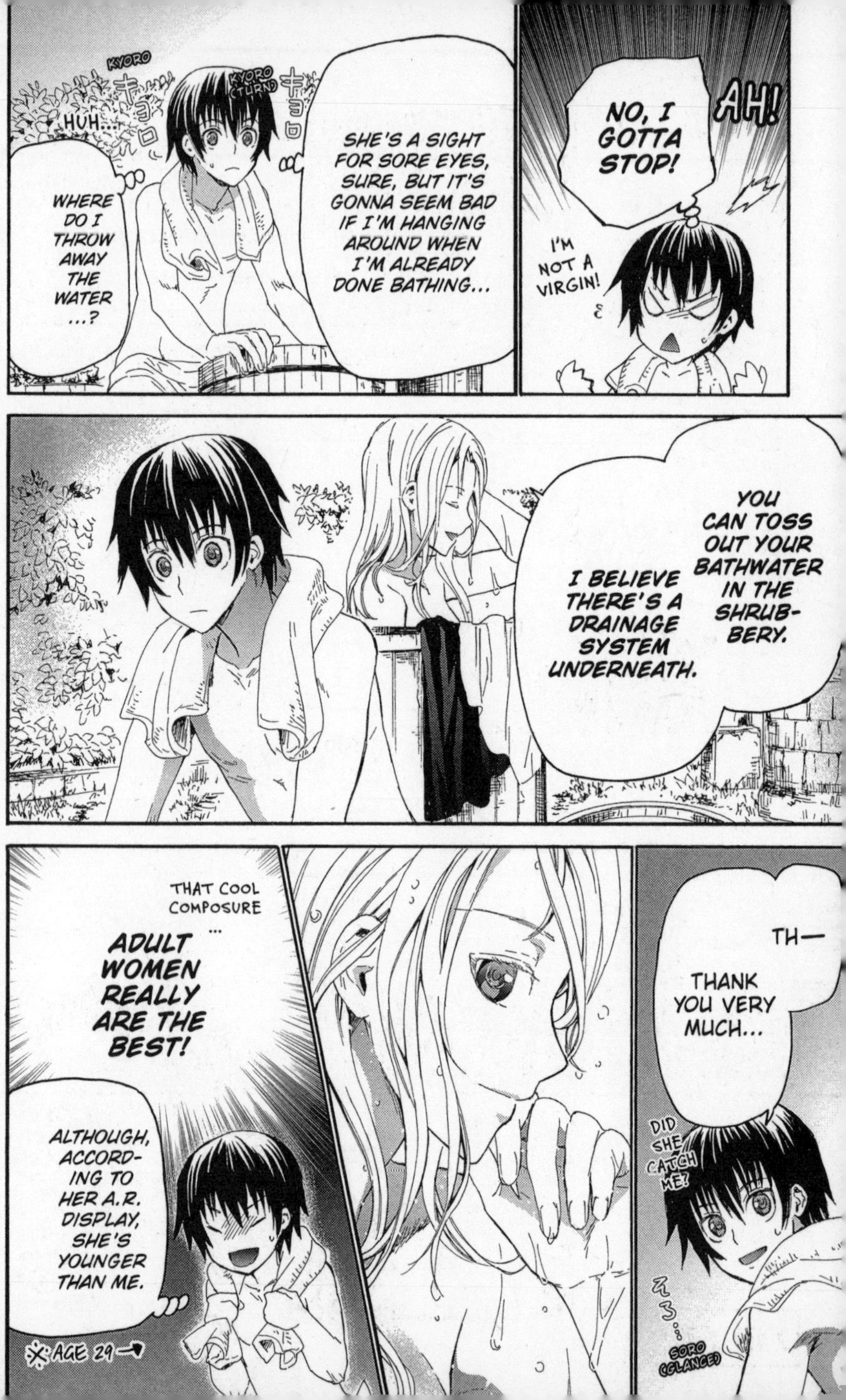
AH!
NO, I GOTTA STOP!
I'M NOT A VIRGIN!
SHE'S A SIGHT FOR SORE EYES, SURE, BUT IT'S GONNA SEEM BAD IF I'M HANGING AROUND WHEN I'M ALREADY DONE BATHING...
キョロ
KYORO (TURN)
キョロ
KYORO
HUH...
WHERE DO I THROW AWAY THE WATER ...?
YOU CAN TOSS OUT YOUR BATHWATER IN THE SHRUBBERY.
I BELIEVE THERE'S A DRAINAGE SYSTEM UNDERNEATH.
TH—
THANK YOU VERY MUCH...
DID SHE CATCH ME?
そろ...
SORO (GLANCE)
THAT COOL COMPOSURE ...
ADULT WOMEN REALLY ARE THE BEST!
ALTHOUGH, ACCORDING TO HER A.R. DISPLAY, SHE'S YOUNGER THAN ME.
※AGE 29→

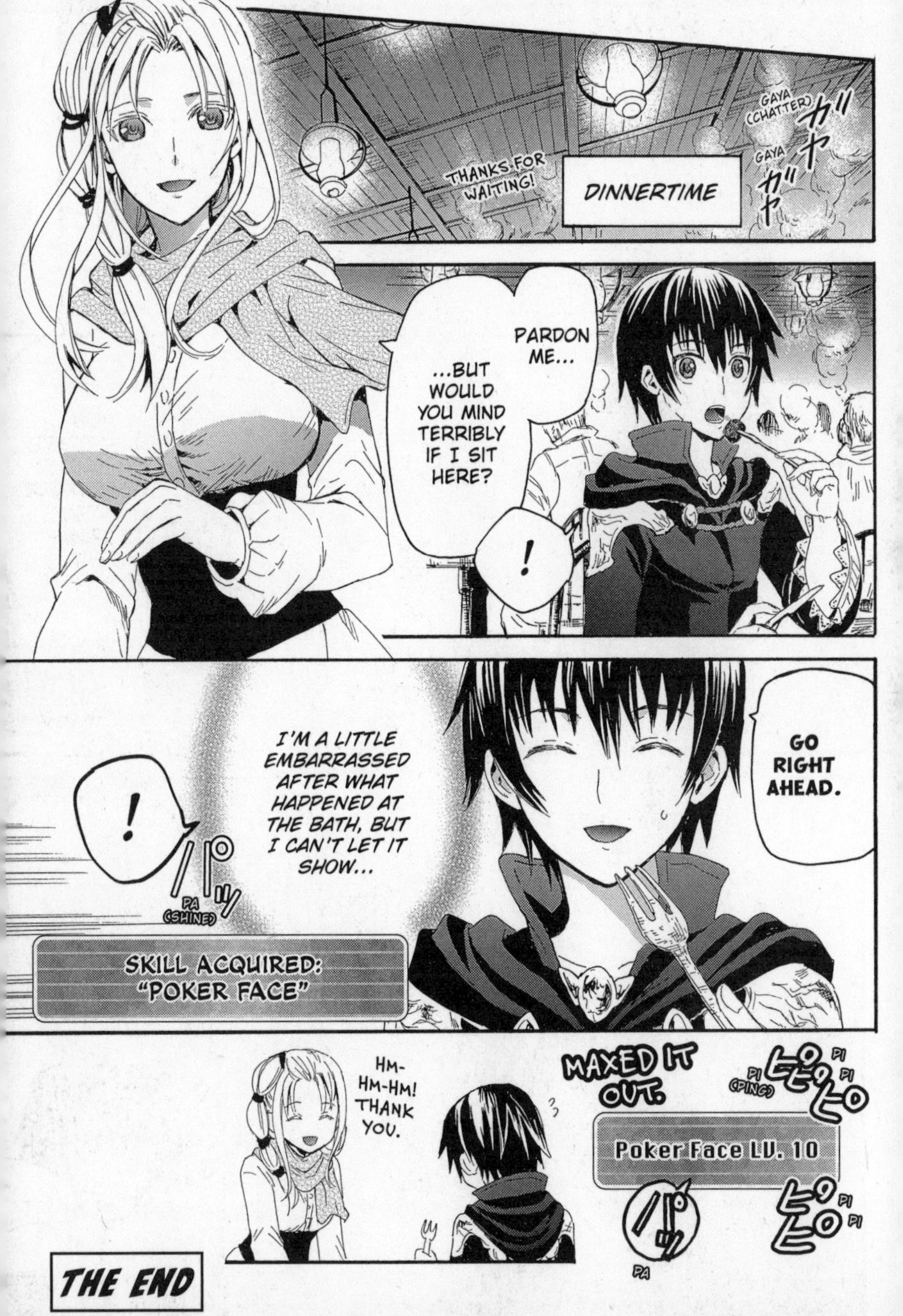
GAYA (CHATTER)
ガヤ
GAYA
ガヤ
DINNERTIME
THANKS FOR WAITING!
PARDON ME...
...BUT WOULD YOU MIND TERRIBLY IF I SIT HERE?
!
GO RIGHT AHEAD.
I'M A LITTLE EMBARRASSED AFTER WHAT HAPPENED AT THE BATH, BUT I CAN'T LET IT SHOW...
!
パッ
PA (SHINE)
SKILL ACQUIRED: "POKER FACE"
PI PI PI (PING)
ピピピ
MAXED IT OUT.
Poker Face LV. 10
ピピ
PI PI
パッ
PA
HM-HM-HM! THANK YOU.
THE END

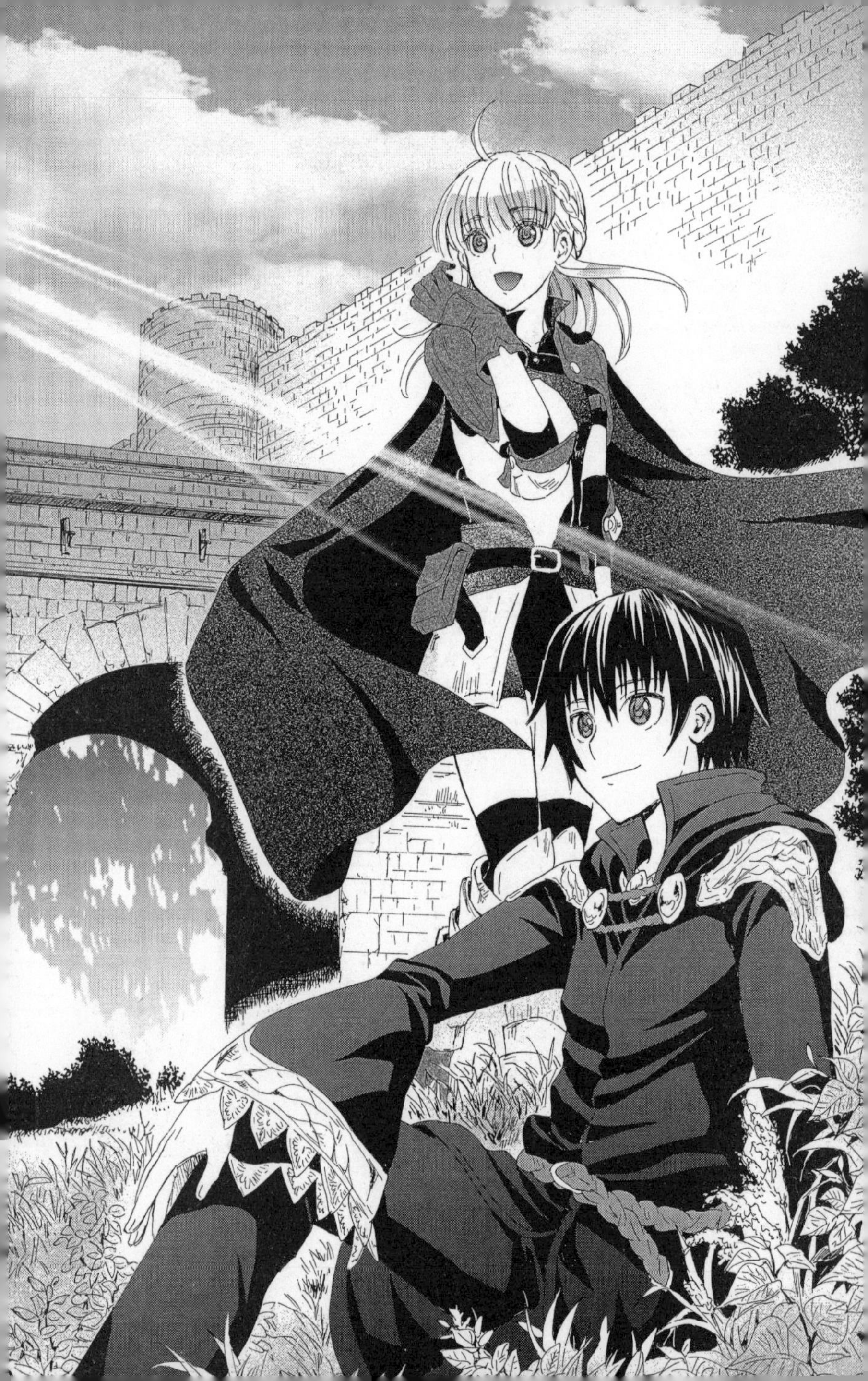

Hello, it's nice to meet you.

We've finally made it all the way to this page.

I say that, but it feels like the time from when serialization was finalized to the sale of this first volume has passed in the blink of an eye. I'm still wrapping my head around these developments...
I'll keep working hard.

I hope we can meet again in the next volume.

Thank you very much.

AYAMEGUMU

...Special Thanks

● Manuscript production collaborators
Yukishiro Kaname-sama
Satoru Ezaki-sama
Yuna Kobayashi-sama

● Editors
Toyohara-sama
Hagiwara-sama

● Binding
coil-sama

● Supervision
Hiro Ainana-sama
shri-sama

● Everyone who helped with the production and publication of this book

And you!

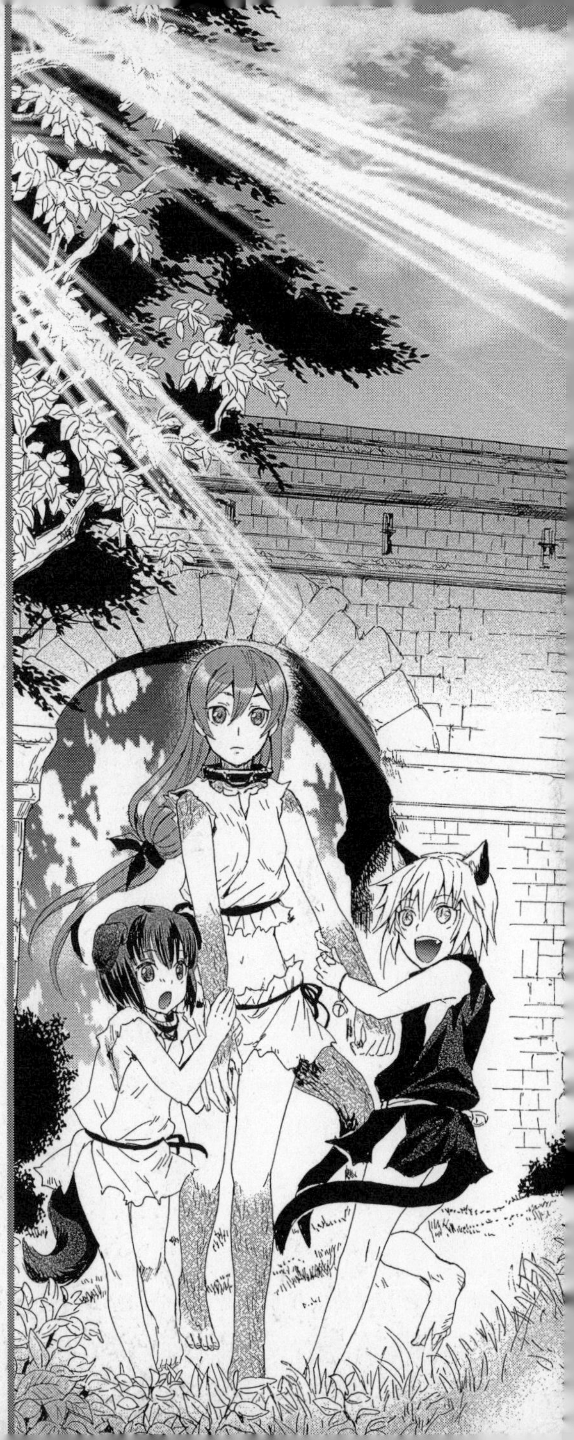

CONGRATULATIONS ON THE FIRST VOLUME OF THE MANGA!

I THINK IT WAS JUST AS I WAS FINISHING WORK ON THE SECOND
VOLUME OF THE NOVEL WHEN TALK OF ADAPTING DEATH MARCH
INTO A COMIC CAME UP. THIS WAS SUCH AN UNEXPECTED DEVELOPMENT
THAT I THOUGHT THE EDITOR MIGHT HAVE GOTTEN THE WRONG E-MAIL
ADDRESS. AND WHEN I FIRST SAW THE ROUGH MANUSCRIPT, I WAS SO
ECSTATIC THAT MY FIRST THOUGHT WAS THAT OF A CHILD: "WOW, A REAL
MANGA ARTIST'S MANUSCRIPT!" IT WAS EVEN MORE AMAZING
THAN I COULD HAVE IMAGINED, AND I COULDN'T WAIT TO SEE THE REST.
(OF COURSE, THE FINAL PRODUCT IS EVEN BETTER
THAN THE MANUSCRIPT!)
ANOTHER FUN ELEMENT IS SEEING CHARACTERS WHO DIDN'T APPEAR
IN THE LIGHT NOVEL'S ILLUSTRATIONS. YUNI-CHAN WAS LOVELY, OF
COURSE, BUT IONA AND THE LADY FROM THE BATH WERE REALLY
WONDERFUL TOO. AND WE CAN'T FORGET THE CHARM
OF THE OLDER MALE CHARACTERS TOO.

I CANNOT THANK MEGUMU AYA-SENSEI ENOUGH FOR EXPANDING
THE WORLD OF DEATH MARCH INTO THE STAGE WE CALL MANGA.
THANK YOU SO MUCH! I'M LOOKING FORWARD TO THE NEXT VOLUME!

HIRO
AINANA

愛七
ひろ

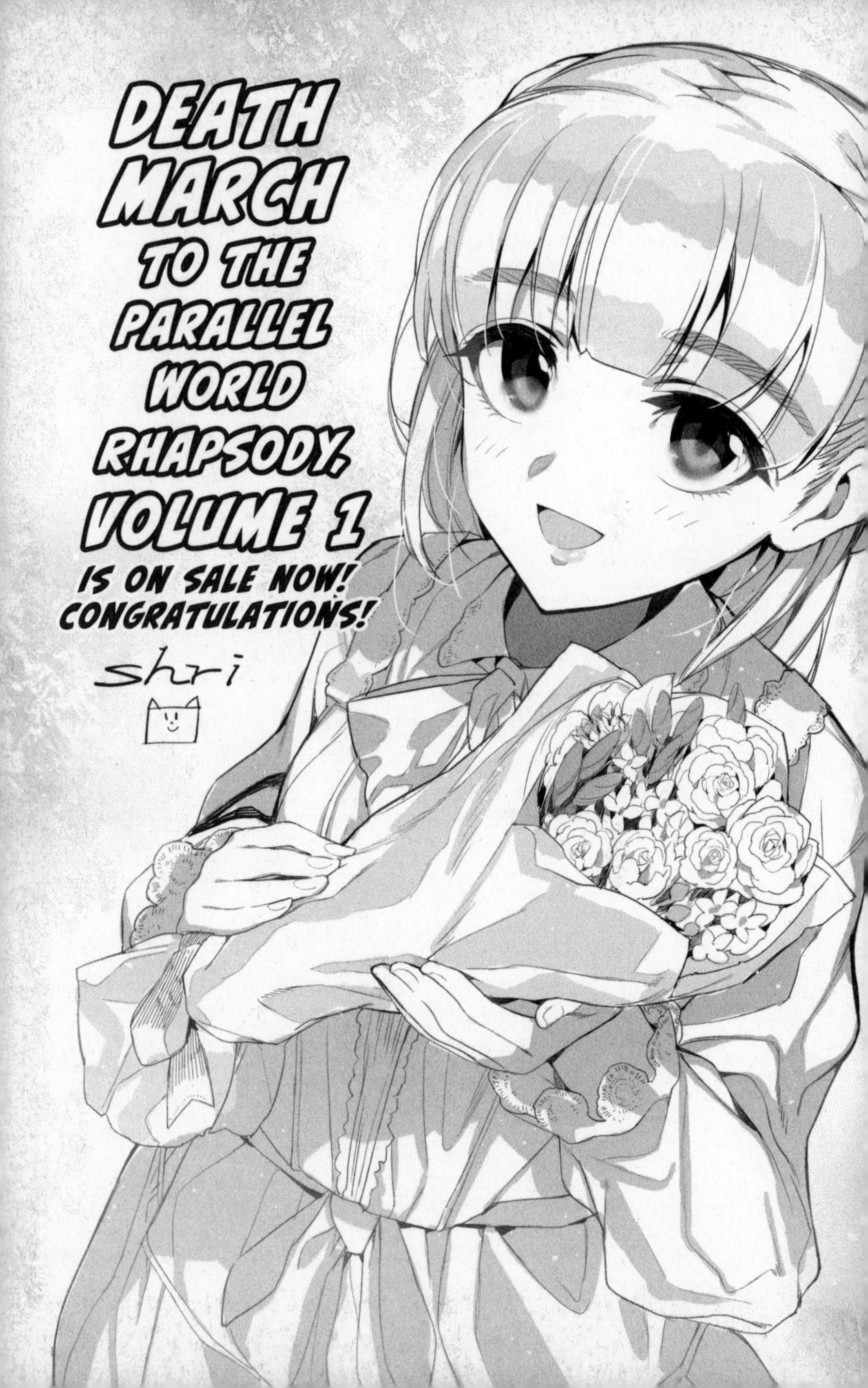
DEATH MARCH TO THE PARALLEL WORLD RHAPSODY, VOLUME 1
IS ON SALE NOW! CONGRATULATIONS!
shri

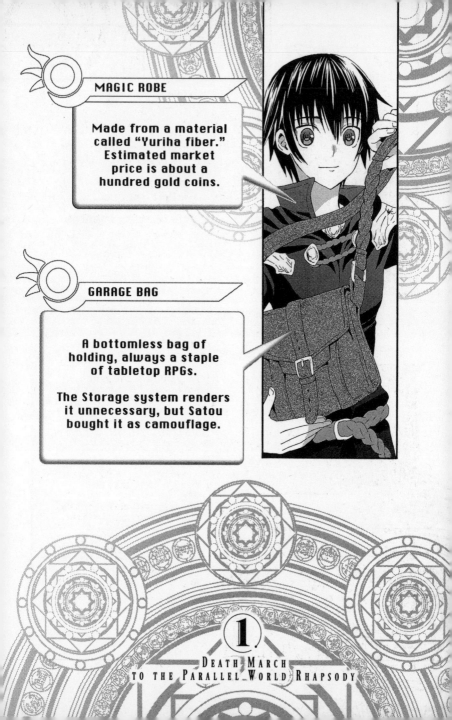

MAGIC ROBE

Made from a material called "Yuriha fiber." Estimated market price is about a hundred gold coins.

GARAGE BAG

A bottomless bag of holding, always a staple of tabletop RPGs.

The Storage system renders it unnecessary, but Satou bought it as camouflage.

1

DEATH MARCH TO THE PARALLEL WORLD RHAPSODY

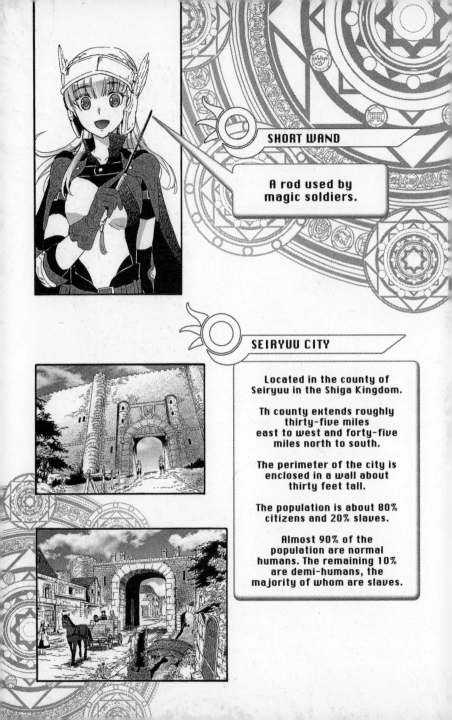

SHORT WAND

A rod used by magic soldiers.

SEIRYUU CITY

Located in the county of Seiryuu in the Shiga Kingdom.

Th county extends roughly thirty-five miles east to west and forty-five miles north to south.

The perimeter of the city is enclosed in a wall about thirty feet tall.

The population is about 80% citizens and 20% slaves.

Almost 90% of the population are normal humans. The remaining 10% are demi-humans, the majority of whom are slaves.

DEATH MARCH ①
TO THE
PARALLEL WORLD RHAPSODY

Original Story: Hiro Ainana
Art: AYAMEGUMU
Character Design: shri

Translation: Jenny McKeon ◆ Lettering: Rochelle Gancio

DEATH MARCHING TO THE PARALLEL WORLD RHAPSODY Vol. 1
©AYAMEGUMU 2015
©HIRO AINANA, shri 2015
First published in Japan in 2015 by KADOKAWA CORPORATION, Tokyo. English translation rights arranged with KADOKAWA CORPORATION, Tokyo through TUTTLE-MORI AGENCY, INC., Tokyo.

English translation © 2017 by Yen Press, LLC

Yen Press
1290 Avenue of the Americas
New York, NY 10104

Visit us at yenpress.com
facebook.com/yenpress
twitter.com/yenpress
yenpress.tumblr.com
instagram.com/yenpress

First Yen Press Edition: January 2017

Yen Press is an imprint of Yen Press, LLC.
The Yen Press name and logo are trademarks of Yen Press, LLC.

The publisher is not responsible for websites (or their content) that are not owned by the publisher.

Library of Congress Control Number: 2016946043

ISBNs: 978-0-316-55276-9 (paperback)
978-0-316-47036-0 (ebook)

10 9 8 7 6 5 4 3 2 1

BVG

Printed in the United States of America

Flip to the back of the book to read the prologue from the light novel of

DEATH MARCH TO THE PARALLEL WORLD RHAPSODY

and a special short story from the under jacket of the manga!

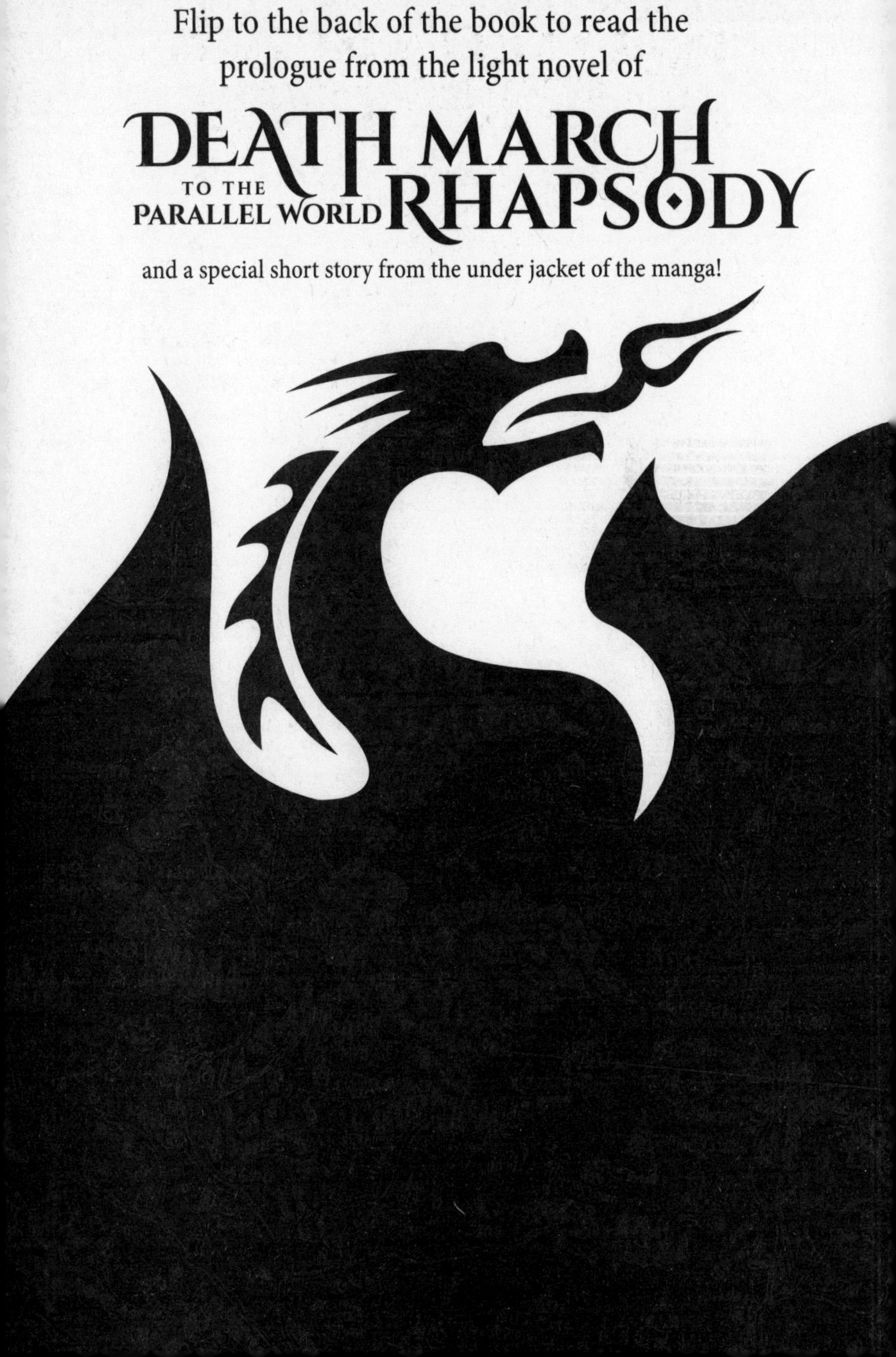

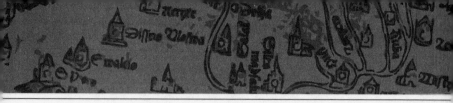

"You there, the splendid-looking merchant! Have you chosen an inn yet? How about the Gatefront Inn, right over there?"

"Sorry, missy. I don't make quite enough money to stay at a place as fine as the Gatefront Inn." The merchant waved his hand to signal that it wouldn't be possible.

I guess there really isn't a point in asking someone like a poor peddler with all his belongings piled on one measly donkey, huh... I tried calling out to at least three other peddlers and travelers, but all of them turned me down. Maybe I'm just no good at getting customers...

"Martha, I'm here to help you!"

Turning toward the voice, I noticed little Yuni standing there with her small fists clenched in front of her chest, full of spirit. As soon as I saw her, I had no choice but to cheer myself up.

I can't very well look uncool in front of a little girl, after all.

"All right, then let's split up the work and knock this out!"

"Yes, ma'am!" Yuni replied cheerfully, and she raced over toward the next wagon that was pulling up in front of the gate.

Suddenly, I saw a black-haired, foreign-looking boy walking from the direction of the gate. With the expression of someone who hadn't yet learned the ways of the world, he was curiously surveying the streets as he went.

Perfect!
I decided to call out to him.

"Hey, you there——!"

GUI
(GRAB)

HEY, THIS IS AN EXCLUSIVE EXTRA!! YOU GOTTA COME READ IT!!

FLIP TO THE MANGA TO FIND OUT WHAT HAPPENS NEXT!

MUNI (SMUSH)

DEATH MARCH
TO THE PARALLEL WORLD
RHAPSODY

(1)

SPECIAL SHORT STORY

Hiro Ainana
illust.AYAMEGUMU

MARTHA'S HELPER

"Ugh, stupid starfaaall!"

"Martha, those cowards aren't coming back no matter how much you whine about it in here! If you have time to complain, then go out and try to pull in some customers or something!"

"Okaaay..."

Clearly, Mom was in a bad mood about the Gatefront Inn losing customers, too. After seeing the rain of stars in the northeastern sky yesterday, our guests shouted something about an "ill omen" and hightailed it out of the inn and Seiryuu City.

But to the people who live in Seiryuu City, wyverns are much scarier than any starfall. Sure, a starfall or a dragon could probably cause more damage, but wyverns are the ones that actually seek out humans and attack them. So none of the locals were going to abandon the city over some silly starfall.

...I can't let Yuni find out that I slept in Mom's bed last night, though. I'd lose all of my dignity.

Oh, a carriage coming in through the main gate! I ran over to fish for customers.

breaking through the clouds, crashing down.

I stared stupidly at the sight.

Thanks for your patience—we're finally back to the scene where all this started.

Real name: Ichirou Suzuki.

Character name: Satou.

This is how my life in another world began.

READ MORE IN
*THE LIGHT NOVEL, COMING
JANUARY 2017!*

my thoughts. The army was firing on me, their arrows raining down in a perfect arc. I quickly slid into a hollow in the rock—well, I tumbled into it clumsily, to be more accurate.

Before I had a chance to catch my breath, a hail of arrows pierced the ground where my body had been just moments before. The first shafts to land snapped and scattered as the arrows behind them struck home. Eyeing the razor-sharp arrowheads, I shivered as if my back had been doused in cold water.

The arrows accumulated within thirty feet of my hiding place. Those lizardmen were talented marksmen, but I had no time to waste on admiring them.

The only thing on my mind was fear.

Those of you who have been chased by monsters in your dreams will probably understand how I felt.

I had very few options. I could stay there squatting beneath the rock and die, try to run away during a break in the cascade of arrows, or *fight back*.

I selected one of the three METEOR SHOWER icons that were still in the corner of my vision. The icon vanished, leaving behind a temporary trace.

But that was all.

"Oh, come on! Are you telling me the command implementation isn't working yet?"

As if to further fan my panic, another wave of arrows rained down. Slowly but surely, the barrage was whittling away my hiding place. "Just how strong are these arrows, anyway? Are these guys Robin Hood's merry band or something?"

Cursing, I selected the two remaining METEOR SHOWER icons. But again, the symbols only disappeared, with no other effect.

One of the arrows finally broke through the rock and grazed my shoulder.

"Damn it! I'm gonna die because of a bug? What kind of sick bad ending is this?" I grumbled, but my anxious complaints soon faded to a weak murmur.

Why? Because I had spotted countless meteorites

level 50. An unarmed level 1 player like me definitely wouldn't stand a chance.

When the group was less than two thousand feet from the cliff, their marching suddenly halted. I ducked behind a rock, out of sight, and peered out at them.

They seemed like some kind of mounted army, but it was no ordinary cavalry. I could tell their mounts weren't horses, but the dust obscured my view too heavily to determine much else.

One of the riders broke away and came closer to my hiding spot, finally giving me a clearer look. The mount wasn't a horse at all but some kind of velociraptor-like dinosaur, and the armored rider was not a human but a lizardman.

"●●●●●●●!●●●●●●●●●●●●!●●●●●●●●!"

The lizardman was shouting something in a language I didn't understand, but there was no question that he seemed to have figured out I was here. I guess I could chalk that up to absurd dream logic, too.

He seemed to wait a moment for my reply. When none came, he apparently grew tired of waiting and took up a longbow, aimed it right at me, and drew the bowstring back with a powerful arm. The outline of his body briefly glowed red, but I had no time to worry about that.

The lizardman let his arrow fly, and it cut through the air, whistling straight toward me. Yes, completely straight—it moved in a perfect line, seemingly untouched by gravity. In that instant, I resigned myself to dying in my dream, but the arrow only grazed my cheek as it flew past.

My face felt hot, as if it had been burned. Unconsciously, I put my hand to my cheek and felt something slippery. Looking down, I saw that my fingers were stained red, just as I'd feared.

I touched my tongue to the fresh blood and tasted iron... *Is this really a dream...?* The question sprang unbidden to my mind.

A thunderous sound like torrential rain interrupted

the ground cut off completely. Figuring it was a cliff or something, I headed toward it.

Clearly, I was pretty high up: I was standing on the edge of a steep drop-off that went down at least three hundred feet. Similar pillars of high land rose up from all over the wasteland. At the bottom, the same reddish-brown earth stretched as far as the eye could see.

In the distance, I could see some kind of rift, possibly a canyon. I tried to check it on the map, but everything outside my immediate area was blank. Assuming this dream had a "fog of war" system like *WW* did, I would only be able to see areas I'd explored. A label in the upper left said VALLEY OF DRAGONS, so maybe that's what the rift was? I squinted as best I could, but I didn't see anything that looked like a dragon.

Instead, I saw something very different.

◆

It was emerging from the shadows of the nearest cliff, kicking up a cloud of dust as it came. Like a cavalry charge in a fantasy film.

My eyes instinctively fell on the four icons in the bottom-right corner of my vision: one that read SEARCH ENTIRE MAP and three that read METEOR SHOWER. The emergency skills for beginners that I'd come up with after the meeting with Mr. Tubs. Driven by a vague sense of unease, I selected the SEARCH ENTIRE MAP icon.

The radar automatically located any enemies, and a cluster of red dots confirmed the approaching group was hostile. Since the radar's scope was limited, I opened up the bigger map to check their configuration.

The advancing army was a group of high-level enemies. There were so many of them, the map's entire upper half was flooded with red.

...Isn't this...a bit over the top? There's way too many.

The approaching band was labeled ELITE LIZARDMEN. There were around three hundred of them, most about

Have you ever heard of lucid dreaming?

It's when you're dreaming, but you're aware you're dreaming.

Right then, I was in a desert wasteland.

Yes, a wasteland. If you can picture the Grand Canyon, that should give you an idea.

How did I know this was a dream? For one thing, I remembered falling asleep under my desk just a few moments ago. For another, there were the four icons in the bottom-right corner of my field of vision along with the gadget labeled MENU and the radar display in the top right. It was the interface from *WW*, the game I had been working on not long ago.

However! This wasn't the first time I'd taken a nap during a death march and found myself working even in my dreams. That I was doing it in a desert instead of the office or my room was a little weird, but it was probably just because the room I was sleeping in was really dry or something.

The scent of the parched earth tickled my nose. A dream where I could smell things... That was unusual. Through a little trial and error, I figured out that I could open the menu just by thinking about it. To my amusement, some kind of bug prevented me from actually touching it with my hand. Luckily, I could operate it with my mind, too.

The menu items seemed to be a mix of *FFL* and *WW*, but I guess you couldn't exactly expect dreams to be consistent. My character name was Satou, as usual. People often call me that by mistake, so it's what I generally name my test characters. My status and such were standard for a new level 1 character, and my equipment consisted of the protein bar, wallet, cell phone, and other things I'd had on me when I fell asleep.

Typical half-assed dream logic.

As I surveyed my surroundings, I saw one area where

"Suzuki, we've got a bug report from the group checking Storage."

"What is it this time? If it's about the infinite free items, I already took care of it."

"No, that was a problem with the inventory in *FFL*. This time it's an item duplication bug in *WW*, they said. Could you take a look at the attachment we sent you?"

"Okay. Damn, duplication bugs are always tough to get rid of..."

Ugh. Working on two projects at once is so complicated. By the way, "Storage" doesn't refer to any external storage or hard drives—it's the name of *WW*'s inventory system.

I continued my work correcting errors in *WW*, dealing with each bug report as it came in from the debug team. At some point in the process, Mr. Tubs sent an e-mail asking me to remove the capacity limitations from *WW*'s Storage for the beta test.

He e-mailed because he doesn't want me to yell at him in person, the bastard. I'm definitely gonna make him buy me dinner or something after all this.

The *FFL* debug team needed to check some limitations, too, and asked me to temporarily deactivate the level restrictions. *Shouldn't that be the server group's job?* I cursed them out under my breath as I worked. *Man, this is going to be another all-nighter, isn't it?*

The error correction continued well into the morning until, miraculously, we were finally able to deliver the *FFL* app to the client. It definitely wasn't bug-free, but fortunately, an advantage of online distribution is the ultimate last-resort weapon known as the "update patch." I could almost hear the users booing me for thinking it, but I was too tired to care.

I made my corrections to the other team's work for *WW* and sent the program file to Mr. Tubs via intercompany mail. After thirty hours without sleep, it was time for a well-earned nap in the peaceful area underneath my desk.

Go ahead and laugh at this corporate slave. Right now, sleep is justice!

difficulty level. I guess all those pointless meetings really were, well, pointless. Great.

"Well, they shot this down before, but what if we added a bonus feature where new players get the ability to find all the enemies on the map, plus a three-use-only bomb spell that can wipe them out? We could give them an extra-special title or something if they get through without using it, so the more-skilled gamers can have an incentive not to activate it."

"We don't have much time, so let's go with that. Set it up, would you please, Suzuki?" Mr. Tubs was as carefree with his requests as ever.

"Wait a minute. I'm working on debugging the smartphone MMO right now, so can you get the okay from the client first? If we just stick it in there without asking, we won't have time to change it later if they don't like it."

"All righty, I'll call them right away!" Mr. Tubs waddled away into the smoking area, cell phone in hand.

I resumed my work, grumbling to myself all the while. Before long, Mr. Tubs gave me the thumbs-up, and it got later and later as I continued working, staving off my hunger with junk food.

Correcting the countless mistakes in Junior's work would take up most of the night before I could finally leave the rest to the debugging team.

What was the name of that game again? Since we always referred to it as "the MMO" or "that RPG," I had forgotten its actual title.

...Oh, right—"Freedom Fantasy World." I guess we'd avoided calling it that because it was confusingly similar to *WW*'s old title, *Fantasy War World*. But I did remember that the old spec documents were always labeled *FFW*"and so on. Eventually, they took the *Fantasy* out of *WW*'s title, and the RPG's name, which had apparently been temporary, was switched to *Freedom Fantasy Life*, with *FFL* as the new abbreviation. So there was no longer any real cause for confusion, but by then it was already too late.

"All right—entry of all classes' input/output and comments, complete. Now I just need to let the auto-documenter prep the docs from the source code and draw up a correlation diagram, and then I can get down to some serious debugging."

I stretched a little, cracking my neck. Looking around, it seemed like all hands were on deck—you never would have guessed it was a holiday. Unfortunately, this was par for the course at my workplace.

At the next desk over, the supervisor for debug commissions was grumbling as he worked, but nobody paid him any mind. Who had the time? The game designers and planners nearby worked alone in silence, all with the same dead, vacant eyes.

By the time I had made coffee and returned to my desk, my PC had finished its processes, and the data needed for debugging was complete. Without this data, it was no wonder my former coworker had done such a terrible job. *I guess it's pointless to complain about Junior when they tossed him into the fray without any on-the-job training, huh? There were four programmers working here only half a year ago when he started, and now there's just me, so I think that says more about this company than anything...*

"Mr. Sa... Er, Mr. Suzuki, the client is complaining that *WW* is too hard for beginners and asking us to fix it... What should we do?" I looked over my shoulder to see Mr. Tubs, the director and lead designer, looking at me helplessly—as always.

I heard you start to call me Satou, pal. Can't you at least get my name right? I've been on the team for over six months! And why do you look sort of happy about even more problems? I don't get why so many developers are masochists.

WW is short for *War World*, a PC browser game we've been developing in earnest for some time. It's a strategy game with some social media elements, set in a fantasy world.

"Didn't I tell them that if we make it any easier, their target demographic won't play it...?" We'd spent countless meetings with the client deciding on this

Because of a choice I thoughtlessly made just ten minutes ago, a meteor shower is gouging out the ground. The meteorites make landfall everywhere, from a few hundred feet away from me to the enormous canyon in the distance, crushing all the enemies within that large radius.

The dots on the radar in the corner of my field of vision disappear like a bothersome stain being washed away. I can't see it from here, but most likely, countless lives are being snuffed out at each meteorite's point of impact.

And shortly after each one disappears into the earth, I hear the sound of the impact and feel a tremor under my feet. And then, just as a massive tidal wave of debris is about to reach me—

Suddenly, a searing pain hits me like the wrath of God. It's as if my skull is breaking open and my body is splitting apart.

As the pain stops, my body is lost in the dust cloud.

◆

Let me rewind a bit.

I was working overtime on a day off in a last-ditch effort to get a long-overdue project completed in time for its final deadline. As a programmer for a subcontracting company, I work on outsourced projects like PC and smartphone games that are commissioned by larger companies.

However shady our company might be, one person never has more than two projects at a time. But because of too many last-minute changes and bugs, the younger programmer assigned to this game had gone AWOL right before it was due! What a loser!

In fact, the job turnover rate here was so high, Junior and I had been the only two programmers in the entire company. Since there was no time to find a last-minute replacement, I got stuck finishing up his projects in addition to my own.

PROLOGUE
Death March to Disaster

Stars streak across the sky.

Dozens and dozens of them.

Have you ever seen a shooting star?

I'm sure many people have. Maybe you've been captivated by their fleeting beauty or made a wish on one as it fell through the night sky.

But have you ever watched a meteorite rip through the heavens toward the surface? Have you seen it tear the sky to pieces with a thunderous roar, crashing into the ground with a terrifying impact?

Maybe some of you have seen something like it on TV or on the Internet somewhere. But even then, I'm sure nobody ever thought they wanted to see a meteor shower up close, hurtling down all around them.

And yet, at this very moment, I'm watching more than a hundred falling rocks pour down right before my eyes, one after the other.

No—I shouldn't say it so passively, as if it's someone else's problem. Because I'm the one responsible for this disaster in the first place.

The prologue
from the light
novel begins
here!

DEATH MARCH
TO THE
PARALLEL WORLD RHAPSODY

★ ★ ★

HIRO AINANA
ILLUSTRATIONS BY SHRI